ODIOUS

AND

CERBERUS

Anyone who enjoys David-versus-Goliath stories should read Julian Raven's *Odious and Cerberus: An American Immigrant's Odyssey and His Free-Speech Legal War against Smithsonian Corruption.*

—Scott Douglas Gerber, Professor of Law at Ohio Northern University and author of, among other books, *A Distinct Judicial Power: The Origins of an Independent Judiciary, 1606–1787*

Julian tells an epic tale of a visionquest and the tangled path endured in attempts to bring it to fruition. Part Odysseus, part Don Quixote, he tells an immigrant's tale of love for his country and reveals the opportunities it offers. Part memoir, part current events, sprinkled with doses of history and jurisprudence, it tells of Julian's tenacious efforts to bring his quest into full light.

—Jim Boden, Artist and Professor Emeritus, Coker University, Hartsville, SC

In a world where presidents "lead" through focus groups, and the rest of us calibrate our opinions and expressions to stay within designated lanes, Julian Raven is an 18-wheeler crashing through our timorous barriers. *Odious and Cerberus* is a forceful love letter to America, the land that Julian chose to make his own. It should, hence, shame Americans and foreigners alike who have lived off its munificent gifts—without replenishing them. A book such as this could only be written by an unabashedly religious man with an extraordinary and catholic appreciation of the world.

—Ashok Panikkar, Founder, MetaCulture, Thinking and Human Engagement Studio

Bold! Entertaining! Julian Raven, the self-proclaimed nobody artist, shares a fascinating tale of his audacious and faith-fused journey to the gates of the gargantuan museum and the battles he found within. Raven's love for God and country are inspiring.

—Dr. Cary Shaw, Head of School at Twin Tiers Christian Academy

ODIOUS

AND

CERBERUS

AN AMERICAN IMMIGRANT'S ODYSSEY
AND HIS FREE-SPEECH LEGAL WAR
AGAINST SMITHSONIAN CORRUPTION

A TRUE STORY BY ARTIST
JULIAN RAVEN

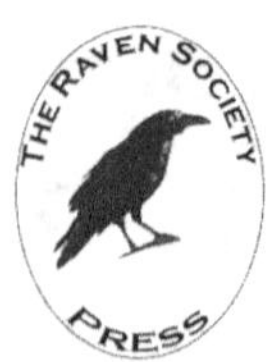
THE RAVEN SOCIETY
PRESS

To Gloria, my friend, wife, and companion on this mysterious American pilgrimage, without whom my story in Odious *and* Cerberus *would never have been written.*

Table of Contents

Acknowledgments

I AM ETERNALLY GRATEFUL TO GOD FOR LEADING ME ON A pilgrimage to America and entrusting me with His friendship's intimacy and the resulting divine adventures, manifestations, and provisions. Those colorful elements adorn and comprise my odyssey.

America's Founding Fathers were those rare individuals whom Providence overshadowed and assembled at a predetermined time to give birth to freedom. That dream could only have emanated from the hearts and minds of people acquainted with the divine revelation that where the Spirit of the Lord is, there is liberty. I give thanks to those Founders and the myriad of other individuals, saints, and soldiers who often paid the ultimate price in freedom's struggle. They have handed to us, the living, this torch of liberty which is to be held with unflinching boldness and courage.

I am deeply grateful to the many Americans I have personally met along my journey who have taught me about this unique nation and—above all—about the faith, values, morals, and ideals they possess and convey. My wife and mentor, Gloria, and our three children, Johanna, Victoria, and Jeremiah, are among these, making up the American family with whom I have shared much of my journey, making my experience precious beyond compare.

Odious and Cerberus's Foreword author, Craig Shirley, and endorsers, Laurence Jarvik, Scott Douglas Gerber, Bill Donohue, Jim Boden, Ashok Panikkar, Cary Shaw, and Richard Sternberg, invested their valuable time in reading my book. They validated my story, anchoring it into the American consciousness, where it belongs. Their contributions are like the icing on a cake, complementing any and every effort I made.

The finishing touch, that red cherry on the cake, which was essential for assembling all the components of *Odious and Cerberus,* was the editor who could refine, prepare, and typeset the entire manuscript for publishing. Michelle Shelfer's services I discovered fortuitously through the Reedsy.com professional book-services marketplace. Remarkably, Michelle became another specific provision from on high, testifying to the divinely curated nature of this story, since she was ideally gifted, experienced, and spiritually suited for the monumental task.

Foreword by Craig Shirley

For more than 170 years, Americans have been enriched by the Smithsonian Institution's incredible archive of artifacts, displays, and knowledge in every field. This excellent resource was bequeathed to the American people by a mysterious English benefactor, and we treasure its museums, galleries, collections, and exhibits. We are the beneficiaries of this donor's will.

However, today the Smithsonian is curated by some whose motives are not in harmony with the benefactor's will and not in the best interests of the people the Institution was intended to serve. What began as a project "for the increase and diffusion of knowledge" has become yet another tool of ideologues who—along with mainstream media, academia, the arts, and other institutions—are dedicated to shaping our knowledge with an invisible hand to further an un-American cultural end.

Institutional transparency and clarity of mission are essential in protecting against those corrupt deeds that thrive under cover of darkness and confusion. In the case of the Smithsonian Institution, we find a conundrum of identity resulting in smoke and mirrors that enables a culture of corruption. It is uniquely ill-defined as a legal entity, which has been an open door for opportunists since its founding. Due to the efforts of dedicated members of Congress seeking Smithsonian accountability, we have received a glimpse into some of the more recent examples of this corruption. We have good reason to be concerned, considering the bloated budget and influence of the Smithsonian.

In the First Amendment of the Bill of Rights to the Constitution, the founders spelled out a protection for the people of the United States against restricted speech. At the time of its writing,

Americans had just broken free from England and declared their independence as a new nation. On the heels of this cataclysmic new birth, the founders looked not to government but to God and natural law as the highest source of authority in guarding freedom of thought, expression, and conscience. Congress shall make no law abridging free speech.

Going back to an even older source for our American legal system, the Magna Carta set forth the idea of due process of law, codified in our Fifth and Fourteenth Amendments. No person shall be deprived of liberty without due process.

You are about to read a quintessentially American story about one man, an immigrant from England, and his struggle against a powerful institution. Was Raven's unalienable right of speech abridged—forbidden by Smithsonian curators with a political axe to grind—and his right to due process curtailed? This is also a story about every American who seeks fairness, free speech, and due process of law. Raven's story cuts to the very heart of America's founding values of liberty for all. What will Lady Justice say in the contest between the influential, moneyed, and conveniently ill-defined Smithsonian Institution and one man backed by the Bill of Rights?

—Craig Shirley,

Acclaimed historian and the author of six books on President Reagan, including *Reagan Rising, Rendezvous with Destiny, Reagan's Revolution, Last Act, New York Times* bestseller *December 1941,* and his most recent book, *April 1945: The Hinge of History.* He is a regular commentator throughout the media and a contributor to national publications and was hailed by the *London Telegraph* as "the best of the Reagan biographers." He has just completed *The Search for Reagan* and is beginning a book on Donald Trump. He and his wife, Zorine, who is also his editor, reside in a three-hundred-year-old Georgian Four Square manor house. They are avid sailors.

Editor's Word

One of the great joys of being an editor is traveling with the author as our guide through landscapes that are novel and unfamiliar to us. We editors learn the language of the author and get to participate in the blessed process of building bridges between author and reader so that communication can occur. This is part of the essential human experience of community. The process can be thrilling when what is communicated has the potential to make real, positive change for the betterment of the community.

In the case of *Odious and Cerberus*, my traveling companion could not have been more passionate and dedicated to his message. Our travels allowed me to see America through an immigrant's eyes and to become, alongside the author, a newborn citizen, a law student, a mountain climber, and an activist. Our journeys brought to mind the parables of Hannah Hurnard in *Hinds' Feet on High Places* and John Bunyan's *Pilgrim's Progress*, which also take us on transformative ascents. Yes, Raven's story could have been written as a dispassionate, "just-the-facts-ma'am" account. But that would have been a very different book and not nearly as exciting a trip. Julian Raven chose to give us the full picture of his American experience, complete with all its life-convulsing vicissitudes and the emotions bound up in it.

Throughout the *Odious and Cerberus* journey, the betterment of our American community was behind Raven's pursuit. Justice and righteousness are at the heart of our American hope and are presently under threat. As we read in Proverbs 2, the Lord "is a shield to those who walk in integrity, guarding the paths of justice, and He preserves the way of His godly ones. Then you will discern righteousness and justice and equity and every good course." Pursuing wisdom will deliver you "from the man who speaks perverse things; from those who leave the paths of uprightness to walk in the ways of darkness." Certainly, in the midst of the departure from "paths of uprightness" that we are currently witnessing in our nation, our ears yearn for the voice of justice to ring through the madness and return us to sound common sense and "every good course."

Julian Raven sounds that urgent call and encourages us to join him in the process of exposing corruption and restoring core American values. He brings the immigrant's perspective that has the audacity (or naivete?) to imagine that America really is all about liberty as our founding and guiding principle. He treasures his citizenship and the responsibilities associated with it far more than most native-born Americans. What if we all cared as much as he does about our American identity and took action to make America the beacon for liberty it was meant to be? That is precisely what we are invited to do in *Odious and Cerberus*. Correcting the corruption at the Smithsonian Institution is as good a place as any to begin the ascent.

—Michelle Shelfer
TheFoundlings.net
June, 2022

Preface

ONE OF THE FEATURES OF THIS BOOK WITH WHICH I AM MOST delighted, proud of, and grateful for is the diversity of thought represented in the persons of my gracious endorsers and Foreword author. We have a Jew, a Catholic, a Protestant, conservatives, a liberal and even an atheist, all of whom are recognized academics in various fields of knowledge, including politics, law, sociology, history, art, democracy, education, and science. We may not all agree on politics, on the purpose of art, or on the best solutions for the problems we face as a nation. Yet, in overcoming differences to give wholehearted acclaim for *Odious and Cerberus*, these people are united in recognizing the problem, and they are willing to speak up about it.

Breaches of trust and the silencing of any person's First Amendment protected free speech within institutions of learning, regardless of that person's political leanings, trip the alarm of injustice inside every lover of justice and freedom. "The increase and diffusion of knowledge" is the primary reason the Smithsonian Institution was established. Mustn't we hold them accountable to that mandate?

As you read, you will discover the answer to the riddle in the title, *Odious and Cerberus*. Who or what is "Odious," and who or what is "Cerberus"? The title evokes images of ancient mythological Greece but is literally derived from a contemporary source that will leave you stunned.

The implications of this narrative-non-fiction story are far reaching and have compelled some (not you, of course) to pull away out of caution. Fear causes many to shrink back, leaving the few to brave the darkness of the terrifying mountain climb, where myths, monsters, and superstitions once blocked their ascent into the glorious light of truth.

JULIAN RAVEN

Prologue

Letters submitted to the Smithsonian in support of Julian Raven's submission painting "Unafraid and Unashamed"

"Julian Raven spent many hours creating this work of art and many more hours displaying his creation throughout the country. To say this creation is amazing is an understatement. This portrait is now part of our country's great history and definitely belongs inside the Smithsonian so many now and many generations thereafter can enjoy this work of art."

—Daniel Mandell Jr., Mayor of the City of Elmira,
November 18, 2016

"As your representative in the New York State Senate, I believe that your incredible work would be an appropriate and impactful addition to the National Portrait Gallery during this time and a truly patriotic tribute to our new President."

—Thomas F. O'Mara, NYS Senator 58th District,
November 16, 2016

"I would ask that the [Smithsonian] selection committee give your artwork every consideration."

—Congressman Tom Reed, New York's 23rd District,
November 21, 2016

"His speech was moving, and he was overwhelmingly elected to be an alternate delegate. Mr. Raven and I were at the convention and his enthusiasm and love of this country is amazing. He represented the 23rd Congressional District with honor. I was proud to have him part of the New York State delegation…. This past fall I had the pleasure of attending the Schyler GOP dinner where Mr. Raven had his artwork on display and was one of the guest speakers at the event. He gave a tremendous speech citing the Declaration of Independence. The room was moved and speechless at both the emotion and joy Mr. Raven displayed as he talked about the founding fathers, their journey to freedom, and his journey to becoming an American citizen…"

—Sandra J. King, Yates County Republican Chair,
November 20, 2016

"I am pleased to write this letter in full support of your application to the Smithsonian National Portrait Gallery…. I feel that your work is more than a portrait and is very inspirational. Just as your portrait has played a signature role in the campaign, it is very appropriate for a prominent display at the Inauguration as a tribute to our new President."

—Christopher S. Friend, Ph.D., Member of the Assembly,
New York 124th District, November 21, 2016

"Thank you for the opportunity to express my strong support for your application to the Smithsonian National Portrait Gallery. We were proud to have this piece prominently on display at the New York Delegation hotel during the 2016 Republican National Convention…. It has already been enjoyed and remarked upon by many, but its display at the inauguration by a New York artist would be an appropriate commendation for our President-Elect."

—Ed Cox, Chairman of the New York Republican State
Committee, November 28, 2016

"As the Chairman of the Chemung County Republican National Committee,…I believe that your incredible work would be an appropriate and impactful addition to the National Portrait Gallery during this time…. It was certainly well received at the Republican National Convention…and at our Annual Fall Dinner…as I witnessed firsthand!"

—Rodney Strange, Chemung County Republican Chair,
November 2016

"Thank you for the opportunity to express my strong support for your application to the Smithsonian National Portrait Gallery…"
—Lest Cady, Schuyler County Republican Chairman,
November 18, 2016

"I am writing to recommend Julian Raven's painting 'Unafraid and Unashamed' to be included in your portrait gallery for the Presidential Inauguration. I have had the pleasure of watching Julian and his painting's 'story' unfold since I attended the unveiling in October of 2015…. Where history was being made this election year, Julian's painting could be found. His painting has become synonymous with this election."
—Frank Acomb, Radio Host,
November 2016

"We support the bid to display 'Unafraid and Unashamed' for art patrons to admire at the National Portrait Gallery. The piece aligns beautifully with the ongoing exhibition 'America's Presidents…. In our minds, art is meant to provoke both emotion and conversation. There is no moment more timely to encourage constructive political discourse than the present. Raven's piece will contribute to the national dialogue regardless of a specific viewer's political leanings."
—Bradley and Andrea Gates,
Art Collectors

"I admire the passion and patriotism that you have displayed through your artwork and I hope that you will be able to share that art with the whole nation through this opportunity."
—Joseph Sempolinski, Steuben County Republican Committee,
November 2016

"It would be a great honor for Julian Raven, and something for all Americans and those who wish to come here to become an American citizen, as Julian did, to be able to see his painting displayed in the Smithsonian as a symbol of freedom…"
—Nanette Moss, 6th District Councilwoman, City of Elmira,
November 28, 2016

Chapter One

POWER AND ABUSE

STANDING WITH MY HEAD HUNG LOW IN MY DIMLY LIT BASEMENT office, I stared into the black screen of my phone. I was shocked. Trying as I did to compose myself, it was a struggle even to swallow. A surge of uncontrollable emotions swept over me. Rising heat rushed up the back of my neck, while the terrible awareness of being powerless alarmed every system in my body. Words even vanished, leaving me grasping for thoughts. Shame burned in my chest, reminding me of when my English headmaster way back in Spain walloped me for being a naughty boy.

It was early December, a clear and brisk morning in upstate New York. The wood stove's oak-scented blueish smoke gently drifted through the bare, wintry woods not far from the American Revolution's Newtown Battlefield. My dear wife, Gloria, and I, along with our three children, Johanna, Victoria, and Jeremiah—and Sammy, our black German Shepherd mix—lived out in the rolling, tree-covered countryside. Staring into the distance through the window, I could see the lazy Susquehanna River through the leafless trees, sparkling in the valley below. The clear, blue sky stretched up to the heavens, resting behind the not-so-distant hills over the other side of the meandering waterway. In the distance, just out of sight and on the banks of the river, was the townish City of Elmira, once made famous as the home of Mark Twain.

In a daze, I wandered around that morning, pretending to go about my business as usual. My wife and children hurried about and got on with the day, as school was winding down for the year. It was 2016, and our eighteenth wedding anniversary was only days away. Thoughts of Christmas had already begun to warm the chilly air. My family had no idea of the turmoil spinning inside of me, which I had just brought up with me from downstairs. Days passed before I could bring myself to share with Gloria what had happened. Strangely, I felt ashamed.

Me—a six-foot-two, 260-pound, then-forty-six-year-old bearded woodsman who hunted, fished, and felled massive trees—ashamed? What had I done? Finally sharing my grief with Gloria felt like confessing to having done something terrible. After unloading, I began to experience a measure of relief. Gloria could not believe her ears as the account of the whirlwind phone call now engulfed her as well. "Yes!" I said. "Director Kim Sajet personally called me, and after an eleven-minute argument—in which she lied, broke the law, disparaged my work, and then, in her frustrated Australian accent, snapped, '*I AM THE DIRECTOR OF THE SMITHSO-NIAN NATIONAL PORTRAIT GALLERY. YOUR APPLICA-TION WILL GO NO FURTHER. YOU CAN APPEAL IT ALL YOU WANT!*'—she abruptly ended the call." Anger, disbelief, and indignation boiled up and over in Gloria, as raw emotions were ignited.

What could I do? Where could I go? To whom could I turn? After all, most people shy away from confrontation, especially confrontation with officials of highly esteemed, influential, and revered institutions. Who was I anyway? Just a newborn U.S. citizen, an insignificant member of "We the People," who had supported President-elect Trump—and to top it off, an artist from out-in-the-woods Elmira.

Wading into a legal battle with a beloved, federally run institution in a city that voted 96 percent for Hillary Clinton would be like a boy in his underpants with a homemade slingshot going out to fight against a giant, armor-clad, spear-chucking, sword-wielding, undefeated warrior! And dare I challenge the largest museum complex in the world, Washington, D.C.'s very own uber-prestigious Smithsonian Institution and the United States of America? In the Queen's English, it was as if my mother's voice sounded off in my head, "What a silly boy to even think of such a thing!"

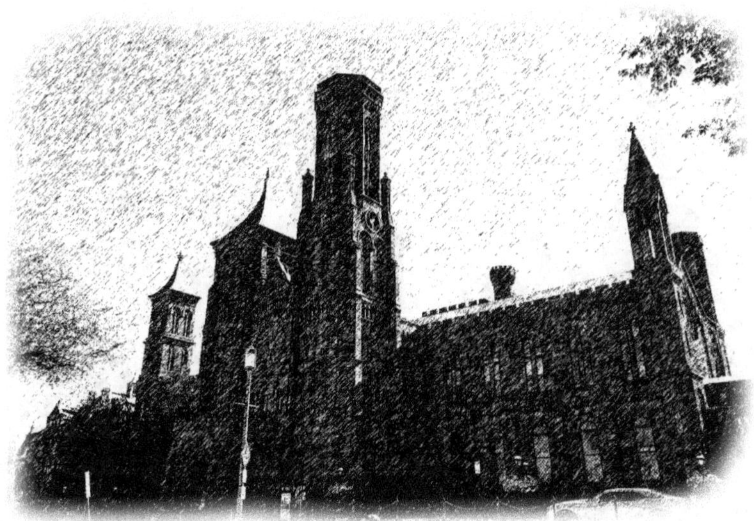

The Smithsonian Institution, Washington, D.C.

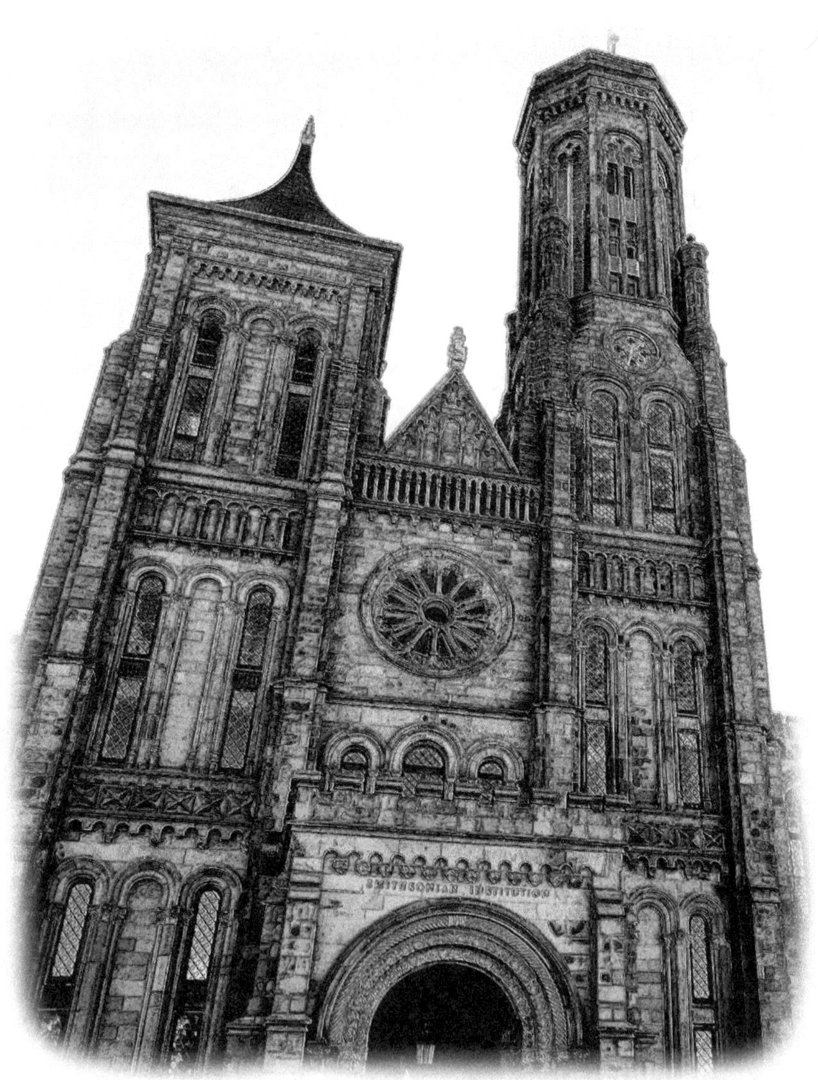

The Smithsonian Castle, Washington, D.C.

Chapter Two

MYTHSONIAN

"**Y**OU CAN APPEAL IT ALL YOU WANT, YOU CAN APPEAL IT ALL YOU want, *YOU CAN APPEAL IT ALL YOU WANT!*" kept barking in my head. Appeal? Was I to appeal? Appeal where and to whom?

Although I was born in Richmond upon Thames in London, England, I had heard about the Smithsonian Institution upon my arrival to America in 1996 as an immigrant from Marbella, Spain. One of my mother's dear friends, Anna Lee Emanuel, who lived in Westport, Connecticut, was married to artist Herzl Emanuel. Anna Lee often told me as a young artist that her deceased husband had a bronze sculpture in the Smithsonian American Art Museum. She spoke highly of the museum and the honor it was to have a sculpture in that collection; it was impressive. Knowing someone whose husband had a sculpture in the Smithsonian American Art Museum was a big deal for me as a budding artist, to the point that people would even hear me boast that I knew someone whose husband had a sculpture in the Smithsonian, as some sort of distant claim to artistic fame.

Once in a while, as a newly arrived immigrant, I would hear about the Smithsonian Institution, either in the news, magazines, or movies, and it always piqued my curiosity. Not having grown up in the U.S., I never knew what the Smithsonian Institution was exactly, other than a colossal museum. I had never been there. Most people, I learned, would visit the Smithsonian when visiting Washington, D.C., as it housed an incredible American archive of science, history, art, and the like. But the mysterious name "Smithsonian" always intrigued me; what did it mean? Little did I know that it would one day become my quest to discover the true identity of the mysterious Smithsonian Institution.

Back in the summer of 2015, when I completed my Trump painting, "Unafraid and Unashamed," I began to hear about the Smithsonian again. On November 1 that year, I unveiled my portrait at the Solid Rock Café in Elmira, New York. One of the guests, a blond woman who was a friend of a friend, came up to me after seeing the patriotic portrait of then-presidential-candidate Donald Trump, saying, "This portrait should be in the Smithsonian!" I thanked her for her compliment and suggestion, not knowing what that actually meant, other than the museum in Washington, D.C.

Once I began to travel the country with the painting, I would hear similar suggestions, and many *other* suggestions as to what I could do with my pro-Trump painting. The 2016 political-art show at Politicon in Pasadena, California, was called "The Art of Politics" and was curated by Yosi Sergant. An elderly gentleman at Politicon also suggested that my painting should hang in the Smithsonian. Yosi, who had invited me to show my Trump painting at Politicon, was an unapologetic left-wing activist and patron, and he was the inspiration behind the Barack Obama "Hope" poster. That poster, by artist Shephard Fairey, was also on display at Politicon that year.

Politicon happened after I had already embarked on my first self-supported, grassroots political campaign. I set out for Iowa in a twenty-foot rented box truck with massive adhesive vinyl prints of the Trump painting on both sides. I aimed to support "joke" presidential candidate Donald Trump for the whole freezing month of snowy January 2016 at the Iowa caucuses. Caucuses? What in the world were caucuses, let alone the Iowa caucuses? And where in the world was Iowa? As a newly minted U.S. citizen, such was my political naivete (having pledged my allegiance to the United States Constitution on "Constitution Day," September 17, 2015, in Brockport, New York). Why on earth would I support a pseudo reality-TV candidate like Donald Trump, paint a massive painting of him as president, and travel cross-country campaigning for Trump on my own dime when very few people took Trump seriously? Most TV pundits and political experts mocked Trump and his candidacy, and people I knew thought I must be stark-raving mad. Was I?

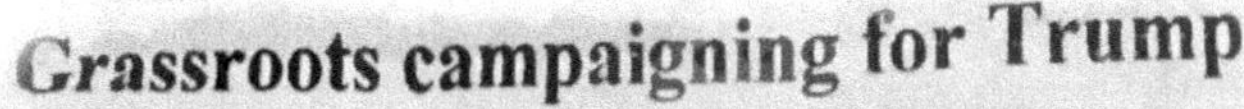

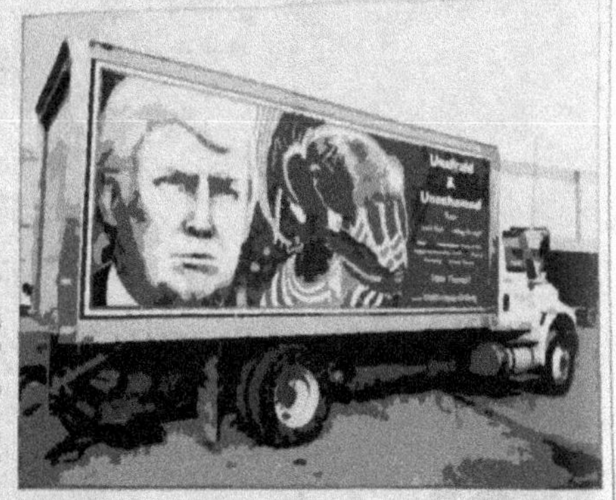

Denison Bulletin, January 20, 2016, Iowa

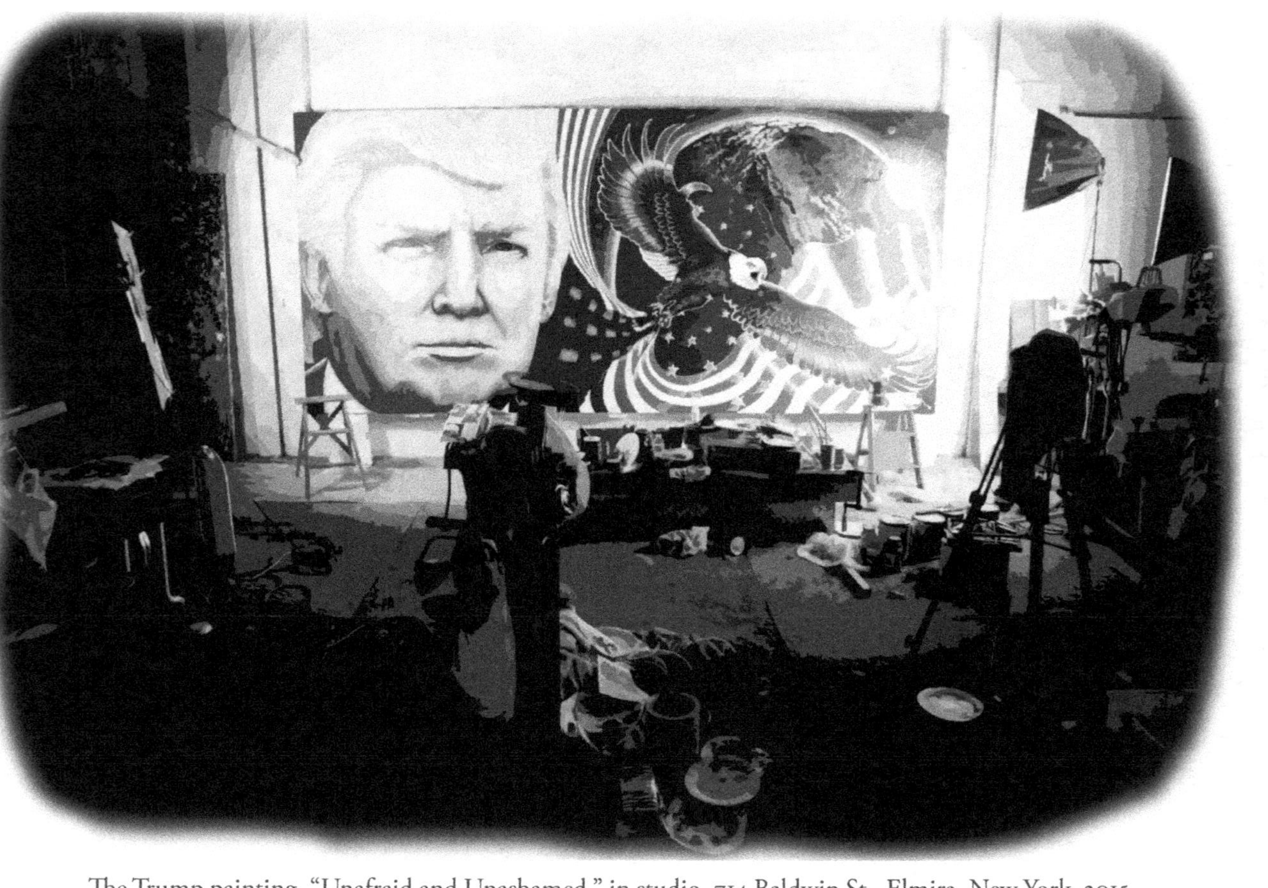

The Trump painting, "Unafraid and Unashamed," in studio, 714 Baldwin St., Elmira, New York, 2015

Chapter Three

TRUMP

My FIRST ENCOUNTER WITH THE NAME OF DONALD TRUMP WAS back in Spain in 1992 when I watched *Home Alone 2*. Another encounter was when I had just arrived in America and ended up living in Nyack, New York. Nyack was a charming and quaint Hudson River town, famous for antiques, small shops, and Manhattan celebrities residing in plain sight. From Rosie O'Donnell to Bill Murray, the Hudson River was a magnet for Manhattan's rich and famous.

Nyack? I had never even heard the name Nyack, nor did I know where it was before the summer of 1996. Yet somehow, I ended up living there. Here's how it happened: it turned out that my mother's best friend in Marbella, Spain, was Janice from Scotland, whose sister was Bernice, whose daughter was Louise. This Louise, whom I had met many years prior in Spain, was now married to a Brit named Stuart and living somewhere in America. That somewhere was Nyack. But to get to Nyack, I had to travel thousands of miles across land and sea in the opposite direction.

All my bags were packed, and I left Marbella, Spain, in February of 1996. I had sold my last item of value, my Canon camera, to buy a plane ticket to America. On the mission field in Almería, Spain, just a year before that, I had met Mark Miller, a minister from California who mentored me in my newfound faith at that time. After an epiphany on a mountain the previous year, I had left a suicidal, self-destructive, atheistic existence. It was a life of sex, drugs, and rock-n-roll while running three hard-rock bars with my two brothers on the Costa Del Sol. We were blessed to grow up in such a beautiful place, so rich in culture. After all, Spain's golden mile was Europe's playground for the rich and famous, neither of which we were.

Marbella, located in Malaga, Spain, was my hometown. I grew up there from age two until I was twenty-six, when I moved to America. My parents had escaped the rat race and crime of Richmond upon Thames in London, England, where I was born back in 1970. Gerald Raven, my entrepreneurial Jewish father, used the then-newly invented fax machine to run his business back in London, while playing golf and drinking gin and tonic under the Spanish sun. My father passed away at the early age of fifty-four, back in 1980, when I was just ten years old.

Sixteen years later, on my approach to JFK International Airport in New York, it was thrilling to see the white, snow-covered U.S. coastline, looking down from the air after the massive snowstorm of '96 had just slammed New York. I arrived at JFK in early February 1996. I headed to San Bernardino, California, to see my friend Mark Miller and prepare for a missionary trip into Mexico, since I was fluent in Spanish.

Landing at 5 a.m. with two hundred dollars in my pocket, I thought I could just hop on a one-way flight to California, since that was what I had heard back in Spain: "Flights in New York are just like buses—frequent and cheap," people would say. Arriving all excited at the American Airlines counter in the wee hours of the morning, ready to get my ticket and just hop on the bus-like plane, I was greeted by some reality and some thick, New York, early-morning, edgy attitude. And No! there were no one-way tickets for two hundred dollars. Tickets cost seven hundred dollars.

Seven hundred dollars, no way! What was I to do? I only had two hundred dollars, my Bible, study books, and a duffel bag with my clothes, and I was three thousand miles from my destination. Bewildered, I wandered around that massive airport like a lost puppy. Something triggered the memory of the name "Greyhound Bus" from a film I had seen growing up. After getting some change, I was soon on a payphone, desperately trying to find out how, and if, I could afford a bus ticket to California. The Greyhound saleswoman on the phone was definitely not from New York! When she heard my lost-puppy sob story, she responded in a high-pitched, "big-momma" Black-woman's voice, "Well son, welcome to the U-nited States of America!" warming my heart and filling my sails for the cross-country journey that lay ahead of me. The ticket I ended up purchasing was a one-way Greyhound ticket for $147. I had some change for food, and that made me glad. Now, I just needed to survive the knife fight that was going on in front of me while standing in line to get on the bus at the 42nd Street Greyhound bus station.

The three-day bus ride was as cramped as it was a blast. Little did I know that my feet would swell up like two balloons after sitting for many, many hours. It was an initiation into all things American: yellow school buses, red barns, huge RV motorhomes pulling cars in tow, and real Western-movie tumbleweeds. Also, struggling people like me, trying to find their way in life, filled those seats on those buses to somewhere. One man named Chuck adopted me as the curious, English-speaking Brit from Spain.

Chuck had a pale complexion, crying out for some sun. Behind his long, straight, strikingly orange hair were two small blue eyes that gave away his lack of sleep. He must have been in his late thirties. He was heavyset, wearing an ACDC T-shirt. On his lap, he carried a large white plastic bag full of snacks that he explained were a gift from his former colleagues, as he was on the way to his new job. He was a likable fellow who happily shared with me the contents of his large sack of goodies. That was to be my initiation into all things "Twinkie": Oreos, cheese puffs, cheese doodles, Tootsie Rolls, etc. Chuck was excited to educate me in this sweet aspect of American culture, amazed that I had never, ever, tasted a Twinkie before.

There was no shortage of characters and examples of human brokenness on that bus. There was the Black mother, out of her mind from her pain of childlessness. She stood in the aisle and cried out for her missing children as if she'd find them up in the escape hatch on the roof of the bus. Then, there was the cowboy with a crafty smirk, wearing his white stetson, bolo, blue jeans, and cowboy boots, in which he hid a suspicious glass flask full of a clear liquid. He would swig on that thing every time we stopped, sneaking over behind the hay bales in front of some seemingly abandoned gas station in the middle of nowhere. There were Mennonites (or Amish folk?) in their black garb, head coverings, straw scribbler hats, and long beards. There was heavy-metal Chuck. And then there was me. I was in America.

After some months in San Bernardino, California, my plan did not materialize as I had hoped. Mark Miller and I spent our time studying the Scriptures and camping on the floor of his empty studio apartment. Time passed quickly, and my three-month visitor's visa ran out. Suddenly, I was in America and out of status, now an illegal alien of sorts. One lawyer from whom I sought assistance offered me a marriage of convenience for ten thousand dollars. He offered to arrange a wife for me, with whom I could live and work, then divorce after a few years, and—voila—I would have a green card.

Well, that was not going to happen. I was going to find a legitimate way of getting my green card. After three months with Mark, I visited some school friends, Nicoline and Sabine from Spain, who lived in Santa Monica. They kindly offered me the floor of their tiny apartment, next to their bed. Nicoline had been a childhood sweetheart of mine. So now, as a wandering and often-lonely young man, seeing her made me fall in puppy love all over again. That emotional roller coaster soon crashed into the icy-cold Pacific Ocean.

My time with Nicoline and Sabine ran out, as did my money. Yet, an opportunity to travel east developed when my mother, now involved with her new partner Joe Berry, visited Joe's two sons, Grant and Craig, who lived in Westport, Connecticut, on the east coast. I was broke, but my dear mother offered to pay my Greyhound bus fare back across the fruited plain. After days of being cramped up on the bus again, I arrived in Westport, Connecticut. Things were looking up, as I was kindly offered the couch.

Now the connection with Louise, my mother's best friend's sister's daughter, became a promising lead. Maybe her husband, Stuart, had some work for me, as he was a contractor in Nyack, New York. I visited Nyack in late June of 1996. I can clearly remember that gloriously bright summer's day that I arrived in Nyack. The sky was a cloudless, deep blue. The intense colors of summer flowers in full bloom adorned people's gardens. It was a perfect summer's day in New York. Oodles of luscious green trees draped the streets, shading the charming Victorian houses, which came in all shapes, sizes, and colors. The slight summer breeze was warm and sweet across my face.

Taking a stroll, I turned the corner and spotted the white columns and pediment of Simpson Memorial Church, dazzling in the sunlight, set against the intense blue sky. The glistening Hudson River behind the church completed the composition. Nyack was beautiful! The sun cascaded through the glowing, dancing leaves, creating scintillating shadow patterns on the street below that would have made even Monet drool! I had the sense that I would move to Nyack, and Nyack indeed was to be my next step. Now, I just needed work to make that happen.

Time was running out. My mother only had a week left in the U.S., and Stuart did not have any work for me at that time. My mother was quite eager for me to return to Spain, so her assistance was very meager. I think Mother would have preferred things not to have worked out for me so that I would have been forced to accept her offer of a free plane ride back to Marbella, Spain.

It looked pretty clear that unless work materialized, I would have no choice but to return to Spain. Before leaving for Spain, Mom invited me to New York City with her. I had never been. We would take the train from Westport Connecticut Station and see the Twin Towers, Central Park, and some art museums, and even have a coffee at Trump Tower.

On that train to Manhattan on that glorious New York summer morning, I remembered someone I had met back in Spain right before leaving for America. In December of 1995, I was working in my brother's cafe in Marbella as a chef. A young man with a swagger walked in. His hair was long, and his talk sounded Americanized. But no, it was Leandro, my younger brother Jonathan's classmate and best friend, who had worked for me in my bar, Locos, some years prior. In America, he studied at Stony Brook University on Long Island, New York—thus his exaggerated American accent. We had spoken briefly, and I'd told him of my upcoming trip to America, at which he'd scribbled his name and number on a piece of paper. He said if I was ever in New York to give him a call.

That morning, on the train heading into New York, I remembered the conversation with Leandro and pulled out the folded piece of paper from my wallet. Excitedly, I turned to my mother and told her that we could call Leandro, and in my mind, I had a vision of actually meeting him.

We arrived in New York City at the 42nd Street train station. Staring upwards, I was immediately captivated by the concrete mountains of glistening architecture, clothed in glass and set against the cloudless, deep-blue summer sky. We walked up to Central Park and then down Fifth Avenue. (And of course, Mom had to have her coffee in Trump Tower just a few blocks down from Central Park.)

Strangely, I began to look for Leandro. I did not even think of calling him. Back then, cell phones were a novelty for me. Instead,

I fixed my eyes on the throbbing summer crowds of wall-to-wall people bobbing as they ebbed and flowed up and down Fifth Avenue. I was looking for Leandro's face and features, especially his distinctive beak-shaped nose and profile. After all, he was in New York—so he'd told me! Since I was in New York, I would now try looking for him, since my vision on the train that morning of meeting him was so clear.

How was I to know that Stony Brook University was hours away at the end of Long Island? We had no way of finding out exactly where he was without calling him. But that did not even cross my mind once we arrived in Manhattan. It was just a burden to keep looking for him, and my mother now protested, since I had already made her walk nearly the entire length of Fifth Avenue toward the Twin Towers.

"My feet are killing me!" Mother insisted, "Let's get a bus or a taxi." To which I responded, "No, we need to keep walking." We pounded the pavement—poor old Mom! The crowds thinned out, and we made a right turn off Fifth Avenue and began walking down a quieter Sixth Avenue, near Washington Square Park.

Mom, who was now walking ahead of me, walked right past three men heading in our direction. A short, long-haired man who walked with a swagger, wearing white-rimmed, mirrored glasses and a striped, long-sleeved white T-shirt, was flanked by two tall, dreadlocked Rastafarians, dressed in green khakis and tea-cozy-styled knitted hats. I walked right up to them and, pointing at the face of the man in the middle, said, "Now that's Leandro!"

He peered over his mirrored shades, perched on his beak-shaped nose, in astonishment. To my mother's complete amazement, we had found Leandro. I was not that surprised. Mom was now jumping up and down in the street, shrieking! She could not believe it. Meanwhile, Leandro and his two dude-buddies were "blown away, man," being super high from having just smoked weed in Washington Square Park. "Whoa! No way, man! Jules, what are you doing here, man?" Leandro asked. To which I replied, "Looking for you!" He gave me his new number, and we parted ways.

Providentially, verging on the miraculous, I had found Leandro amongst the nearly eighteen million people in the metropolitan New York City area. Little did I know that the phone number he had previously given me would not have worked, since it was late June and college was closed for the summer. He had moved back from Stony Brook to the lower East Side in New York City and lived with his fake wife in her apartment. She was a classmate whom he'd married to get his green card.

Time was ticking. Mother was still dangling a free ride back to Spain in front of me, with only days to go. But now, Leandro was part of the equation. So, I called him up and told him my scenario of needing a place to stay, "rapido," to which he replied, "Let me ask my wife." He called me back minutes later and said his fake wife said I could sleep on the other couch next to him, as she slept with her boyfriend in the bedroom. Leandro had to live in the apartment just in case the INS (at that time, the immigration services) popped by for a surprise inspection to see if they were really married and living together. You can see why the '90s movie with Gerard Depardieu, *Green Card*, was such a hit. Yet this was real life.

Mother was not impressed; her plot had been foiled! She dropped me off at the Westport Train Station. As we awkwardly said goodbye, Mom gave me twenty dollars. I now had just enough money to buy an eight-dollar one-way ticket to Manhattan and some change for a sandwich. The rest was in God's hands. Leandro kindly took care of my needs. He looked up to me, as he was my younger brother's age and had formerly worked for me in my bar back in the day. He saw it as an honor to help me out, generously giving me sixty dollars in cash to keep me going.

About ten days later, my mother's best friend's sister's daughter, Louise, finally got back to me with good news of a summer job painting their house in Nyack, New York. Louise also had arranged a place for me to stay in a friend's basement on a pull-out bed, which I could afford after working a whole week for Stuart. Leandro drove me to Nyack from Manhattan and dropped me off at my new digs.

It was in Nyack, after a year, that I met my precious wife, now of twenty-three years, Gloria. We never dated a day, and then we were engaged, and then we married! We became friends, best friends, and then God intervened, and our lives changed forever. Now, it would be a disservice to you not to share this story. Although the minutiae of details would fill a whole book by themselves, a decent overview you must hear.

On the heels of three failed romantic endeavors, the emotional pain had pushed me to a place where rejection and betrayal had convinced me that maybe a life of celibate mission work was my calling after all. I now boldly proclaimed to all (especially to single women) that my celibacy and singleness were a special calling from God, as a defense mechanism to keep them far away from my wounded heart.

I attended Simpson Memorial Church in Nyack, New York, and was enrolled part-time at the Alliance Theological Seminary, where I fine-tuned some of my theological beliefs. I was heavily involved as a lay minister and lived on the premises as sexton of Simpson Church. This position opened up the opportunity of applying for a mission-worker green card, which could have resolved my legal status. I always made sure people knew my legal status, since I wanted to be transparent. Pastor Ed Mangham and his dear wife, Sharon, took me under their wing and did what they could to help me. It was also to be a critical season of spiritual formation, which culminated in some of the most demanding and most challenging times of my life.

The mission-worker green card required a Bachelor's degree, something I did not have. Since the church was affiliated with Nyack College, a Christian ministry school in Nyack, I pursued a degree to solve my embarrassing and glaring out-of-status problem. Because I was involved in ministry and desiring to be enrolled full-time, people I knew would remind me that it was "unrighteous" to be in America illegally, citing Romans 13:1 in the Bible: "Every person is to be subject to the governing authorities." I had my ways of self-justifying my status issue and refused even the thought of going back to Spain, as I had fallen in love with America. It was my new home; I did not want to leave.

Events transpired later that year that shook my life to the core, culminating in me seeing the errors of my ways in different areas of my life, especially in the area of my legal status. My conscience was tormenting me because of being illegally present in America and breaking the law. I had overstayed my welcome and overstayed my visa—something had to change.

My problem was then bigger than ever since I was also falling in love with Gloria. My ivory tower of singleness was crumbling, even though I made it clear to Gloria that I did not want to get married, since I was called to a life of singleness, of course.

Well, God is in the business of thwarting man's best-intended plans, you know. Just remember, if you want to make God laugh, tell Him your plans. Well, mine were working well enough, I thought. God must have been chuckling as He sent Gloria into my life. The wheels began to come off my bold assertions of singleness. Gloria and I had become such good friends that I fell in love with her. Not wanting to be in love, but at the same time wanting nothing more than to be in love, I desired that the loneliness and longing of my heart would be filled. I was in an existential quandary—to be, or not to be, in love?

One night, having seen Gloria at a Bible study and rejoiced in her presence there, I went to prayer. Kneeling at the foot of a large cross, I was just about to begin speaking with the Almighty when suddenly I was overwhelmed. I can only describe it as a giant piece of invisible sponge, compressed and then released inside my head. It expanded and filled every corner of my mind, as the presence of God so overwhelmed me.

Then, I began to hear these words: "She's to be your wife…she's to be your wife…she's to be your wife," at which point I called out to God and exclaimed, "Excuse me, Lord, do You mind, I am trying to pray here!" The response was immediate: "She's to be your wife…she's to be your wife…she's to be your wife."

"That's it!" I said, getting up in a huff. "I'm going to bed!" I was angry. Not only because I was trying to pray, but because I also was doing my best to fight off this "love stuff" that I was feeling toward Gloria. I woke up the following morning with peace and quiet in my mind, so I sighed with relief until I heard, "She's to be your wife…," as it started all over again. For days, a battle ensued—a struggle of wills. It was as if I were boxing with God. After a few days, I began to relent and to express sorrow at my fighting with God. I would repent and apologize, and then I would repeat, "But no, I am called to be single!" followed by, "I am sorry, Lord!" On and on it went until finally, by the fourth day, I said to myself, "What is wrong with me? What an idiot I am!" Here was this wonderful, godly woman whom I admired, respected, and with whom I had become best friends, and now I was fighting against her and God. What in the world was wrong with me? Marriage could even solve my green-card status.

That evening, exhausted from the battle and from remodeling work, I threw down my tools and walked out to the edge of the Hudson River. It was dusk and hazy, as the sky melted into the blueish river. The wide river was very calm, the water moving like oil in slow motion. Suddenly two swans, bright as white can be, set against the mysterious blended horizon, swam toward me. The river slopped and clapped as the waters kissed the shore. Male and female, faithful partners for life, on their journey together, one by one, they fed together. Their elegant, exquisitely beautiful long necks disappeared in slow motion as their heads submerged into the viscous, watery shallows. I was transfixed. God was painting a beautiful picture for me. He comforted me with His divine order and the wonders of nature. It was not good for a man to be alone. God had brought me my life's partner in Gloria. In perfect peace, I surrendered.

On the morning of the fifth day, I arranged for Gloria and me to go for a walk to share our faith. Before we set out, I suggested we pray together, which we did. Gloria prayed how, as iron sharpens iron, we could bless each other. She also sang the song, "By My

Side," by Peggy Gordon, which she had learned growing up from the 1973 movie *Godspell*. ("Where are you going? Can you take me with you? For my hand is cold and needs warmth. Where are you going? Oh please, take me with you. By my side...") I was continually moved as Gloria innocently shared, seeming to know what was going on, yet not knowing anything about the emotional turmoil swirling inside of me.

Then, Gloria shared a dream she'd had. In the dream, I was this life-sized, scary cat sitting at the top of a staircase, not letting anyone pass. The cat was growling and clawing, showing its sharp teeth. Gloria innocently came up the stairs in the dream and tossed me (the cat) a huge tootsie roll, which I caught in my mouth. The giant, sticky-and-chewy candy gummed up my teeth as I tried to eat it. As I ate the tootsie roll, in a puff of smoke, I turned back into myself and asked her why she was feeding me, to which she replied, "I didn't want you to bite me!"

I immediately knew what the dream meant. It was God showing Gloria the defenses I had constructed around my wounded heart, not allowing anyone to get too close because of the pain. She would bring healing to my heart, and I would once again become a healed version of myself. I was now angry at God again, as I muttered under my breath, how could God dare do such a thing, showing Gloria my secret wounded heart?

As we walked together, I pretended everything was fine though it was not. We walked out onto a floating boat dock in the Hudson River. Dark gray clouds hung low over the river. It began to rain, and the dock rocked and bobbed in the wind and choppy waters. I turned to Gloria and told her I had something to say to her, at which she told me to "just get on with it," as she expected some lecture again about me being single and not wanting to get married. She said bluntly, "Just spit it out," to which I replied, "God has told me, you are to be my wife."

Everything at that moment froze, it seemed. Gloria said her feet felt like cement blocks. As the dock swayed, the rain came down, and I began to bang my head on the dock post. Gloria responded,

"I always wished that something like this would happen to me, but I never thought it would!"

From that day forward, we were betrothed, engaged to be married. But the fun was only about to begin. God seemed to delight in interjecting Himself into our divine romance. As everything around us seemed to be falling into place, people would give us strangely apt love-related gifts, such as angels and cupids, though they had no knowledge of what was going on. Out of the blue, strangers would say things to us, like, "Are you two married?" echoing this mysterious union of two souls, as if another note in a melody were being plucked on God's harp in divine delight. It was truly intoxicating, as we both accepted the will of God and then embarked on a fairy-tale romance that can never be truly expressed. The love of God surrounded us, infusing us with ecstasy. We were tempted many times to jump the gun and open the gift prematurely. By the grace of God, we remained chaste until our wedding night eleven months later, when we consummated our marriage in celebration. But this would happen only after passing the fiery trials that came upon us before that joyous day.

We were head over heels in love with each other, and I was also in love with my new home, America. But as soon as things looked too good to be true, the storms rolled in. Gloria's family, especially her father, got wind of our romance. I approached him to ask for his blessing, at which he balked—especially after I told him I was out of status. He immediately thought I wanted to marry Gloria either for her money or to get my legal status resolved. Before long, Gloria quit her job as a teacher, and Gloria's family tried to perform an intervention of sorts. Gloria's father now called the INS to get me deported, and he called the police to try to get Gloria committed to a mental hospital, since they could not fathom why she had left her job. The blowup happened around the same time that I had become deeply burdened with being out of status here in the U.S. One family member took it upon herself to go around Nyack, even to the furniture store where I worked, spreading terrible falsehoods. (Years later, Gloria's family did finally sort of accept me, even though we were banished to eating at the kiddie card table in the kitchen when we visited for Thanksgiving, while the rest of the family celebrated in the dining room.)

In one way, it made sense to get married and solve my legal status. Yet the church, Beth Israel Messianic Congregation, Gloria's home church where we attended, would not marry us for eleven months. That was their policy. We seriously considered eloping, and I even considered getting married in Las Vegas. We would do anything that would cool the flames that raged around and within us. But no, feeding the accusations by eloping would only fuel the speculation. There was one way to silence the allegations, and that was just for me to pack up and leave, get my status resolved outside the U.S., and then get married. However, just leaving avoided any accountability for my having broken the law.

I reasoned that the only way to silence all of the noise was to hand myself in to the INS and let them decide what I needed to do to make the situation right. So, with Pastor Ed Mangham and my sweet fiancée, Gloria, we made the trip to 26 Federal Plaza in New York City, to the Immigration and Naturalization Services. After waiting for hours, we made our way up through the very tall building to a dimly lit room, where I waited for my turn. When it came up, I walked up to the desk with Gloria and Pastor Ed, put my hands together as if ready to be cuffed on the spot, and told them my story. They laughed! No one had ever turned themselves in that way. They told me just to leave the country, with the warning that at the airport, Immigration could stamp my passport with a five- to ten-year no-return stamp for overstaying my visitor's visa.

That dreadful day came when I was to leave my sweet bride-to-be, Gloria, and my country that I now called home. We were shaken and hurt beyond belief at the prospect of being separated for who knew how long. The passport desk awaited me, where I could get the five- to ten-year no-return stamp. In tears, we both said so long, and we hugged tighter than ever before, never want-ing to let go. Finally forcing ourselves apart, I turned and walked through that door.

The Immigration passport officer, looking sternly into my face, looked at the passport and flipped through the pages, then closed the passport, looked me again in the eyes, and handed it back to me. NO STAMP! Yes, that is right! For reasons unknown to me, that challenging day had an unexpected silver lining.

I was free!

A huge relief came over me, as the prospect of marriage still glimmered ahead. Six months in Spain and six months of late-night phone calls added up. We often wept in our pain at being so far away from one another. It was at the height of our intoxicating romance that we were separated by land and sea. Gloria would finally visit me six months later in Spain, as we charted our next steps toward marriage. Gloria brought a wedding dress, just in case we eloped in Gibraltar, and a letter from Florence McGarrity, a friend back in the U.S. who had reached out with her husband to help me with work at different times. That letter contained clear directions for me to return to the U.S., as she prayerfully believed it was God's will for me to return to America. My boss in Spain at the time, Chris McCarthy, responded by saying, "Go west, young man!"

The door flung open for me to return to the United States lawfully and finally get married, which we did on December 5, 1998, at Beth Israel Messianic Congregation. The wedding was officiated by Messianic Rabbi Jonathan Cahn and Pastor Ed Mangham.

Gloria and I lived in Nyack and started our own business together on February 14, 2000. It was a custom-painted furniture business called Raven's Custom Creations. We were there for six years, during which time we started a family. God blessed our marriage with four beautiful children—Johanna, Victoria, Jeremiah, and Benjamin. Sadly, we lost our baby son, Benjamin, at six months when we moved to Elmira, New York.

During this time, I became more familiar with the name and person of Donald Trump. But then, it would become more personal as I would visit Manhattan for business now that I lived in Nyack, New York, right outside of Trump's stomping grounds.

It was impossible not to see the name Trump emblazoned here and there, whether a road sign indicating Trump was sponsoring clean-up of some road, like the West Side Highway, or some massive construction project on Manhattan's West Side, draped in Trump's glistening banners.

I think the most memorable story that I heard about Trump was the limo story. It was a typical tale, folklore that drifted out of New York City. It was during the massive 2003 Northeast blackout one summer, when parts of New York City were without power for nearly the whole day. I can remember sitting outside with my employees, chatting for hours while waiting for the power to return.

One of them began to discuss the remarkable story of Trump's broken-down limousine. How some guy in a pickup truck stopped to help, fixing the problem. The tinted window of the limo rolled down, and it was Donald Trump inside. Trump asked for the fellow's address so that he could send some flowers to the guy's wife as a token of appreciation. Trump not only sent flowers but allegedly paid off the mortgage on the man's house! I thought, "Wow! It would be great to meet Trump. Maybe I could do custom cabinetry work for him. And maybe even something like that limo story could happen to me!"

It was also then that *The Apprentice* TV show started, in 2004; we would watch it here and there. I can remember enjoying the show, especially Trump's no-nonsense dealing with contestants. Years later, in 2014, it was exciting when Trump explored a potential run for governor of New York, now that I was a New Yorker. It made sense to me that a no-nonsense, successful, straight-talking businessman from New York City with name recognition would run the state better than Democrat Governor Andrew Cuomo. Trump's business skills would attract businesses to New York, creating a thriving business environment, rather than driving millions of people and companies away. However, since Trump could not get Republican Party support he needed across the state, it was not to be.

A year later, excitement and anticipation filled the air. On June 16, 2015, Donald Trump made his iconic and historic escalator descent at Trump Tower. This would immediately precede Donald Trump's announcement of his candidacy for president of the United States.

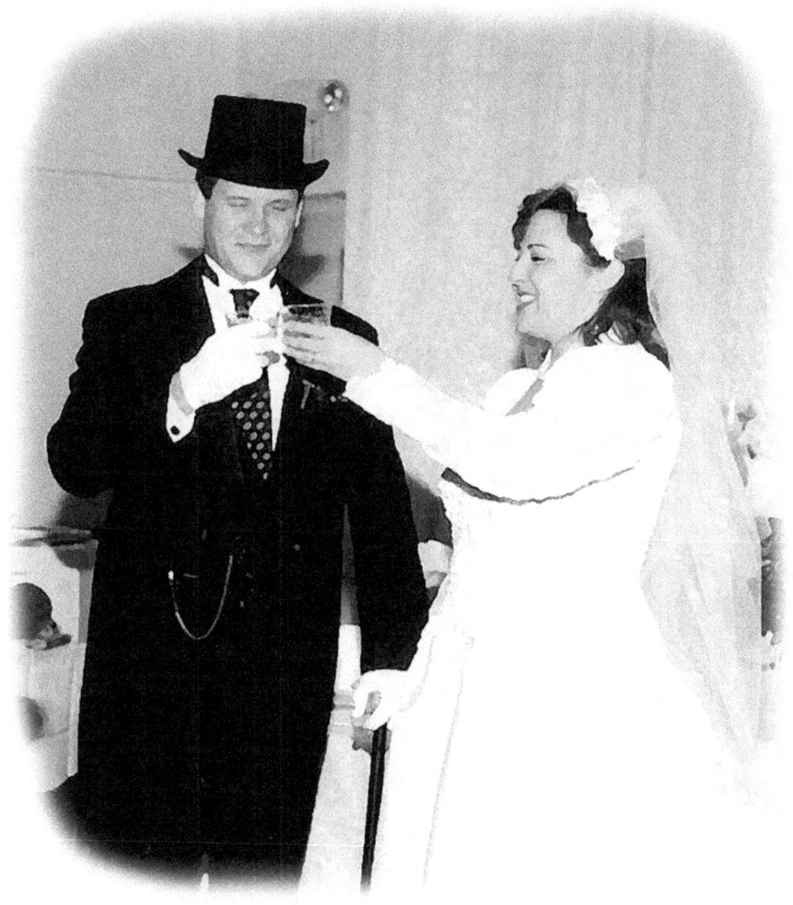

Julian and Gloria Raven, December 5, 1998

Chapter Four

COMMON-SENSE APPEAL

CANDIDATE TRUMP'S FIRST STATEMENTS, ESPECIALLY REGARDING illegal immigrants entering the United States, set the world on fire. They were very personal for me. I wholeheartedly agreed with the sentiment about the need to fix an ever-increasing illegal-immigration problem. I understood that rape was a significant part of that problem—not because all Hispanics are rapists, but because the illegal human-trafficking and rape industry originating from Latin America was run by evil people who happened to be Hispanics. I had come to America to take the Gospel of Jesus Christ to Mexico, being fluent in Spanish and having great affection for Latin Americans. But the rape issue struck a nerve in me.

Back in Nyack in April of 2005, Mary Nagle of New City, New York, was brutally raped and murdered by an illegal Salvadorian. Her suffering is best left only broadly described out of respect for her family and memory. Her husband's brother was one of our clients at the time, and the story tore through our world. I had several Salvadorian workers over the years. We helped one young man get his legal status. This young man, named Ismael, was the hardest-working person I had known in my life—a treasure of a human being, deserving of all of the help we could give him.

Evil people exist in every culture. Managing them in our own land is hard enough. But deliberately leaving the back door open to our country at night, knowingly allowing wolves to come in and kill our sheep, is insanity and a dereliction of duty.

The fact that even one illegal Salvadorian could sneak into America and commit such a heinous crime upon one American citizen, having been left alone and unvetted at the home of Mary Nagle by the contractor who hired him, still today makes me sick to my stomach. It made me change my hiring practices concerning who could come with me on the many jobs I had installing custom cabinetry in private homes in New City, New York.

Trump was right about the need to address the problem, no matter how ugly the truth was. Was Trump's choice of words deliberate, aimed at igniting and focusing racial hatred against "them" (disparaging a minority, as some claimed), using them as scapegoats for our cultural woes? Or was he just pointing out the elephant in the room? That answer each person needs to decide for themselves.

Personally, the vast majority of Hispanics I have met are humble, decent, and hardworking people who have become an integral part of the American economy. For me, it had nothing to do with race; it was about law and order and enforcing reasonable and humane border laws. How in the world could there be anything wrong with that? Turning a blind eye to the problem was just another expression of American capitulation in the face of lawlessness, which only emboldens lawlessness and disrespect for the rule of law and American sovereignty.

Hispanics who enter America illegally come with all sorts of backgrounds, many being criminals. A left-leaning *Huffington Post* story[1] from 2014 (updated in 2017) by writer Eleanor Goldberg documents the tragic story of Hispanic women and girls making their way to the United States. Goldberg documents that 80 percent of women and girls are raped on their journey to America. Knowing this in advance, the women and young girls take birth control pills as pregnancy prevention, knowing there is an elevated chance they will be the victims of rape. This means that some of their male couriers, companions, or coyotes are their rapists who also come into America.

My personal immigration story and experiences with the shadowy immigration underworld (with its dehumanizing effects on people) directly affected my support for Trump. Shutting down the border and building a wall (which would later be featured in my Trump painting), not because we wanted to but because we had to, would cut off a considerable percentage of the criminal, seedy, illegal, and dark human-trafficking underworld. It would also dramatically impact the illicit-drug trade and sex trade and other attempts to cross the border illegally. Also, it would close a wide-open door to Islamic terrorists plotting to enter the U.S. for their sordid ends. Now, if an equally effective solution could be achieved without building a wall, then great—even better. But no such solution was in sight.

In my own personal and painful experience of self-deportation, I developed a solution for helping solve the ongoing immigration crisis in America, while also dealing with the massive amounts of people who live in the shadows—a solution that could even become a viable policy. Incentivized self-deportation would allow the government to vet, number, and document all who participated, with a required time outside the country (political penance) and a guaranteed pathway of return. Legal working papers would be given to those who returned upon their arrival, legitimizing those hard-working immigrants who wanted to make things right. This would dignify those who wanted to legitimately participate in the American Dream. It would give them a way to demonstrate respect for our laws. It would also create in them a determination to succeed legally, as the road would be open. Those initial working papers would turn into a green card after five years and eventually into citizenship after twenty years. Granting green cards to people who are here illegally only rewards lawlessness. It is also an insult to those who wait in line, legally seeking entrance into the United States.

Upon my arrival in the United States, I marveled at how people's lawns just blended into each other without any fences or walls. Every house in Spain, where I grew up, had walls—even tiny houses like my family home. Every property had walls, iron gates, or even broken glass embedded into the concrete on top of the walls. I would have to do a double take whenever I saw how even mansions often did not have walls here in America. In Spain, the bigger the house, the bigger the walls. Theft and break-ins were so prevalent because of people's lack of lethal options to defend themselves and their property—primarily, I believe, because gun ownership was so restricted. This deprivation of people's power just emboldened criminals.

Americans and their lack of walls revealed something extraordinary and yet naive about America. Trusting, open-hearted, and law-abiding citizens express their values in how their homes are built next door to each other. But for America to build an entire country without walls (i.e., efficient law enforcement at the border) just leaves them vulnerable if a criminal wants to break in, because disrespect for the rule of law is encouraged by turning a blind eye to lawless entry into the U.S.A.

Now, of course, the Second Amendment in America makes criminals think twice about breaking into someone's home in most parts of the country. Criminals know that the chances of homeowners owning more than one gun are very high. The potential of the criminal getting shot and dying is very high, and so down goes the motivation for breaking in.

Donald Trump's no-nonsense, say-it-as-it-is approach to politics was a thunderous, rushing gust of fresh air. Juxtaposed against the typical political peddling of putrid, half-baked policy ideas and forked-tongued windbags filled with empty promises, Trump was an instant phenomenon on a meteoric rise. He was unafraid to say what he believed was necessary, echoing what people were thinking. His approach was like diving headfirst off a cliff into the ocean. Once he leaped off the rocks, there was nothing left for him to do but fly through the air with no restraints. Desperate times called for desperate measures!

Because of Trump's wealth and self-financed campaign, he could say what he wanted and get away with it; his money purchased great freedom to speak. Trump was unashamed to buck everybody who was anybody who demanded to be coddled, obeyed, or even revered. He bulldozed through institutional norms, expectations, and established decorum, the likes of which usually hamstring and emasculate men, converting them into institutional weasels rather than reformers.

The sound of Trump's unvarnished and often brutal honesty had the power to cut through every other sound bite, constantly sucking the oxygen out of every story. People everywhere and the media were either shocked, stunned, amazed, energized, or horrified, as this "New York builder of buildings" began to ram and demolish every tower in his path.

Trump's America-first approach, with the promise of tightening the sagging belt buckle of an already sloppy national identity (with its sluggish economy), was an inspiration. Promises made would be fulfilled. Tax cuts and deregulation would eventually set the economy on fire. Caring for and prioritizing the military, veterans, and first responders—especially the boys in blue—was met with a gasp of "finally!" Fighting for the forgotten American men and women—whether Black, Brown, Red, Yellow, or White—in cities and towns across the nation, who were crippled by globalism and American job-destroying trade deals, was a win-win-win for Trump.

Trump's foreign policy was in its infancy. It would evolve on the fly, with a mixture of uncertainty, showmanship, braggadocio, and shocking decisiveness, depending on who would become the Secretary of Defense or Secretary of State for the week. Getting NATO members to cough up and pay their fair share would be a hit. Abandoning the Kurdish fighters and people would be a disaster and an unfathomable betrayal.

Once Trump became president, his common-sense approach to policy had a mixed bag of results. Unreservedly recognizing Jerusalem as Israel's capital, recognizing Israeli sovereignty in the Golan Heights, and moving the American embassy from Tel-Aviv to Jerusalem without hesitation were historic. Trump's strange meeting with Vladimir Putin in Helsinki, however, was disturbing. Trump's long-game economic trade wars with China seemed to make sense, even if farmers had to be bailed out in the short term. Digging America out of decades of compromise and squishiness would take years, but Trump, the new kid on the block, rapidly put enemy nations on notice. Being unpredictable and inexperienced, his hard-line approach caused America's enemies to freeze and hold their breaths for a season. Walking away from President Obama's Iran compromise put Iran back in its place.

Trump's eventual withdrawal and reduction of troops from Iraq, Afghanistan, and Syria appealed to American sensibilities about war. But retreat was both naive and isolationist since it undermined American sacrifice and denied the need for a strong American global-leadership presence, especially in the face of ever-changing and evolving threats against America and our allies. Conducting a historic photo op with Kim Jong-un in the Korean DMZ and bragging about having a "bigger button" was a high-risk gamble. It was a radically new approach to foreign policy when dealing with despots. The end game was hard to fathom; North Korea is still North Korea.

Trump's growth on social issues, especially abortion and the battle for a Christian America—even if it was as superficial as unashamedly saying "Merry Christmas"—was music to believers' ears all across the country. An ungodly man was fighting for Christian causes. It was revolutionary!

That unusual combination of characteristics inspired millions of Americans to get on board the Trump train. Looking at everyone else who ran for president, there was no comparison. There he was, a self-funded man in open political warfare against anyone, everyone, and anything that might get in his way. This was Trump's allure but also his liability. I extended my prayers and grace where Trump's checkered and immoral past clouded his path. All in all, it was exciting and entertaining and produced hope that maybe Trump really could save America.

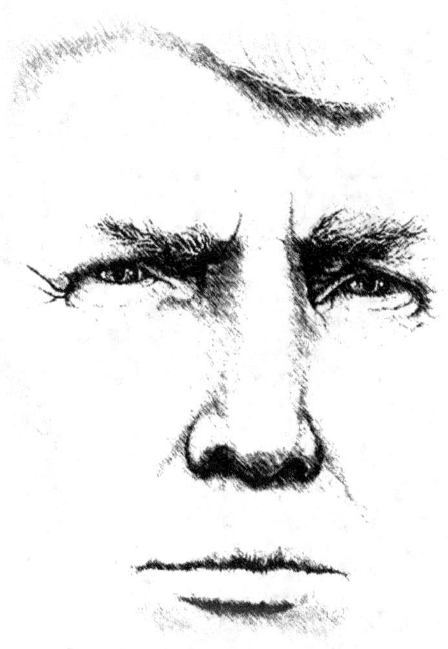

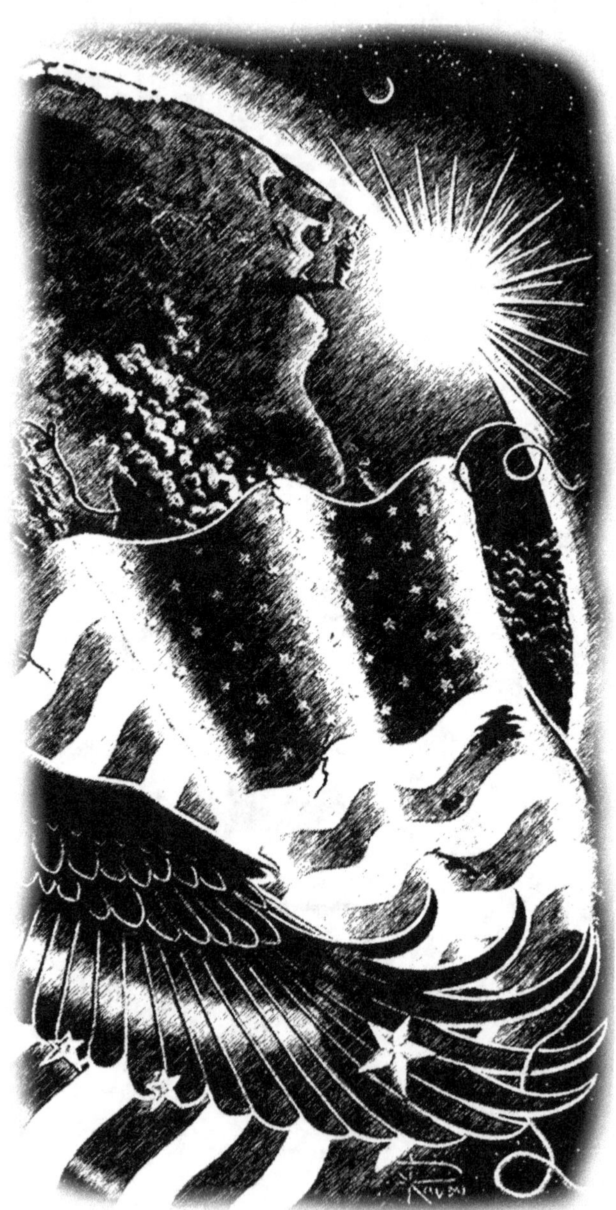

"Unafraid and Unashamed," stylized detail

Chapter Five

AMERICA FALLING

On the morning of July 9, 2015, I was sitting at my desk, captivated by a Trump speech charging through the speakers on my computer. Immediately, a creative response to what I was hearing began bubbling up inside of me. On my computer screen was a picture of Trump's face staring at me. His expression was full of determination, as his words resonated with my heart and mind. Suddenly, the words "Unafraid and Unashamed" ticker-taped across the screen of my mind, as it were. In that moment, an image appeared—a vision of a torn and faded American flag billowing in the wind on a flagpole falling to the ground. Before the flag touched the ground, a speeding bald eagle swooped down and snatched the falling flag with saving action.

What did this mean? Could Trump save America? Was it a picture I was to paint? Was this just another good or bad idea?

President Obama's "Hope" poster, created by artist Shepard Fairey, became a historic image attached to a historic presidential campaign, establishing Fairey as a nationally recognized artist. Before that poster, Fairey spent his late nights pasting guerrilla graffiti art posters of André the Giant on abandoned buildings in Los Angeles. Now he will forever be associated with Obama's presidency. Nothing was going on in the art world that was pro-Trump. Could this be my moment to create something? Would creating a pro-Trump painting help my emerging art career, or would it destroy it?

Only a few weeks into his fledgling and freewheeling campaign, Trump was already a polarizing figure. Trump constantly created controversy, which polarized people and made those on the left boil with rage and hatred. He was already labeled as a racist, misogynist, homophobic bigot and fascist. That same fierce reaction was already being smeared onto anyone taking a public stand in Trump's support. At that time, his candidacy was considered a PR stunt. He was largely considered a fool, and very few people took him seriously. Fewer still would show any public support for him. People I knew, especially in the Christian community, despised him. After all, Trump was a casino and gambling tycoon, philanderer, and adulterer. In short, Trump was a hardened, unrepentant sinner!

Painting the Trump painting would be a gamble and costly for sure. I had already experienced how being an outspoken Christian and conservative had caused me to be blacklisted in the leftist-controlled local art community. So, painting the Trump painting would be like a red flag to a bull, ensuring the darkest and most enduring of all blacklisting. But what was I to do? America's bold red, white, and blue colors were fading. America was falling into the abyss of globalism, corruption, lawlessness, and debauchery, and somebody had to do something about it. Could Trump be God's man for the job? Could Trump right the ship?

Perhaps it would be worth creating the painting, regardless of the guaranteed grief and hostility that would come at me from all sides—leftists, liberals, Republicans, and Christians—leaving me standing all alone. Maybe there would be a big payoff for me?

Time passed. Days turned into weeks as I pondered the image of the eagle, the falling flag, and Trump's face that was seared into my mind. Every day, the vision just sat there. At the time, I was consumed with a new artistic discovery: welding steel sculptures out of scrap metal. However, the image would not fade. Listening to the radio daily kept me abreast of the news and Trump's meteoric rise, which showed no signs of slowing down. The radio maintained the image fresh in my mind, reminding me and dangling a carrot of what might be. I knew that I had to do something with this image, but I kept pushing it off.

When inspiration happens, it is like a form of spiritual or mental pregnancy, starting with a seed idea growing deep within that builds pressure until that vision must be birthed, expressed, and created in order to move forward. But I was swamped and focused on my steel sculptures, a trained focus I have developed that requires a considerable force to shift onto something else.

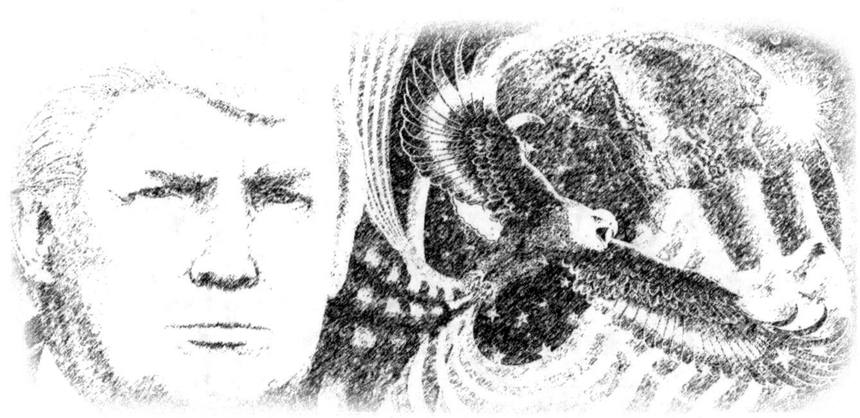

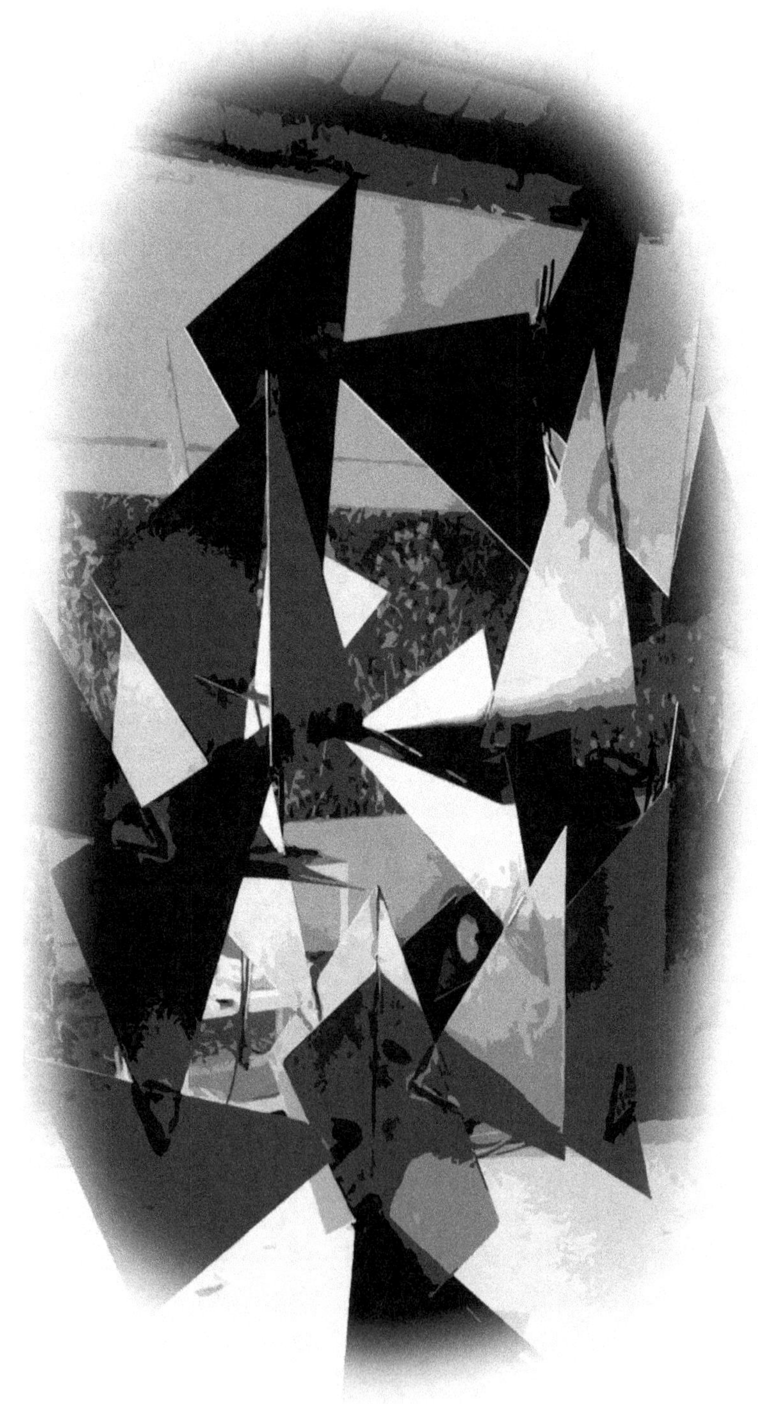

Steel, 2015

Chapter Six

SCINTILLATING SYNCHRONICITY

Weeks passed, and the internal pressure kept building. My dithering was now nagging and aggravating me because the image lingered. "Just get on with it," I would say to myself, until finally, one evening, on August 20, I sat down at my computer to work on a sketch that incorporated Trump's face, an eagle, and a flag. I sought a pleasing composition, beginning with the eagle and moving other elements around. Bald eagles snatching fish from rivers are common subject matter, but eagles never scream when they snatch their prey, so I began to create a bird that would be doing both.

My thirteen-year-old daughter, Victoria, walked into the office, looked over my shoulder, and said, "Dad, what are you working on? Are you going to build a sculpture of an eagle?" Victoria had seen the angular steel sculpture that I was working on at the time. I replied, "No, Darling, I'm working on a painting," not saying much else. All of sudden, as Victoria was leaving the room, she turned around and uttered, "Dad, why don't you paint the painting of the eagle and give it to Donald Trump, so that when he becomes president, he can hang it in the White House?"

Victoria somehow had connected the dots without knowing anything about what was going on inside my head. Victoria knew about Trump, as we would often discuss politics at the dinner table. But she knew nothing of the weeks of internal struggles I had gone through or the image of the eagle, the flag, and Trump that was seared on my mind. Sitting on the edge of my chair, I stared into her large brown eyes in awe. Looking back at me, as a thirteen-year-old teenager, Victoria innocently shrugged her shoulders and walked out of the room.

Waking early the following day, August 21, 2015, it was exciting to find out what Trump was saying, whom Trump was scorching, or who was scorching him, as was the daily ritual. Opening my Internet browser to CNN and clicking around, there in front of me was a brand-new video from that morning. The caption was Trump saying something like, "I had a visitor this morning." Clicking on the video clip, I watched as it began to roll. *Time* magazine had been to Trump Tower that morning for a photo shoot in Trump's office with Trump and "his guest."

"No way!" In unbelief, I pushed back from the desk, staring at the photo on the screen. It felt like I was getting pranked—it was surreal. After weeks of daily seeing this image in my mind of Trump, a bald eagle, and an American flag—and the night before, my daughter saying I should paint an eagle and give it to Donald Trump when he becomes president—there on my screen, in Donald Trump's office the very next morning, was Donald Trump in a blue suit with a live bald eagle perched on his left arm! It was so well lit that it looked artificial, like a photo montage that had been created in Photoshop. It seemed impossible that all these events and elements had synchronized in such a grand manner. After collecting my children from school later that day, I hurriedly led Victoria into my office and showed her the photo on the screen, and she stood and stared with amazement.

I rushed down to my art studio and began constructing a giant seven-by-fifteen-foot wooden stretcher frame. Upon this giant frame, I would stretch the preprimed cotton canvas for my magnum opus that I was about to create. By the afternoon, the canvas had been stretched and I had begun to paint the painting. My next challenge arose—what exactly was I going to paint? I had only sat down the night before to begin composing the image, and here now the massive hundred-square-foot blank canvas was staring down at me. Whatever it was going to be had to be worked out on the canvas as I painted. The creative inner impulses directed me from the moment my brushes touched the primed surface. The motivation within me was explosive compared with the prior weeks of procrastination. The internal pressure felt like a spitting volcano that was about to blow a massive hole in my chest. Before, it had been just one of many visions in my head, but now it was all that I could see.

When that sequence of events unfolded, they switched something on inside of me that would change my life. "This is it!" I said to myself. Inspiration is what artists dream of—that moment when the sails that hung low and slack in the morning dew for weeks on end suddenly become filled with a mighty gust of wind. Clinking and clanking, the rigging wildly thrashes as all the creaking ropes tighten up, thrusting the vessel forward. That level of inspiration eclipsed everything else in that moment, as I believed that Donald Trump would become president of the United States. I had to paint that painting; I had to paint that painting. I worked with absolute focus and undivided attention, with a drive I had never experienced before.

This focus would engulf my life night and day for the next six weeks. Could this painting be the one that would establish me as an artist? My wife, Gloria, was working full-time in the medical field as a phlebotomist at the time, allowing me to pour myself into the painting without any distractions.

At night, I would lie awake in bed, struggling to sleep, developing the composition in my mind as the image burned brightly within. I was often like a zombie, going to the studio at all hours of the day and night. At times, Gloria became concerned and did not recognize me, because I ignored many of the basic daily routines of life. I slept at the foot of the painting at times, working on it sixteen to twenty hours a day, drinking substantial amounts of coffee, and eating roast chicken and nut bars that I picked up from the grocery store nearby. (That focus was similar to the inspiration I experienced when writing this book you are currently reading.)

The painting was developed by blocking out large areas of color with my brushes, the outline of Trump's full-sized face on one side and an eagle snatching the flag on the other. The rest of the imagery emerged as I painted, the brushes getting smaller and smaller as I went along to handle more detail. Most of the time, it was a struggle not knowing how to paint what I wanted to paint. As a result, there are many practice layers beneath the painting's surface—the problematic sections were redone over and over and over again.

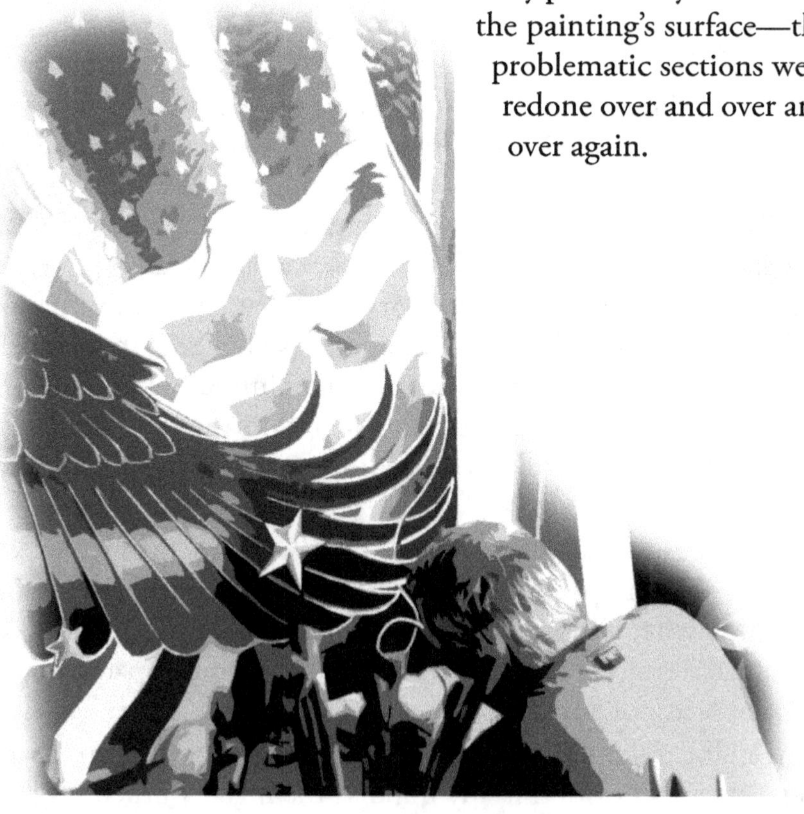

Chapter Seven

GOD WITH TRUMP?

THE SYNCHRONICITY OF EVENTS COULD ONLY HAVE BEEN interpreted as divinely orchestrated. Associating Trump with any divine orchestration was anathema to most Christians initially, as Trump was known as an unrepentant sinner, and "How could God be using such a wretch of a human being?" But learning to discern the voice of God has been a lifelong goal of mine. Testing to see whether something is inspired by God or just an excellent human idea takes practice. The prevalence of so many people claiming God said this or that makes me extremely cautious to proclaim with certainty that God has spoken at all.

Ideas—particularly artistic ones—and their origins are mysterious. Many ideas come from deep within, from a fountain of knowledge that just bubbles up. What makes something more than just an excellent human idea and potentially a "God idea" is how the idea develops and conflicts with one's own views at the time. If from God, an idea will have a specific quality about it. Since God knows one will struggle with the concept on the inside, He will confirm it on the outside in ways that would make it impossible to be one's own idea.

The sequence of events in my life, my spiritual journey, and the discovery of God and His ways, coupled with my seeking to know God's voice, prepared me for this idea. Marvelously, since God knows our weaknesses, He will make sure the specific idea He wants us to pursue will be highlighted more than all competing ideas and sometimes even be crystal clear. When my daughter spoke without knowing what I was thinking, it was an external confirmation of the direction I should take. Then, the very next morning, the dramatic image of Trump with a live bald eagle was all of the unsolicited external confirmation I needed in discerning the times and seasons in which I was living. But, what did it mean? For me, having been immersed in the imagery for so many weeks, to finally resolve to sit down and begin the painting's composition and just then to have a series of related "coincidences" was all I needed to discern the leading of God.

As I feverishly proceeded with the painting at the end of the summer of 2015, I began to question how God could be using such a man as Donald Trump. Immediately, I was reminded of the Scripture in the book of Isaiah, chapter 45, where God calls Cyrus the Great. I knew that verse very well, as it had taught me so much about God's dealing with man and how mistaken we are when we think we know whom God could be using and what God should be doing. People by nature project their idea of God onto their ways of doing things and think God will act accordingly. But God's ways are higher than our ways, and who can know them?

The calling of Cyrus, the sixth-century-B.C. king of Persia, as the deliverer of Israel demonstrated that God is no respecter of persons. Cyrus did not even believe in God—he was an idolater and had a harem of wives—yet this man was specifically called and chosen by God. Yes, God even calls him Meshiach, His Messiah. Cyrus was God's choice to be the savior of Israel. God calling and using a godless sinner like Cyrus shows us that He can choose to overlook a man's sins to accomplish His greater purposes.

Trump was no different. Trump was a Cyrus-like figure in prominence and influence, a sinner used by God. In time, Trump became the most widely recognized and powerful leader on earth, like Cyrus was in his day. However, Trump was not Cyrus, as some would mistakenly come to believe.

Without a doubt, Donald Trump's faith took a turn during the campaign season and beyond. What was indeed a political position at the outset, to pander to believers and garner votes from conservative Christians, would begin to rub off on him. I observed a genuine turn in Trump toward God's direction. His mentions of faith went from mere talking points to echoing a ring of increasing confidence and genuine faith.

My painting went on to have a solidly symbolic Christian theme, as my conviction increased of Trump's divinely ordained role in human history. This symbolism was crafted deeply into the composition. The image became Trump as president of the United States as a converted man, having a conversion on the scale of the Roman Emperor Constantine. That was my hope and prayer for him, for America, and beyond. In 2015, I made a few YouTube videos to this effect, explaining how I believed this Trump phenomenon could play out. Trump had the stature, guts, and presence to become as influential in human history as the Roman Emperor Constantine. The latter experienced a dramatic divine intervention as the Roman gods failed him. According to the writings of Eusebius, Constantine prayed to the God of his earthly father, who had become a Christian.[2] As a result, Constantine experienced an open vision and the voice of God directing him to conquer under the sign of the cross, at which he draped his armies in Christian symbols and won. As a result of Constantine's victories, Christianity, which once was savaged by the Roman Empire, now became a protected religion. In Rome, Christians used to be burned alive to light up the city or fed to the lions for sport and entertainment, but that all changed.

Upon becoming president, Trump was declared by Franklin Graham as the most pro-Christian president we've had in the last fifty years. But my faith filter also put Trump in another possible scenario, where he could go mad like King Nebuchadnezzar. King Nebuchadnezzar became so puffed up with pride that God stripped him of his kingdom and made him eat grass like an animal of the field for seven years before being restored to his throne. Or, Trump could end up like King Saul, chosen and anointed but in the end rejected as king of Israel, only to fall on his own sword.

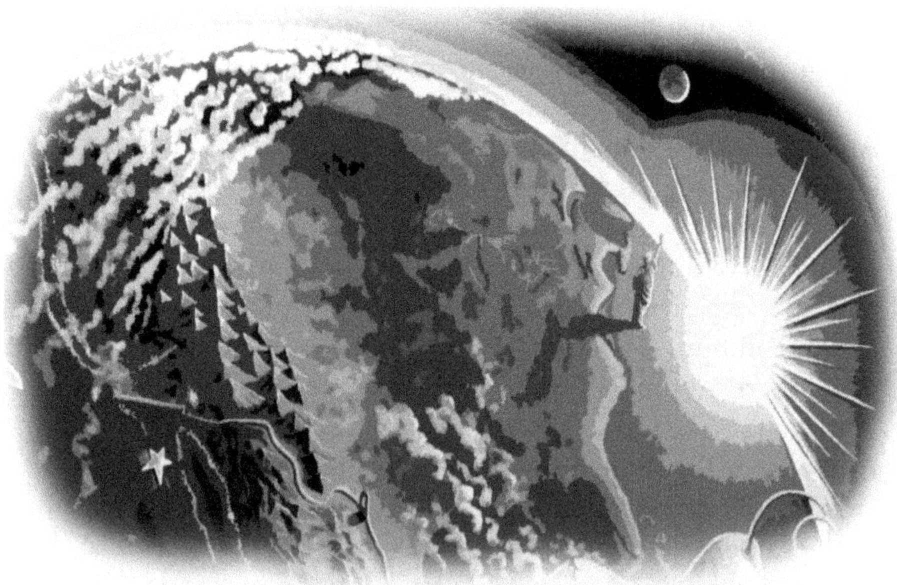

The rising sun in the east, posterized detail, "Unafraid and Unashamed"

Chapter Eight

AMERICAN, IMMIGRANT, CITIZEN

As the Trump painting came together, the cool of September 2015 arrived, as did correspondence from the USCIS (United States Citizen and Immigration Services, formerly the INS). I had applied for my citizenship back in 2010, when my original green card expired. The USCIS letter's arrival and the timing seemed providential. The letter scheduled me to be naturalized into the American family through a ceremony in Brockport, New York, on Constitution Day, September 17, 2015. Yes, finally, I was to become an American.

My love for America, already being expressed in the painting before me, would now be sealed in a naturalization ceremony, as my seven-by-fifteen-foot magnum opus, "Unafraid and Unashamed," was nearing completion. My naturalization as an American citizen was the perfect complementary event after being so profoundly involved in painting American patriotic and political elements, symbols, and colors, such as the red, white, and blue of Old Glory, the majestic bald eagle, and the historic presidential candidate.

What a perfect time to swear allegiance to the U.S. Constitution, an image of which was depicted in the painting. It was a moving ceremony. Gloria and I had been through so much together to get to that day. Together with our children, we cried. I was honored by being invited to lead the hundreds of new citizens at the ceremony in reciting the Pledge of Allegiance.

Having sworn an oath to protect the Constitution and the laws of the United States against enemies both foreign and domestic, duty came upon me to be active in carrying out my oath. Getting involved in politics was as good as any path to do this; campaigning for what I believed and using my gifts and talents for the same end would be fulfilling my oath. I believed that becoming an American required being active in defense of the constitutional American ideas and values that had wooed me.

America once stood tall in a world ruled by despots, tyrants, and demigods, a world of shifting and corrupt regimes. America now suffered from eroding Christian values and sentiments. If left unchanged, this nation would waste away and ultimately end up on the ruins of human history, piled high with immeasurable tragedy and human suffering. America once stood as a beacon of hope and freedom, like a rock where moral and traditional Biblical values and virtues could be defended and were defended. Those values and virtues had become catastrophically eroded over the last half-century.

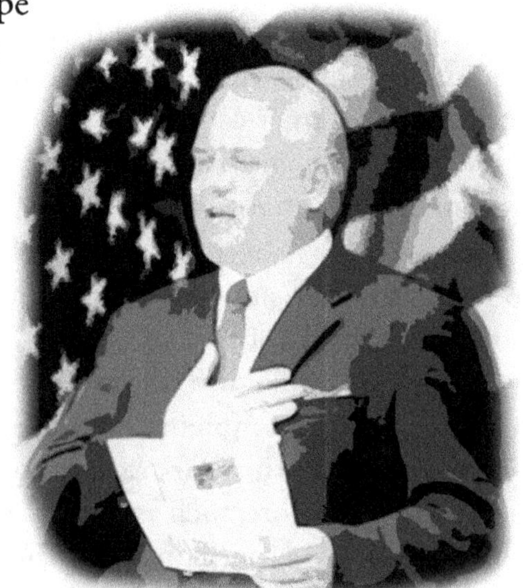

Chapter Nine

SYMBOLICALLY SPEAKING

A MAN OF THE PROMINENCE OF TRUMP, CONVERTED TO CHRIST, could resoundingly affect the morals of America and the world, as was the case of the influence of the converted Emperor Constantine. Constantine outlawed the abominable pagan practice of child sacrifice, among other ancient barbarities. Constantine's defense and promotion of Christianity enabled the birth of Western Civilization, which would develop over the centuries, influenced by the ideas and values of the Christian faith.

Trump would become a champion of the pro-life movement over time, culminating in the appointment to the U.S. Supreme Court of the pro-life jurist Amy Coney Barrett to replace the late pro-abortion Justice Ruth Bader Ginsburg. This support of the pro-life agenda was proof of Trump's ability to stand without wavering, either conveniently or courageously, in support of a baby's right to life. I could only imagine the influence and eternal impact a converted Trump could have in other critical areas of national morality. Redeemed national morality is essential for ensuring God's continued blessing upon America.

As crass as Trump seemed at times, believers rejoiced that a fighter in the presidential race promised to fight for them. Trump's support for Christmas and simply saying "Merry Christmas" were a welcome breath of fresh air in our crippling, politically correct society. In the book of Philippians, found in the Bible, chapter 1, verse 18, the apostle Paul writes: "The important thing is that in every way, whether from false motives or true, Christ is preached. And because of this I rejoice. Yes, and I will continue to rejoice" (NIV).

"Unafraid and Unashamed" would symbolically embody many of these critical themes that were dear to Christians. These themes would distinguish the Trump presidency, yet I conceived of and painted them before Trump made them major campaign issues. These Christian themes were also embodied and galvanized the following year in Trump's selection of Governor Mike Pence as his running mate.

Let's take a closer look at some of the hidden symbolism in my painting, "Unafraid and Unashamed":

- Abortion is depicted as a baby-shaped tear in the flag.
- Our fading voice is depicted as the fading ink in the words, "We the People."
- Our unwavering support for Israel is depicted as a blue Star of David tucked securely beneath the eagle's wing.
- Our support of the military and first responders is seen in a lone military star.
- The rising of the white sun in the east, which bathes the whole composition in white light, speaks of the dawn of a new day of hope, also illustrating the hand of divine sovereignty upon the entire drama playing out.
- The rising of the white sun also speaks of humanity's only true and lasting hope, that being the return of Jesus Christ, as celebrated every Easter at the Sunrise Service.
- White is the color of holiness and righteousness. Matthew 24 Biblically speaks of the east when the Son of Man returns. He will be like lightning shining from the east to the west.

- The array of the twelve principal rays of the sun evoke the Biblical number twelve, representing perfection and governmental authority.
- The light from the east alludes to the Messianic prophecy of Ezekiel 44:1–3, where the returning Messianic Prince will enter through the east gate.
- The sun's rays also evoke many ancient Christ-centered paintings, where Christ is arrayed with the sun's rays behind His head.
- The reversed, torn, and faded American flag, fluttering aimlessly in space, describes the weakening of the fabric that once made America great, unmoored from its moral and political founding values.
- The tears in the flag speak of civil unrest, hatred, and division that could tear America apart.
- The upper severed halyard rope is one coil of the Gadsden snake from the "Don't Tread on Me" Revolutionary flag from 1776. It is upside down, symbolizing that the spirit of that age, expressed in the Declaration of Independence and Revolutionary War, has died.
- The lower severed halyard rope, coiled in the shape of Ichthys, is the ancient Greek fish symbol that Christians used to identify themselves while under persecution. It represents Christian values, especially the sanctity of marriage between one man and one woman.
- The immigration issue is captured in the Christ-like Statue of Liberty walking on water, welcoming the rising of the sun in the east, evoking New York's Ellis Island port of entry for immigrants to enter legally into the United States.
- Lady Liberty also reminds us of the different periods when immigration was suspended to allow assimilation to occur in America.
- The "huge" wall, with the "beautiful" gate between the United States and Mexico, is depicted in the painting, clearly showing America's need to protect its borders.

- The key for the keyhole in the gate is hidden in the "W" of "We the People," speaking to the fact that "We the People" must determine who enters and who does not enter our country.
- There is a trinity of luminaries depicted twice in the painting: the rising sun, the waxing new moon, and the Statue of Liberty's beacon. The trinity of luminaries is reflected in Trump's eyes, and both these depictions remind us that our country's origins are rooted in the faith of the Triune God of the Bible.
- The trinity of luminaries reflected in Trump's eyes symbolizes hopeful expectation that Trump will genuinely look to God and be converted.

During the time I was painting, Trump's hair was often in the news. People were perplexed by its artificial appearance and wanted to know if it was real. While painting, I made the meteoric shape of Trump's hair symbolic of his meteoric rise. The sides of Trump's hair were deliberately painted gray (even though Trump colors his hair) to depict Trump as the future president. The color symbolizes the aging process brought on by the stresses of the presidency. Yet, the two-tone coloring of Trump's hair symbolizes that he will not be overwhelmed, since his executive abilities make him fit for the job.

The aggressive snatching of the flag by the eagle, the central part of the vision, represents the rescuing or saving of America. Initially, as I was painting the image of the eagle snatching the flag, I did not see all the layers of meaning that could be hidden within it. Upon studying the eagle's talons, it dawned on me that those talons would tear at the very fabric of the flag. The razor-sharp talons piercing the flag, and the shadows they produced (which could resemble running blood), could be broadly interpreted. I gulped as I painted that scene because of its possible foreboding implications.

The overall composition of the painting is descriptive of Trump's vision to save America and the attitude, toughness, and resolve it would take to accomplish that. This can be seen in Trump's silent stare of determination. The waves of the flag were an attempt to represent the thoughts coming out of Trump's mind. The scream of the eagle represents a cry of alarm, expressing the urgency of the hour. Swooping in, he powerfully snatches the falling flag, which flutters aimlessly. The painting depicts Trump as a man of action, a builder, and a doer who gets the job done.

"Make America Great Again" is a complex concept to visualize or depict graphically, but the image captures the ingredients necessary to accomplish that goal. As I painted, the flag evolved into a timeline, a continuum of American history. America's founding starts on the faded, severed end. The present day, which includes the Trump presidency, is depicted where the eagle snatches the flag. The timeline continued on from there.

In the eagle's wake come the new stars, stripes, and blue ink necessary to restore the bold colors of the faded glory. The components of "Make America Great Again" were now all in play.

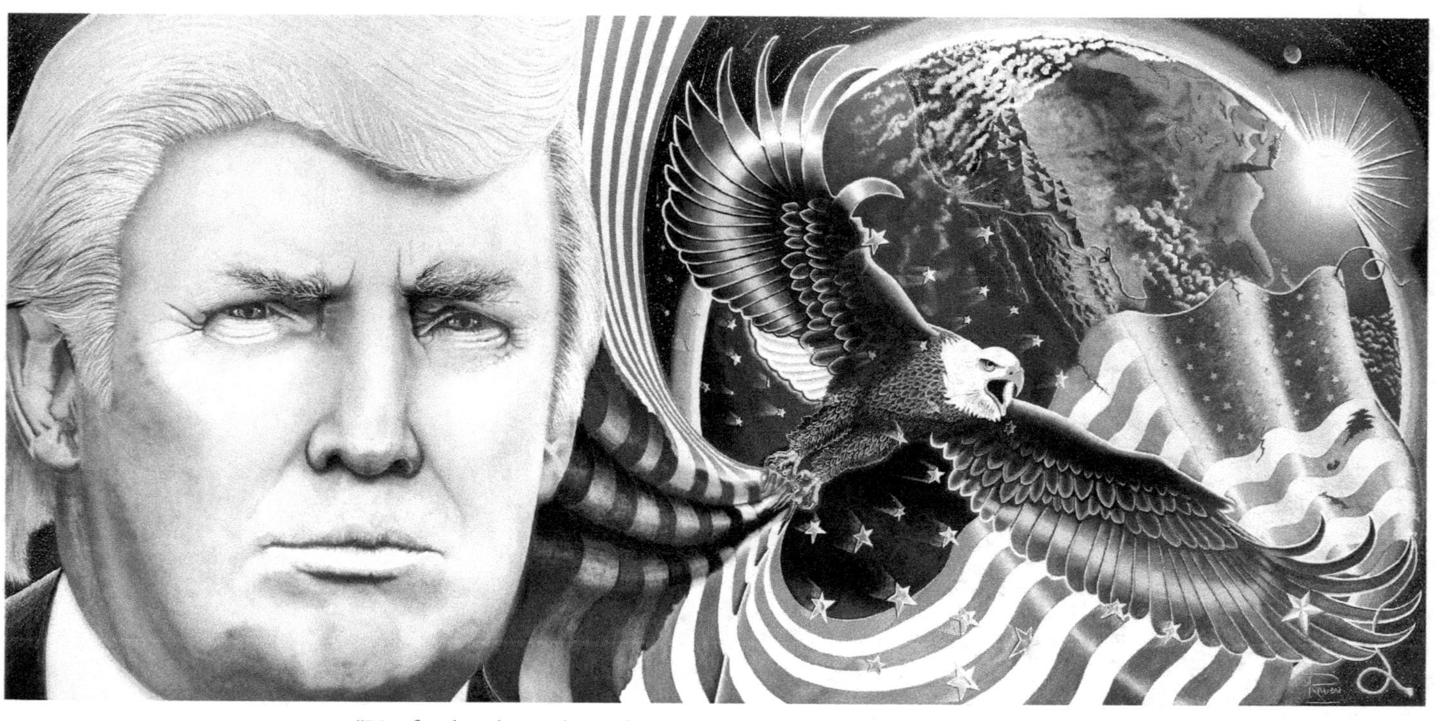

"Unafraid and Unashamed," 7' x 15' acrylic on canvas, by Julian Raven

Chapter Ten

AMERICAN DREAMING

POLITICS NEVER INTERESTED ME BEFORE I ARRIVED IN AMERICA, but that was about to change. American politics began to intrigue me because it is an unavoidable part of American life. Upon arriving in America, I started making money by painting houses. When up on the scaffolding, I was fascinated by conservative radio hosts like Rush Limbaugh, Sean Hannity, and Mark Levin, having never heard anything like what they were saying before. They helped me better understand American politics and develop my political point of view. I listened to them for years before moving on to create my own beliefs without the constant influence of theirs or anyone else's opinions.

After arriving in America, the first election I experienced was in 1996, with the reelection of President Bill Clinton and the third-party Ross Perot split. In 2000, it was the Bush-Gore hanging-and-dimpled-chad fiasco, followed by the historic Barack Obama win in 2008. Following those campaigns, I became curious about the national conventions held to nominate the presidential nominees. Those conventions were gargantuan American expressions and celebrations of political power, wealth, and patriotic fervor. Delegates dressed up in all manner of patriotic attire from their home states, even dressing up in cosplay as Abraham Lincoln. There were delegates from Texas waving huge white cowboy hats and wearing sparkling white cowboy boots. Others wore ridiculously sized political buttons, flags, and political slogans plastered onto any surface that would hold paint. Partisans got caught up in the affair, intoxicated with fervor and more, showering themselves in glitter and rivers of gaudy makeup. Money flowed like wine, and the shrewd capitalized on the chaos, selling truckloads of "merch." Those conventions, of course, burst with showers of red, white, and blue balloons and patriotic confetti. I was utterly intrigued by the American political chaos, wondering if and how I could ever get to a convention to experience it firsthand.

Little did I know that one day, emerging from the shadows of my illegal status and the scaffolding of Nyack, New York, I would find myself at the 2016 Republican National Convention in Cleveland, Ohio. Yes, just nine months into becoming a newly minted American citizen, I would be sitting on the very front row, right before the podium, as an alternate delegate for the State of New York!

Once my painting was complete, at the end of September of 2015, and once I had become a naturalized American citizen, I began to chart the next steps for exhibiting the painting. What in the world was I to do with the massive seven-by-fifteen-foot painting (eight-by-sixteen with the frame) of the controversial and much-despised presidential candidate Donald Trump?

Showing the painting was the whole point of the painting. Letting people see it and watching the reactions were to be the artist's delight. I had virtually disappeared for the two months it took me to finish the Trump portrait. Not even my mother knew what I was doing. My already-sparse social life as an introvert had all but dried up. I had vanished, swallowed up by my giant painting in my massive studio. Slowly, I began to invite people to my studio to see their reactions. I would not tell them anything, building the suspense and then dropping the massive sheet that covered the painting. The impact was powerful. A painting that large is already powerful, but this was a megawatt-power painting. Not just the Trump content, but the bold colors, the red and white stripes, the deliberate compositional lines of beauty, the action, the depth, and the drama. People did not know what to say. One elderly gentleman resorted to waving his arms, yelling, and cursing aloud, as he could not contain his emotions.

These reactions were just a foreshadowing of the multitude and wide variety of responses that would come to me throughout the years. The painting generated intense responses from all sides of the political aisle. One man paced back and forth in front of the giant display, rubbing his arms, as he exclaimed, "I have goosebumps all over me!" Another woman stood silently and abruptly departed. I was left somewhat disturbed. Had she been offended? I wondered, only later to get a text with an apology, explaining that the painting had left her speechless.

Standing in the anti-Trump protest park at the Republican National Convention (RNC) in Cleveland, Ohio, thousands of people saw a smaller, four-by-eight-foot printed version of the painting. The park was filled, especially with those protesting the convention—especially those who despised Trump. One Black Lives Matter protester wearing a "F*** Trump" T-shirt yelled at me, "Yo, I hate Trump, but that painting is wack [great]!" Those on the left were critical of the content, but some admired and respected the painting as a work of art. Others cringed.

At Politicon, the anti-Trump art show in Pasadena, California, one female liberal artist came up to me, making sure no one was watching, and whispered to me that she despised Trump, but that it was a great painting. By and large, those who opposed Trump and saw the painting in person were surprisingly respectful. The painting commanded both attention and respect.

As you already know from the outset, I received that particularly shocking reaction from Kim Sajet, the Smithsonian National Portrait Gallery director (who never even saw the painting in person). Was Sajet's reaction biased? Why did Sajet, the director of the

Smithsonian Art Gallery even call me? Her reaction would thrust me into a legal battle that would last three years and take me all the way up to the United States Supreme Court in Washington, D.C.

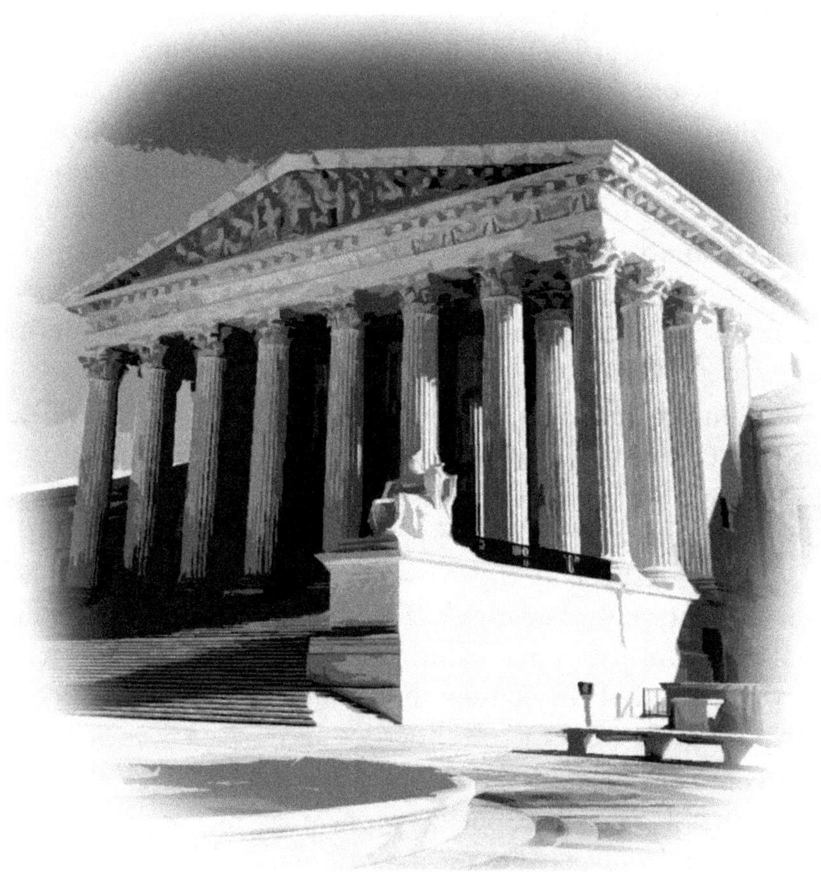

Chapter Eleven

STAIRWAY SUPREME

T HE STEPS WERE MANY, THE CHALLENGES OFTENTIMES EXTREME, along the unfolding odyssey that would eventually take me up the iconic Algerian-marble steps and through the sixteen sumptuous, fluted, Corinthian-marble columns of the U.S. Supreme Court. Never could I have imagined such was to be my destiny. That lofty destination was a long way off—the stages just ahead of me were just beginning to materialize.

Early in October 2015, soon after the painting was finished, a gentleman named Tom Freeman of Elmira, New York, was one of the first people to see the portrait. Mr. Freeman had a private viewing of the painting at the recommendation of local media guru Tom Brown. He was so impressed that he offered me the use of the entire Elmira hockey arena for free for the unveiling of the Trump painting, if I could get Donald Trump to come in person.

Without hesitation, I made a small, eight-and-a-half-by-eleven-inch print of the painting, and with a letter in hand, took off on the two-hundred-mile journey south to Trump Tower in Manhattan. My friend from New City joined me, and we arrived at Trump

Tower at eight in the morning, right as the doors opened the following day. Approaching the desk, I informed the concierge that I was an artist from upstate New York who had come to deliver an invitation to Donald Trump and his campaign. Before long, they put me on the phone, and I began to chat with John McEntee, a new, young volunteer staffer at the Trump Campaign HQ. "John, the portrait is finished, the arena is ready and free, and the only thing missing is for Mr. Trump to turn up, have a rally, and accept his gift." (McEntee would become personally involved with Trump when he became president, becoming his main personal attendant, or "body man." He was then promoted to White House presidential personnel director.)

A few minutes later, the gilded Trump Tower elevator chimed, and its doors opened. A youthful, well-groomed John McEntee, dressed in dark slacks, white shirt, and tie, appeared. His bewildered look was priceless and could only be described in these words: "Who is Julian Raven? What in the world is he talking about? What painting? What arena?" and "Where in the world is Elmira?" After hearing what was going on, McEntee received the small print of the painting and the letter. (The image appeared shortly afterward in a CNN article on November 12, 2015, about art in the Trump HQ.)[3]

On Sunday, November 27, a controversial, public Black-pastors' meeting with Trump had been scheduled at Trump Tower and then abruptly canceled. The Trump campaign had moved it forward to Monday, November 28, as it had stirred fierce controversy within the Black churches, risking an embarrassing no-show pastor response. Instead, they chose to make it a private meeting to protect the identities of those who were curious and who would attend, ensuring some would come. This rescheduled meeting coincided with my next visit to Trump Tower on Monday, November 28, this time with a twenty-two-by-forty-four-inch print on canvas in hand, beautifully framed in a tri-color, antiqued, ornate, red, white, and blue frame. The framed canvas print was a gift to the Trump campaign, as I was not satisfied with them having just the small paper print. They had not seen the original, as the campaign declined the invitation to the arena.

As my visit coincided with the controversial Black-pastors' meeting, and having been a lay minister myself for many years—even though I was short on melanin—I could be of support. I was going to be at Trump Tower anyway; including my face in the crowd at that time would help the barely-there Christian presence, adding to the few who were scheduled to meet with candidate Trump.

The campaign had already rebuffed my efforts to meet Trump personally by not accepting the hockey-arena invitation. I was an unknown, emerging artist, lacking the fame necessary to get past the centurions guarding the gilded, golden elevators. But would the hand of Providence bypass their stonewalling to orchestrate a divine appointment in the giant conference room on the twenty-sixth floor in Trump Tower between the unknown artist and candidate Trump? (Piqued your curiosity, have I? I will have to leave you dangling for a wee bit if you don't mind.)

As an artist, working from various photos from the Internet, one can only get a limited amount of information for a painting. My artist's eye craved the intimate details in the specific subject of Trump's eyes. Artistic curiosity can be seen in the macabre practice of Renaissance artists sneaking into morgues at night and taking corpses apart by candlelight in their quest for understanding the mechanics of the human body. I had to see the man's eyes.

Making Trump's eyes look convincing on the scale that I had done was already challenging; the eyes in a portrait are everything. But, seeing them in the flesh would clear up any questions. What hue of blue? How light or dark was the tone? What expression did Trump convey through his eyes? I was constantly left hungry for the answers. Looking into a person's eyes can also reveal volumes about who they are. If I could just meet Trump and get that information, it would significantly help me with my painting. Even though complete at that time, there was room for tiny corrections, especially in the essential details of the eyes. Meeting him in person would also help share my story while supporting Trump on the campaign trail.

That same month, I had begun to plan a cross-country, grass-roots political campaign supporting Trump, as Ted Cruz had established a commanding lead at that time in the primary, especially among Evangelicals. It was early December, right before the Iowa caucuses in January of 2016. At that time, I was convinced that it was my Christian, civic, and patriotic duty to go to Iowa. Being so invested in supporting Trump with my painting—also since I had just become a citizen—Iowa had to be my next stop. It was thrilling to be part of history in the making. I wanted to show the painting and share with Evangelicals and Christians in general my personal experiences and conviction that perhaps God Himself was voting for Trump. And that they too could vote for someone like Trump. My journey would also serve as a great promotional opportunity for my art and provide needed exposure for the Trump painting. What an epic journey lay ahead of me!

After renting a massive twenty-foot box truck, I headed to Iowa. Once in Iowa, with the help of a new friend and fellow Trumper, former Marine Sergeant Jeff Moorman, I wrapped the sides of the truck with vinyl decals of the Trump painting. My grassroots campaign was one of the very few that were for Trump at that time. There was little Trump ground game in Iowa; Trump focused on rallies. It was candidates like Ted Cruz who had tremendous grassroots support and a vast machinery of volunteers. I traveled the length and breadth of Iowa, clocking three thousand miles. My goal was to end up in the town of Denison, in west Iowa. Little did I know that this small town was also home to Kronk's Cafe, a politically historic venue through which every candidate and his brother had passed over the years while barnstorming the Hawkeye State for the Iowa caucuses.

At Kronk's Cafe, I held a couple of campaign events, as was the political tradition there. Carly Fiorina had just passed through at the time. Also, Ben Carson held a meet and greet. Then, it was my turn. I was excited! I informed the Trump campaign in Des Moines of my event in case they wanted to direct anyone our way by chance.

The assistant director of the Trump campaign in Des Moines was resistant to my efforts for some reason. At one point, I directed a local man, who was seeking yard signs, to call the campaign HQ, since there were no yard signs available out in western Iowa. Shortly after, I received a call from this assistant director, berating me for doing so. I could not figure out why. Were we not trying to get Trump elected? I needed yard signs!

Having a monster truck, I was off to Des Moines to get some. I thought I could paint the snow-covered Iowa countryside with hundreds of blue Trump yard signs, giving them out like freshly baked cookies. After the long schlep to their headquarters, I met this same assistant director, who took what appeared to be an envious disliking to me. I drove my huge truck over a hundred miles to get some of the 1,500 yard signs sitting in their office. He gave me ten—yep, just ten! This was the same guy who snubbed me at the Trump rally at Dordt University in Sioux Center. It was a freezing north-Iowan January. I stood for hours at the front of the line in the dark and wee hours of the morning in that bitterly cold weather. The assistant director let all the other volunteers in ahead of me and never invited me in. He looked at me, staring right in my eyes from the warmth behind the glass door, and firmly locked the door, leaving me out in the cold.

My pro-Trump town-hall-styled meeting, to be held at Kronk's Cafe the following week, managed to get the attention of others at the campaign headquarters in Des Moines, because it just so happened that there was nothing on their calendar scheduled for that day. Trump was not holding any events, so mine was it. As a result, they put the word out to show that something pro-Trump was going on that day, and CNN arrived at the event with one of their satellite trucks. I arrived super excited to see the satellite truck sitting there for my event, believing that my story was about to get some serious coverage as the only event for Trump in the state that day. The media narrative of the day was that Trump did not have a ground game. CNN would have to contradict themselves and report that Trump did have a grassroots ground game from New

York. And, however small that operation may have been, the Trump painting was huge!

Before their reporters even set foot outside their sleek, black, tinted-windowed SUV, they and their satellite truck pulled out of the parking lot and left without an explanation. I had already learned that the leftist media did not want to carry anything positive for Trump. They probably decided that my story did not fit theirs.

Later on, I held a meet and greet for Eric Trump, at the request of the Trump campaign's Chris Hupke—a great honor for me at the time. The well-attended gathering had all of the eight precinct captains (local volunteer caucus leaders within the different voting precincts) present, which I had enlisted, as well as media and security. I was told by the campaign not to have any of my merchandise present, which I honored. It was disappointing to have to hide my painting, since I was hoping at least one Trump family member might finally see the painting. But, wanting to comply with their request, I parked the truck off in the corner of the lot and coordinated the event without any images of my painting. The event was a great success. The full house and great atmosphere made Eric and Lara feel very welcome. Denison, Iowa, was a predominantly Republican stronghold supporting Cruz at the time, so there was no party support for anything Trump. After the event, as I escorted Eric and Lara to their car, Lara spotted my truck on the other side of the parking lot and made a beeline to it. "WOW!" she exclaimed, "Whose is this?" At that point, I shared some of my story and how I had come from New York with the painting. I told Eric it was a mission in support of his father. Eric took my arm and had his assistant take a photo of him, Lara, and me in front of the truck. He tweeted out the picture, calling me the MVP of the day.

My daughter Victoria suggested I give Trump my painting so he could hang it in the White House. Giving Donald Trump the original painting to be used for his campaign made sense. Maybe it would have an impact similar to the Obama "Hope" poster for Obama, helping Trump win, and maybe it would be a win for me personally because of the publicity it would generate. I made the

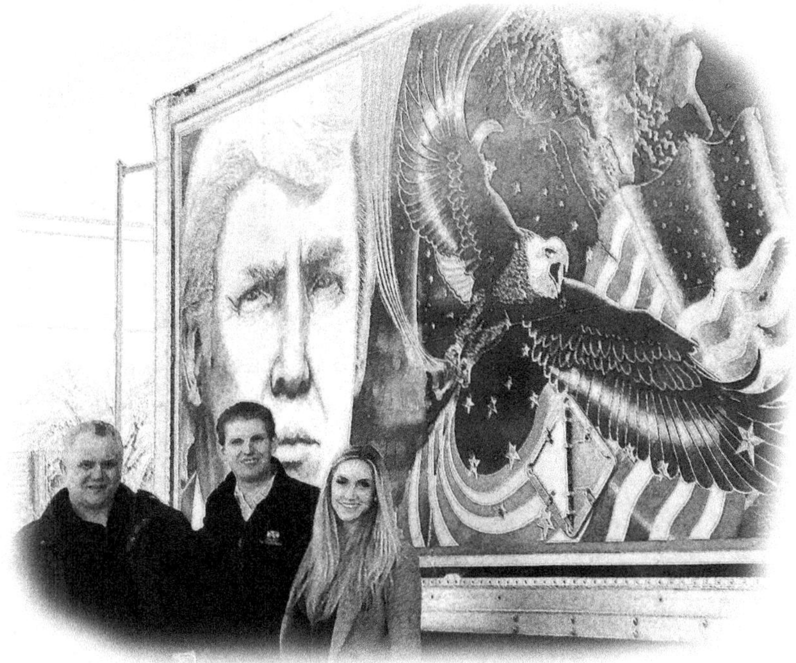

Eric and Lara Trump at Kronk's Cafe, Denison, Iowa, 2016

offer to Eric, who excitedly said "Absolutely!" and that he would "make it happen!" Giving Eric my contact info on one of my giant printed postcards, he took off with Lara to his next event.

Now that was the big break for which I had been hoping. Driving a thousand miles out into the tundra of Iowa in the unpleasant winter looked like it was going to have a great payoff. My painting would finally find its proper place and the recognition it deserved. I would get a photo with Trump in front of the painting, and the prints I would sell as a result would, in turn, fund my campaign for him across the country right up until the election in November. After all, what good is a portrait if the subject does not even acknowledge it? Artists have historically sought the patronage of the rich and famous because of their ability to artistically immortalize their subjects with their brushes. Eric's enthusiastic response was encouraging, fueling energized and expanded campaigning efforts. At the same time, I waited for Eric's response, which I hoped would inform me of the day I could present the painting to Trump—maybe even at a rally. That would have been amazing!

After showing the painting in Des Moines, Iowa, I received pretty good media coverage from Japanese media, thanks to Jeff Moorman. Photos of the painting also began to appear all across the media in print and online. I continued to campaign vigorously in Denison right up until election night, attending the caucuses in person as an observer. I thought it would be a great idea to park the Trump truck right in front of the entrance of the polling station, not to intimidate voters of course but to strengthen their last-minute resolve. Not a good idea! As the novice, I knew not about the rules requiring all promotional material be a certain distance from the polling place. I was viciously blasted by caucus attendees who were definitely not voting for Trump. I moved, parking a few hundred feet away. I went in. Seeing caucus-voter participatory democracy in action further educated my newborn citizen's brain in the greatness of American political freedom and political free speech. On election night, a large town meeting was held at the local high school where the town of Denison voted. The entire voting population was present and divided by precincts, meeting in different classrooms all over the school. The volunteer precinct captains representing their party and specific primary candidates were responsible for speaking in turn before the assembled caucus, explaining why their candidate deserved their vote. Campaign staffers, or even candidates themselves, made their last pitch to the voters, running from room to room. A bucket was then passed around, into which the voters dropped their handwritten ballots. The numbers were tallied on the spot.

Nearly the whole of Carroll County voted for Ted Cruz, except for the town of Denison, which went for Trump. My efforts had paid off by winning the Denison caucuses for Trump. Anyone who wanted a printout of the tally could get one. This was my trophy, and I grabbed it and wasted no time that evening, jumping back into the truck and heading to New York. After a month in Iowa, I returned home to Elmira.

The very next day, I decided to take my "trophy" to Manhattan. Yes! I headed to Trump Tower to celebrate my victory, but this time with the Trump truck (emblazoned with the Trump painting) and the Denison, Iowa, results in my hand. My previous trip to Trump Tower had left me so discouraged. This time, it was different. Trump came in second place in Iowa overall but first place in Denison, making my trip undeniably worthwhile.

The painting was loaded into the truck. Maybe Eric would jump at the opportunity to come down and finally receive it, or at least he could see the original. He could then schedule some sort of meeting where I would officially give "Unafraid and Unashamed" to the Trump campaign. Driving into New York City in the Trump truck was nerve wracking. In Iowa, most people were friendly toward the truck, with a few glaring exceptions; in New York City, things were very different. People in New York never smile much. They smiled even less when they stared at what I had plastered on

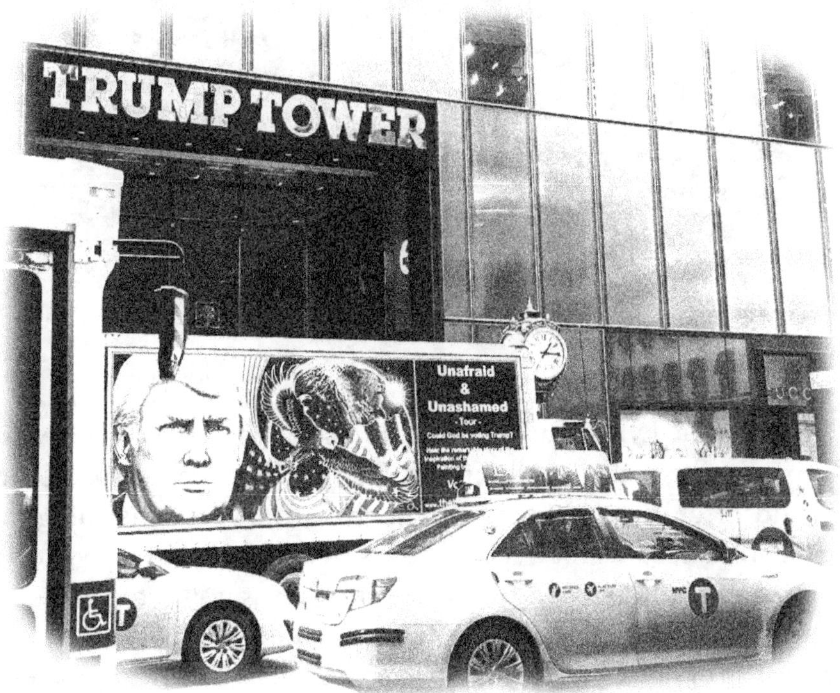

Trump Tower, New York City, February, 2016

the side of my truck. Pulling up outside Trump Tower was an absolute blast, though. Outside Trump Tower, people loved the truck once again. John McEntee and another staffer, Daniel Gelbinovich, stared in amazement, "You did it!" they exclaimed. I had told them of my plan to go to Iowa with the truck back in November. Proudly, I handed the staffers the paper trophy of my documented win for Trump in Iowa, and they took off upstairs in the golden elevator.

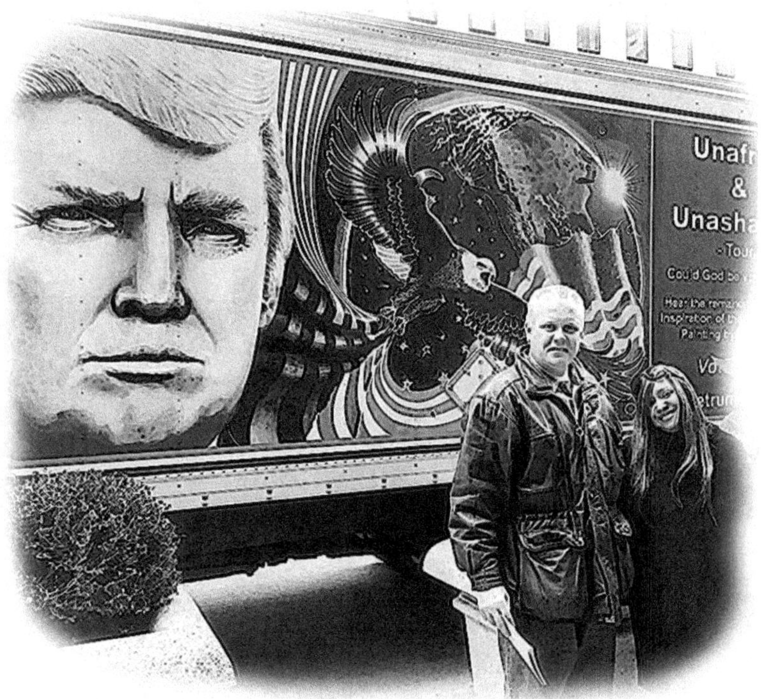

Outside Trump Tower with Lynne Patton, February 2016

Eventually, Lynne Patton came down. At the time, Lynne was the personal assistant to all three of Trump's children, Ivanka, Don Jr., and Eric. I thought for a moment that maybe I was going to be escorted upstairs for a spontaneous welcome due to my victory report—not to mention that Eric said he was going to "make it happen!" Unfortunately, it did not happen. Instead, I was given a goody bag of gifts, some Trump hats, chocolates, and Trump's latest book, *Crippled America*, and that was that.

It was disappointing, but I had done my part. People are busy; seeing me that day was not their priority. Lynne Patton later created a video called "The Trump Family That I Know"[4] in support of Trump and his family, as she recounted her experiences with them over the years. The Trumps helped her through some tough personal struggles. It was an intimate video containing many images of Lynne with the Trumps. A local friend, Tom Brown, emailed me the video link when it first came out, telling me to watch it. The black-and-white video was professionally produced, and to my pleasant surprise, early on in the video appeared a photo of Lynne standing with me in front of the Trump truck outside of Trump Tower. That was completely unexpected. The video went on to have over five million views. I emailed Lynne thanking her and asking her why she included me in such an important and personal video. Her reply was, "You deserved it!" It was as if she was saying, "Even if they would not recognize your efforts, I did." (This viral video would be shown later, at one of the most important events of the historic Trump campaign.)

To my disappointment, Eric never followed through with his offer to "make it happen." It was an extremely anticlimactic end to my Iowa adventure. After several months of trying to get the ball rolling by writing to Eric and patiently awaiting his response, I finally gave up and rescinded my offer in a letter. It would have been monumental to have had my painting received by Donald Trump personally, but it was not to be. However, what was to be took me down an uncharted and unexpected path that I will never forget. Even in the deeply discouraged state in which I found myself after that trip, I had to keep going. Like being at the bottom of the barrel, all I could do was look up and start again.

And look up I did. Now back in Elmira, I used the front of my six-thousand-square-foot art studio located in a commercial building to hoist a freshly printed giant twelve-by-twenty-five-foot vinyl banner of my Trump painting. With the help of my wife and kids, we hosted a handful of local grassroots Trump rallies, with local politicians and Elmira Mayor Dan Mandel in attendance. Local

Trump enthusiasm began to increase. New York would eventually fall to Hillary Clinton because of the massive voting blocks in New York City, Albany, and Ithaca. However, the whole state of New York, county by county—especially my home of Chemung County—voted overwhelmingly for Trump.

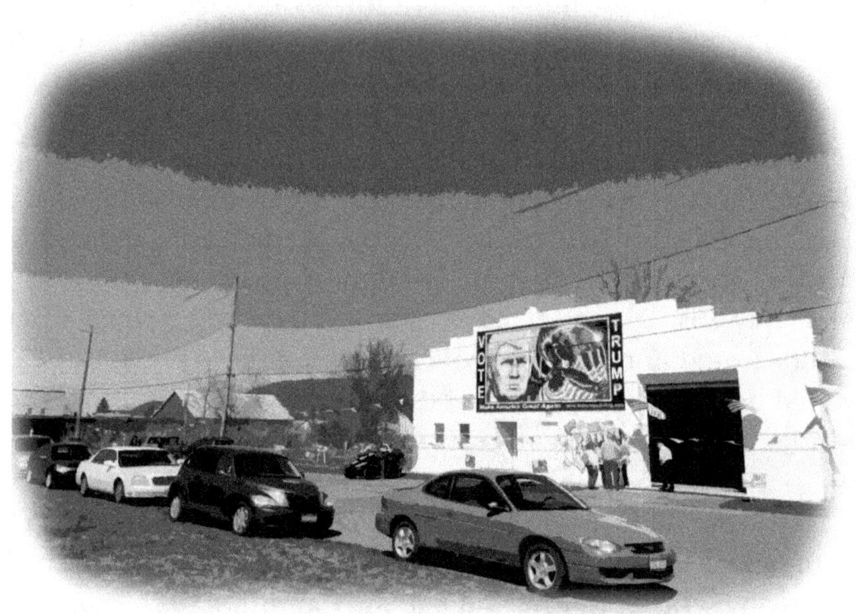

Grassroots Trump Rally, Spring of 2016, Elmira, New York

Locally, the left-leaning media refused to cover my pro-Trump story, except for the one story told by reporter Tanner Jubenville.[5] When he interviewed me for the story, he made it a point to identify himself up front as a conservative who worked for WETM 18 News. His story was about the huge Trump banner on the front of my studio. Tanner also informed me he would be back to cover the upcoming Trump rally at my studio. But as it turned out, the day of the rally, he was assigned to a road race miles out of town. No other journalists came. At the unveiling of the painting on November 1, 2015, the local *Star-Gazette*, WETM 18 News, and WENY TV were invited, but all refused to cover the story. Only Spectrum

News[6] from Binghamton, New York, (fifty miles away) traveled to cover and document the beginning of what would become the Trump-painting odyssey.

Conservative talk-radio host Frank Acomb, from "Frankly Speaking" on WENY radio in Corning, New York, became the first local media personality to cover the story consistently over the years. Thanks to Tom Brown, I spoke on his show multiple times, sharing the many stages of my independent epic journey all the way up to the Supreme Court.

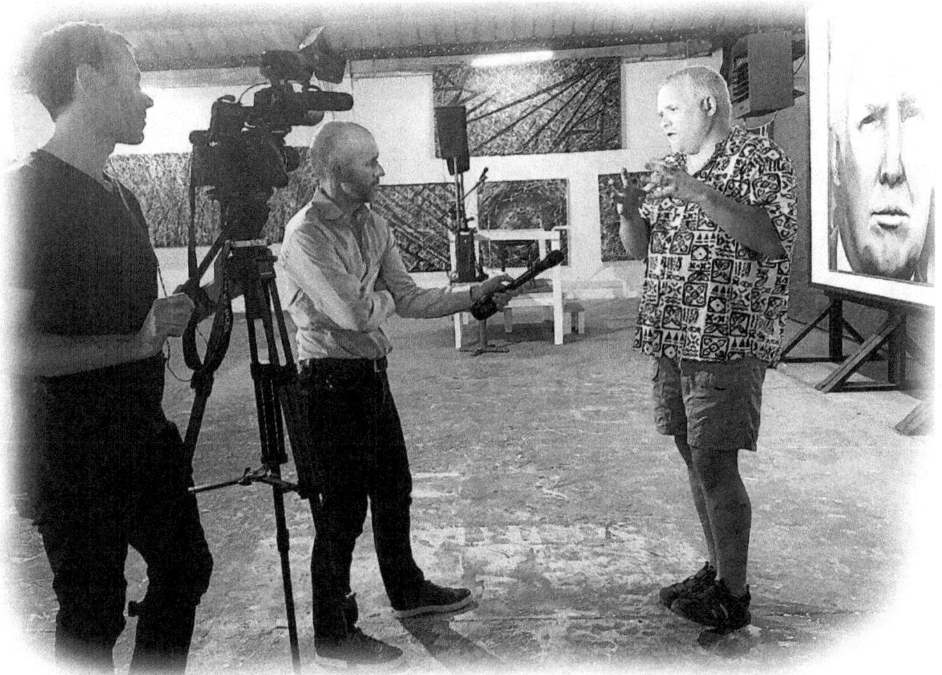

German news crew, art studio at 714 Baldwin St., Elmira, New York

Understanding the media's mind became another challenge for me along the road because I could not fathom how they functioned when they claimed to be reporters of the truth. The media as an institution is neutral in itself, and yet its faithfulness to its journalistic purpose depends on the moral character of each of its member journalists. Journalistic codes of ethics mean nothing to agenda-driven ideologues, who could care less about the truth or the facts because they constantly seek ways to twist stories into their preconceived narratives. My numerous personal experiences with bias, dishonesty, and deception at the hands of so-called trusted journalists have been disheartening. Imagine a scenario where, after an in-depth story of your journey comes out in print in a major publication, the journalist who wrote the story tells you straight to your face that the reason he twisted your story was that it was too "good," and he had to knock you down to size because he was a Democrat. That was my reality.

Chapter Twelve

BIG BREAK OR BUST

IN MAY OF 2016, I RECEIVED AN EMAIL OUT OF THE BLUE. THE email caused me to push myself away from my desk in disbelief, in a similar manner to other moments that stand out distinctly like mile markers along the road. I walked away from the computer to compose myself, preparing to go back and carefully reread the email to see if it was so. Gloria was in the next room and realized something significant had transpired. She was excited to see what it was all about, having stood by me through all of the discouragements life had cast my way. As always, she was hoping for the best for me, ready to cheer me onwards.

2016 had been up to that day a novice's political adventure, with many highlights and lowlights. I was at a place in the campaign where I was in New York and actively promoting my Trump painting, but nothing "big" was happening. Part of the Achilles' heel of political art, or any art in Republican or conservative circles, is that there are no galleries to show conservatively themed work. It became a side campaign for me to challenge and educate the politically right of center about the power, importance, and necessity of the language of art to communicate political ideas. Virtually none of the available systems that recognize, promote, and certify art and artists, especially from a Christian, conservative, or Republican perspective, are run by people who are right of center ideologically. Left-of-center ideologues primarily run Hollywood, the music industry, the contemporary-art world, etc. To succeed in those environments, you must either hide your political and religious beliefs or goose step in total ideological sync with the driving leftist woke ideologies of the day. Neither of those options was me.

My personal experience in the local Elmira, New York, art scene was that being outspoken for Jesus Christ, Biblical morality, and the Christian worldview was enough to get one banned for life. Add to the mix a megawatt dosage of Trump, in the form of an eight-by-sixteen-foot magnum-opus patriotic, unapologetic painting, and one quickly discovers how people who once were cordial will swiftly dodge you in the grocery store. It has always baffled me how people in the art world who so ardently proclaim their virtues of being open minded and tolerant are absolutely not! It was through a local, well-known, prestigious art gallery that I was to experience another mind-numbing dose of rejection, blatant hypocrisy, and anti-Trump political bias, prompting my swift rebuttal. But first, let me backtrack to the "email of disbelief."

In my inbox was an email from Yosi Sergant, patron and inspiration behind the Obama "Hope" poster created by artist Shepard Fairey. Sergant was the former White House Liaison for the Arts and National Endowment for the Arts Communications Director. He had seen my Trump painting and other works of mine online. In the email, he was inviting me to participate in the Art of Politics art show, which he was curating at Politicon 2016 in Pasadena, California. America's top political artists would be showing, and on display would be one of the three original finished screen-printed Obama "Hope" posters.

I was floored! The email was a massive boost because in New York the doors to the art world were tightly closed. This invitation was a game changer—*a big deal*—with all sorts of possible pivots, opportunities, and outcomes. To travel to Pasadena, California, to have my magnum opus on display with the nation's top political artists, political candidates, activists, and pundits was epic! Sergant was no fan of Trump—he made that perfectly clear. But we concurred in other areas, as he recognized my painting as a vision of hope. Like everything else operating at this level, the turbulent seas into which I would then navigate were raging, and my ship was about to experience some severe heaving, pitching, and rolling.

My painting was immense. I told Sergant it would travel in an eight-foot-tall, sixteen-foot-long, one-foot-deep plywood crate that would weigh about eight hundred pounds. "No problem, we move art all over the country," he told me. Wow! They were going to pay to ship my magnum opus across the country and back. What a gig! Landing that type of coast-to-coast, white-glove art service made me suddenly feel like an established artist who was about to fly into Pasadena, California, and make a huge splash. I was super impressed. Someone, please hold my cup of tea!

My phone rang steadily as Sergant's Task Force logistics team began inquiring from Pasadena, California, about the shipment details. I told them the crate dimensions—eight feet tall by sixteen feet long by one foot deep, weighing eight hundred pounds. "Ok, ok, we get it, no problem!" I hung up the phone and proceeded to build the gargantuan custom crate to carry the 120-pound framed Trump painting. I used ten full sheets of four-by-eight-foot, half-inch-thick plywood, weighing sixty pounds a sheet, for the sides, top, and base of the crate. The three-quarter-inch pine framing was an additional fifty pounds. The crate was so tall that it would not fit out of our roll-up bay door at my loading dock. It was also too top heavy to tilt and too big and long to roll out the front of the building to fit onto the liftgate of a truck. I had no choice but to take drastic measures.

The concrete floor under the door had to be cut out. Renting a concrete saw, I cut a four-inch-deep, twenty-inch-wide, twenty-foot-long gully into the concrete floor under the eight-foot loading door at the loading dock. This way, the crate could slide out upright on rollers and into the back of the delivery truck, which would be parked at the loading dock. The truck would have to be extra high to accommodate the internal eight-foot height requirement.

The day before the scheduled pick-up, the trucking company called to confirm the dimensions and weight—you know, "eight hundred pounds, eight feet tall by sixteen feet long by one foot thick." Everything was a go. I was barely able to sleep that night, as I was restless with excitement.

Early the next morning, the driver from the trucking company called me to tell me that he was on his way and would be at my studio soon. Politicon was a big deal. I kept telling myself this was the big break I needed. I had built a bomb-proof crate to ensure that my magnum opus would make it one piece. The painting was shrink- and bubble-wrapped, bolted tight into the mega box, and ready to go. It was Monday, and the show started on Friday. Five days to get there, no problem.

My phone rang again. This time, it was Task Force. "Uh, we have a problem." They told me that they had canceled the pickup. "What are you talking about?" I blurted out. "The truck is on its way and will be here very soon," I said. "No, it will not," they said. It turns out that the shipping company told Task Force at the last minute that it would cost an extra five thousand dollars to ship my painting, and that Task Force did not have the budget for it. One would have thought that they would have known this for weeks, since I kept telling them very deliberately—you know, eight feet tall, twelve inches deep, sixteen feet long, and weighing eight hundred pounds! I knew how shipping worked, and I knew it would take a specialized service.

No go, no show! Talk about getting broadsided by a massive breaker, leaving you stunned and teary eyed as you try to find your balance and composure. There was no time to get angry. Through my blurry eyes, I called a friend of mine from New City, New York, who was already going to fly out with me to the art show and also had expressed a lifelong desire to drive cross country. When he answered the phone, and with little explanation, I said, "I am leaving for California by the end of the day in a truck. If you want to come across country, get here as soon as you can." He jumped in his car and drove two hundred-plus miles from his home. By the time he arrived, I had rented a sixteen-foot Penske box truck. I had unpacked the painting from its crate, since it could neither be moved nor fit into the truck, and I hastily got it ready for my unexpected emergency cross-country trip.

We were on the road by late afternoon the same day. We had to swap out trucks in the Clintons' Arkansas, unloading and reloading the painting due to a breakdown, causing Tom to quip that it must have been the curse of Hillary upon our journey. We slept for a couple of hours here and there. Finding a flat surface on which to sleep was easy—the painting leaned diagonally up against the wall in the back of the truck, so we slept right under it. It took us two days and nine hours to arrive in California. We arrived in California from New York early Thursday morning. We delivered the painting to the conference center, to the surprise of Sergant and his staff. Politicon did eventually chip in to the cost of the trip, to the tune of $1,500. The truck rental alone cost $3,000, some of which my friend kindly lent me since I was artistically short of cash.

Sergant said there would be a VIP showing on Friday night for the political candidates, celebrities, TV pundits, artists, and the media. He also told me there would be an art discussion with Shepard Fairey, Ilma Gore, and other artists. None of the planned art events took place, to my great disappointment, even though I was billed as one of the speakers.[7] Apparently, leftists seemed to be avoiding me and did not want to engage in dialogue. The art show was predominantly anti-Trump. Even conservative artist Sabo was a hardcore anti-Trumper back then, displaying his anti-Trump creations. Because I had the VIP armband, I got to meet Sarah Palin, Anne Coulter, Michael Steele (who was no fan of Trump), and actor Robert Davi, *none of whom* came to the art-gallery section of the political conference. This no-show seemed to confirm my theory that art was politically irrelevant in conservative circles and that I was simply a nobody with no pull. Not very VIP!

However, Sarah Palin made a beeline to meet me as I sat in the crowd of about a thousand people, listening to her speak. I stood out to her because I was one of only two people in the crowd wearing a red "Make America Great Again" cap. (Welcome to liberal Pasadena, California!) I invited her to see the painting twice, to no avail. Recognition is what legitimizes a painting. When people whose opinions are valued recognize your work, it gives life to your work. Because art in the conservative world is such a dud—for now—artists like myself just drift in a no-man's-land, devoid of validating opinions and moral support.

But I did receive another email around the same period—a weird, tempting email with an offer to get me into a green room with candidate Trump in a rally in North Carolina. It was so weird that I thought it was the FBI probing, maybe even setting me up, à la Papadopulous. The pitch came from a company in California offering me a promotional product for sale that, once purchased in quantity, gave me access into a private meeting with Trump. The emailer became the caller. This person knew all about me, my painting, and my efforts to get my work recognized, which was intriguingly alluring, flattering, and alarming all at once. But who were these people, and what were they really selling? Was it a scam? Was it Trump's golden door to access, fame, and attention? My problem was not understanding the language of a quid-pro-quo, celebrity access peddling, and preferring apples for apples, not for oranges! I passed on the bait sandwich, hanging my hopes on a Politicon big break.

The ghosting and the lack of coverage of my Trump painting were blatantly evident in the leftist media stories that came out of Politicon. Did I imagine this? An example of this was that I stood with two *Rolling Stone* magazine journalists for about fifteen minutes in front of the painting, as people interacted with it and took photos. Even their photographer was shooting excitedly, catching people interacting with the painting, as was often the case throughout the day. The journalists looked very uncomfortable. In fact, they looked like stuffed penguins suffering from a severe case of gastric-bowel retention. They refused to interview me. There were excellent pieces of art on show, and there was also a whole load of junk art. Yet, my painting trounced everything around it because of its subject, scale, and graphic power. Instead of acknowledging my Trump painting, all the media could discuss was the fifteen-foot, inflatable KKK Trump doll. Sergant even hung my painting on what he called the "hero wall" (or main wall), ensuring it was unavoidable.

The following week, the *Rolling Stone* story was published. There was plenty of anti-Trump imagery from the art show, yet not a single mention of my painting. Would it not have been journalistically honest to give a little balance to the art show, demonstrating there was another side to the story? Thankfully, some publications did use the Trump-painting image for their stories,[8] which became critical to the documentation of my painting's journey.

It was apparent to me that the Left understood the power and language of art. They knew that reproducing the image, even with a negative story, would allow the image to speak for itself. Thus, they chose to ignore it. On the other hand, those on the right, not understanding the language or the power of art at all, just ignored it altogether.

To have my painting on show and photographed alongside the Obama "Hope" poster was the most significant part of this whole season artistically and historically for me. The personal invitation by Yosi Sergant and learning firsthand the story of the creation of the Obama "Hope" poster would turn out to be providential, as that would be a critical part of the fateful phone call I was to have with Smithsonian National Portrait Gallery Director Kim Sajet.

Other than that, the art show was underwhelming. The media did not want to share my story, and the event organizers shut down any speaking and presentation avenues that would have allowed me to share my story. I wondered if my political artistic path would always be a wilderness. "Conservative art" seemed to be an insurmountable oxymoron—or maybe I was the moron? Would an art show ever materialize where my painting would finally be celebrated?

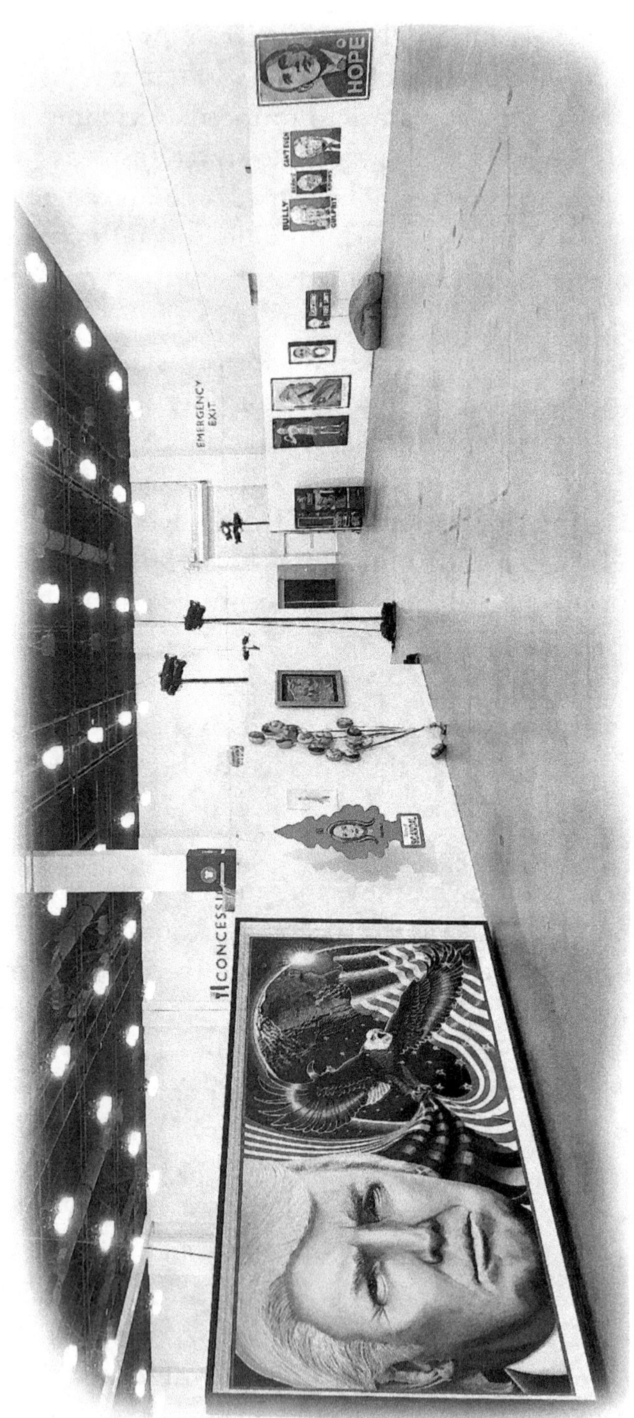

The Art of Politics Show, Politicon Conference, June 2016, Pasadena, California

Chapter Thirteen

CONVENTION HOPPING MAD

Since I was on the road out west in big-sky country, on my way back to New York after Politicon, it made sense to take a slight detour to enjoy the magnificent artistic handiwork of the Grand Canyon and its environs. Yosi Sergant had given me directions to an off-the-beaten-track scenic drive toward the Grand Canyon. Carefully following his directions, we took a little side road into the hills. Sergant's suggestion did not disappoint. The landscape was vast and breathtaking, the weather was perfect, and the views were spectacular. Indeed, that was God's country and a refreshing reset from Politicon's mixture of emotions and anticlimax.

With my painting on show in California in June 2016, I also sought another venue to display the painting: the July 2016 Republican National Convention. Destiny's compass already pointed in the direction of my next step. Earlier that year, I had made inquiries about serving as a delegate for New York at the 2016 RNC. Preparations were now underway in June in Cleveland, Ohio, at the Quicken Loans Arena. I submitted a request to have the painting on display for the convention, but I never heard back from the RNC organizers. Since I would be in the area on my way back from Politicon in California with painting in tow, I decided to pop by and attempt to drop it off.

Arriving in Cleveland at the Quicken Loans Arena, wearing my red "Make America Great Again" cap, I pulled up around the back to the underground loading entrance. Security asked me about my business. I said I was there to deliver the Trump painting. Without even checking to see if I was on the agenda, they just waved me through and down into the belly of the arena, where all the construction activity was happening. My traveling companion could hardly believe his eyes as we descended under the arena. I laughed. He chuckled and gasped and chuckled some more.

Upon arriving in the massive basement, where a full-sized tractor-trailer could turn around, a receiving manager approached me with a clipboard asking me about my business. "Dropping off the Trump portrait," I told him. He looked at his clipboard and, not seeing it there, off he went to speak with his supervisors. He returned clueless. I explained to him that I had submitted a request and had not received a response, so I took the initiative to pop by to see if they had made a decision yet, maybe even helping them make a decision.

No joy! The painting was not on the agenda. "It was worth the try!" I retorted, throwing up my hands. After distributing some prints to the guys in construction, I went into the offices and did the same, requesting in person to display the painting. They never responded. But once again, the mysterious hand of destiny was to ensure that the image of the Trump painting would be part of the historic RNC convention.

Earlier that year, in May, I had received a Facebook message from a grassroots Trump supporter in Des Moines, Iowa. Loni had been kind and helpful in my campaign during the caucuses. She had also encouraged me to become a New York delegate for Trump. Not having any clue what that meant, I followed her recommendation and asked Rodney Strange, the local Elmira Republican

Party chairman, how to become a delegate for Trump. At first, he was reluctant to help me, even trying to blow me off. He told me that there were so many people lined up for only three delegate positions, insinuating that I had no chance of getting in. Don't even bother was his unspoken advice, sounding like he wanted the spot. But I pressed him all the same; if becoming a delegate was the next step in my odyssey, no one was going to thwart the plan. As I was not backing down from my request to try for the position, Strange finally acquiesced, informing me of my next steps.

The delegate-selection ceremony was quite an official occasion, I was to discover. I also learned that there were many people trying to become delegates—even Rodney himself (as I had suspected). Rodney had been a Ted Cruz man and was a late bloomer for Trump. But then, he wanted in, since the convention was coming up. For long-term politically active Republicans, the RNC was verging on a holy convocation—no wonder there was so much enthusiasm.

As the ceremony got underway, people began to share their stories, explaining why they should be elected as a delegate for Trump. Displaying Trump yard signs on their lawns, telling people here and there of their support for Trump, and making Republican Party contributions all seemed trivial to me. When it was my turn, I shared the story of my painting and my campaigning locally and across the country. But I was unknown to the local party brass and never a donor. Raven, the starving artist, a Republican Party donor, sounds like an oxymoron all over again. I did not make the cut as a New York delegate in the first round of voting.

Then to my surprise, I discovered that there were also three alternate-delegate positions available, sort of like spare tires on a car, just in case the primary delegate died, got sick, or simply failed to show up. The candidates who had tried and failed the first time and the contenders for this spare-tire position went up. I requested to speak again, to which there was some resistance from the director. But since I was contending for a different responsibility, I argued that I should be allowed to make another speech, and eventually, I was.

Without delay, I jumped up and began to speak, taking the audience back to the unforgettable day when I traveled to Trump Tower to give the campaign the twenty-two-by-forty-four-inch beautifully framed stretched-canvas print of the Trump painting. Remember, the day of the controversial Black-pastors' meeting at the end of November 2015? Let's go back to that day.

On my second trip to Trump Tower, you'll recall I was dragging the crate around the streets of Manhattan. I ended up handing over the Trump-painting print to the campaign at the reception desk. The receptionists would not let me go upstairs and personally deliver the gift, insisting it had to be examined by the secret service. That was the last I saw of it until it began to appear in photos of the Trump campaign headquarters in the media throughout the campaign. Also, when the campaign moved to a more finished space inside of Trump Tower, staffer Daniel Gelbinovich sent me a picture of the painting hanging on a brand-new, no-longer-bare wall somewhere inside of their new offices.

After that, coffee at Starbucks in Trump Tower was the order of the day for me. I sat around enjoying the atmosphere and giving out some of the bumper stickers I had made. One kitchen worker ran up to me, showing me photos of the painting that he had taken on his phone when the box was opened downstairs by the secret service.

After giving the painting to the campaign earlier that morning, I met with Daniel Gelbinovich downstairs by the waterfall. He was a campaign staffer with whom I was in contact. I told him that as a minister of the Gospel, I was happy to be of support in any way that I could while I was there—being appropriately dressed in a black suit, even wearing a black shirt and silver-and-black tie. I was ready for divine intervention. I shared my story with Daniel and how the Scriptures in the book of Isaiah told the story of Cyrus the Great, an unbelieving man mightily used by God for God's purposes regarding Israel, and that Trump could be a man that God would use similarly. He told me that he had recently started to read the book of Isaiah, rekindling his Jewish faith. Before he left, he asked for another thick stack of attractive bumper stickers with the image of the painting, which I gladly gave. Would he return the favor? Biding my time, I waited to see how the pastors' meeting would materialize but learned that the meeting was canceled again.

After waiting some more, it appeared that I was just wasting time. Since I was in New York City and only a few blocks from St. Patrick's Cathedral, I seized the moment and went to spend some quiet time inside that magnificent, sacred space. In that place of peace, amid the New York City hustle and bustle, I prayed and regrouped in my mind as I prepared for the journey back to Elmira.

As I left the church, walking down the steps, I called Gloria and told her what had and hadn't happened. God must have tugged at my wife's spirit as we spoke. She became excited and said that the day was not over; I should head back to Trump Tower—that God had a divine appointment waiting for me. When God moves upon my wife, Gloria, like that, I pay attention.

Trump Tower was en route to my car anyway. As I approached the building, I could see a large crowd of journalists gathered outside. I walked through them and into the lobby. Strangely, the lobby was empty, except for three men standing by the elevators. They were Michael Cohen, Pastor Darrel Scott, and another Black pastor I did not recognize.

Walking up to the group to introduce myself, I wanted to inform them that I was the artist who had given the campaign the painting that morning. To my surprise, Pastor Scott turned to me as I approached and said, "You're late!" To which I responded, "I thought the meeting was canceled." "No, it's just about to start," he replied. Scott had no idea who I was. And yet, at that moment, God took over. (My wife was right!)

I later read an account by a minister who was in the meeting upstairs precisely at that time the three men went down to the lobby to gather any stragglers to join them. They apparently wanted to make sure the meeting was well attended for Trump's sake, since some ministers were still reluctant to attend. I happened to walk into the lobby right at that moment. That was no accident.

"Come with me," Scott said, directing me and another minister who had just arrived. He, too, was short on melanin. Into the once-elusive gilded elevator we went. By now, my heart was pounding, as I didn't know what would happen. Maybe they would toss me off the top of the building, or perhaps they had the painting and would show it. I had no idea. Life had taught me that when a door opens, keep walking through it unless it closes. This door opened all by itself, and I was most certainly going to keep walking. I talked with Pastor Scott briefly, telling him my story of coming to America. He and I, along with the other minister, traveled up to the conference room on the twenty-sixth floor.

The doors opened with a ding. A line of people were getting wanded with a metal detector by the Secret Service agent before they were allowed to enter through the double sliding-glass doors to the conference room. Pastor Scott looked at my transparent-green art portfolio, now empty of bumper stickers, and said, "What is that? Leave that there by the wall," which I did.

Now my heart was pounding out of my chest as I approached the Secret Service to get scanned. They did not ask any questions as to who I was; they just passed the metal detector all over me, with my arms stretched wide open, front and back, and ushered me through the sliding doors. What a relief. The conference room was full of ministers and their wives, all standing around this massive cream-colored, speckled-granite conference table, just waiting. The conference table was splendid—it must have been three or four inches thick and could seat at least forty people. Black leather upholstered executive chairs flanked its vast sides.

Following behind the guests in front of me, I ended up at the table with the name tags. "This is going to be fun," I thought to myself as my heart started to pound once again. The other guests looked through the names, selected their tags, and walked off, pinning them to their jackets. I looked over all the names as if looking for mine, and surprise of all surprises, there was my name tag! No, just kidding. The attendant asked me if I needed help since I looked bewildered, not finding my name tag. She told me not to worry since the meeting was all over the place, with guests just like me coming at the last minute. Sweet relief blew across my brow like a kiss from an angel.

No one knew who anyone else was, so no one knew who I was or was not. Then, Pastor Scott called the meeting to attention, laying out the ground rules. Since Trump was not a believer, he would have no understanding of "the moving of the Holy Ghost," so we were instructed not to go off the rails and roll around on the floor. (No, he did not say that, but in charismatic-to-charismatic code talk, I knew what he was saying: "Behave yourselves and don't scare Trump out of the room!")

Then, my heart skipped a few beats as he raised his voice, pointing in my direction and announced that there were "five honorary Black brothers" there with them that day. One by one, Pastor Scott introduced by name the other four White ministers, whom he knew personally. Then he came to me, the last of the last guests in the room of about a hundred people. Taking a deep breath, I braced myself.

"And this is Brother Raven…, a…a…a brother from England…who…who…who became a citizen…and now is here with us today…" I was dying inside as everybody in that room was looking right at me, nodding their heads, and I was looking at them. Small applause followed, yet I felt mortified and wanted to hide under a chair somewhere. I smiled and sheepishly half-waved. The truth was I was meant to be there, even though no one knew who I was! We mingled some more, and I seized the opportunity to encourage one pastor who had severe doubts about Trump. I shared my story and the story of Cyrus the Great from Isaiah 45.

Then, the moment we had all been waiting for arrived. I had positioned myself at the far end of the conference table near the windows, thinking Trump would sit at the head of the table at the other end by the doors. Trump walked in, and without hesitation, waved his Bible, saying, "I brought my Bible!" He then proceeded to walk around the whole table and sit down about three feet from where I stood. Pastor Scott sat to his right, and another pastor sat to his left. Also present were some well-known, money-hungry televangelists that I vaguely recognized, causing me even to question my being there with these new unintentional associates. Undoubtedly, Trump's billionaire celebrity status was a huge draw to people of all sorts of stripes, even mine. It was business for me too, along with the sense of mission. Omorosa, Trump's friend at the time, sat at the table near him, and Michael Cohen hurried about making sure things were in order.

Being this close to Trump allowed me to observe him behind closed doors and get a real sense of who he was as a person. The meeting was private—no press and no recordings were allowed during the "thirty-minute meeting," which lasted nearly two hours. Trump was very engaged and open, even tolerating flack from a Black Lives Matter activist pastor in attendance. He claimed Trump, who was comfortably sitting between two Black pastors, was a racist for ejecting a Black BLM protester from one of his recent rallies. Others complained about Trump apparently mocking a journalist who was crippled. Other issues came up, hot and quickly. Trump made most in the room laugh by calling himself an "equal-opportunity offender," as he responded to the accusations.

Overall, Trump's demeanor was very different from what I was used to seeing in the news. He seemed seriously interested in learning and at one point sat quietly for about half an hour, listening intently to the litany of problems facing the inner-city African American community. This firsthand encounter with Trump would prove golden when sharing my story because he was so different in private. I wished Trump would have shown some of that other side to the public.

Trump suggested that if elected president, he would reduce corporate tax rates to incentivize companies holding billions of dollars overseas to return to America. Corporations could then reinvest the money, creating desperately needed jobs for the African American community. (Upon becoming president, Trump did indeed do what he said, and the African American jobless rate became the lowest it had ever been in history.)

At one point in the conversation, Michael Cohen tried to "canonize" Trump, painting him as a "very Christian man," highlighting some of the ways Trump had given money to people in need. That made me cringe, as what he was saying rang hollow. (Today, Michael Cohen sings a different tune, claiming it was all a scam.)

A time of comments arrived when attendees could speak. So, knowing the fears and doubts that lingered in the room, I chimed in and encouraged my brothers in Christ to read Isaiah 45 to see an example of how God could use a man like Trump. Other times in the meeting, the same Scripture had come up, echoing this same opinion that Trump could be a Cyrus-like figure, even highlighting that the Cyrus chapter in Isaiah was number 45 and Trump would soon become the forty-fifth president of the United States—a very curious coincidence.

The meeting finally ended. As Trump stood up, I was the first to greet him, being so close. I tapped him on the right arm, approached him from his right side, and introduced myself as "the artist who had painted the painting" delivered earlier that day. Whether he had seen it or not, I did not know, but he said something like, "Thank you, very nice." I informed Trump that I was going to the Iowa caucuses to use my painting to persuade Evangelicals to vote for him. He was grateful. I would later meet Trump again at a rally in Iowa, engaging him about coming to Denison because the local media in Denison wanted to know if he would come. Trump never did come.

Speaking with Trump, I paid close attention to his eyes. They were as blue as I had painted them. It seemed like he had stars in his eyes as the conference-room ceiling lights reflected in them. Looking him squarely in the eye, I perceived that God was with him, in that room amongst those Spirit-filled believers. Trump had opened his heart, and you could see it in his eyes. For me, that was unexpected and added further fuel to my assurance that Trump would indeed win and become the forty-fifth president of the United States.

People were now lining up behind me to get photos with Trump. I resisted taking a photo of myself with Trump unless Trump knew who I was—the artist who had painted "Unafraid and Unashamed"—and he was willingly giving me his endorsement. I did not want to be just another guy in the room posing next to someone famous. However, I took a selfie over my shoulder a few feet from him, wanting to document the story and prove that I was there, as I knew people would not even believe it. Upon leaving, I rode the elevator down with the same pastor with whom I had spoken at the outset. Convinced he could support Trump, having heard the echo of Isaiah 45 bounce around the room, his demeanor had changed. Not only that, but he shared with me that he had also read that same passage himself that morning.

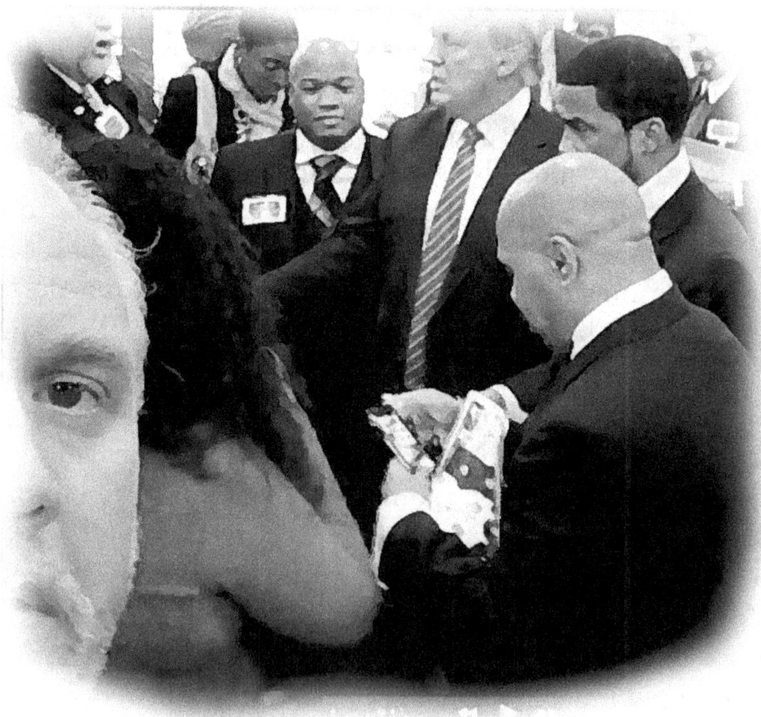

Photo over my left shoulder of Pastor Mark Burns, Donald Trump, Pastor Scott at Black-pastors' meeting, Trump Tower, November 2015

Elated, I bounced and virtually skipped down the street back to my car. This providential encounter further galvanized my conviction and determination to go on the road and campaign for Donald Trump, a sinner and yet chosen of God for God's purposes at that particular time in history. I even went straight to the local ministers' prayer meeting back in Elmira, at a church called the Church of the Twin Tiers. I offered to share with them the story of what had just happened, along with my Biblically significant painting, to help them get a sense of how to pray for Trump. They received me with polite indifference and a "thanks, but no thanks," so I left. Most believers I knew at the time were for Cruz, Carson, or Fiorina. I often heard how they would have to hold their noses in disgust to vote for Trump.

Now, getting back to the New York delegate-selection ceremony, I had attendees sitting on the edges of their seats listening to my every word. I continued with the story of my campaign in support of then-candidate Trump:

My dear wife, Gloria, was not on board with me selling my tools and other equipment to fund the campaign. This understandably caused severe tension and arguments. But I had no money and no choice but to sell and go. If I did not go, my painting would sit in my studio. Locally, I was already blacklisted, with little chance of a showing. If I went, the whole country could see my painting. Gloria insisted that for her to support my campaign, I had to get Trump's endorsement. For the third time, I packed my car with my camera, put on my suit and tie once again, and took off on the two-hundred-mile road trip to Manhattan.

My requests to have some form of official acknowledgment, such as a photo with Trump and the painting, were never granted. They would accept and hang the painting but were reluctant to acknowledge me as the artist. The campaign thought I was seeking money, which I neither wanted nor requested. Being fiercely independent, who would want the controlling influences that receiving money could create? Instead, I preferred to pay my way, roughing it at times and even struggling financially rather than compromise and beg, selling my soul. Neither did I want to be seen as an opportunist hitching a ride on Trump. However, I did request an endorsement, which I could use to generate sales of prints. That would, in turn, fund my cross-country grassroots campaign for Trump. To me, that was a fair and reasonable transaction, benefiting all parties involved. With no endorsement, sales were slim. I had labored for hundreds of hours, creating what at the time was my life's most important work of art, and they had received it, hanging the beautifully framed copy on their wall.

Arriving at Trump Tower yet again, I called Trump staffer Daniel Gelbinovich and asked if we could meet. I was now getting frustrated at the whole situation. I explained that the Trump campaign could simply endorse the copy of the painting they had hanging on their wall upstairs and that could help my campaign. I kindly asked Daniel for a photo with me and my painting upstairs, maybe with the staff or even Trump, to which he apologetically said it was not

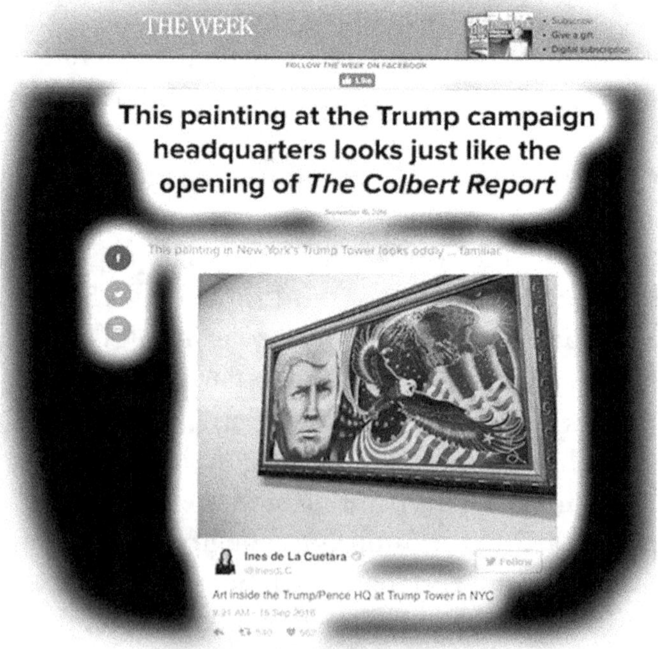

A mocking article in *The Week* magazine,
showing the painting in Trump Tower

going to happen. (When I was in Iowa, journalists did not believe me that a copy of my painting hung in Trump Tower until other journalists visiting Trump Tower started posting pictures of it.) It was very disappointing. The last time I'd left Trump Tower, I was skipping down the streets; this time, I was dragging myself along the New York City sidewalk. That was one long, long walk back to my parked car. My quiet and gloomy two-hundred-mile drive back to Elmira seemed like it took days.

It was back to ground zero. I informed Gloria that I had to generate the funds through my sale of tools and go, even though she disagreed. Reluctantly, yet wanting to support me because of our love, Gloria came on board as my primary support and encourager. Gloria would keep the home fires burning and take care of our three children as I embarked on my month-long, five-thousand-mile campaign in Iowa.

At the tool sale, Bill Stewart and his military-veteran son, Tyler Stewart, of Horseheads, New York, were the first to make a purchase, giving me the chunk of change that I needed to fund my journey. They had initially come just for the tool sale. Yet, after seeing the original Trump painting and hearing about the patriotic journey I was about to embark on, they went the extra mile and bought two of my paintings. Bill even bought a third painting when I was on the road in Iowa, giving me another greatly needed cash injection.

Not many, but a few faithful people stood up to assist me. Some of the people who bought tools or art would later become friends. People like local veteran Bob Brill would often pop by to give words of encouragement. Pat Sager Wall and Perry Treu also stand out for their support and generosity.

In Iowa also, I met wonderful patriots who assisted me: Simon Fitzpatrick and Paul Shook from Denison, also Jeff Moorman, Charles England, Tammy Kobza, and Grant Gardener, who kindly welcomed me into their homes, fed me, or had me stay over. One man, Roger Roseke, treated my Trump truck to a full double-tank load of diesel fuel in central Iowa. God provided for all of my needs.

Even though it was very tough and brutally cold in the middle of the Iowa winter, it was an epic adventure. Some of the perks were the deliciously huge portions of apple or pecan country-made pies with ice cream or the full-sized hungry-man's breakfasts. The pies were sold at the gun shows where I would campaign for Trump, displaying the painting. Those small-town gun shows resembled a modern-day Wild West on the Iowan snow-covered plains in the middle of nowhere. Characters right out of the movies strutted around in their boots, toting their weapons. The Old-Timer, with a revolver holstered on his hip, a long white beard, and wearing a baseball cap, gave me the chills. He was keen to inform me about the modified AK-47 assault rifle he had under the front seat of his pick-up truck, making me wonder if there was a wanted poster of him hanging on a tree somewhere. Iowans, in general, were red hot for Trump. Yet some were viciously opposed.

One smiling woman came up to me as I sat in the truck and asked if she could take a picture, at which I said, "Of course." Driving that Trump truck around was a people magnet; everywhere I went, people would honk, wave, take photos, take selfies with me, or just yell and scream. After taking a picture of me smiling and giving the thumbs up because I thought she was a fan, she suddenly snapped into her true mode and began viciously insulting me and the painting. She yelled out how she just wanted to get a photo of how a @#$%!)&$# looked. The woman got so heated that I had to take a photo of her license plate, fearing she would get violent. One other unhinged man circled the gas station in which I had parked. Screaming wildly out of the window of his car, he drove around and around, getting louder with each lap. That was disturbing!

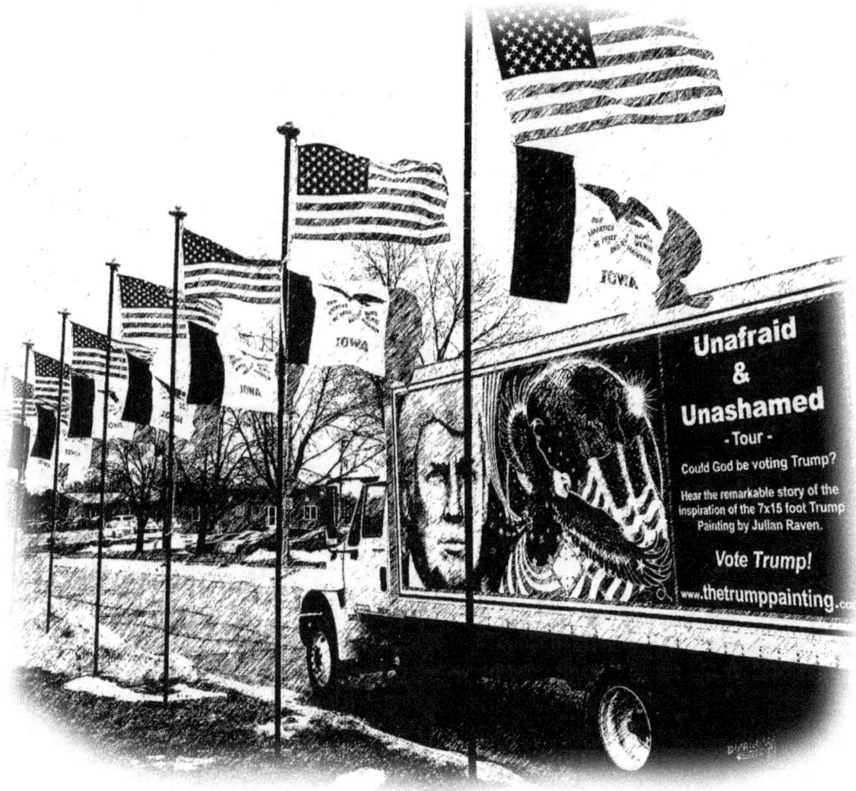

Trucking across Iowa, January 2016

It was so cold at times that the ropes I used to hurl over the Trump truck to drag the massive tarp over the entire truck every night would freeze and become like stiff wire. It was brutal. Covering the truck was necessary to protect the image from getting vandalized. At one point, even death stared me down on the road in the middle of a snow blizzard. Heading up one of the very few hills in Iowa, a tractor-trailer came toward me over the brow on the wrong side of the road. The driver could have been drunk or asleep. That morning I had prayed specifically for protection on the road from drunk drivers. My truck shook violently as the massive tractor-trailer, barely missing me, hurtled past, pushing me onto the hard shoulder. Those single-lane roads had narrow hard shoulders and six-foot drops into the fields below. If I had not been vigilant, it would have been a head-on collision, or the truck would have flipped onto its side and into the snow-covered Iowan field.

After sharing this detailed chapter of my epic campaign for Trump with the audience at the Republican delegates ceremony, a round of applause went up. Some business was conducted, then votes were cast by the Republican chairpersons and counted for each contestant. The gentleman officiating the meeting came and sat next to me to whisper something in my ear. I thought, "Uh oh, what have I done?" Surely he was there to turf me out of the meeting, but no! To the contrary—I was going to Cleveland as an alternate delegate for New York State. Hurrah! He told me to leave the room and join the parade of delegates that was about to enter. I went out into the lobby. People were congratulating me, shaking my hand, and lining up for the procession. A uniformed flag bearer led the way. They all marched, chests puffed up, looking very official and important. I followed behind, tagging along, not knowing exactly what I had signed up for, but I did not care—I was an alternate delegate for Trump. I just smiled and waved!

The next big shock was that it would cost me three hundred dollars a night for five nights. You must be kidding—that's fifteen hundred dollars! I was a starving artist of sorts who could not afford to stay at the Grand Plaza Hotel in the center of Cleveland, where New York's top political brass and delegation would stay—because Trump, after all, was a New Yorker. Yes, New Yorkers were the bomb at the Republican National Convention because Trump was a New Yorker.

On the first night in Cleveland, I read online that Cleveland had opened up overnight parking to accommodate the anti-Trump and anti-RNC protesters. I thought I would try camping in that parking lot. Arriving first, I went to sleep, only to be awakened by a knock on the door; it was the cops. They did not realize that the overnight parking started that night, so they harassed me until I showed them the press release from their mayor. It took awhile to convince them that I was not an anarchist but actually an alternate New York delegate sleeping in his old truck. They finally believed me, yet warned me that it might not be the best place for me to park after all. I took their advice.

My old faithful Dodge 1500 pickup truck would serve me well on that trip. I took a large four-by-eight-foot copy of the Trump painting, printed and stretched on canvas, and slept in my pickup truck at a rest area twenty minutes outside Cleveland each night. Showering in the rest-area bathroom using a wash bucket worked just fine.

Arriving super early each day for the daily New York delegation meetings ensured I landed a parking spot right in front of the Plaza Hotel for twenty dollars a day. In that way, I did not miss the unlimited delicious complimentary breakfast, courtesy of the New York delegation. The ample buffet breakfast at the hotel was for all the New York delegates and people attending the daily morning meetings held at the hotel before the convention activities started later in the evening.

When the evening session started each day, I had to be in my assigned seat if the official delegate needed replacing. Kindly, the bona fide delegate for whom I was the backup did let me sit in his seat right up front for a brief twenty minutes over the four-day convention. He told me of the sign he'd built in his front yard made of bricks, representing Trump's wall. He told me of the wads of money he had given to the local Republican Party. He even offered me money in support of my campaign if I would give him a ride in the front seat of the Trump truck the next time I went to Trump

Tower! Passing greenbacks was how the game was played—no wonder I was so out of place.

Those morning meetings at the Plaza Hotel were loaded with Republican heavy hitters. Rudy Giuliani, Newt Gingrich, and a host of other leaders and politicians from New York, and even billionaires like John Catsimatidis, were in attendance. At the time, I did not know who Catsimatidis was. Sitting down at those spacious and empty round tables early in the morning before anyone else arrived was my daily ritual. Catsimatidis appeared at my table one morning, sitting down next 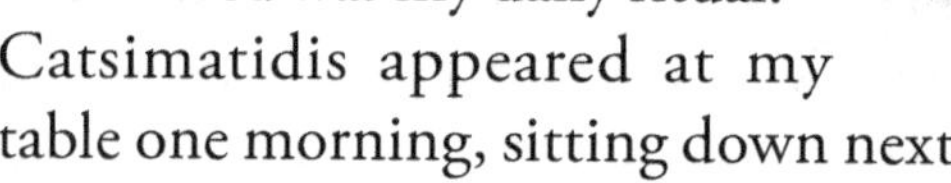 to my empty place setting while I was busy loading up at the breakfast buffet bar. When I returned, I just went ahead and sat down right next to him in my place—all cozy, elbow to elbow.

Mrs. Catsimatidis sat down on the other side of him and gave me a look of indignation, as if to say, "How dare you sit next to us! Don't you know who we are?" No, I did not, and to make it worse, I was wearing khaki shorts and a Hawaiian shirt, not the formal suits and ties that abounded. The billionaire couple was dressed up to the nines as if going to an inaugural gala. (I did wear my suit on the last day to demonstrate that I had one and that I even knew how to tie a full Windsor knot.) But that day, I was not winning any brownie points with the local brass by offending oil magnate Catsimatidis.

Politely, I introduced myself but then paid no mind to the man as I tucked into my piled-high breakfast banquet. For reasons unbeknownst to me, greeters seemed to be coming up to kiss his proverbial ring. Even Congressman Tom Reed, my representative from upstate New York's 23rd District, came up, genuflected before the man, and greeted both of us, thinking I was friends with big John. I popped up and introduced myself to him, "Oh, Congressman Reed, my name is Julian Raven—we finally get to meet!" Reed stood there awkwardly staring at me sitting right there next to big John, wondering, I imagined, how I knew him. Why else would I be sitting right next to the billionaire at a vast, otherwise-empty table? Later learning that Catsimatidis was the source of unending campaign cash for politicians up for reelection explained everything.

At the five-star Grand Plaza Hotel, I enjoyed these daily morning breakfasts, flowing with freshly brewed coffee, gourmet platters of exotic fruit, melted cheddar-cheese-covered scrambled eggs, and toast, draped in crispy bacon. It was just the hobnobbing and political jockeying that I could not wait to flee. In my Hawaiian shirt and shorts, I would take my four-by-eight-foot Trump painting print and position myself on a wall in Public Square, in the center of town. That was where the fun was for me. I loved observing the ever-flowing throng of political agitators and engaging with people who disagreed with me. I carried out a social experiment of sorts, observing people interacting with the painting throughout the day. I did my best to stay quiet and let the painting speak for itself, and it did!

The RNC and Public Square came with their own tempting associations. I got wind of a Trump rally organized by Roger Stone, the ever-creepy political dirty trickster that circled the Trump campaign. Stone triggered a sixth-sense warning in me whenever I heard his name. But he was shepherding all the MAGA supporters off to my right and away from Public Square. People would come up to me and tell me about the rally going on and that I should go and get involved. Should I stay alone on my wall among the hostilities or go where maybe I could get some recognition? Stone had Trump's ear, and he was mobilizing the street support for Trump. But I was there to build bridges with the antagonists on my own marketing mission. Even conspiracy weaver Alex Jones, who flew an anti-Hillary sign in the sky around the arena all week, sauntered through Public Square, causing a huge confrontation, commotion, and media attention from which he needed to be dramatically escorted out of Public Square. Associating with those characters could have been profitable. Yes, but at what cost?

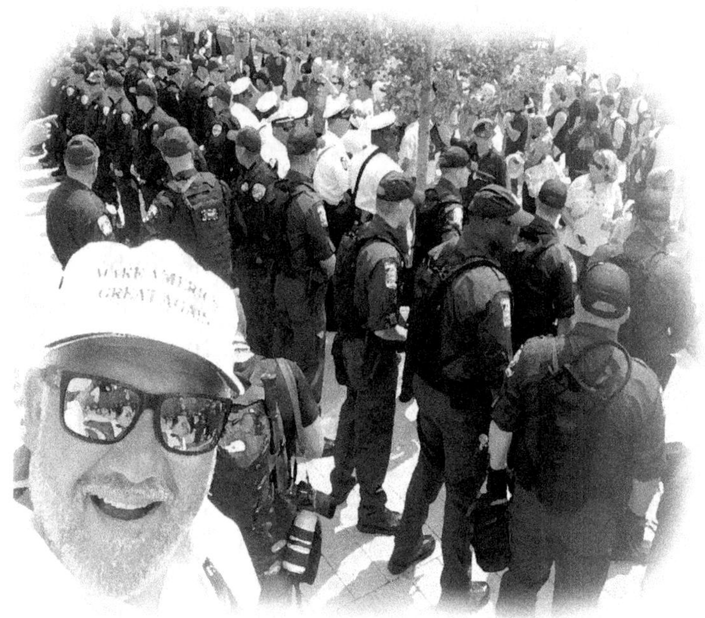

No shortage of law enforcement at Public Square, Cleveland RNC, 2016

The convention became a circus because Trump was to become the nominee. It was a madhouse. Fifteen thousand journalists from all over the world scurried about, seeking their next scoop. At the same time, 5,500 law-enforcement officers from all over the country maintained order, while thousands of convention attendees, delegates, protesters, and Cleveland residents packed the streets. The convention for some reason attracted every type of group with a gripe or group with a gun. Armed militia members paraded their outfits, wearing mirrored shades, tactical gear, guns, and plenty of swagger. Protesters yelled in every direction, while preachers preached repentance. Black Lives Matter marchers chanted as Westboro Baptists condemned, insulted, and hated on everyone equally. There was something for everyone at Cleveland! Snaking through the crowds and corralling them, anti-wall protesters were dressed up in one colossal canvas banner painted with the image of a wall that seemed to be a mile long. At one point, these canvas-clad anti-border-wall provocateurs surrounded me and my Trump painting. I was standing on the back of a tall concrete bench, as the leader of the walled mob, a man of the cloth, stared up at me. He harangued me about Trump and the wall in my painting. I'll never forget the short, shiny-faced sweating priest, dressed in a black robe and white collar, hollering up at me in Spanish under the scorching summer sun. Yes, the human experience, with little restraint, was on full display. It was both a marvelous and disturbing sight to see.

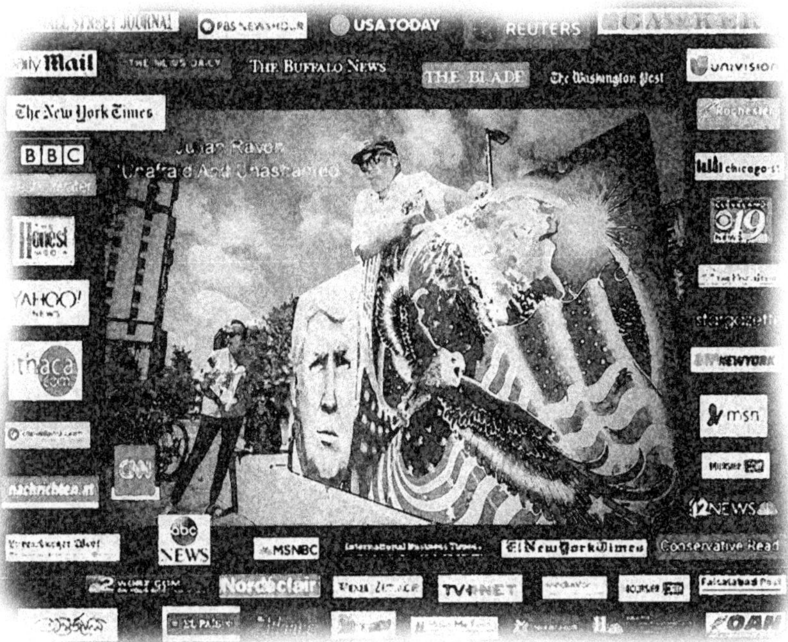

Media coverage of Public Square, Cleveland RNC

At one point, a gaggle of journalists and photographers mobbed me. Over their heads, I proclaimed, "Behold what an incredible view." That view was of the sea of people freely expressing them-selves within the freedoms we enjoy under the U.S. Constitution. It was beautiful and ugly all at the same time, but it was freedom! One journalist, wanting to make me look superficial, twisted what I said through his tainted lens in a typical effort to disparage and distort my story. He wrote that the beautiful view I was referring to was the view of the gaggle of journalists writing my story and taking pictures of "moi," as if that was all that mattered to me.

Truth be told, it was wonderful to see the continuous attention my painting was receiving, which was one of the reasons I was there. Journalists from all over the world were waiting in line to interview me. But the beauty I was referring to was the freedom of speech, specifically the political free speech of the People. The biased journalist did not want to admit that I could see that sweet freedom.

Passions boiled over in Public Square, but violence was short lived because of the police presence everywhere. I was startled at one point, turning my head to find a man wanting to eat my paint-ing. Starting on the upper left corner and then on the upper right corner, he opened his mouth and gnawed on the canvas-covered wooden frame. I waved urgently to a group of policemen who were standing under the shade of a tree. It was like a law-enforcement buffet. It was just a matter of deciding from which group, which uniform, which color, or which state you wanted help. They rushed over like a football team to intervene. The man with the strange taste in art tried to explain to the police why he was trying to eat my painting. Unconvinced, they arrested him.

Another man proclaimed he did not know whom he was voting for. He stepped in front of the painting, examining it up close for about five minutes before popping up and proclaiming, "I'm voting for Trump." Wow! The power of art. My social experiment was working!

My story was told worldwide, even in *El Pais*, Spain's premier newspaper. The people I knew growing up in Spain were all too familiar with that paper. Journalists, seemingly from every country under the sun (even from Iraq) lined up to interview me in their broken English. It was massive exposure. Local, national, and international papers printed a portion or all of the Trump painting to either tell my story or bolster their own—except, that is, for CNN and other mainstream TV news networks. They would wait in the park, looking for screaming and yelling Trump supporters so that they could weave their biased tales. The mostly silent Trump guy on the wall with his painting just did not fit their prescripted narrative, since he was engaging in civil dialogue with protesters—even finding common ground with BLM members who despised Trump yet admired his painting.

When I first arrived in Cleveland, four days before the convention started, I was the first one to arrive at Public Square. A CNN news crew arrived one day. It was just me, them, and some people milling around before the massive crowds arrived. They saw me carrying what appeared to be a large sign. From the back, I think they imagined it was some kind of anti-Trump poster. They appeared excitedly interested. They looked like meerkats on a dirt mound bobbing up and down to get a good look. But the moment I unwrapped the painting and showed them the image, they lost their steam. Like deflating blowup Christmas lawn ornaments, their interest melted away.

The Public Square exposure solidified my portrait as the main pro-Trump image created by an independent artist. The identical four-by-eight-foot copy I displayed at the Public Square in the afternoons I also displayed at the New York delegation headquarters at the Grand Central Plaza Hotel every morning. Before the convention, I had asked the New York Republican chairman, Ed Cox, about displaying the Trump painting at the hotel—another request that was never answered. So, I just took it upon myself to display it on an easel every day when I went to breakfast. Immediately, people would gather around and take pictures of and with the painting. Eventually, even Chairman Ed Cox himself started using it as his background when interviewed by the media. Out of the fifty states at the convention, only New York had the painting of Trump.

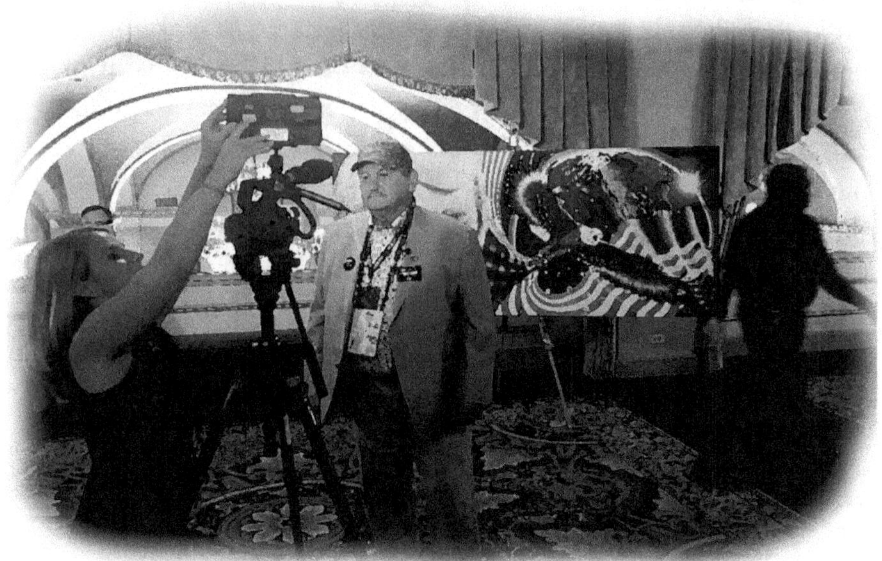

Media setting up for an interview in front of the
Trump painting, Plaza Hotel, RNC, 2016

But the defining moment came when Lynne Patton spoke. On the third day, I was sitting in the convention hall, acting in my alternate-delegate, spare-tire role. Reviewing the schedule for the day, I saw that they were going to play Lynne Patton's viral video, "The Trump Family That I Know." For a moment, I wondered if they had edited me out, since I seemed so out of place. Lynne spoke from the heart, and then the video played. I watched as if in slow motion, ready to take a picture of the jumbotron in front of me. There it was! For four seconds, my painting appeared on the screen, being watched by millions of people. From that moment on, I was getting all sorts of congratulatory remarks from media people and New York politicians. My phone rang—it was Sharon Mangham, Pastor Mangham's wife, who was watching the convention live from their home. She saw me and the painting for herself on TV and congratulated me with excitement.

That moment was historic. The image of my painting, the only recognized political Trump painting at the convention—even

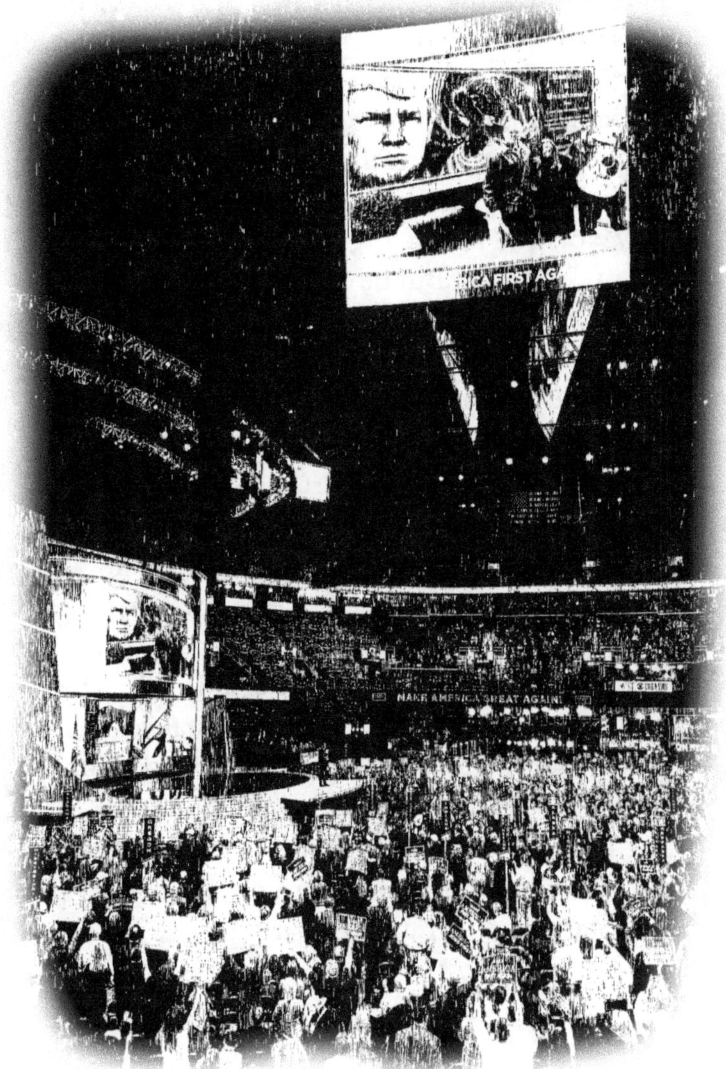

Republican National Convention, 2016, Cleveland, Ohio

though it was the version plastered on the side of my truck—was sealed into the historic nomination of Donald J. Trump at the 2016 Republican National Convention in Cleveland, Ohio.

Back at the hotel, during a speech by Newt Gingrich, I was afforded the opportunity to ask him a question. Pursuing my other

objective of reinjecting the visual arts back into conservative politics as a necessary and persuasive language, I asked Newt to explain
why he thought the use of visual arts was nonexistent in the conservative movement. He responded by mentioning the '40s and
'50s, when conservatives successfully used art. But since the '60s
and '70s, leftists and Democrats had developed a monopoly on
using the power of art. His statement left me wanting since it didn't
really answer my question. But he did acknowledge the deficiency.
The ongoing failure of conservatives to harness the power of the
arts today remains an enigma that my experience illustrates. It is a
reality that I hoped and still hope to change.

The convention was incomparable to anything I had ever experienced. I'll never forget when Ted Cruz was hysterically booed off
the stage for his continued opposition to Trump. Then the moment
came when candidate Donald Trump made his show-stopping
entrance. The space-age door slowly slid upwards, as billowing
smoke rolled onto the stage. The electric teal-colored backdrop lit
the fog from behind, cutting the unmistakable silhouetted figure
of the man of the moment—the silhouetted stance, the side profile, and hairdo shape—all amplified by the creative drama. That
performance art was iconic and ironic.

Candidate Donald John Trump became the anointed leader of
the Republican Party and the Republican nominee for president
of the United States of America.

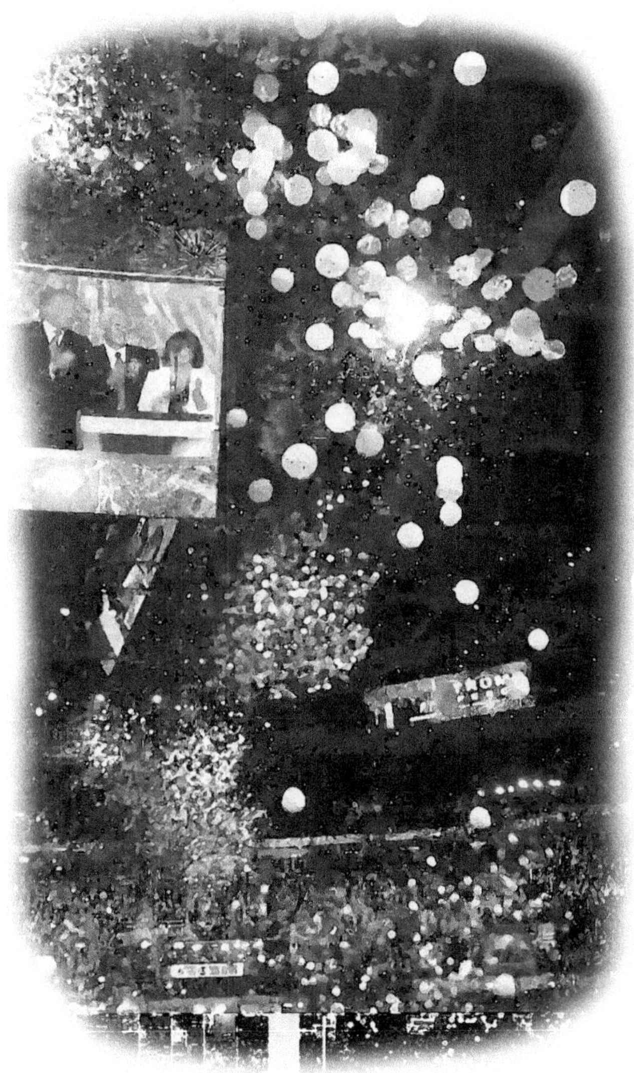

Convention balloons celebrating the nomination
of Donald Trump, RNC, 2016

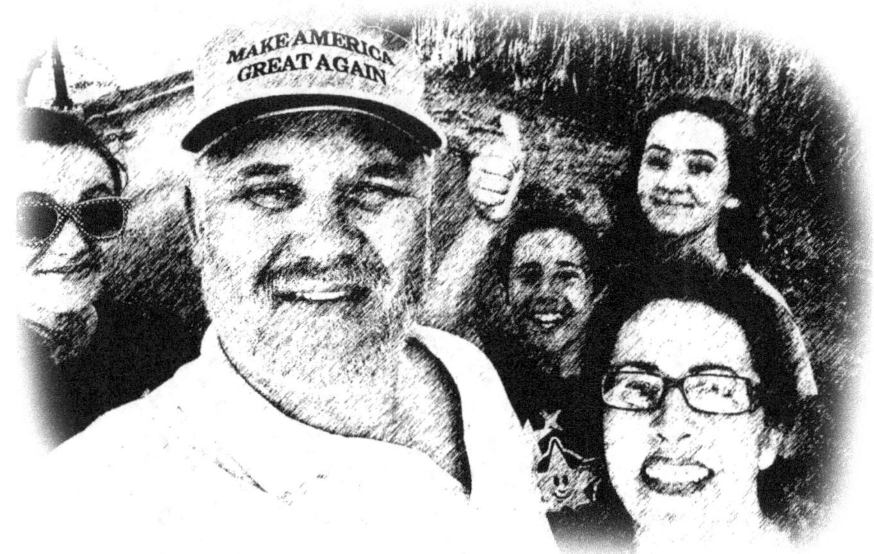

My family, July 2016

Chapter Fourteen

INTERMISSION

The Republican National Convention came to an end, and I was exhausted. The convention was thrilling and informative but emotionally draining. How wonderful to head home to Gloria, our beautiful children, and our dog. The Elmira summer countryside, blooming with greenery and colorful wildflowers, called to me with open arms. I needed a heavy dose of rest and relaxation. Maybe I could even slow down enough to mow the lawn, paint a picture, or perhaps go fishing with the family along the lethargic Susquehanna River.

The demanding and agonizing ordeal that I was unwittingly navigating toward was still a few months down the road.

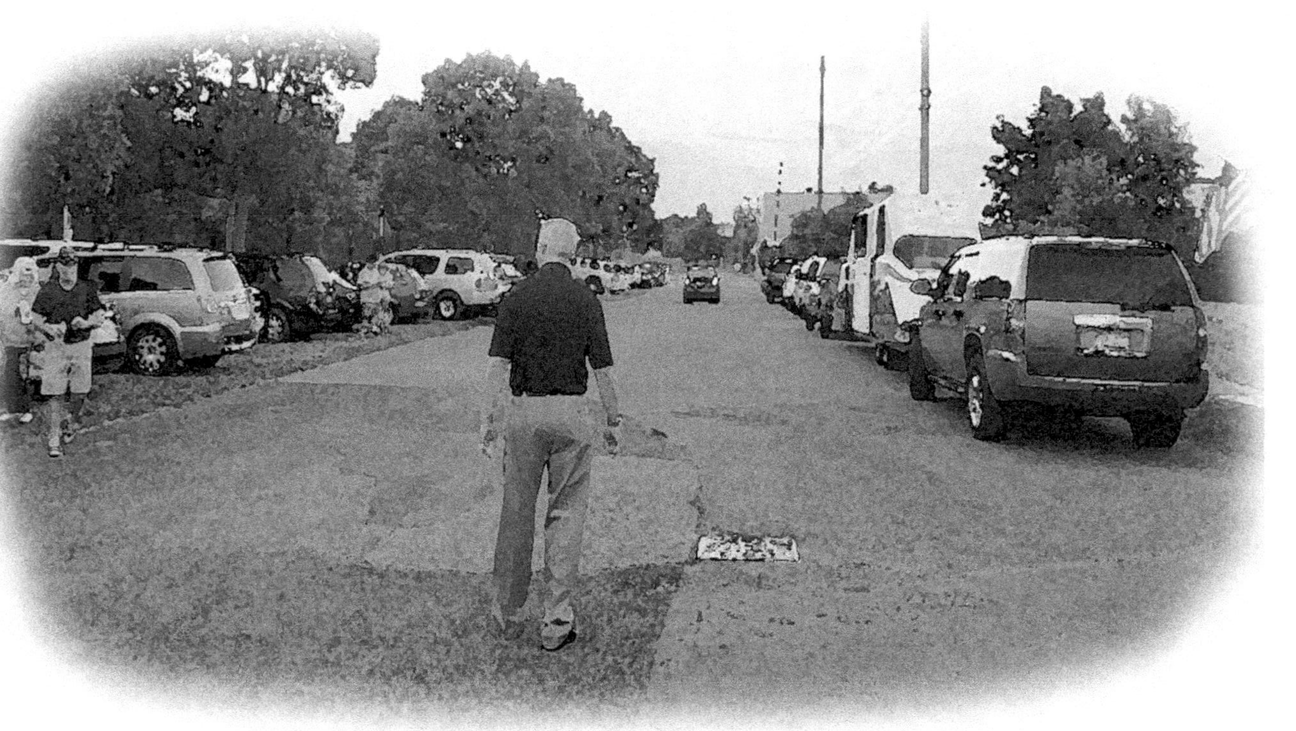

Parking for Tea Party Rally at my art studio, 714 Baldwin St., Elmira

Chapter Fifteen

FINAL STRETCH

THE TRUMP CAMPAIGN CONTINUED TO SURGE INTO THE LATE summer and early fall as the candidates prepared for their final push. There was no time to waste, as the election on November 8, 2016, raced toward me. In early September, it was time to bang my drum, hosting the local Twin Tiers Tea Party Rally for Trump at my art studio in Elmira. That conservative event was a hit, with over one hundred people present. For my area, that was a well-attended rally. As usual, it was ignored by the local media. Ghosting by the media could be excused if there had been a host of other more significant or exciting events going on that Saturday night that took preference. But no, the rally was in Elmira, New York, somewhat of a ghost town when it came to events of any importance.

My art studio sat behind a fenced area on Baldwin Street, which runs parallel to Clemens Center Parkway, the main thoroughfare through Elmira. On the afternoon of the rally and into the evening, Baldwin Street was jam-packed with cars. It was impossible to miss, not to mention that the front of my dome-shaped studio was adorned with a huge vinyl banner of the Trump painting.

Trump was front-page news every day, coast to coast. Multiple invitations and press releases had gone out to the media from the Tea Party, including to the left-leaning *Star-Gazette*, WETM 18 News, and WENY. There were even a couple of anti-Trump protesters outside the rally. The media's absence and their silence were disingenuous, giving credence to Trump's clarion call against the mainstream media as fake news. The local media ignored a total of three grassroots Trump rallies that were held at my art studio that year—anything, it seemed, to dampen any perception that there was local enthusiasm for Trump.

Later that month, the local Republican Party was organizing its preelection dinner events. Since I was considered at that time somewhat of a Trump artist celebrity, Chairman Rodney Strange invited me to show the painting at the upcoming Republican dinner. Marc Molinaro, the Westchester County Executive who was running for governor against incumbent Andrew Cuomo, was slated to speak. Attorney and Republican candidate Wendy Long was also invited to speak—she was running for the New York Senate seat against Democrat political dinosaur Chuck Schumer.

Wendy Long canceled her appearance at the last minute, and Rodney Strange invited me to share my painting and speak in her place. It was an honor to be invited to speak at such an auspicious event. This helped me decide to get further involved with the Republican political machinery, hoping to be a catalyst for change, especially in the arts, in a reluctant conservative system.

November 1 arrived quickly, with election day glistening just around the corner. It was not unusual for foreign media outlets from Germany, Switzerland, Japan, and even South Korea to travel to Elmira to see the Trump painting and interview me in my studio. That week, a news team from South Korea traveled from New York City to cover the preelection events. I had met them in Iowa, and they were following my story and wanted more.

After a year of cross-country campaigning for Donald Trump, including many hardships and disappointments, arriving at the Republican dinner flanked by my beautiful wife and blossoming teenage children was like victoriously crossing a finish line. The camera team from South Korea filmed my every move. It was also great fun. That night, the local Holiday Inn event in Elmira,

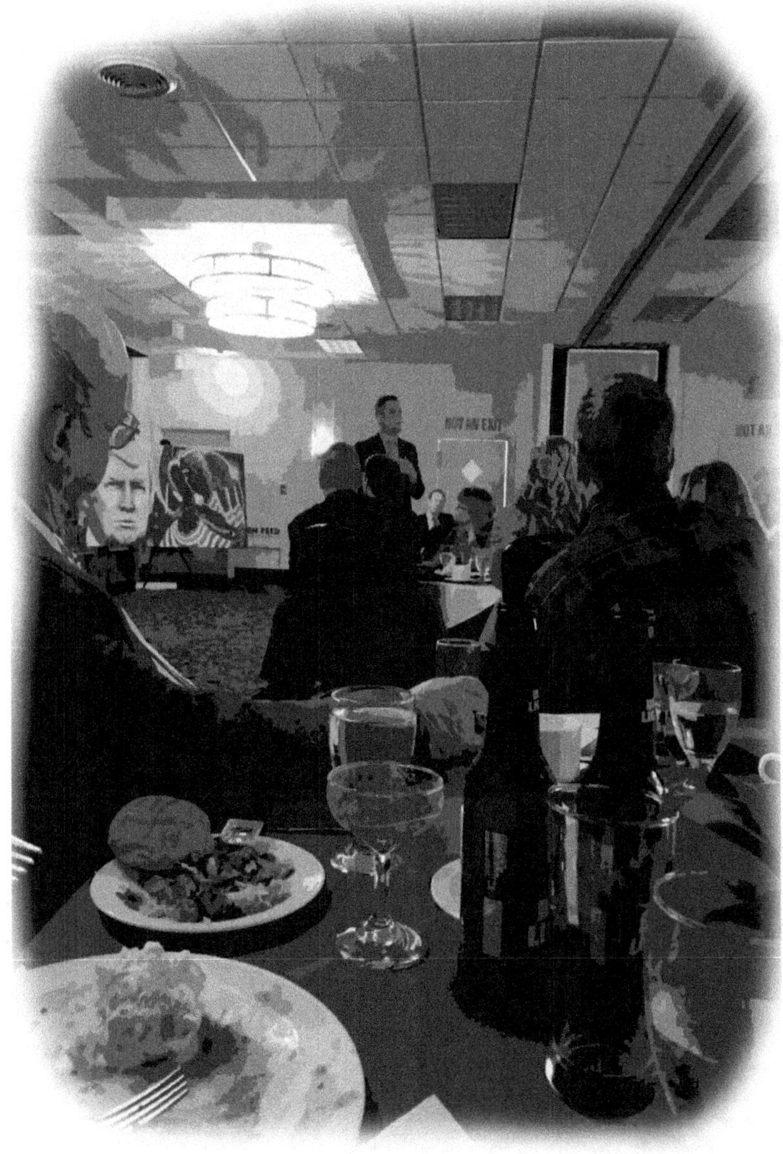

Marc Molinaro speaking, Chemung County Republican Dinner, November 2016

New York, was the closest thing I had experienced to a Hollywood red-carpet arrival. It certainly was a redeeming moment, delusions of grandeur aside.

We were seated in a place of honor up front near the podium and treated with great respect. My wife and children were very proud of me that night. After some announcements, it was my turn to speak. Before long, I was reciting the Gettysburg Address in full dramatic voice, embellished with my English accent. People sat up in their seats to pay attention. In the audience were Senator Tom O'Mara, Assemblymen Friend, and Elmira Mayor Dan Mandel and his wife, Sherry. Also present were Chairman Joe Sempolinski, Chemung County Legislator Joe Brennan, and radio host Frank Acomb. Amongst the guests were many other people whom I had come to know that year. My speech was a call to finish Lincoln's work, the ongoing work of defending our republic and the precious values and freedoms for which those brave men fought and died. The danger I foresaw was crippling complacency among the people—that they would prefer to leave it to Trump to fix America once he won the presidency rather than take action themselves.

My speech was met with a rousing crescendo of cheering and a standing ovation. One old-timer came up to me excitedly, declaring, "That was like a tent-revival sermon!" Westchester County Executive Marc Molinaro was next up, speaking right after my well-received political sermon. Molinaro brought the house down when he quipped that "no one ever remembers the guy who spoke after Lincoln at the Gettysburg Address." Everyone laughed! The laughter lit the spirit in the place, as gladness of heart filled the dining hall. It was a great evening of food, inspiration, and hopeful expectations—what a fitting end to a historic and unprecedented election year.

Chapter Sixteen

AMERICAN PRESIDENT

Election day, November 8, 2016, arrived. This newborn American citizen would be voting for the first time ever in a presidential election. Living out in the country guaranteed casual attire would be acceptable at the voting booth. But not for this patriotic and meaningful occasion. I was the suit-and-tie man, making sure to wear my red tie. Fall had arrived that day with its perfect weather in upstate New York. Harvest colors and spice-flavored coffee made the morning bounce, while the fresh morning air filled my lungs, invigorating my step. A cloudless bright-blue sky welcomed us as Gloria and I headed out early to the polling station.

It had been twenty years since I had arrived at JFK International Airport to start the American chapter in my odyssey and just over a year as a newly minted U.S. citizen. My immigrant artist's political pilgrimage, including the American values, ideals, and laws to which I had pledged my allegiance, all came together on that blessed day.

Together with my wife and fellow American citizen, Gloria, who showed me the ropes, I cast my vote for Donald J. Trump and all of the Republican candidates I had supported. Voting for the first time thrilled me. The profound significance, my purpose in America, everything I had learned and embraced, boiled down to one tiny black dot on freedom and democracy's ballot. My vote became a source of great joy and satisfaction. I had participated in the race, fought in the campaign, participated in the democratic process, and then I could sit back with a bowl of popcorn and watch the horses come in.

Bernie Murray's Irish Pub in downtown Elmira held the watch party that night. A loud, even boisterous, and merry atmosphere welcomed me as I entered the pub that evening. All of the local Chemung County elected officials were present, along with their families and friends. They all ate and drank as they watched and waited to see the results of their individual political battles and then the result in the main event. They all won that evening: Congressman Reed, Senator O'Mara, Assemblyman Friend, Attorney Baker (who became County Judge), and others. Raucous cheers went up while applause rang out as each race's results came in. What a victorious night.

The main event, the race between Trump and Clinton, dragged on through and into the night. Most in attendance were exhausted by late evening and by midnight had already gone home. No one could make heads or tales of the unfolding results they were watching on the screen. I sat there waiting and watching too, with butterflies within, not understanding much or able to make sense of the data.

The last week of the campaign had its trials as Trump ran into significant headwinds. Scandals blew up in his face as his checkered past came back to haunt him. The crude last-minute Billy Bush audio stunned the campaign and for a while looked like it would derail Trump's juggernaut. The pro-Hillary polling propaganda paid off for the Democrats. It muddied the waters and at times caused me to doubt my up-until-then-unwavering assurance that Trump would win. I kept my doubts to myself. I had learned in my walk of faith that when doubt comes in, you have to set your mind on the goal and keep going no matter what you see with your eyes. Without wavering, I kept trusting that the result for which I had believed would come to be. After all, faith is the assurance of things hoped for, the evidence of things yet to be seen (Hebrews 11:1). I ran out of fingernails to chew on the longer the night dragged on. I had watched other elections on TV, but I was never invested in the outcome. The ongoing roller coaster of uncertainty all of a sudden slammed on its brakes, coming to a dead stop.

Some time after 1 a.m., the call came in for the new president of the United States. Exhausted and bleary eyed, I stood up and punched the air, uttering the words "President Trump!" Peace rested upon me as I drove home, eager to wake my family with the great news. Upon hearing my restrained but excited proclamation, they grunted acknowledgment, rolled over, and fell back asleep.

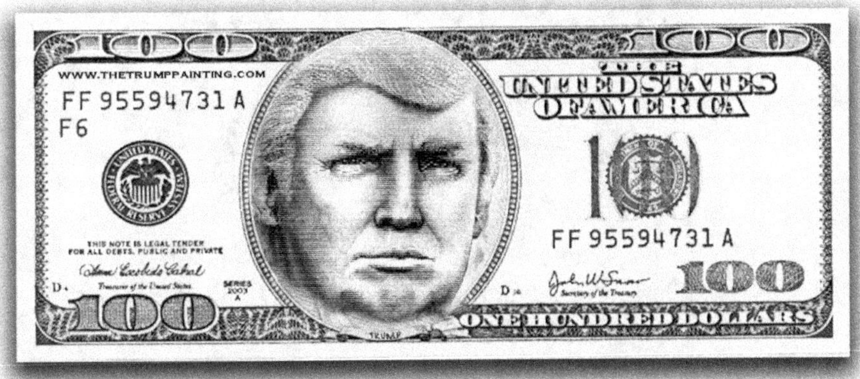

The President of the United States of America

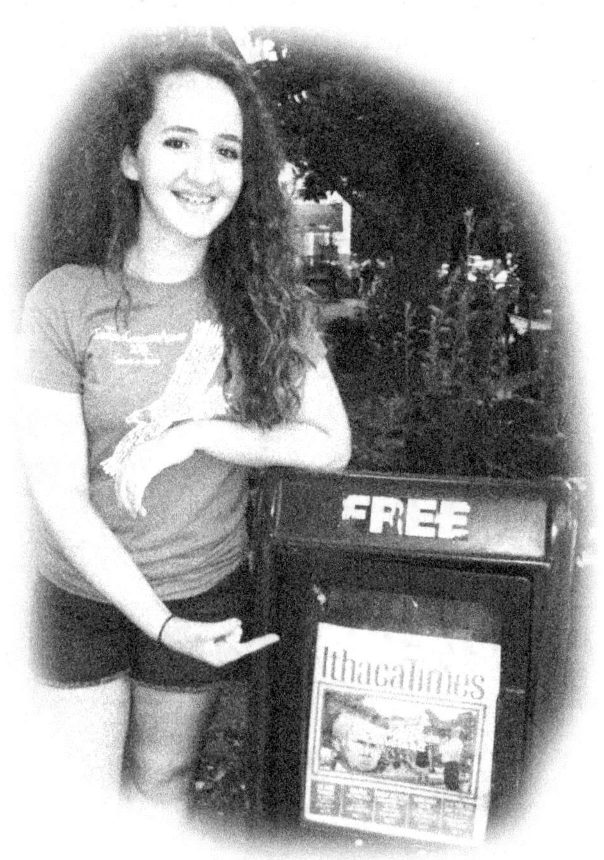

"Elmira Artist Prophesying Trump Win," July 2016,
Ithaca Times, Ithaca, New York[9]

Chapter Seventeen

TRAUMATIC SILENCE

STUNNED! DEJECTED HILLARY SUPPORTERS SHOOK THEIR HEADS in disbelief. Their hands cradled their weary heads, as the paralyzing grief, coupled with weeping, was juxtaposed against the ecstatic celebration of Trump supporters. Those images flooded my computer screen the day after the election. A bloody knockout blow of political blunt-force trauma to the nose of Hillary Clinton, the fake-news media, the propaganda pollsters, and the legions of raging, hateful, leftist radicals (especially in the art world) had been released.

As the liberal world reeled in agony, stripped of their hope, a sinister rage also began to boil. The Left was not going away without a fight. Their recourse in that bloodied, bitter, and wounded state was to band together to form a resistance—an insurgency of sorts.

Rather than go away and accept defeat (and prepare for another electoral season, when the Left could once again contend for the powers of government, deriving their just powers from the consent of the governed), an eerie chant began to rise like sulphuric smoke from the ashes of Hillary Clinton's campaign. "Resist, resist, resist," they cried as they donned their "p**sy" hats. They plotted and schemed at every opportunity to hinder or sabotage any progress the president or his supporters would try to make.

There is no need for me to repeat the litany of continuous accusations and the anonymous sources that the mainstream media quoted without hesitation—not to mention the subsequent investigations that went on for much of Trump's presidency. Over time, it was hard to tell whether President Trump had brought on all the scandals by himself (which he did do often) or was just haplessly navigating through a mine field—a mine field laid by active players throughout the government and the media with one objective: resistance.

This resistance could be felt by the average man on the street, even a newborn American citizen and artist like me. The resistance was already embedded in Washington, D.C., left over from the Obama administration. The precious democratic institutions that undergird our republic in many instances became hotbeds of Trumpian resistance. One can understand why many came to believe in the existence of a so-called "deep state."

For example, law-enforcement agencies were involved. The FBI had Peter Strzok and Lisa Page as its star agents of the resistance. Both their adulterous love affair and their personal hatred for Trump were revealed in their passionate tweets on FBI-issued cell phones. Those became front-page fodder for the ever-salivating and pot-stirring media. Right after the election, former Speaker of the House Newt Gingrich said, "This is essentially the opposition in waiting. He [Trump] may have to clean out the Justice Department because there are so many left-wingers there. State is even worse."[10] The Left brought the deep-state conspiracy theory, and others, on themselves. The Smithsonian Institution had its own poster child of the Trumpian resistance: their director of the Smithsonian National Portrait Gallery.

Chapter Eighteen

RITE OF PARTICIPATION

THE GREATEST OPPORTUNITY IN A GENERATION FOR AN AMERI-can reset was handed to us on November 8, 2016. To make America great again would require the engagement and full participation of We the People. Restoring America was a task way beyond the power of any one man to accomplish, compelling me to get involved.

What was I to do after the election? What was the next step for my painting? Was my journey over? Should I sell or donate the painting? Not sure of the answer, I prayed and asked God for direction. A few days later, I remembered the American citizens I'd met across the country who'd said my painting should be in the Smithsonian. Yes, the Smithsonian was to be my next step. It was the will of the people I had encountered on my travels, who wanted to see my painting displayed in their Smithsonian.

Without delay, my research began. At the time, I knew nothing of the Smithsonian Portrait Gallery except that it was in Washington, D.C. My googling brought up Shepard Fairey's Obama "Hope" poster and many stories from 2009 covering then-President-elect

Barack Obama's inauguration. I was elated. Not only did the Smithsonian have a National Portrait Gallery, but they displayed significant and relevant political-campaign portraits to honor the inaugurations of current presidents.

Shepard Fairey had expressed his political speech in his Obama "Hope" portrait, a political-campaign poster displayed not just once but twice, for the inauguration and reelection of President Barack Obama. That was established practice at the museum. That was precedent.

In my thinking, that practice guaranteed my painting would be displayed at the Smithsonian National Portrait Gallery for the inauguration of President-elect Trump. My political-campaign portrait was the most recognized political painting of Trump at the time. Was there another, more prominent political portrait documenting Trump's historic campaign and election worth considering? Even if there were, why could there not be two or more displayed for the inauguration?

With all the recognition I'd received from the New York Republican political brass, they would surely support my application to the Smithsonian. Without delay, I sent off a series of emails explaining my plan, seeking their prompt attention in support of my application to the Smithsonian National Portrait Gallery to display my political portrait as a tribute in the arts to Trump's historic inauguration. The clock was ticking, driving hard toward the inauguration on January 20, 2017. A flurry of emails filled my inbox within a few days, expressing wholehearted support for my application.

Was there a better way for the sleepy upstate portion of New York where I was from to participate in the historic inauguration of President Trump? Having a painting created by a Chemung County resident on display in Washington, D.C., would have been a high honor for the region. Letters on official government stationery arrived in the mail, one after the other, from U.S. Congressman Tom Reed, New York Senator Tom O'Mara, New York Assemblyman Friend, Elmira Mayor Dan Mandel, Republican Chairpersons

Rodney Strange, Lester Cady, Sandra King, and Joe Sempolinski, Councilpersons Joe Brennan and Nanette Moss, radio host Frank Acomb, and art collectors Bradley and Andrea Davis, all of whom were eager to express their support in writing.

It was now the beginning of the third week in November—time waited for no man. I drafted my detailed application letter to the director of the Smithsonian National Portrait Gallery, Kim Sajet, highlighting the story of creating the painting and its journey. In my research, I discovered that the local Rockwell Museum of Art in Corning, New York, about twenty minutes away, was a Smithsonian Affiliate museum. That was great news, as Affiliate museums served as Smithsonian connections to local communities to facilitate participation. My application could thus be submitted at the local level. Not only could the politicians participate but the local art institutions and community could join with me in this celebratory artistic triumph.

The painting exhibition at the Smithsonian could then serve as an excellent opportunity for political dialogue. And it could promote understanding, as art has the power to transcend the typical obstacles that hinder constructive conversation. Displaying my painting could be a way to participate in bridging the political divide and to motivate others to participate in the democratic process in a redemptive manner, paving the way to a more civil and respectful local and national political atmosphere, especially in the arts.

Was that just wishful and naive thinking on my behalf? The Bible teaches in the book of First Corinthians chapter 13 that love hopes all things and believes all things, and that love never fails. Did love even play a part any longer in our American brotherhood? Did Lincoln's Gettysburg exhortation to be dedicated to the unfinished work and the great task before us still apply? Indeed, could I even play a part in bridging the gap? What about all the hostility and opposition I had experienced from the outset of my political campaign? Was that not a measure of the temperature of the political climate? Maybe, but did that mean I shouldn't even try? Or should I just abandon my local initiative involving the Smithsonian Affiliate, the Rockwell Museum of Art?

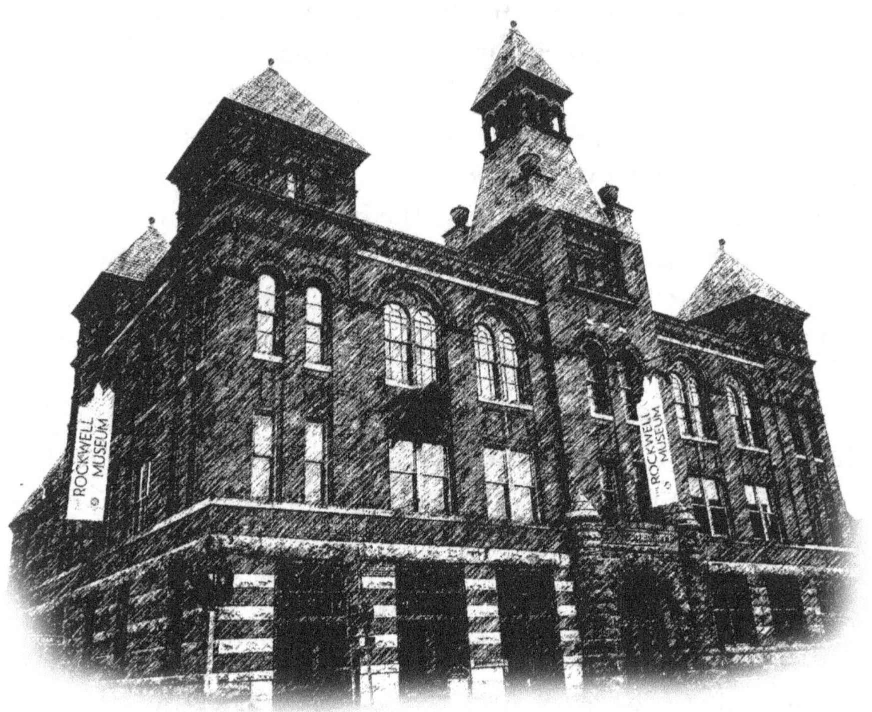

The Rockwell Museum of Art, Corning, New York

I had already encountered hostility and opposition in Iowa in January of that year. I requested a showing of a canvas copy of the painting in the Iowa State capitol building in Des Moines. The Iowa capitol building would display political paintings of the candidates participating in the Iowa caucuses. Having fulfilled the application, I was approved. The female officer told me what size the painting could be and how the easel displaying the painting was to stand. It was a straightforward affair. At first, the official did not ask to see who was in my painting. But after approving my application, the official requested to see the image of the painting. After emailing the photo of the Trump painting, I never heard back from her. She refused to answer my emails, and my phone calls just rolled over to her voicemail.

Remembering that biased encounter made me extremely cautious about approaching the Rockwell Museum. When meeting one morning with Elmira Mayor Mandel about his recommendation for my application, I asked him if he knew anything about the director of the Rockwell Museum. I shared my concerns that they might be biased against Trump and stonewall my application, causing me to miss the fast-approaching inauguration. He did not know the answer. In good faith, I went ahead regardless of my notions and emailed a cover letter to the museum director, Kristin Swain, with my Smithsonian application. It was turkey time, Thanksgiving break. The director had my application for over a week; there was no reply. I had expressed the time-sensitive nature of the application in the letter, asking them to swiftly at least indicate if they would help me forward the application or even participate. No response.

The end of November drew near. December 1 was a couple of days away, and still I had heard nothing. This meant action. It was suit-and-tie time again as I disappeared into my bedroom closet and then took off for the Rockwell Museum of Art in Corning, New York, to investigate what could be causing the delay. Upon my arrival, I greeted the receptionist and explained the reason for my visit. She told me the director and managers were out to lunch. It was close to midday, so I told the receptionist that I would go have a slice of pizza and come back after lunch.

Upon my return, surprise, surprise, they had all taken the rest of the day off. I knew what that meant. I left the pile of letters, applications, and prints with the receptionist, politely asking her to give them to the director and the Smithsonian Affiliate manager. Once home, I began to dig deeper online into the Rockwell Museum and its activities to see if I could get a reading on their politics. Holy Toledo—I found revealing information online.

Not wanting to miss a beat since the clock was ticking, the next morning before the sun was up, I did a Clark Kent and put on my suit again and took off to Corning. Arriving super early, right as they opened their doors, gave them no time to scatter, as certain bugs do in the light. The Smithsonian liaison manager, Patty Campbell, came out of her office, hunched over and dragging her feet. "Top of the morning to you!" I said in a bright and cheery tone, extending my salutations. She looked like she had just seen a ghost. Her expressionless face was as long and pale as a dead, white horse. I knew right then that sinister scheming and skulduggery were at play.

Employing my finely honed skills in Socratic irony, I set a trap for her, into which she clumsily tumbled headfirst. Campbell's claimed objections to the Rockwell Museum participating in a political art exhibit were swiftly rebutted as I laid bare their naked hypocrisy and anti-Trump bias. "O really," I said. "Did you not just have a preelection political event last month called 'Art & Politics,' which was hosted by Kal Penn, who is both a leftist Hollywood actor and the Obama White House Liaison for Cultural Communications?" Campbell's pale cheeks now flushed crimson red with shame at being ensnared in the hypocrisy trap.

Regardless, the Smithsonian liaison manager did not change her tune or color. Snatching up my hard copy of the application and the copies of the Trump-painting print from the counter, I was gone. Later, with more googling, I discovered that their political event, hosted by former "Bernie-guy" but then "pro-Hillary-guy" actor Kal Penn, was strategically held on the twenty-eighth of October, right before the election. That event had peculiar stipulations, one being that no one was allowed to record it, eliminating the evidence of conflict of interest of a White House employee cashing in while on the job. Also remember the Rockwell Museum was a 501(c)(3) non-profit organization that by law must give equal time, presenting all sides at a political event, which they never did. As a local artist, I would have loved to have engaged in civil debate with Mr. Penn about art and politics.

Soon after my visit, I received an email from the then-retiring museum director, Kristin Swain. It was short and to the point and went something like this: "Sorry, Mr. Raven, we do not have the resources to help. Goodbye!" Oh, really? Out of mere curiosity, I wondered how much it had cost the Rockwell Museum to have celebrity actor Kal Penn come for that weekend back in October. It wasn't long before actor Kal Penn's talent agent was on the phone answering my questions. Since I missed Penn's event, how much would it cost for him to come and do another similar one in Elmira at my art studio? Their response: sixty thousand dollars.

Scratching my head, I wondered what in the world the director meant by saying they did not have the resources to help me? Clicking "send" on her keyboard by simply lifting her finger and forwarding along my emailed application was just too difficult, painful, and expensive, I suppose. The eerie chant to resist echoing up from the abyss needed no further explanation. Was I to tuck tail and run? Absolutely not!

Right away, I filed an official complaint against the Rockwell Museum for anti-Trump bias with Harold Closter, the director of Smithsonian Affiliate museums nationwide. To my pleasant surprise, he became the first official in a long line of officials to do his job. Closter responded without hesitation and with professionalism. It was the afternoon of November 30, 2016. The same day I wrote him, Closter replied to my email, informing me that he had forwarded my application to the Smithsonian National Portrait Gallery director, Kim Sajet. If Closter forwarded my entire email to Sajet, she would have my application and my official complaint against the Rockwell Museum, blasting them for their anti-Trump bias. Fresh on the heels of Hillary's spectacular loss, my potentially provocative email, if received by another left-leaning liberal, could trigger a terrible episode of what would become known as Trump Derangement Syndrome.

Fifty-one days remained until the historic inauguration. Knowing Sajet had my application excited me and filled me with expectation. The crowning moment of my artistic and patriotic journey seemed inevitable as the inauguration fast approached. Shepard Fairey's artistic career was cemented as a result of the publicity and attention the Smithsonian National Portrait Gallery gave him when they displayed the Obama "Hope" poster for Barack Obama's inauguration. Recognition from such a prestigious institution would be a game changer for my emerging artistic career as it had been for Fairey's. Elmira, a forgotten city in the depressed region of upstate New York, along with its people and representatives, would get to participate in the honor of the inauguration festivities as President-elect Trump would be celebrated in the arts in the People's Smithsonian National Portrait Gallery.

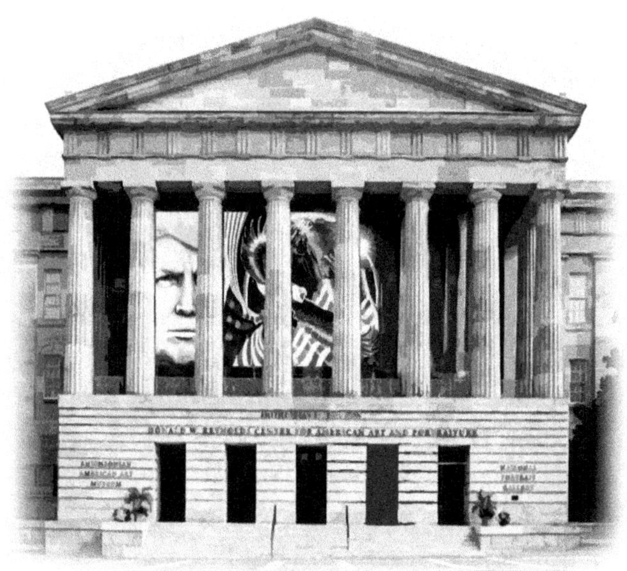

The Smithsonian National Portrait Gallery, Washington, D.C.

Chapter Nineteen

ODIOUS RESISTANCE

BRIGHT AND EARLY THE FOLLOWING DAY, I POPPED OUT OF BED. It was not Christmas, but it sure felt like it. It was December 1, 2016, and the expectation of making contact with Smithsonian Director Kim Sajet added plenty of pep to my step. First, I rushed to open my email just in case I had received a reply during the night. Donald Trump was president-elect, promising Christmas that year would be outstanding. The Christmas break, when many institutions would grind to a halt, was on its way. Sajet had the email, and no, she had not replied. This prompted me to make a follow-up phone call to see if she had read the email. Since time was of the essence, I needed to know if anything was lacking in my application.

With trepidation and excitement, I made my way downstairs to my basement office. The carpeted space was also a recording studio where Gloria recorded her music. The room had better soundproofing than lighting, making it super quiet—perfect for the important call and away from the family's morning hustle and bustle going on upstairs. Google supplied me with Director Kim Sajet's phone number. I made the call, and Kim Sajet's assistant answered the phone. Right away, she informed me that Sajet was unavailable that day and that she would pass along my message, getting back to me if there was anything else I needed to do. Kindly, I thanked her and hung up the phone.

Within ten minutes, my phone rang. Staring at the phone, I saw the call was coming in from the same Washington number I had just dialed. It was Kim Sajet's office calling back. Anxiously, I answered the phone. The voice was that of a different woman. To my complete surprise, the woman introduced herself with an Australian accent, throwing me off. "This is Director Kim Sajet." My surprise was piqued because the assistant had blown me off, telling me Sajet was not available that day. I was caught off guard, not expecting a call directly from the director and not expecting her to be a foreign national.

I stood up from my chair and composed myself. The call was from the director of the Smithsonian National Portrait Gallery, deserving the utmost respect and deference. "Thank you for getting back to me so soon. I was calling to find out if you received my application from Director Harold Closter?" Sajet replied in the affirmative, and then in a snooty tone, she condescendingly referred to the painting as "the one with the eagle and the flag in it?"

"Yes," I replied.

"*It's too big*," Sajet objected.

At that time, I did not have any knowledge of the written standards for portraiture acceptance at the Smithsonian Institution. Sajet invoked a supposed standard by objecting to the painting's scale. Because of available space and the logistics and complications of managing large paintings, many art galleries have size limitations for participating artwork. Was this the case at the Smithsonian? Supposedly it was at that moment, according to the director.

I respectfully pushed back, requesting clarification on the scale standard, at which point Sajet backtracked and even apologized for objecting to the scale. How strange! Sajet appeared to have arbitrarily invented her objection to the scale of the painting—otherwise, why the sudden change of mind? Now, Sajet was the director, so one would expect her to know the standards for portraiture consideration. I trusted her and thought that if anyone knew, it was the director.

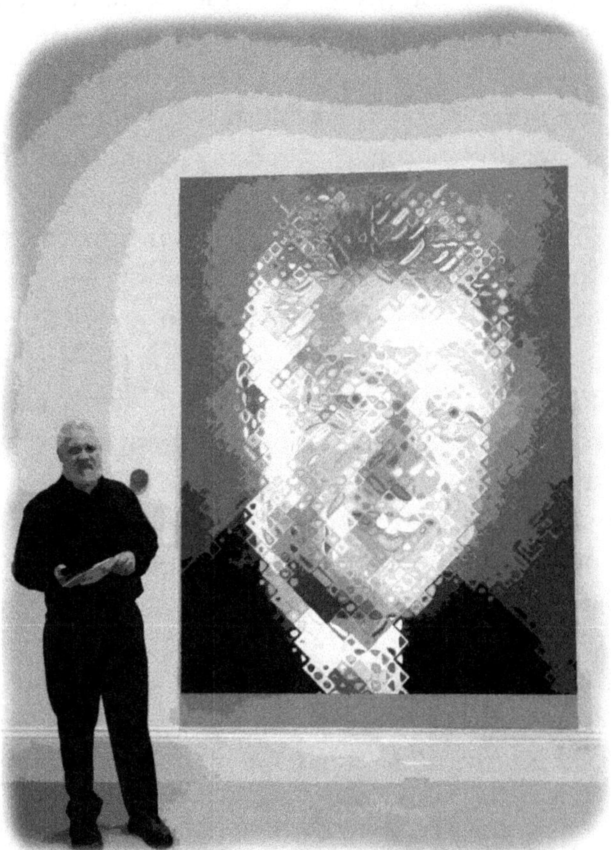

Example of scale: Chuck Close's Smithsonian portrait of Bill Clinton, seven-by-nine feet

Something seemed out of place. Remember, Sajet's call to me came about ten minutes after my call. Why was Sajet so eager to personally return my call when she was supposedly not available? Why was the director herself calling me? Had she rushed to respond to my email and follow-up call once she found out who had called?

Having abandoned the scale objection, Sajet continued. "*The portrait is not from life,*" meaning that I did not paint the portrait of Trump with him sitting down in front of me at my easel. That was a fact—the painting was not from life. Now, that's where the conversation began to go off the rails. Sajet was erecting objections; she was not trying to assist me—she had already made up her mind. I humbly went along, with her as the director, trusting her objections to be legitimate, based upon standards she must have known. And yet something in my mind told me this did not make sense. Sajet had either not thoroughly read my application or assumed that I was just ignorant, as a deplorable Trump supporter. She did not realize from my application that I was intimately acquainted with the Obama "Hope" poster and its creation.

"Neither was the Obama 'Hope' poster created from life," I retorted, pushing back with the facts about the showing in the Smithsonian of the "Hope" poster. "My Trump painting has been exhibited with the 'Hope' poster. I spent four days with its patron and inspiration, Yosi Sergant. Sergant personally told me how he found the artist, Shepard Fairey, and commissioned him to do the poster based on a photo Fairey used from the Internet. Shepard Fairey was convicted of a copyright violation for using a photo of Obama without permission that belonged to AP photographer Manny Friedman. Because of destroying the evidence, Fairey received a six-month sentence. The whole world knows that the Obama 'Hope' poster was a copy of a photo that was photoshopped. It was *not* a portrait painted from life."

"*Yes, it was created from life!*" Sajet snapped back. Sajet twisted reality to support her arbitrary objection. Sajet lied, escalating the tense exchange into a full-blown argument, and throwing down the gauntlet in the process. I later discovered that one of the originally written standards for Smithsonian portraiture consideration and acceptance said, "Original portraits from life, *if possible.*"[11] Sajet was deliberately using the convenient half of the written standard to enforce her objection until I called out her contradiction. And as author Robert A. Heinlein wrote, "The first way to lie artistically is to tell the truth—but not all of it."

Sajet then deflected, creating another arbitrary standard for acceptance to explain away her glaring contradiction. In her supercilious tone, she claimed the Obama poster qualified for acceptance and display (regardless if it had been created from life) because it was *an iconic image*, adding with disdain that my painting was not. I later discovered that one of the written standards for portraiture acceptance at the Portrait Gallery was that a painting's artistic merit or the fame of its creator should have no bearing on its acceptance—instead, it was the historical significance of the individual and the moment that mattered.

Trying to comprehend what was happening, my mind traveled back to a time I was a young boy and an avid naturalist. The teacher was discussing insects and had included spiders into that category. I knew that spiders were not six-legged insects; they were eight-legged arachnids. My hand shot up, and I unintentionally embarrassed the teacher, contradicting her and showing her to be in error. Rather than thank me for the correction, she proceeded to bark at me, belittling me in front of the class. Sajet was responding similarly. Rather than back down, apologize for her tone, and take some time to check that maybe what I was saying could be true, Sajet dug in her heels. Still defiant in her attempt to refute my arguments, she continued.

Sajet jumped to another objection: "*It's not neutral enough,*" she complained. Aha, Sajet was beginning to reveal what was underneath her incessant objections. The painting's content and the content of my speech had struck a nerve with the dear director. Sajet was not opposed to the tonality of the colors I had used as being not neutral enough—for example, the blue is too blue; the red is too red—because she did not mention the colors. Objecting to the characteristics of the painting—its size, its style, its creation, etc.—that could be measured against written objective standards, if there were any, would be legitimate. On the other hand, the issue of the painting's subjective content crossed over into the realm of constitutionally protected artistic expression and freedom of political speech. Did Sajet have the written standards to use as the basis for objecting to the painting's content, concluding its content was not neutral enough? Content neutrality is as vague and subjective a standard as when a police officer enforces a speed limit on a road where there is none.

In law, the "void-for-vagueness" doctrine exists precisely to prevent arbitrary enforcement of laws. The U.S. Supreme Court declared that the law must "provide explicit standards…to policemen, judges, and juries" so as to avoid "arbitrary and discriminatory applications."[12]

Was the Obama "Hope" poster neutral? Obama's poster was political speech representing hope only for those who voted for him—maybe half the population. How was that neutral?

In my painting, was it the bold red, white, and blue flag or the giant nine-foot eagle, both cherished patriotic American symbols, that were too intense for the "National" Portrait Gallery? My painting captured and embodied the zeitgeist of the unprecedented and dramatic 2015-2016 presidential campaign and election of the forty-fifth president of the United States of America. Again, it only represented the political hope of the people who voted for Trump—maybe the other half of the population. Was the painting too American for Sajet's taste as an Australian (actually she was a Dutch citizen)? Perhaps Sajet wanted to emasculate and tone down American boldness and spirit. She had opted for a twenty-six-year-old dreary and boring photo of Trump tossing an apple in the air—a photo about which no one would care and which no one would go to see.

Further clarifying her vague objections and revealing the depths of her personal opposition to the painting, Sajet then trampled the First Amendment's free-speech clause with her following more precise objection.

"*It's too political!*" Sajet hissed. The intense argument now nosedived, as I stood there in my basement office in shock at what I was hearing. As a result of my posture of humility and deference to the Smithsonian official's authority, I suddenly felt like I was having my face shoved into the mud under Sajet's boot. We had already discussed the Obama "Hope" campaign poster, and now Sajet was blatantly objecting to the political content of the painting. Was I hearing that correctly? Political free speech was usually the highest protected form of free speech under the U.S. Constitution; it was not to be the case that day for me.

The Obama "Hope" poster[13] was a political campaign poster made famous during the 2008 presidential campaign that contributed to the election of Barack Obama. It was pure politics— left-wing Democrat politics, but politics nonetheless. My painting could not be displayed because it was too political? This was an outrage, and I could not fathom how Sajet could reconcile in her own mind such a statement. You had to be a shameless hypocrite to say such a thing. But Sajet could say such a thing, because apparently, she could determine what type of political-speech content was permissible in her gallery and get away with it. Her own political bias, seething animus, and the pressure to resist were forcing her to reveal her true colors.

I was reeling from Sajet's tongue-lashing. And please remember we are talking about an artist trying to display a tribute for the inauguration of the president of the United States of America in the People's Smithsonian Institution in Washington, D.C.

Could it get any worse?

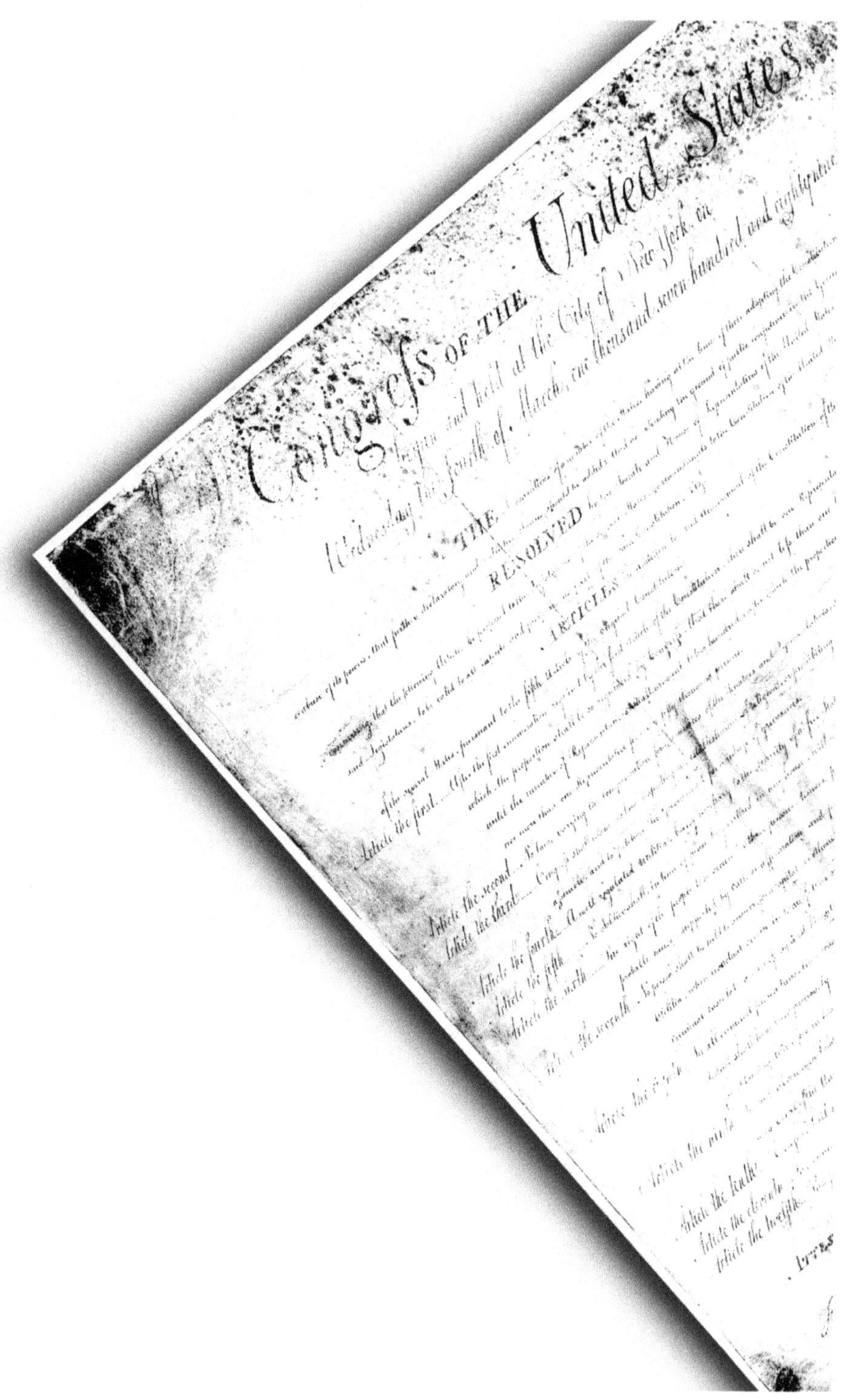

The Bill of Rights

Chapter Twenty

ABRIDGING TOO FAR

WHY ON EARTH DID SMITHSONIAN DIRECTOR KIM SAJET PICK up the phone and call me? Why didn't she reply to the email, putting her objections, "*Too big…not from life…not iconic…not neutral enough…too political…*" on the record?

She was not done. Sajet's determination that my painting was too political was a personal objection from a government official who used her authority to abridge or diminish my conservative, pro-Trump, political free speech, in violation of the First Amendment.

Further honing her viewpoint discrimination, Sajet now added this clarification as she tried in vain to refute my arguments: "*It's too pro-Trump,*" Sajet snipped.

Yes, a portrait of Donald Trump was too pro-Trump. Now, what did she mean? How was the Obama poster not pro-Obama, or how was it just the right amount of being pro-Obama, so as not to be too pro-Obama? I mean, what on earth did that mean? Was there too much of Trump? Did Trump appear too handsome for her liking? Did it make him look too presidential? What was it?

This behavior is what the framers of the Constitution intended to prevent with the First Amendment, the curtailing or abbreviation of speech because someone in government objects to the quantity—*"too big,"* the quality—*"not neutral enough,"* the ideology—*"too pro-Trump,"* or the intensity—*"too political"* of an opponent's political speech.

Every free-speech legal precedent[14] established in the United States judicial system clearly says that if the government permits some political free speech in a venue they control, they must permit all political free speech in that venue. They cannot discriminate against the viewpoint—in this case, the conservative, pro-Trump content in the political speech. The government can determine the viewpoint in specific forums; they can exclude all political speech, which means *all.* They cannot permit just some political viewpoints.

I never got any clarification or answers to my questions. Sajet's tactic was to continuously drag red herrings across the argument to divert attention from the critical issue: her lack of legitimate reasons to ban my painting. Her red herrings only made the issue at hand more obvious. Firstly, nothing was disqualifying about my painting—thus, her need to fabricate objections. And secondly, she just hated Trump and now me, for that matter. I would become the victim of her Trump Derangement Syndrome.

In general, people do not like to lose an argument. When distortions, lies, and falsehoods fail, losers resort to hurling the lowest stones in their rotten sack of ideas at their adversary. Sajet's next stone was ad hominem—attack the person. Sajet, being familiar with the art world and the sensitivity of artists and their work, resorted to attacking my skill as an artist and the quality of my painting.

"It's no good!" Sajet sneered.

"No good" was a personal attack against me, the artist. Sajet even tried to rub salt into the wound by saying how she knew "how hard it is for artists to be rejected and hear that their work is no good," in that now-all-too-familiar patronizing tone. I asked Sajet if she had ever seen the painting in person, for her to have accumulated enough information to make such a qualitative judgment, at which she became further irritated.

Whether something in art is good or no good is an objective and subjective assessment based on a wide range of qualitative judgments. Having witnessed hundreds of people interact with the painting from coast to coast, I never could recall anyone seriously saying that my painting was no good. Many leftists had expressed their hatred of the content and disliked the imagery, thus disliking the painting. But some even reluctantly admitted to their appreciation of the painting as a serious and substantial work of art.

For the director of such a prestigious art institution to make such a statement without actually seeing the original painting in person was a mockery of the art-critiquing process and the trusted position she held as a curator of American historical images. Her conduct was especially reprehensible since the written Smithsonian standards of portraiture acceptance say, "Thus the standards for accepting portraits varied considerably from other galleries. Even today, in every instance, the historical significance of the subject is judged before the artistic merit of the portrait."[15]

Sajet never mentioned or considered the historical significance that a portrait must possess to qualify. The purpose of the Smithsonian National Portrait Gallery is to document history. It is a historical pictorial archive. Therefore, even if the painting was no good, it still qualified as a historical pictorial record since artistic merit is not the primary concern. To prove my point, at that time, there were four other portraits of Trump in the Smithsonian from different seasons in his controversial life, three of which would never qualify as good art. One of them was a cartoon sketch that appears to have been drawn on a napkin. It depicts Trump as Icarus falling from the sky, his wings made of dollar bills ablaze. The image describes an American public figure and a specific event in time: Trump's catastrophic loss of wealth as a billionaire. Two other portraits were crude computer-generated graphics from what looked like a dot-matrix printer from the 1980s or '90s.

The last portrait was a 1989 photo of apple-tossing Trump in a business suit. The photo's historical significance was regarding a period in New York City's history when Trump not only resided in New York but also worked in New York, running his hugely successful real-estate business. The Big Apple and its conquest were depicted by Trump tossing an apple in the air. This photo, which the Smithsonian chose to display for the 2017 inauguration, was a betrayal of the museum's historical imperative. What relevance did that photo have in the context of the historic presidential election? What will your great-grandchildren learn from an irrelevant photo chosen as the archived pictorial record of the 2016 election?

Sajet had gone for the jugular with her disparaging comment that my painting was "no good." I replied, "All you saw was a small reproduction of only a few square inches. My painting is one hundred square feet in size, and you can determine from that small image on the screen that the painting is no good?" The technical attributes of a painting can only be examined in person. Sajet did not back up her assertion with a single critique—it was just "no good." I wondered, was it stylistic? Was it the genre? Was it the artist's skill? Was it because it was acrylic instead of oil? Was it the surrealist-spiritual content? Was it the way I used symbolism? Was it the composition or the subject matter? Was it because the painting was a prescient image of President Trump before he became president? Come on, what were the criteria against which Sajet was judging the painting? To what did she compare the painting to make that value judgment?

Sajet's comment was offensive and injurious coming from someone in her position. Not because she said my painting was no good, but because she refused to qualify her comment. It was sadistic.

Sajet could have hung up the phone at that point, ending on a "no-good" note. But it was as though her own conscience was pointing at her right in the face, condemning her conduct. She had to silence her conscience too, I imagine. Trying to illegitimately block the participation of the person she should have been serving by twisting the truth, bending the rules, and personal insults had failed. Would Director Sajet resort to the tyrant's handbook? Every "no-good," corrupt official whose schemes have been exposed always resorts to an authoritarian use of power—the final act that sears the conscience. Smithsonian National Portrait Gallery Director Kim Sajet was no exception.

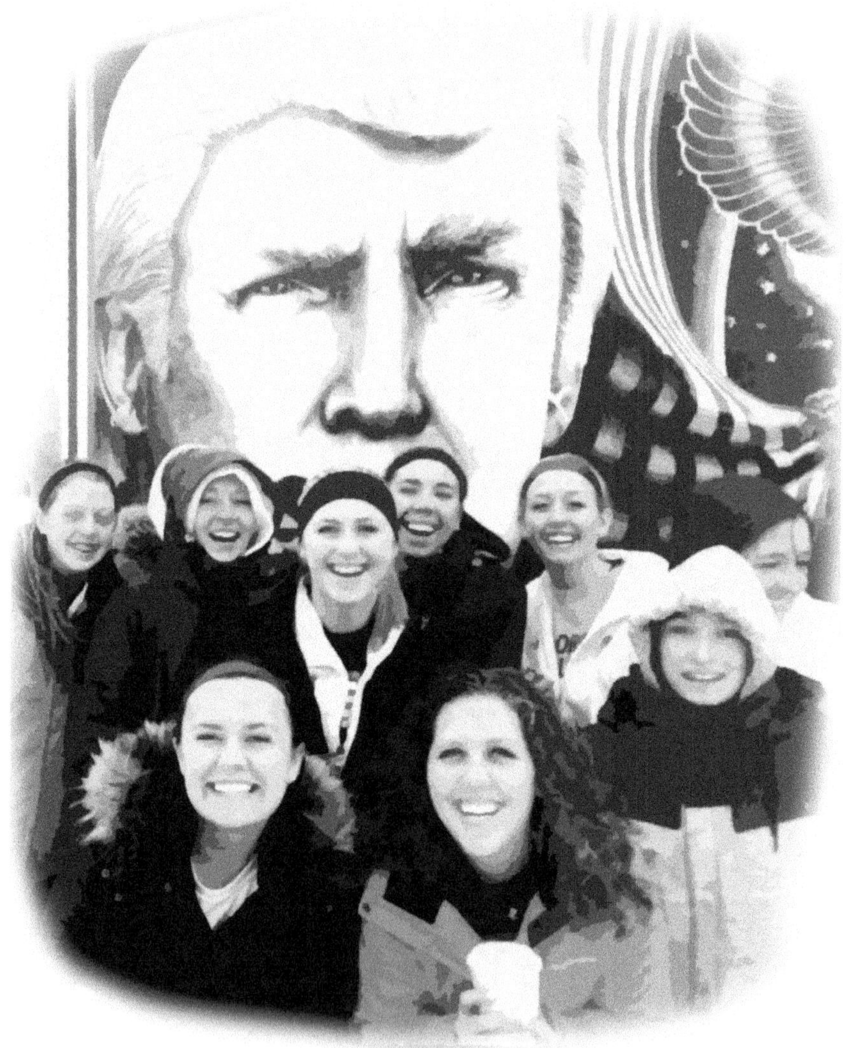

Students at Dordt College, Iowa, 2016

Chapter Twenty-One

AUTHORITARIAN DILEMMA

THE MORAL HIGH GROUND THAT LEFT-LEANING ACTIVISTS OFTEN embrace, portraying themselves as wanna-be resistance fighters against authoritarianism—in this case before Donald Trump was even president—can have a particularly nasty twist. This leftist dilemma is often noble in theory but sometimes bizarrely hypocritical in practice—just ask Fidel Castro (or his brother) and the people of Cuba. This strange lip service to selective antiauthoritarianism buried deep within the well-meaning yet crippled human condition was to come into play as my argument with Director Kim Sajet came to its dramatic conclusion.

Sajet's futile efforts to resist all of my legitimate efforts to participate in the People's Smithsonian National Portrait Gallery had crumbled to the floor, exposing her not-so-hidden anti-Trump agenda. Sajet had run out of objections, and I had not tucked tail and run. She had to use the nuclear option to cancel me, tacitly admitting defeat since any remnants of the lawful process lay in the wreckage of our heated exchange.

After attempting to tear up my painting by declaring it was no good, Kim Sajet raised her frustrated voice to a crescendo: "*I AM THE DIRECTOR OF THE SMITHSONIAN NATIONAL PORTRAIT GALLERY. YOUR APPLICATION WILL GO NO FURTHER. YOU CAN APPEAL IT ALL YOU WANT!*" Then she abruptly hung up. She might as well have shrieked, "Over my dead body will your Trump painting ever be shown in my gallery!"

The director had invoked her federal authority, abusing its power and trampling due process. By the audacious manner in which Kim Sajet behaved, she revealed far more than her personal bias. It was as if Sajet thought she could disparage my work, arbitrarily reject my application, taunt me, and get away with it precisely because of who she was and for whom she worked. In other words, she was untouchable because the Smithsonian was untouchable. Was she untouchable? Was the Smithsonian Institution untouchable?

I began to research the Smithsonian—what it is, where it is, and who runs the Institution. That was necessary because I needed to know to whom I was going to appeal. A fascinating season of historical research and discovery would take me back in time, across the Atlantic to Victorian England in the 1800s.

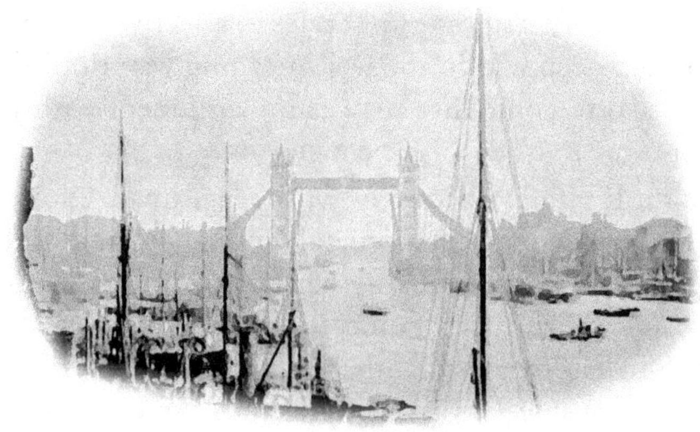

London, England

144

Chapter Twenty-Two

GOLD IN THE COURT OF CHANCERY

AFTER WEEKS AT SEA, RICHARD RUSH ARRIVED AT THE FOGGY London docks in the United Kingdom of Great Britain to carry out the duties of the United States. It was September 14, 1836 (134 years to the day before I was born). President Andrew Jackson had appointed Rush as an emissary from the United States due to an act of Congress accepting a generous bequest originating in England. His mission was to secure the funds bequeathed to America by a certain Englishman, a Mr. James Smithson.

Smithson was the illegitimate son of Hugh, the first Duke of Northumberland, and Elizabeth, heiress of the Hungerfords of Studley and niece to Charles the Proud, Duke of Somerset. America, by a series of strange circumstances, would become heir to Mr. Smithson's fortune.

James Smithson was proclaimed a great philanthropist because of the bequest he made to the United States that resulted in the Smithsonian Institution's creation. Still, the fact remains that he had left his entire fortune to a whole series of relatives who, over time, were unable to receive the fortune, either because they did not have children or because they died. At the end of Smithson's will, he left a fail-safe in place, lest the English law of "escheat" went into effect, giving the state the power to gobble up his fortune as unclaimed property. Smithson would give his entire fortune (less a hundred-pound annuity to a so-called Mr. Fitall) to the United States of America. In his will, Smithson wanted his fortune to "found at Washington, under the name of the Smithsonian Institution, an establishment for the increase and diffusion of knowledge among men."[16]

In England, his money was worthless for any publicly acknowledged use because he was an illegitimate child. Due to his unwed parents wanting to escape public shame in Victorian England, he was born in Paris, making him a persona non grata back in Old Blighty. Smithson died in Genoa, Italy, at the age of sixty-four. No amount of money on earth would have persuaded Victorian England to build Smithson an institution of learning with his name plastered all over it. His fortune would have simply been absorbed into the British Commonwealth and his legacy dissolved and forgotten.

On the other hand, America was now the New World, and yet it had its own "bastardy laws" early on while under British rule that could have been a problem. But after 1776, the bastardy laws and their punishments slowly changed. At the time of consideration of the Smithson bequest, Smithson's illegitimacy was mentioned but did not become an obstacle to receiving the fortune. Around the same time, President Andrew Jackson was having quite a gold rush of a presidency, after driving settled Cherokee and other Indian tribes off in a Trail of Tears because of gold discovered in Native lands in Georgia.

It would take two years of litigation for Mr. Rush to secure Smithson's gold. The correspondence is well documented between all parties, as they tried to work out who could receive the funds on behalf of the United States and how, since the will was short and vague. Then there was Madame de la Batut, a relative of one of the heirs who got deeply involved in the litigation, as she, too, tried to secure a chunk of Smithson's gold for herself. This complicated and extended the litigation. De la Batut eventually shaved off roughly five thousand pounds from Smithson's gold—a handsome sum, if I may say so.

After what seems to have been an agonizing and frustrating two years, Mr. Rush and his English solicitors were victorious. On May 12, 1838, Mr. Rush sent a letter to John Forsyth, the U.S. Secretary of State, informing him of the victory. Rush would begin proceedings to secure the fortune that was tied up in stocks. He would liquidate the stocks and cash out in British gold sovereigns—104,960 of them. In the end, the 87,620 British pounds were turned into 105 sacks of sparkling gold coins. There were eleven crates, ten sacks per crate, each sack holding one thousand gold sovereigns. At that time, that amount was the equivalent of 541,379.63 USD, which today would be over sixty million dollars.

You can read the entire documented correspondence, see the legal bills, the ledgers, the invoices, and the integrity that governed business transactions in that era (juxtaposed against Smithsonian Director Kim Sajet's opaque conduct). Also, you will find the Smithsonian establishment documents in the first volume of William Jones Rhees's *The Smithsonian Institution*.[17]

Richard Rush arrived back in the United States, in New York, on August 28, 1838, gold in hand. His voyage was a great success, allowing the United States to deposit the gold in the U.S. Treasury. Unsurprisingly, Congress then borrowed the money at 6 percent yearly interest. Congress dithered and debated the Institution's establishment for eight years while the gold ballooned in value. By the time the Smithsonian was established, the interest owed on the borrowed money was hundreds of thousands of dollars. It was the interest that was used to establish the Smithsonian Institution. The original monies borrowed from Smithson's bequest still appear to be owing.

Director Kim Sajet's taunt to appeal led me to discover facts that created questions, and my research swelled as a result. Even back in 1836, before securing the Smithson funds, the congressional debates regarding whether America should or could accept the money, and then how to fulfill the will of Smithson, had raised serious questions. The debates also revealed aspects of the Institution's legal identity that were to greatly assist me in my appeal. For example: Whom did Kim Sajet work for? Who paid her salary? Was it the federal government? What was the federal government's role in receiving the sacks of Smithson gold, since he was a private citizen from a foreign country? Could the government nullify the private Smithson will and keep the gold as its own? Did the Smithsonian Institution become a national government agency to further the objectives of the federal government? Exactly what was the Smithsonian? A public trust whose mission was to fulfill the will of the private and foreign testator, James Smithson? Or something more? Research into Smithsonian history would have to answer my questions.

In 1836, former President John Quincy Adams argued eloquently to Congress in favor of accepting the bequest. Not only was Smithson from a prestigious family line but the apparently virtuous objective of the donation constituted "the assumption and fulfillment of the high and honorable duties involved in the performance of the trust committed with it."[18]

Regarding Smithson's lineage, Adams argued that Smithson was "a descendant in blood from the Percys and Seymours, two of the most illustrious names of the British Islands."[19] Adams was at times excessive in his flowery and flattering portrayal of the man's family line, seemingly in an attempt to neutralize Smithson's illegitimacy and enigma. Adams did go on to make a profound argument for the acceptance of the bequest and justification for "the attainment of knowledge":

> The attainment of knowledge is the high and exclusive attribute of man, among the numberless myriads of animated beings, inhabitants of the terrestrial globe. On him alone is bestowed, by the bounty of the Creator of the universe, the power and the capacity of acquiring knowledge. Knowledge is the attribute of

his nature, which at once enables him to improve his condition upon earth and to prepare him for the enjoyment of a happier existence hereafter. It is by this attribute that man discovers his own nature as the link between earth and heaven; as a partaker of an immortal spirit; as created for a higher and more durable end than the countless tribes of beings which people the earth, the ocean, and the air, alternately instinct with life, and melting into vapor or moldering into dust.

To furnish the means of acquiring knowledge is therefore the greatest benefit that can be conferred upon mankind.[20]

Furthering the understanding of the duty of trust incumbent on Congress, Adams continued:

In the commission of every trust there is an implied tribute of the soul to the integrity and intelligence of the trustee; and there is also an implied call for the faithful exercise of those properties to the fulfillment of the purpose of the trust.[21]

Now that, ladies and gentlemen, was a massive pile of "free" gold—in a sense, just dumped on the floor of Congress. It would take huge restraint and sterling moral character not to be bedazzled and hypnotized by the beauty and allure of the sparkling treasure.

Was the fortune in gold really free money?

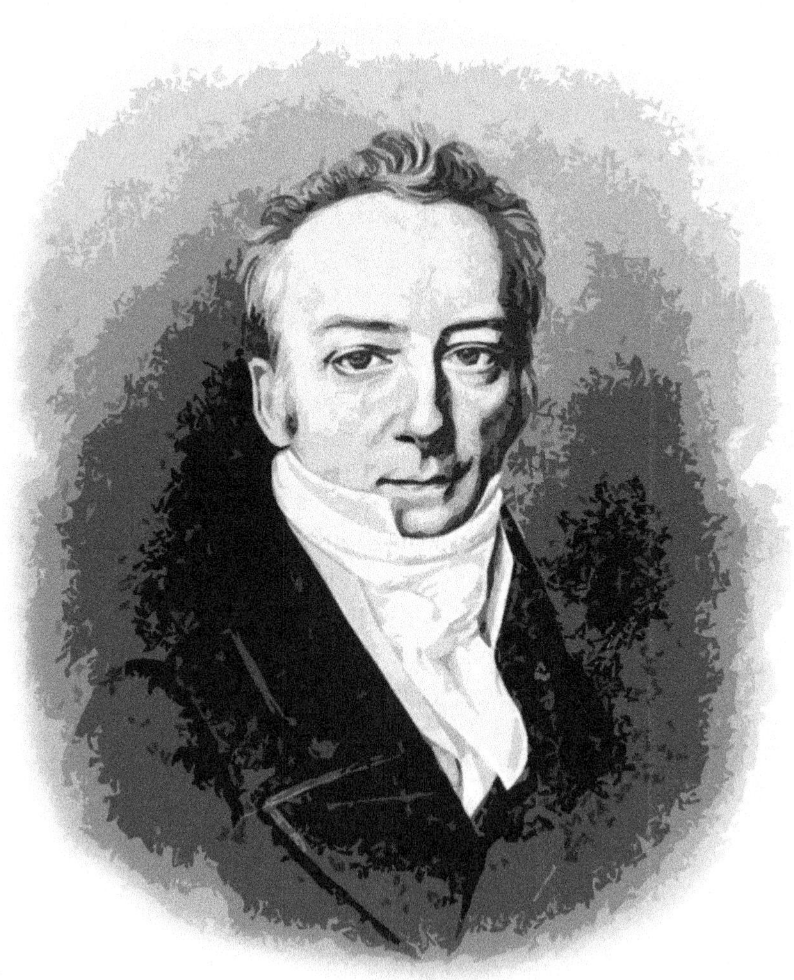

James Smithson (1765–1829)

Chapter Twenty-Three

BASTARD-SON WHIPPERSNAPPER SMITHSON

James Smithson's fortune was not free money. Receiving the gold came with preconditions, requiring the creation of a trust and raising ethical questions that dogged the debates. Some members of the House of Representatives were not convinced regarding the appropriateness of receiving Smithson's gold. Senator William C. Preston from South Carolina had some choice words to say about James Smithson. Rhees writes:

> He [Preston] thought this donation had been partly made with a view to immortalize the donor, and that it was too cheap a way of conferring immortality. There was danger of their [Congress's] imaginations being run away with by the associations of Chevy Chase ballads....
>
> If they [Congress] accepted this donation, every whippersnapper vagabond that had been traducing our country might think proper to have his name distinguished in the same way. It was not consistent with the dignity of the country to accept even the grant of a man of noble birth or lineage.[22]

Senator John C. Calhoun also protested. He believed Congress could not accept the gift, not having the authority and arguing that "it was beneath the dignity of the United States to receive presents of this kind from anyone."[23]

On May 2, 1836, the resolution passed with thirty-one yeas and seven nays. On August 10, 1846, a decade later, Congress finally established the Smithsonian Institution with the Smithsonian Act of Congress:

James Smithson, esquire, of London, in the Kingdom of Great Britain, having by his last will and testament given the whole of his property to the United States of America, to found at Washington, under the name of "Smithsonian Institution," an establishment for the increase and diffusion of knowledge among men; and the United States having, by an act of Congress, received said property and accepted said trust; Therefore, for the faithful execution of said trust, according to the will of the liberal and enlightened donor; Be it enacted...[24]

Before going any further, I must say that while doing my research, I became aware of the complexity of issues relating to the historical Smithsonian and its founding documents that developed over time. An unexpected task presented itself as a result, like an age-old riddle that had remained a mystery for over a hundred years. Just what the Smithsonian Institution is became the big question. The answer to that question would come to answer all other questions. It is imperative at this early stage of the discovery to make a note of the guiding purpose of the Smithsonian Act of Congress—also, the independence of the actors or the organizational components.

I became absorbed by the Smithsonian mystery as a result of a hostile encounter with a Smithsonian official. I entered a season of research from a point of complete ignorance. Was that a random clash or my destiny, I would ask myself. That mystery, comprising an unknown, wealthy bastard of British royal lineage, the vague instructions in his will about knowledge, a national treasure worth millions of dollars in gold, and even a castle in Washington, D.C., began to consume me with an Indiana Jones–like excitement and curiosity. But as a heads-up, the learning curve at times may be as overwhelming for you as it was for me when I first tried to understand it. Let me encourage you with the ancient yet sacred words of a poorly educated fisherman named Peter to "gird up the loins of your mind." I imagine you will be as astonished as I was. So without further ado, let's get back to the business of finding to whom I was to appeal.

The Actors

The Testator: James Smithson exercised his right to express his will regarding his private property in his last will and testament.

The Will of James Smithson: His speech was expressed in his will that in Washington, "an establishment for the increase and diffusion of knowledge among men" be founded.

The Trustees: These are the individuals who accept the duty to carry out the will of the testator—in this case, Congress, the elected representatives of the people of the United States. Back in 1846, they understood their role as trustees of the will of a private foreign citizen on behalf of the Smithson trust beneficiaries, the American people.

The Smithson Trust: The legal arrangement created by the reception of and agreement to the terms of the will of James Smithson by the trustees.

The Smithsonian Institution: The organization necessary to carry out the objective of Smithson's will.

The Board of Regents: The leadership structure appointed by the trustees to oversee the operation of the Institution.

The Smithsonian Chancellor: The head of the Board of Regents.

The Smithsonian Secretary: The principal manager is appointed by the Board of Regents to manage the Institution's day-to-day operations.

The Smithsonian Officials: Employees like Kim Sajet and others are hired as directors to manage specific branches of knowledge in the Institution.

The Beneficiaries: The American People.

> Be it Enacted By the Senate and House of Representatives of the United States of America in Congress assembled. That the President and Vice-President of the United States, the Secretary of State, the Secretary of the Treasury, the Secretary of War, the Secretary of the Navy, the Postmaster-General, the Attorney-General, the Chief Justice, and the Commissioner of the Patent Office of the United States; and the mayor of the city of Washington, during the time for which they shall hold their respective offices, and such other persons as they may elect honorary members, be, and they are hereby constituted, an "establishment," by the name of the "Smithsonian Institution," for the increase and diffusion of knowledge among men; and by that name shall be known and have perpetual succession, with the powers, limitations, and restrictions, hereinafter contained, and no other.[25]

The Smithson trust, created from the Congressional Act, was separate from the trustees. The trust was the legal arrangement itself that needed to be established. The trust was neither the trustees nor the beneficiaries, nor did it have members of the House or the Senate, because they were the trustees. Both the executive and judicial branches of the government were represented in the trust, and a series of bureaucratic positions were also added, including the attorney general and the elected mayor of the federal district of Washington. Also, anyone else who was elected by the officials became established as the Smithsonian Institution in perpetuity, having its physical expression in the literal Smithsonian Institution and its buildings. This establishment could have been composed of anyone the constituted members decided should be part of the Institution. Those individuals had no function other than bearing their titles, upon which the legal framework rested and functioned, facilitating the will. The business of running the Institution was left to the Board of Regents and the secretary:

SEC 3. And be it further enacted, That the business of the said Institution shall be conducted at the City of Washington by a board of regents, by the name of regents of the "Smithsonian Institution," to be composed of the Vice-President of the United States, the Chief Justice of the United States, and the Mayor of the City of Washington, during the time for which they shall hold their respective offices; three members of the Senate, and three members of the House of Representatives; together with six other persons, other than members of Congress, two of whom shall be members of the national institute in the City of Washington, and resident in the said city; and the other four thereof shall be inhabitants of States, and no two of them of the same State.[26]

Congress, acting as trustee, created and appointed a Board of Regents, a cross-section of the three branches of government and members of the public, responsible for overseeing the fulfillment of the will of Smithson. The Board consisted of just the vice president, the chief justice, three Senate members, three members of the House of Representatives, and six members of the public. The formation of the Board of Regents has changed little over the years, except for the increase in members of the public from six to nine and the removal of the mayor of Washington.

It became clear to me that it was to the Board of Regents, especially the chancellor, that I had to appeal regarding Director Kim Sajet's egregious conduct and arbitrary refusal of my painting. The Board of Regents looked like the place where my appeal would be heard and I would find relief. All of those esteemed members of the different branches of the government would assuredly grant me definitive relief. But would they? And to what exactly was I appealing? Was it a government agency to which I would redress my grievances, maybe even under the U.S. Constitution? Notice how representatives of the three branches of government, the executive, judicial, and legislative branches, and unelected, appointed members of the public, are brought together around one table to oversee the operation of the Institution. Think about the meetings, requiring a minimum of eight board members to be present, to make binding decisions in what I learned was called a "quorum." Now ask yourself again, What type of institution could this possibly be? Could it operate as a government agency without violating the separation-of-powers doctrine? In other words, if the appointed representatives, who were members of the three branches, acted in their official capacities when they sat down together to conduct business as Smithsonian regents, did their decisions in unison constitute the singular will of the federal government? The regents' decisions would become a conflux of executive, legislative, and judicial power, creating new hyperauthoritative "Execu-legis-judicial" orders. Was it a multi-headed federal agency? Would that not be better called a monster?

Or, could it simply be that when the Board of Regents met to hear my appeal, the officials would leave their titles, offices, and robes at the door and sit down together as regular American-citizen trustees? After all, they were sitting with six (now nine) members of the unelected citizenry. It would not matter if the regents were policemen, congressmen, doctors, judges, lawyers, vice presidents, politicians, mothers, fathers, gardeners, or pastors; they all became and/or functioned simply as trustees. Was it not their sole obligation to carry out their fiduciary duties as expressed in the will of Smithson?

Whatever it was, the Board of Regents would soon receive my appeal.

Chapter Twenty-Four

HELP ME, JUSTICE ROBERTS, YOU'RE MY ONLY HOPE

"Justice will be done. Justice will be done," I sang to myself. I was exuberant upon discovering that the chief justice of the United States Supreme Court, John Roberts himself, also happened to be the chancellor of the Smithsonian Institution's Board of Regents. Yes, the nation's top law diviner, the big kahuna of justice, a man who had sworn this oath:

> I, John Glover Roberts Jr., do solemnly swear (or affirm) that I will administer justice without respect to persons, and do equal right to the poor and to the rich, and that I will faithfully and impartially discharge and perform all the duties incumbent upon me as Chief Justice of the United States Supreme Court under the Constitution and laws of the United States. So help me, God.[27]

John Roberts may not have been bound by his judicial oath in his capacity as Smithsonian chancellor, but surely it affected his conduct, I imagined. Since the Smithsonian was a trust, then the trustee duty prescribed in trust law would apply to the chancellor.

And that responsibility was one of the highest fiduciary duties and responsibilities placed upon an individual. Esteemed Justice Benjamin Cardozo, who was also chief judge of the New York Court of Appeals in 1928, helped me better understand the binding duty of integrity placed upon a trustee, in a court case by the name of *Meinhard v. Salmon*:

> Many forms of conduct permissible in a workaday world for those acting at arm's length, are forbidden to those bound by fiduciary ties. A trustee is held to something stricter than the morals of the market place. Not honesty alone, but the punctilio of an honor the most sensitive, is then the standard of behavior. As to this there has developed a tradition that is unbending and inveterate. Uncompromising rigidity has been the attitude of courts of equity when petitioned to undermine the rule of undivided loyalty by the "disintegrating erosion" of particular exceptions.... Only thus has the level of conduct for fiduciaries been kept at a level higher than that trodden by the crowd. It will not consciously be lowered by any judgment of this court.[28]

Trustee duties and their "undivided loyalty" to the testator and the will are not only expected but precisely prescribed and codified, in this case, into the Uniform Trust Code for the District of Columbia. The body of trust law and related case law is broad and historic. Our American laws rest upon British criminal and civil legal history, reaching back nearly a thousand years to the Magna Carta, when property rights, including inheritance rights and guardianships (trusteeships), became statutory law. Reading the Magna Carta was encouraging, and the ancient document shed light on my situation as I navigated the seas of grievance in search of redress. In Article 60, we read:

> If we, our chief justice, our officials, or any of our servants offend in any respect against any man, or transgress any of the articles of the peace or of this security, and the offence is made known to four of the said twenty-five barons, they shall come to us—or in our absence...to the chief justice—to declare it and

claim immediate redress. If…the chief justice, make no redress within forty days, reckoning from the day on which the offence was declared to us or to him,… [the barons] may distrain upon and assail us in every way possible, with the support of the whole community of the land, by seizing our castles, lands, possessions, or anything else…until they have secured such redress as they have determined upon.[29]

Trust law is particularly personal; it deals with people's hard-earned wealth and property accumulated over their lifetime that remain when they leave this world, in the care of a trustee. That amounts to a lot of dead people and a lot of property. Who benefits from the property? What did the testator desire to be done with the property? Who shall administer the property left in trust delineated in the last will and testament? These questions were answered by creating the laws that govern the administration of the deceased person's property on behalf of the beneficiaries. Without laws to guide and ensure the transfer, all hell would break loose, as the lust for a relative's gold makes even family members forget themselves. Imagine when the gold left in trust is not even a relative's, and politicians are left drooling over it. Everyone wants a part of the dearly departed's gold—even the IRS, in the form of death taxes, estate taxes, and inheritance taxes.

Over time, the codified fiduciary duties for trustees developed. Those duties were broad and binding, requiring strict adherence to the will. They provided legal remedies for the beneficiaries if the trustees got caught with their hands in the cookie jar. It would be very tempting for trustees to embezzle or misuse the testator's property for their own selfish, sordid, or corrupt ends, because usually the testator was dead. Who then would remain to ensure the testator's will was honored if the trustee breached the trust?

What was also interesting about the role of trustees was that they became co-titleholders of the property, greatly amplifying their need to be trustworthy. The trust was not like a legal corporation where the title to the property could be held. The trustee held legal title equally with the beneficiaries of the will (public trusts were more complicated, as beneficiaries were not always explicitly named). This entitlement gave trustees the legal power as title-holders to carry out the testator's will in the best interest of the beneficiaries.

In Washington, D.C., those trust duties are beautifully spelled out in the Uniform Trust Code for the District of Columbia, the legal jurisdiction for the Smithsonian Institution. It is necessary to review some of these laws to determine who was doing their job in my case. Once you know what to expect from those acting as trustees or trustee agents, it is easier to see when they breach their trust. In Section 19-1308, we read about the duties and powers of trustees:

The Duty to Administer Trust, in good faith in accordance with the terms and purposes of the trust, in this case, the increase and diffusion of knowledge

The Duty of Loyalty, a trustee shall administer the trust solely in the interest of the beneficiaries

The Duty of Impartiality, the trustee shall act impartially

The Duty of Prudent Administration, a trustee shall administer the trust as a prudent person would

Trustee's Skills, the trustee who has special skills or expertise shall use those special skills in executing the trust

Delegation by Trustee:

> (a) A trustee may delegate duties and powers that a prudent trustee of comparable skills could properly delegate under the circumstances. The trustee shall exercise reasonable care, skill, and caution in: (1) Selecting an agent; (2) Establishing the scope and terms of the delegation, consistent with the purposes and terms of the trust; and (3) Periodically reviewing the agent's actions in order to monitor the agent's performance and compliance with the terms of the delegation.

> (b) In performing a delegated function, an agent owes a duty to the trust to exercise reasonable care to comply with the terms of the delegation.

(c) A trustee who complies with subsection (a) of this section is not liable to the beneficiaries or to the trust for an action of the agent to whom the function was delegated.

(d) By accepting a delegation of powers or duties from the trustee of a trust that is subject to the law of the District of Columbia, an agent submits to the jurisdiction of the courts of the District of Columbia.[30]

Ahhh, what delightfully straightforward, righteous, and caring written standards have developed over the years. It was exciting to think that Chancellor John Roberts, having expertise in law, would be the exemplar par excellence of principled trusteeship. So much so, in fact, that I could just lie back, arms behind my head, toes dangling in the crystal-clear, turquoise-colored warm tropical water on a bright-pink flamingo-shaped floaty, bronzing myself under the sun's golden rays in the Caribbean. Yes, there I would be, slowly sipping a layered, multi-colored fresh-fruit beverage through a red-and-white striped straw out of a green, frosted-rimmed, and elegantly stemmed cocktail glass with an orange parasol sticking out the top. The sharpened toothpick end of the parasol pierced the bright, red, plump cherry floating in the sweet cream accumulated at the surface of my libation. Slurping away my concerns about the outcome, my mind would sip at the sweetness of justice, trusting implicitly that this man of law would get me satisfaction.

After all, Chancellor Roberts not only worked (without pay, that is) in the sprawling Smithsonian museum complex, but he also worked as the Chief Priest in a beautiful and ornate white-marble temple devoted to the god of law and justice. Even the creed "Equal Justice Under Law" was carved into the temple's marble facade in giant letters right across the front.

Five days after the December 1 phone call with Director Kim Sajet, I drafted my appeal to Chancellor John Roberts and the Smithsonian Board of Regents. Time was moving quickly. On December 7, 2016, now only five weeks from the inauguration of President-elect Trump, I mailed my appeal regarding Kim Sajet's outrageous and grievous conduct. I simultaneously sent the letter by email to Smithsonian Board of Regents Chief of Staff Porter Wilkerson. The forty-plus-page appeal packet included the original Smithsonian application, all of the letters of recommendation, and eighteen copies of the twenty-by-thirty-inch full-color, high-resolution glossy print of the Trump painting, "Unafraid and Unashamed." Mailing the eighteen packets was not cheap. In trying to send all of the eighteen official appeals to the chancellor of the Smithsonian Institution and the other seventeen Smithsonian trustees individually in USPS priority-mail envelopes (plus the eighteen posters in their own priority-mail poster box), I ran out of money, as every struggling artist frequently does. Fortunately, the large envelopes fit inside one of the large priority-mail boxes, so I could stack nine envelopes in each box, costing me a fraction of what it would have to mail them individually. I sent them registered, signature required, stamped, insured, and to the attention of the chancellor of the Smithsonian Institution, John Roberts.

Ahhh, back to the beach scene. Seeing those bulky packages being huffed and puffed by the mail handlers was as sweet as the freshly squeezed juice I was just sipping. In mere days, the trustees would have their packages. It would be like Christmas, as they eagerly tore them open. Soon, the trustees would be indignantly banging their fists on the regents' round table, outraged at the breaches of trust and violations of my free-speech rights at the hands of that venomous Kim Sajet. And soon, the phone would ring or some official letter would arrive from Chancellor Roberts himself, expressing his sorrow at the way I had been treated, saying that he personally had taken it upon himself to resolve the issue, and assuring me that without delay, justice would be served. I just wanted to drift away on my pink floaty into the sunset forever.

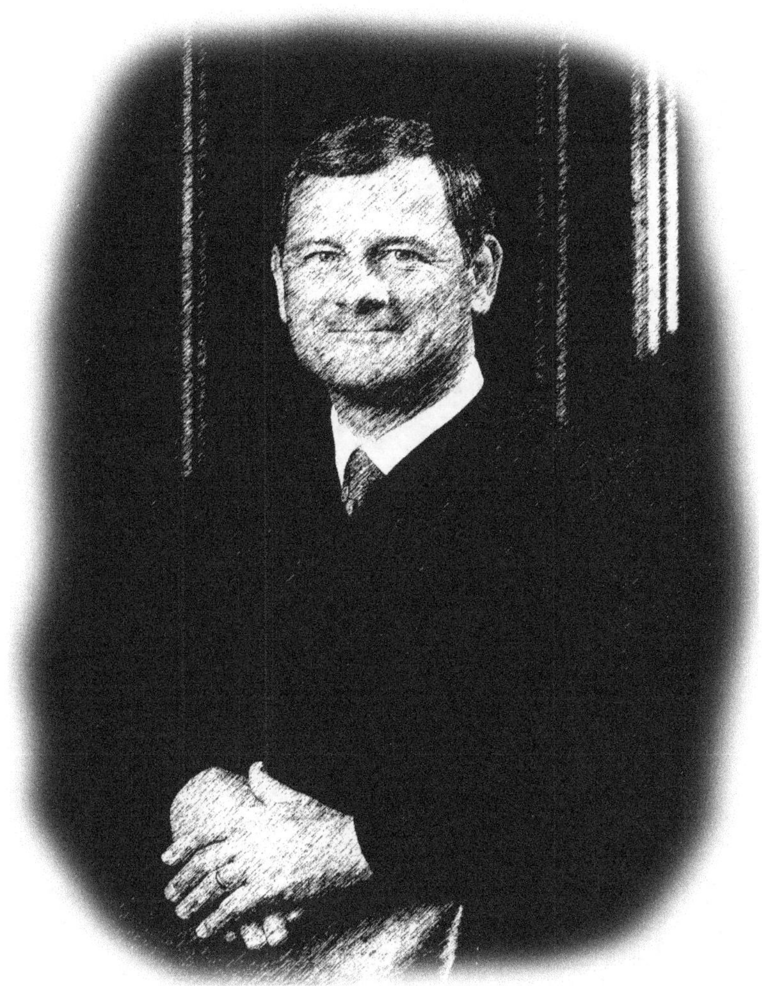

Chief Justice John Roberts

My appeal to Chancellor Roberts and the Smithsonian Board of Regents

Chapter Twenty-Five

DOUBLE AGENT

ABOUT TEN DAYS LATER, TO MY SURPRISE, A LETTER ARRIVED. Although the official Smithsonian envelope was regular in size, it felt like a sack of cement. My heart was pounding. Who had replied? What did it say? Was it just an acknowledgment that they had received my appeal? Was it going to begin to restore my faith in the system? Was it going to bring healing to my aggrieved condition? Was it going to restore my artistic voice and my rights of free political expression in our public Institution? Was it going to pave the way for me to show my painting as a tribute to the historic election of Donald J. Trump at the fast-approaching 2017 inauguration in Washington, D.C.?

The letter was from a Dr. Richard Kurin,[31] dated December 9, 2016. He was the Acting Provost and Under Secretary for Museums and Research. I had just discovered who the Smithson Board members were, and Kurin was not one of them. The date indicated that the response had been made swiftly and caused me to wonder how the Board members could have responded so quickly.

In his letter, Kurin completely ignored the fact that my letter was appealing Sajet's egregious actions. He refused to acknowledge that Director Sajet had both injured me and indirectly instructed me to appeal. Thus, Kurin cut off any process for me to redress my grievances. Kurin added insult to injury, waffling on about how "we appreciate receiving your letter." This was like admiring and complimenting the color of a man's shirt while he drowned and clawed at the side of the boat, crying out for help. This letter seemed deliberately disconnected from reality, and that threw me off balance. I had appealed to Chancellor Roberts and the other sixteen regents. Had he or they even seen my appeal? Had Roberts handed me off to Kurin? Ignoring my appeal revealed a profound dissimulation. Was the whole apple poisoned at the Smithsonian Institution? Was I the only one to experience this? No, in another discrimination case from 2006 that we shall examine later, in the U.S. House of Representatives Committee on Government Reform, under Congressman Mark Souder, Congressional staff reported:

> Unfortunately, Secretary Small and Deputy Secretary Burke have exhibited a head-in-the-sand attitude toward the wrongdoing committed toward Dr. Sternberg at their agency. They continue to engage in stonewalling and spin rather than dealing forthrightly with the discrimination that has occurred....
>
> Tellingly, the Deputy Secretary's statement completely failed to address the central question of whether the harassment and discrimination identified in the OSC report took place.[32]

A different time, different officials, but same behavior, same chancellor, same Smithsonian Institution, and same systemic corruption!

Kurin then explained how they had "long planned" to hang a portrait of President-elect Trump. It was mid-December, just over a month after the election, yet this was a long-planned event? Now truth be told, in amongst all the pretense, Kurin might have been telling the truth—I cannot prove otherwise—but I highly doubt it. Even if that were the case, the Smithsonian hung three portraits for President Obama's second inauguration in 2013. One was the original "Hope" poster that was part of their collection, by donation from pro-Obama lobbyists. The other two were giant, six-foot by eight-foot "jacquard" photo prints by artist Chuck Close, which were on loan to the gallery from some famous billionaires. Ahhhh, yes, the power and influence of money, without which you are treated like—well, like me!

Kurin now incriminated himself by saying that he had spoken with Kim Sajet and concurred with her decision to "decline" my offer without a single explanation according to the standards of the process. I was appealing Kim Sajet's egregious conduct, which Kurin ignored and with which he concurred. Would someone, somewhere—like a federal judge—eventually condemn Sajet's actions?

Once again, I was brushed aside by a government employee living high on the federal hog, either getting paid by our tax dollars or deriving his pay from the Smithson trust, whose first responsibility was to the beneficiaries, We the People, and to the fulfillment of the trust. Where was the duty of care? How was it an increase of knowledge to use an outdated Trump photo from their archive? Kurin's silence regarding Kim Sajet's actions, my appeal related to those actions, and my injured condition at the time was contemptible. In the light of the fiduciary duties owed the American people, it was disgraceful.

Kurin's letter was as reprehensible as Sajet's actions, just in reverse, as he politely abused the People's trust. We the People pay these Smithson trust agents and government employees to do their job. They have sworn an oath to the U.S. Constitution as covered executives. Both Sajet and Kurin were expected to follow the law. By concurring with Sajet's treatment of me and my painting, he agreed with everything she had failed to do, every law she had broken, and every process she had violated.

The Smithsonian Institution has clearly defined processes to determine whether a submission by a member of the public qualifies or not for acceptance. Ask yourself this question: When the

Smithsonian opened, where did it get all of its collections? The Congress and the Board of Regents, as trustees, were responsible only for the building; the content of knowledge had to come from somewhere. The Smithsonian did not create its own content. It invited and welcomed it from the public, who flooded the empty hallways and storerooms of the new Smithsonian buildings with specimens, samples, artifacts, and original works of art—especially portraits, most of which came by way of donation at the outset. The Institution's job was to process the donations, organizing them for display for the benefit of the American public.

The will of Smithson is very broad, not stipulating any specific field of learning or knowledge, which James Smithson could have done. And so, the trustees had the discretion of determining what fields of knowledge, in their judgment, were to be increased and diffused. They were responsible for establishing the objectives and standards by which the selection processes could determine whether a painting like mine would or would not fulfill the will of Smithson by increasing and diffusing knowledge in the arts, American history, and specifically, political art.

The trustees created a portrait museum by commissioning a committee in 1962 that established portrait objectives and written standards to fulfill those objectives. In 2009, the gallery directors set a precedent by displaying political art revolving around the presidential-election campaign and then displaying it in honor of the winning candidate. They confirmed this by repeating and amplifying the exhibit in 2013. This then created a theme of knowledge to be increased and diffused in which the public could participate by submitting political works for consideration. The presidential portraits displayed for Obama's 2009 and 2013 inaugurations came from average members of the public, lobbyist Tony Podesta, brother of John Podesta, Hillary Clinton's campaign manager, and a pair of billionaires, Ian and Annette Cumming. (John Podesta then became Obama's transition co-chair at the time of the inauguration.) Since this was the People's gallery documenting the history of the People of the United States in portraits, the National Portrait

Gallery director and curator's job was to select, through a rigorous process, the most historically relevant qualifying portrait. Director Sajet's job was *not* to inject her personal political opinions and trash the sixty-plus million members of We the People who voted for Donald Trump because she despised him.

To help the public understand how relevant items could be submitted for consideration to the Smithsonian, they have a Frequently Asked Questions and Answers section on their official Smithsonian website that addresses this topic. This is how it initially read before it mysteriously changed:

> The Smithsonian acquires thousands of objects and specimens each year for its collection holdings through donation, bequest, purchase, exchange, and field collecting. The Institution accepts only items that truly fill a gap in the collections and then only after careful consideration by museum curators and directors. Because of this rigorous selection process, the Smithsonian adds to its collections only a tiny percentage of what it is offered.[33]

By their own definition, there is a "rigorous selection process," and "only after careful consideration by museum curators and directors," items are selected, but only if they truly "fill a gap" in the collections.

Where in Kurin's letter did he describe participating in this rigorous process of selection? Nowhere. Where in Kurin's letter did he describe the standards for portraiture consideration that had been applied and explain how my portrait did not qualify? Nowhere. And as to filling a gap in history—in my case, the historic election campaign of 2015-2016—could Kurin have said that my portrait did not fill a gap, when in fact there were no other portraits of Donald Trump submitted for consideration that corresponded with this historic period of time, documenting this specific period in history, filling this specific gap? He could not! There was only one portrait submitted that could have filled that gap—mine.

The reason neither Kurin nor Sajet could cite any written standards for portraiture consideration to legitimately process my painting for consideration was because there was no way on earth it did not qualify. Everything about it made it a legitimate candidate as a pictorial record of that particular historical period and historic individual. These two just happened to despise Trump and the patriotic subject matter in the painting. The Smithsonian has remained untouchable by the law, emboldening the officials to do and say as they please. Not only have they trampled their oaths, but they have violated the Constitution and the federal and Smithsonian standards of employee conduct and code of ethics and hijacked the will of James Smithson.

Kurin's refusal to acknowledge my appeal and do his due diligence in investigating my claim was a cold and calculated breach of trust that further injured me. Kurin's refusal to answer my reply to his letter only further amplified the corruption. He slammed the door in my face without a single word of justification.

As cited above in the Uniform Trust Code for the District of Columbia, when an acting trustee (John Roberts) commissions a non-trustee agent (Richard Kurin) to carry out a task on his behalf, the trustee can be found liable for the agent's actions unless there is follow-through to see if the commission was accomplished faithfully. If not, the sins of the agent become the sins of the trustee. Hence, Chancellor John Roberts and the rest of the trustees became complicit because Chancellor John Roberts and the Board of Regents concurred with Dr. Richard Kurin. Kurin concurred with Director Kim Sajet's actions and statements that broke the law.

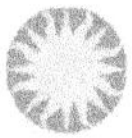

Smithsonian Institution

Dr. Richard Kurin
Acting Provost/Under Secretary for Museums & Research

December 9, 2016

Mr. Julian Marcus Raven
2524 County Route 60
Elmira NY 14901

Dear Mr. Raven:

We appreciate receiving your letter of December 7 to the Smithsonian's Board of Regents, regarding your proposal to exhibit your portrait of President-elect Trump at the National Portrait Gallery. The Board has referred your letter to me for a response.

Consistent with recent tradition, the Gallery has long planned to hang a portrait of the President-elect before his Inauguration. A portrait of Mr. Trump from the National Portrait Gallery's collection will be on display at the Gallery beginning January 13, 2017.

The decision about whether to acquire or display a work of art at the National Portrait Gallery rests in the first instance with that museum's director, curators and historians. I have spoken with Kim Sajet, director of the National Portrait Gallery, and concur with her decision to decline your offer and continue with the museum's plan to display a portrait of Mr. Trump from our collections.

Thank you for your interest in the Smithsonian and the National Portrait Gallery.

Sincerely,

Richard Kurin

Chapter Twenty-Six

FEDERAL FOIBLES?

MY ESTIMATION OF THE GOVERNMENT-RUN SMITHSONIAN Institution disintegrated. Everywhere I turned, it seemed rotten to the core. Was this how federally run institutions treated regular people, or was I just caught in the crossfire of their hidden yet palpable hatred of Donald Trump? After all, at that time, Trump was about to triumphantly ride a wave of conservative, flag-waving populism into a city that had voted overwhelmingly against him (96 percent for Hillary Clinton, that is).

Was Washington's Smithsonian Institution now divorced from the people it belonged to, having become an ideological leftist stronghold, a bastion of elitism, godless academia, and political liberalism? Could it be likened to some sort of unchained mythical beast that I had provoked? Was I now fodder for their cannon, at which these individuals would blast their seething animus, personally deriving the salivating satisfaction of cutting down a deplorable Trump supporter?

And no, what I experienced was not mere foibles but something far more sinister than just human failings within the Institution.

The Smithsonian Institution trustees' handling of my treatment at the hands of Museum Director Kim Sajet and Senior Museum Provost Dr. Richard Kurin was profoundly disappointing and depressing. No closure, no recourse, no restitution, no apology, just the taste of gravel in my mouth.

Now what? What were my options? What was originally a civil or criminal encounter—or both—with a Smithsonian official was beginning to look like systemic institutional disease.

Time was not going to wait for me. January 17 approached fast; I needed closure, a remedy for my injured condition. Also, I wanted to show my painting as an artistic conclusion to a victorious and historic presidential campaign.

People said to me that I should appeal to President Trump. I briefly considered that path at one point, but that was not my style. Being fiercely independent, I was not going to ask anyone for help. I did not want anyone's fingers on the scales of justice, not even President Trump's. Blind justice, as a matter of law, had to be served without influence. That is when justice is pure and truly beautiful.

This was my fight. This was my painting. This was my right to participate in the Smithson trust as a beneficiary member of We the People, even if that participation meant having my application lawfully processed and then lawfully rejected. Lawful consideration was the minimum I expected. This was my country. This was my odyssey. This was my patriotic journey to engage in a country whose ideals and values I cherished and had sworn an oath to defend.

God alone was the One to whom I would turn in my pain and disappointment. I had faith that He was with me, that He had led me, and that He would continue to lead me. And that someday, in some form, justice would be served.

I needed resolution. My wounded condition had not improved; in fact, it had festered. I was frustrated at being violated, cast aside, and treated with contempt. The Smithsonian Institution in Washington, D.C., may have silenced me and ignored my appeal, but I was not done.

I picked myself up from the gravel driveway just outside the gates of the Smithsonian Castle, where I had been tossed. I brushed off my grazed knees with the bloodied palms of my hands. My lip was split, and my right eye socket throbbed. Though beaten and downtrodden, I was ready to fight on. With appeal in hand, I marched off down the street, looking for a judge or a court where I could file my appeal. What type of court should I be seeking? I did not know. Which court would hear my appeal? I had no idea.

Could I even sue the Smithsonian Institution?

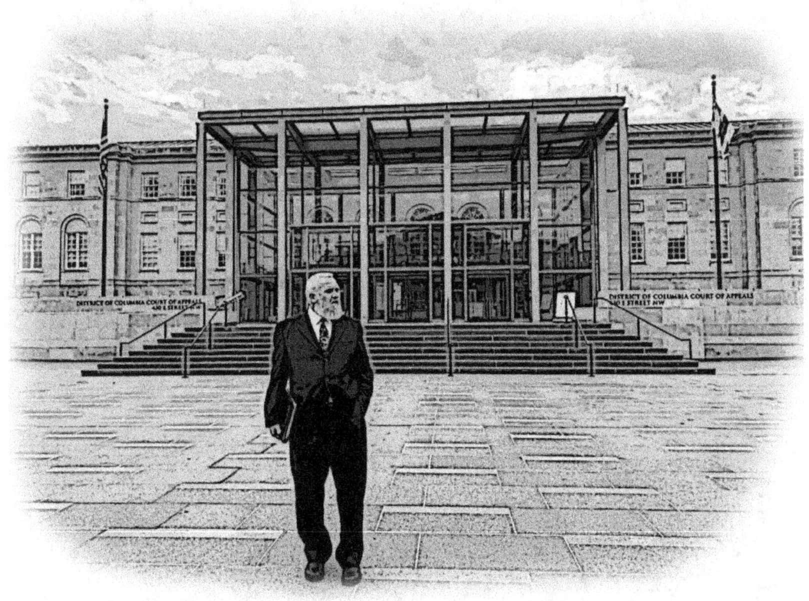

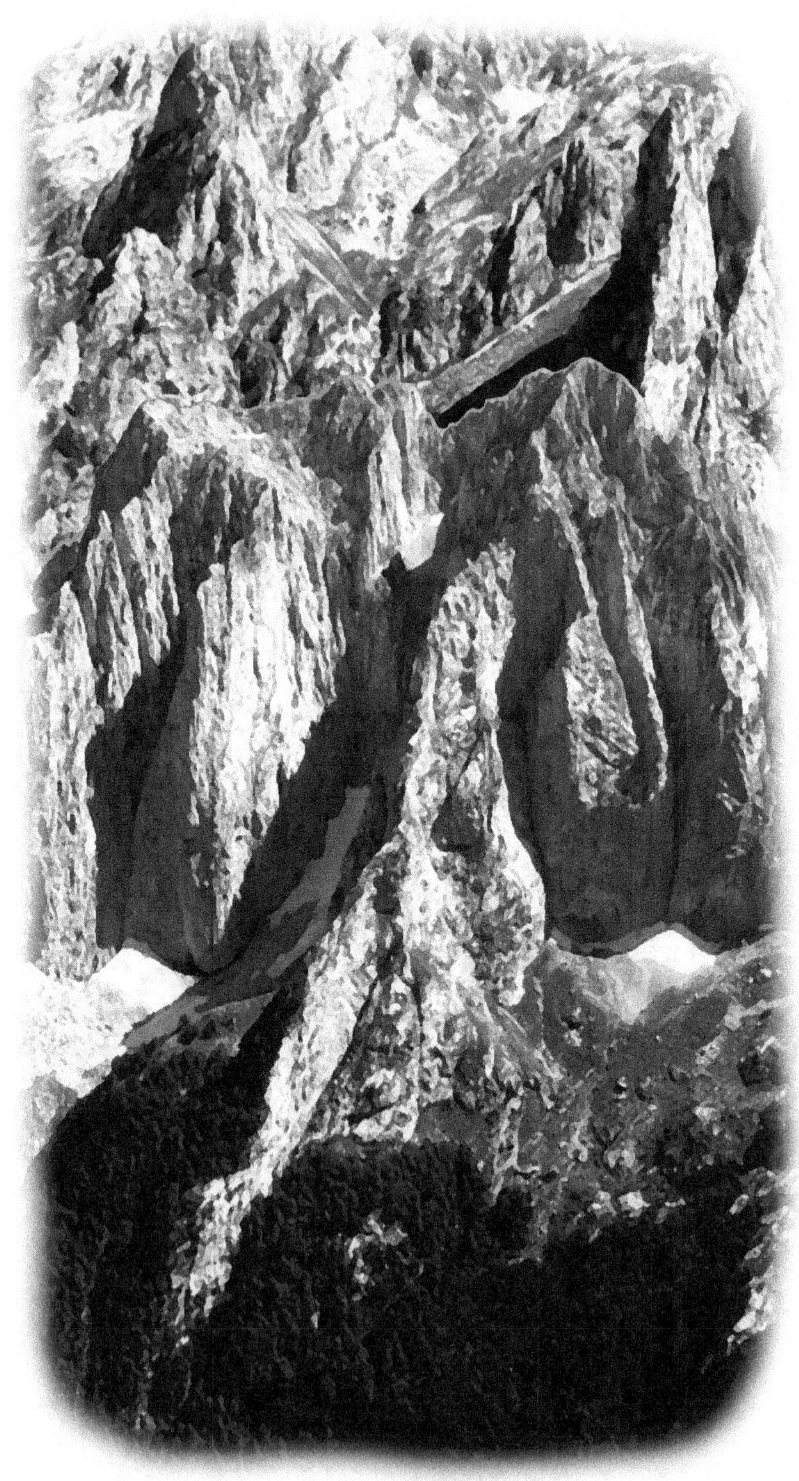

Mount Justlaw

Chapter Twenty-Seven

ASCENDING MOUNT JUSTLAW

I WAS NOT A MOUNTAIN CLIMBER. THE DARK, JAGGED FACE OF Mount Justlaw stared down at me as I stood at its foot. An acute awareness of my smallness and weakness gripped me, and it was dreadful. I could only see about a third of the way up. The rest was wrapped in fast-moving, heavy-laden rain clouds, stretching miles into the distance. I was all alone at the beginning of a dirt path. It was just me and the stone face of Mount Justlaw. I didn't have to climb the mountain; no one was forcing me. I could have turned around, retreated into the woods, and gone home. But no, staring for the last time into my backpack, I again went through the items I thought I would need: ropes and climbing hardware, some tools, sleeping and severe-weather gear, a solar charger for my phone, a small stove, a stainless flask, utensils, a variety of power foods, and of course, tea bags. Water I would find on the mountain. There was no time to waste. I had to climb. I had no choice.

This was how I felt as I prepared to file my lawsuit against the Smithsonian Institution in federal court. Google was a fantastic tool that rapidly led me to the stepping-stones I would need to follow. Vigorously, I searched for a court in which to file my suit. Not being a lawyer and without legal training, my passion and determination for seeing justice served were the only legal equipment I had. I was indignant that government officials living off taxpayer money were getting away with this type of treatment of a U.S. citizen and beneficiary of the will of Smithson. That indignation was all the fuel I needed to embark upon a treacherous mountain climb that would become the most demanding and challenging endeavor of my life.

It was December 19, 2016. Time had ceased to be my friend and had run away in front of me. In less than four weeks, President-elect Donald Trump would be sworn in at the U.S. Capitol in Washington, D.C. The ominous mountain continued to stare me down, taunting me. If there was to be any hope for justice, it was up fearsome Mount Justlaw.

Finally, some good news. After my search, I found a court where I could appeal and file my first lawsuit: the United States Court of Federal Claims in Washington, D.C. As a struggling artist, I would qualify as a legal pauper. By filing in *forma pauperis* status, I would be exempt from any filing fees I would encounter. Since I could represent myself against the federal government, I would now be classified as a *pro se* litigant. Yes, there was a whole vocabulary before me that I did not yet understand. The legal world of the federal court system was complex. Unless I could speak the language, there was no functioning within the system. Read and reread became my ritual until I could grasp enough to keep climbing up the mountain.

Simple successes became powerful morale boosters. Receiving my first filing confirmation by letter from the court with my name on it and the accompanying docket number 16-1682C was a great milestone. I made it in; my lawsuit was born! I was a citizen in the greatest country on earth, where the common man could redress his government on his own, without a lawyer, for grievances suffered. Justice was a distant, flickering light in the cloud-covered darkness of the mountain. Great struggles to understand persisted, however, and it was still very tempting to walk away. Did I need the self-inflicted headaches? In my heart, at times I wanted to toss the whole stinking ordeal, go back to my studio, and paint beautiful pictures, leaving the corruption to the corrupt. That is probably what most people do when staring up the side of Mount Justlaw. But if I did not speak up, then I would join the ranks of who knows how many before me who had been silenced and never spoken up. Thank God, the will to persevere remained. I just needed to keep going and get to the top.

It was evident that not everyone succeeded in ascending the mountain of justice, as I climbed over the bones of others who had tried and failed. I became acutely aware of the masses who had been denied justice in this world. Nevertheless, I rejoiced, confident in knowing that in the end, no one gets away with anything on this earth. All people, rich and poor alike, will one day stand accountable.

Not everyone could venture up that dark, shadowy mountain alone, and not everyone had the means (myself included) to hire costly expert mountain climbers to guide them to the top. But some had the will. I had the will.

As time passed, I learned enough that I became confident at mountain climbing. Over the next three years, my skills greatly increased, as it would take me that long to climb Mount Justlaw. I was to learn many stories of injustice that would deeply disturb me. Also, stories of remarkable triumphs of justice that would transform my life and my thinking, deepening my appreciation for my new country.

The law language, legal concepts, and terms had to be figured out and learned. But learning the ins and outs of how the federal court system worked and all of the particulars of the Federal Rules of Civil Procedure and the particular rules for each particular court were challenges on top of the monumental challenge of just understanding the law.

Placing my boot on the stone ledge in front of me, I pulled myself upwards. My ascent of the formidable Mount Justlaw had begun.

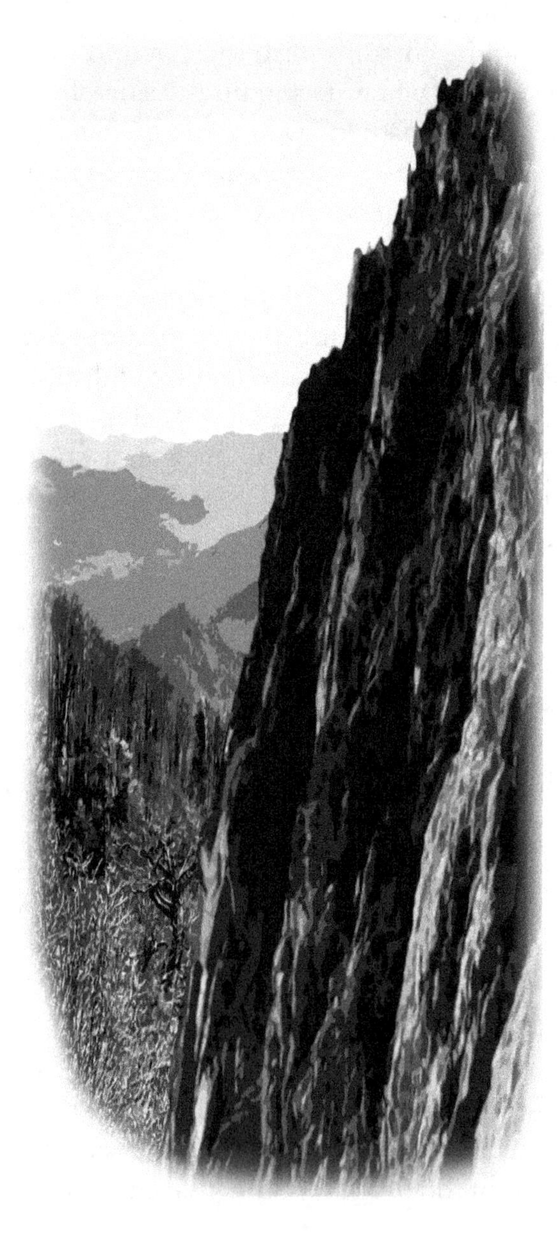

Chapter Twenty-Eight

O FLICKERING LIGHT OF CRASHING HOPE

AT FIRST, MOUNTAIN CLIMBING WASN'T AS BAD AS I THOUGHT IT would be. But then the steady rhythm of my initial ascent ground to a halt. Entering the federal court system slowed me to the court system's clogged-up pace. All of a sudden, it felt like I was crawling up the mountain. There was no way to jump to the front of the line, and time waited for no man. Scrambling frantically, I continued my research, discovering to my delight that I could try filing for an "injunction," or even a "motion for an expedited hearing." That was a motion I could file with the court, appealing for an emergency intervention, suspending the actions of the Smithsonian and its director because of the fast-approaching inauguration. Yes! There was still a chance.

Wrong! Thinking I could make up for lost time by scampering up that perilous-looking shortcut was a pipe dream. I did not have the skills necessary for that endeavor. A lawyer might have pulled those strings, filed the correct motion, and perhaps caused an intervention. Not me though—I was holding on by my fingernails. At that time, I needed to just survive and remain on the mountain.

Like the ocean's rising tide washing away a boy's sandcastle, the days vanished, and my hopes of displaying my portrait as the capstone of an incredible political and artistic journey faded. My participation in the arts, paying tribute to the historic event and the historic candidate Donald Trump in the People's Gallery was shut down. Could I find a place elsewhere in D.C. to exhibit my painting—perhaps right next door to the Smithsonian? Maybe stand on a wall once again? No. I was angry, and I was discouraged.

To make matters worse, I did not receive an invitation to the inauguration. Others I knew who had been active in helping get Trump elected did receive their invitations and were jubilantly posting them on Facebook. The campaign had my information, but for some reason I was not invited. Going to Washington without an invitation was not going to happen, especially without my painting. It was too much of an effort in my discouraged and injured state of mind. Thus, I purposely scheduled an art delivery for the week of January 20, 2017, in Chicago. I had sold a fourteen-foot painting titled "Intelligent Design" to a spine surgeon who wanted the painting to display for his upcoming party. After an initial shipping fiasco damaging the painting, it was returned to me, lying flat on the bed of the truck with crates piled on top of it. I repaired the painting and drove it out to Chicago myself in a sixteen-foot box truck. This trip was very encouraging, and it paid well, easing my profound disappointment and replenishing my exhausted wallet. You see, someone somewhere wanted to show my art, O sniveling, pity-pouting, and quivering bottom lip.

For whatever reason—maybe just plain disorganization (as was rumored within the Trump campaign)—I eventually did receive my invitation to President-elect Trump's inauguration. It arrived on January 23, 2017.

There was no time to mope in my pool of wallow. The challenge of learning the mountain-climbing ropes drove me day and night, consuming my attention. My only hope was up Mount Justlaw. I had to learn fast or fail. Rereading what I had just filed with the court and simultaneously researching online, I noticed deficiencies in my filings, causing me to refine my arguments. So I motioned the court, requesting to amend my claims, which motion was granted.

Deep in my gut, I knew that I was on to something about the Smithsonian. But, at that early stage of the game, I was still barely hanging on. And yet, I could perceive through the dense fog that something significant had happened, magnifying the Smithsonian mystery—that something there was in error, even upside down. Yet, I could not put my finger on it or express it in words because I did not know the words.

The fog began to clear once I discovered the components of that mystery. To my surprise, I learned that the Smithsonian Institution is only a public trust and nothing more—in other words, not a federal agency. I discovered that although the Smithsonian is simply a trust, it is believed by most people to be something else, causing the Smithsonian mystery. Yes, because the federal government established the trust and is the trustee, and because it is run by federal appointees and employees, it had become an institutional enigma. Had I, through my interactions with the Smithsonian officials, inadvertently waded into something that in the end would eclipse even the specific legal issues related to my painting?

As the Smithsonian mystery began to loom over my lawsuit, all of a sudden I realized that the section of mountain I was climbing had become precariously narrow, coming at last to an untraversable end. I was in the wrong court! Yep, I had filed my lawsuit in the wrong federal court. That caused me to panic, not knowing if my error would be catastrophic. Was I about to fall off the mountain? Did I get a second shot against the Smithsonian? I wondered. I glanced across the gorge at the pathway I should have been on— how in the world would I get over there?

Back to the books (or Google) was the answer, searching for how to fix my dilemma. Aha! Get the judge to transfer my case from the U.S. Court of Federal Claims to the correct court, the District Court for the District of Columbia, with a motion to the court. Was my opponent at law aware of my blunder and would they be able to take advantage and terminate my suit?

U.S. Attorney Amanda Tantum had my briefs and drafted the Department of Justice's response. Yes, Mount Justlaw suddenly became all the more ominous as I learned that none other than the United States Department of Justice was the legal organization in charge of defending the Smithsonian. My adversary at law was no longer the largest museum complex in the world; the Smithsonian was defended by the most powerful government-run law firm in the world. A shuddering and shrinking sensation gripped me as I clung like an ant to the side of Mount Justlaw, and the climb grew darker, steeper, and more frightening.

It was up to Judge Victor J. Wolski to decide whether to transfer my case. He would have to scrutinize my claims in the light of the law. If he found my lawsuit frivolous, incoherent, or baseless, would he order the transfer? That would be like sending a crate of rotten fish to a neighbor. I held my breath as my hopes of redress flickered.

Chapter Twenty-Nine

HIGH-MOUNTAIN ECSTASY

AT THE END OF MY LENGTHY GRAVEL DRIVEWAY, MY MAILBOX stood waiting. Two or three times a day, it would find me peering inside. Federal court orders come only by mail to pro se litigants. Pro se litigants like me, along with thousands of self-represented criminals within the federal prison system, are not allowed into the online federal court system. I imagine this is for security reasons, just in case one presses the wrong button and deletes everything—or at worst, hacks the system.

My climb had come to a standstill. Being stalled in the darkness of a storm cloud at the impasse was intense while I anxiously awaited Wolski's order. Months had passed since I began my climb up Mount Justlaw. Spring was nearly over as June rolled in. The Elmira countryside was in full bloom, with summer only days away. A letter dated June 5, 2017, from the U.S. Court of Federal Claims finally arrived. It was early evening by the time I collected the mail. Sitting at the top of my driveway, I stared at the letter before tearing into the envelope. The two-page order was the first official legal opinion on my claims about what had transpired at the Smithsonian Institution. I did not even bother to read Judge Wolski's opinion at first, as the legal jargon was still intimidating; what I cared about was the order. I flipped the pages over to the end, where the order in bold letters was typed:

> Mister Raven's claims appear to have sufficient factual support—he has alleged specific instances of government actions, which could plausibly form a basis for relief....
>
> The plaintiff's motion to transfer this case to the United States District Court for the District of Columbia is GRANTED....
>
> IT IS SO ORDERED.[34]

For a moment, the storm clouds parted. Peering out from beneath my hood, the brilliant golden sunlight pierced through the darkness, illuminating the entire mountain and valley below. Stretching into the distance, the golden fields stroked by the gusting wind, the rolling hills, and the meandering rivers never looked so crisp and vibrant. Radiating with warmth, the sun's rays caressed my soul, and my weary frame straightened.

Judge Victor J. Wolski's order became one of the handful of moments of pure ecstasy that would come to me on Mount Justlaw. It was the type of moment that silences any nagging voices of doubt from within and without. That order was a shot in the arm right when I needed it. It gave me the energy to "keep on keepin' on" up that ominous mountain in front of me. Reading his order as I sat in my truck at sunset produced pure joy. I'll never forget that day. I was in the trial of my life, and up until that day, there had been no joy—only darkness, discouragement, and struggle. "Consider it all joy, my brethren, when you encounter various trials." The first chapter of the book of James sprang to mind with the admonition to persevere joyfully through hardships. By the grace of God, I persevered. I kept on, and when joy came, it was intoxicating. A tiny dose of judicial validation goes a long way in the pro se wilderness of the federal legal system. Scripture also says in the book of Proverbs, "Like apples of gold in settings of silver is a ruling rightly given" (Proverbs 25:11 NIV). Did I ever finally understand what that meant, after receiving Judge Wolski's order!

During those months, as the climb went on day after day, I would find myself at places where for a moment I thought I could see the summit through the clouds. Not being an experienced mountain climber, I would often get excited and tell my family I could see the summit, raising their hopes and mine. "It's ahead of me!" I would say to them, "I can see it. I am going to be there soon," only to rush through the clouds and find myself tumbling down the other side into another valley where the sun seldom shines.

Climbing up then falling down, appearing then vanishing behind the clouds, was the natural rhythm of the mountain and my experience of Mount Justlaw. Thankfully, my family put up with me on my odyssey. Family dinnertime became the whetting stone upon which I would sharpen my arguments. My ideas were tested in conversations and developed in the air in front of me. I needed a sounding board. My attentive teenage children and my dear wife sat there enduring their father and husband's figuring and fathoming. I spun every facet of the ever-increasingly complex legal issues daily in front of them. "You see it, you see it?" I would ask as they smiled and nodded politely in agreement. I apologized to them often, as at times it was very taxing and tedious for them— and remember, that continued for three years.

"Stare decisis" (precedent or preexisting legal decisions) is a big deal in law, as legal themes and rulings are constructed case upon case, on the backs of previous decisions. First-time cases that raise unresolved legal issues are rare, and the legal issues they present are harder to argue, as there are no direct precedents to stand on. My case was such a case. Although the key issues were not well-defined initially—since I did not know how to formulate my arguments correctly—they became crystal clear over time. Finding supporting cases was difficult, but when I did find them, it was beyond marvelous.

As my case entered into the U.S. District Court for the District of Columbia, I was assigned a new jurist—Judge Colleen Kollar

Kotelli, and a new case number, 17-cv-01240. Kotelli became famous as the presiding judge over the now-well-known Microsoft antitrust case and later as the presiding judge in the FISA (Foreign Intelligence Surveillance Act) court. That was the big leagues of law. Kotelli had dealt with Bill Gates and Saddam Hussein, and now she had to deal with yours truly! I felt like a tiny minnow swimming amongst giant killer whales and plenty of sharks. But boy was I impressed! Little old Julian Raven was swimming with all his might in the surging legal seas as the barely born American citizen who was about to have his case adjudicated by such a well-known and respected jurist.

… Not!

Chapter Thirty

SWAMPY AND SPOOKY

Just as I made the precarious maneuver of climbing across the gorge separating where I stood from where I should have been, high winds began battering me. Upon becoming aware that my filing with Judge Kotelli was deficient, I motioned to amend my arguments. That motion was granted. While correcting my work in the District Court for the District of Columbia, my case was transferred again—although within the same court—to the desk of an unknown rookie judge, Trevor N. McFadden.

The biting wind on the mountain continued to assail me. The setting sun had nearly disappeared, causing me to seek refuge in a nearby cave for the night. My well-insulated sleeping bag comforted me, pea-in-a-pod style. Surprisingly, there was excellent cell service on the mountain, allowing me to catch up on my reading. The wind still howled outside. Tightly zipped into my cocoon, I scrolled through McFadden's story, as the light from my phone illuminated my snug space for the night.

Judge McFadden was a Trump appointee—maybe that was more good news. Formerly a federal prosecutor at the Department of Justice, McFadden had sunk some pretty large and ugly mafia operations. It was impressive, but he had little experience dealing with free-speech issues and trust law. When I found out that he was from the same Department of Justice that was now defending the Smithsonian against me, I was left scratching my head. Mine was one of the first cases that he would decide as a federal judge, making me very concerned and causing me to wonder if I would get an accurate and fair ruling. Could McFadden take my pro se side against the DOJ if I was right? His conservative credentials were well established, giving me great confidence that anti-Trump bias would not shade his thinking. He had been a member of the Federalist Society for many years, which has produced many fine conservative judges. But did he have the stomach to overturn the applecart, throwing the beloved Smithsonian Institution, Chancellor John Roberts, etc., under the bus at such an early stage of his career as a judge? He was just thirty-eight years old at the time. His youth and inexperience on the bench caused me to wonder.

Washington, D.C., which some believe was built upon a swamp, is the seat of national and global power, the center of the American political and judicial world, and the home to virtually every major federal-government and law-enforcement agency. It is a city that, block after block, is mainly owned by the federal government, with one glaring exception. The federal courts are located a stone's throw from the sprawling Smithsonian Institution museum complex and down the street from the Department of Justice, the FBI, the National Archives, Congress, the White House, and the Supreme Court. So you see, it is a small, tightly knit town, where everybody knows somebody who is working for somebody or some agency but ultimately is working for "the feds."

The media gossip-and-leaking industry is a sprawling and insatiable enterprise in Washington, D.C. The city is also the ladder-climbing, flattery-gushing, and groveling capital of the world. It is a place where careers are cemented or destroyed, as the ever-circling federal gravy train slops its engorged load over the sides of its railway-wagon walls, to the drunken delight of its soiled and stained passengers. Yes, this federal font reminded me of the swollen nipples of the Capitoline Wolf who suckled the founders of Rome—except in American Gangnam style.

That was the context in which my lawsuit would be tried, an environment where influence, power, and prestige were golden, affecting everything—even the decisions of blind Lady Justice. In such a place, it is hard to imagine that those within it are *not* under pressure to comply with external forces that are constantly driving with a specific end in mind.

Could the young, rookie Judge McFadden see and hear the truth and rule accordingly, surrounded by such a cacophony of powerful and competing interests? Federal judges nominated by the president stick around for a long, long time—way longer than sitting presidents. So careful navigation would be required not just to endure as a judge but to ascend the judicial ladder. A judge's career in the federal court system is for life and can even end up with a lifelong appointment on the bench in the U.S. Supreme Court.

Would the rule of law prevail, or would the status quo derail the justice I was seeking? With what I had experienced already at the Smithsonian Institution, there seemed to be an aura of untouchability surrounding the mysterious place. Would that spell affect the judges in the federal courts? Washington, D.C., was, after all, a place of great intrigue, corruption, and murder. A place where ten thousand spies and spooks from all over the world are believed to operate. A place where men in dark trench coats, mirrored glasses, and fedora hats leave cryptic threats folded into newspapers dropped at your feet as you sit on a park bench eating lunch on the mall—a place where speeding vehicles with dark, tinted windows deliberately cut you off, swerving as if to hit you, sending you silent warnings.

Remember, rookie Judge McFadden was at the very green bottom of the federal judge's seniority ranking, while Smithsonian Chancellor John Roberts, a defendant in my case, was at the tippy-tippy top as chief justice. And that's not all. Adding to the concoction, Smithsonian Chancellor John Roberts was not only the chief justice of the U.S. Supreme Court, he was also head of the federal judicial branch of government, chairman of the Judicial Conference of the United States, supervisor of the Administrative Office of the United States Courts, and chairman of the Board of the Federal Judicial Center.

> Other duties include appointing two members of the Judiciary to the Commission on Executive, Legislative, and Judicial Salaries, reporting to Congress on changes in the Federal Rules of Criminal Procedure prescribed by the Supreme Court and, under the Foreign Intelligence Surveillance Act, appointing 11 federal judges to the Foreign Intelligence Surveillance Court.[35]

Basically, John Roberts was Trevor McFadden's daddy, judicially speaking. Being responsible for a controversial judicial decision early in your career could make you a pariah in Washington. Judicially tarnishing the prestige and status of the beloved Smithsonian Institution and its chancellor required a particular type of courageous individual. Would McFadden be that man? Would all of the stops be pulled out to maintain the Smithsonian's facade of prestige? Had the Smithsonian already been tarnished? Was it perpetually polished by D.C. bureaucrats determined to maintain the status quo?

The wind died down outside the cave, ushering in an eerie silence. Aching and bleary eyed, my head bobbed with fatigue while my yawning whisked me away into my dreams.

Chapter Thirty-One

EVOLUTION DEVOLUTION

I FOUND MYSELF WALKING THE IMMACULATE AND BEAUTIFULLY KEPT grounds of the Smithsonian Castle, wondering if the Smithsonian Institution had devolved into something unrecognizable from what its founding secretary and visionary, Joseph Henry, created during thirty-two years of his life. From the appearance of the gorgeous and luxurious gardens, everything looked amazing. Gazing up at Henry's dignified and commanding bronze statue standing in front of the Smithsonian Castle, Kim Sajet's smug voice interrupted and stung me again, leaving me shuddering and cupping my ears. The noble statue's influence had been reduced to that of an outdated curiosity, a glorified garden gnome, or a trellis upon which to cultivate ivy. A fall breeze whipped up the fallen leaves that tumbled down the well-manicured paths. Drawing closer to the statue, I could hear a faint whisper, the words of warning from an ancient holy text about honoring the righteous prophets, only to be betrayed by the corruption of their contemporary pseudo-disciples.

Those were different times when Joseph Henry walked the castle's gardens, when influences of a different kind weighed on the hearts and minds of people. Principled, virtuous, and spiritual influences produced a type of character that is deeply missed today. His sterling attributes caused Joseph Henry, first secretary of the Smithsonian Institution, to be eulogized like few others of his day. Professor Henry's funeral in itself was a remarkable testimony to that fact. It was attended by officials from every branch of government, as well as scientists, writers, diplomats, business leaders, professionals, and even the renowned General William Tecumseh Sherman. The assemblage of dignitaries, too long to list here, was so extensive that only a tiny number of the citizens and visitors could gain access to the church.[36]

Who was Joseph Henry? How did his life of service as a museum manager (and his death in 1878) impact so many people, causing such a distinguished funeral ceremony?

Secretary Henry's legacy stands in jarring contrast to that of Smithsonian Secretary Lawrence M. Small in our modern era in 2007, just as an example. Under the chancellorship of John Roberts, Secretary Small precipitated a major Smithsonian scandal, subverting its leadership and threatening its very existence. The scandal prompted an investigation into allegations of corruption and a "champagne lifestyle" that Senator Grassley of Iowa addressed directly in a scathing letter to Chancellor John Roberts.[37]

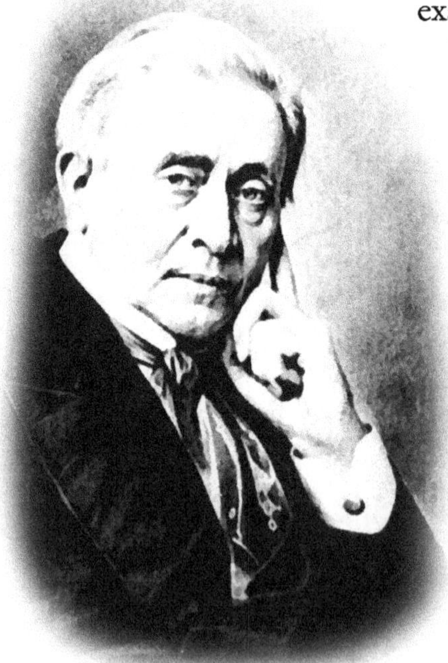

Joseph Henry (1797–1878)

Chapter Thirty-Two

SPARKLING BUBBLY CORRUPTION

Senator Chuck Grassley of Iowa had the character, guts, and platform, beyond the reach of Washington's pernicious influence, to directly rebuke Chancellor Roberts and the Board of Regents for turning a blind eye to the champagne lifestyle of Secretary Small. In his assessment of the handling of the corruption allegations and the general management of the Smithsonian Institution, Senator Grassley, in a lengthy eleven-page letter, slammed the Smithsonian Board of Regents under the chancellorship of John Roberts for its "anything-goes" culture.

Under the heading, "Bend the rules; Break the Rules; Change the Rules," Grassley hammered the chief justice, saying that

> instead of enforcing the rules, the Audit Committee and the Board of Regents change the rules to conform with the actions of the Secretary....
>
> To be blunt, I have been conducting reviews of tax-exempt organizations for a number of years, and the actions of the Smithsonian Board of Regents raise as many red flags as some

of the worst boards I have investigated. The American people expect and deserve much better.[38]

Now that alone, ladies and gentlemen, is an indictment that should fuel a Congressional-committee investigation and reformation of the Smithsonian Institution.

Since 2007, as a direct result of the report, Congresswoman Eleanor Holmes Norton, a representative for the District of Columbia, has dragged multiple bills through Congress—so frequently in fact, that it would seem a yearly festival could have been created in her honor for her persistent yet futile efforts. Through Congress, Holmes Norton's multiple Smithsonian modernization bills have attempted to assist the People in wresting control from the Board of Regents (under John Roberts) and reforming it.

Even the self-prescribed internal colonoscopy (the basis for Holmes Norton's bills), which the Board of Regents ordered to be performed upon itself, was an eloquent, well-informed, well-documented diagnosis of the Smithsonian's sickly condition. But it fizzled. The Independent Review Committee's report was a thoroughly engaging read, a job well done, and nothing more—since nothing has changed. The IRC Report became another historic document to be granted sacred space on the online Smithsonian Historic Archive, inadvertently and partially fulfilling Smithson's will, since the 392-page report provided "an increase in knowledge." The "diffusion" part of the will, however, where the public is supposed to learn of the corruption scandals through public record, is another Smithsonian story all its own.

Eminent nonprofit experts (the Honorable Charles A. Bowsher, the Honorable Stephen D. Potts, and A. W. "Pete" Smith Jr.) were hired to evaluate the leadership crisis at the Smithsonian. In their report, they said, "There was a clear indication that the Secretary and those whom he selected deemed themselves outside the Smithsonian's otherwise recognized ethics standards."[39] Even after reviewing the role of KPMG (Klynveld Peat Marwick Goerdeler), an outside firm that audited the Smithsonian for thirteen years, the investigation determined that while the Smithsonian agreed with the recommendations, "it apparently took limited action to develop the policies and procedures manual."[40]

Even the Office of the Inspector General (the last line of internal institutional accountability) came up short. The IRC investigation stated, "The OIG performed no audits or investigations of any matters"[41] that related at that time to the ongoing leadership crisis for six years. The investigators said they were "surprised." This is not surprising—this is shocking.

A decade later, I encountered the same prevailing systemic cultural beliefs and practices. The Smithsonian Office of the Inspector General is the same office to which I appealed along the way, and from which I never received replies to any of my letters requesting an investigation.

The IRC Report, consisting of over three hundred pages of investigative research into the corruption allegations, reports, and documentation relating to the events surrounding the crisis of leadership and the champagne lifestyle of Secretary Small, exposes the systemic rot in the Smithsonian. The IRC Report clearly defines the fiduciary duties incumbent on the secretary, regents, and director:

> The duty of loyalty requires a director to act in the interest of the entity rather than in the personal interest of the director.... More importantly, the duty of loyalty encompasses an obligation of directors and key employees with financial or other decision-making authority to avoid conflicts of interest. For a director, a violation of this duty may result in personal liability for a breach of fiduciary duty....
>
> These duties of care and loyalty are heightened for the Regents due to their status as trustees of the Smithsonian trust. In short, Regents owe the highest possible fiduciary duty to the Smithsonian and the American people.[42]

Maybe I was confused? Were there two Smithsonian Institutions? It seemed that I must have applied to the wrong Smithsonian. It was mind bending and bizarre to read these accounts, having gone through the treatment I suffered. I was not the first to witness the system's complete failure under the Board of Regents and Chancellor John Roberts.

Undoubtedly, there were many factors contributing to the ongoing mystery. The impotence of every self-correcting internal effort only perpetuated the impenetrable shield of untouchability. Holmes Norton and Grassley's efforts from both the Senate and the House, failing year after year, further elevated the impregnable walls against public accountability. Surely, there had to be a way to compel institutional compliance, since it also came to light that vast amounts of taxpayer dollars were being funneled into the Smithsonian coffers.

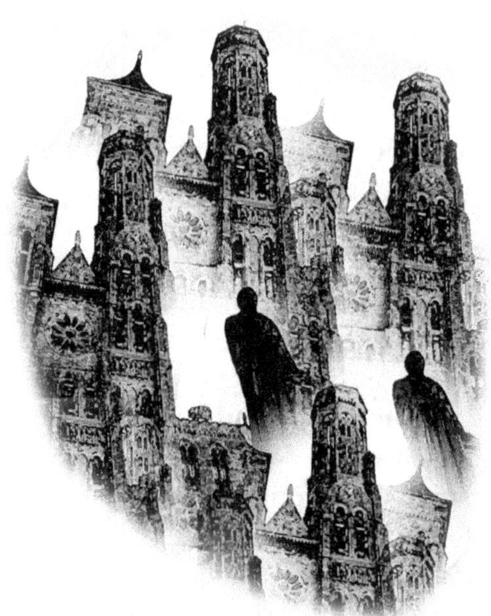

Smithsonians

Chapter Thirty-Three

THE TALE OF TWO SMITHSONIANS

IT WAS THE DUTY OF LOYALTY—IT WAS THE BETRAYAL OF THAT duty. It was the trust—it was the breach of trust. It was the will— it was the violation of the will. It was the law—it was the breaking of the law. It was the appeal—it was the denial of the appeal. It was a public trust—it was not a public trust. It was the duty to care—it was the refusal to care. It was the truth—it was the lie. It was the tale of two Smithsonians. While editing this chapter and after I already titled it "The Tale of Two Smithsonians," I found another Smithsonian report from 1977. That report dealt with the same entity-confusion issues at the heart of the mystery. The report by Phillip Samuel Hughes (which I shall discuss later) states on page 7: "Theories have been advanced…that there are two Smithsonians, a 'private' and a Federal."[43] You see, it was not my imagination.

The Smithsonian Institution was caught in the age-old dilemma of living by the adage, "Do as I say and not as I do." Their website is currently replete with updated, gilded versions of lengthy statements of lofty values and detailed codes of ethics.[44] Yet, when one holds those up against the conduct carried out by its directors—and regents in my case—they turn a blind eye, instead choosing to violate every binding law, standard, and ethic applicable to the Smithsonian Institution. No one in 1977 could enforce the law against the Smithsonian, not even themselves.

The power of the perception of untainted prestige in the public's eye was maintained at all costs at the Smithsonian. Lawlessness was excused to obfuscate any evidence of corruption that could besmirch the carefully curated money-generating facade. The Smithsonian had become a walled city of impenetrable legal confusion cloaked in secrecy, either by design or by default.

And just when you thought that the news of the scandals was getting thin, another scandal belched to the surface of this bubbling and stinking swamp (imagine for a moment all the secret scandals that do not make it to the surface). Kathryn Tully from *Forbes* magazine, on July 13, 2015, shed light on the schizophrenia, writing the following:

> More organizations are distancing themselves from Bill Cosby since court documents were unsealed last week in which the entertainer admitted under oath that he had obtained quaaludes [methaqualone] to give to women with whom he wanted to have sex....
> Not the Smithsonian, though.[45]

Yes, as hard as it has been to stomach the stench we have endured so far, convicted and released felon and serial rapist Bill Cosby (who at the time was under federal investigation and was still to be convicted) could peddle his powerful celebrity and wealth influence over the ever-so-eager Smithsonian Institution's vortex of insatiable lust for celebrity copulation and corruption.

Chapter Thirty-Four

AMERICA'S WORST DAD

CHARMING DR. HUXTABLE (AKA BILL COSBY) AND HIS DEAR WIFE Camille O., who coincidentally sat on the board at the Smithsonian Museum of African American History and Culture, hatched a scheme. Hand in hand, Bill and Camille donated, out of the goodness of their hearts, $716,000 to the museum. Camille O. casually suggested an exhibition of the Cosbys' vast African-art collection. The show would, of course, serve to promote those poor, starving, and once-unknown artists, according to the Smithsonian's Under Secretary for art, history, and culture at the time (remember the Smithsonian Museum that initially barred any mention of the existence of Justice Clarance Thomas but did not fail to mention his accuser Anita Hill? That one![46]), who was none other than our old friend Dr. Richard Kurin. Kurin, once again center stage as chief scandal coordinator, rapidly told the Associated Press[47] the exhibit was "not about the life and career of Bill Cosby. It's about the artists."

Now hold on a second, Dr. Richard Kurin—the same Dr. Richard Kurin appointed by the Smithsonian Board of Regents to hear my bleeding-artist's appeal? An appeal that detailed the egregious treatment I endured at the hands of Director Kim Sajet, and yet Kurin dismissed my accusations against her conduct as if they did not even happen? That Dr. Richard Kurin who concurred with Sajet's arbitrary and lawless rejection of my painting? That Dr. Richard Kurin who slammed the door to the Smithsonian in my face and refused to answer my follow-up letter? That same Dr. Richard Kurin was all about caring for artists?

According to the *Hollywood Reporter* article from July 13, 2015:

> Noah Kupferman, an art market expert at Shapiro Auctions who has taught about the economics of fine art…said, "It just raises a little eyebrow that a trustee of a museum is lending (her) own collection,…and the exhibition is highlighting works…by less well-known artists whose work is considered by some to be undervalued…. Repositioning these artists' works as suddenly important could have significant positive effect on their economic value."[48]

Who would've thought that such a scheme to ride on the back of the famous and prestigious American taxpayer-funded nonprofit public trust could possibly be the brainchild of America's best dad? It was a master class in premeditated calculus, since their hyper-generous $716,000 donation, which greased the skids of access (paying for the whole exhibit), would be a drop in the bucket, especially when compared to the Smithsonian-stamped exhibit, which would inflate the value of their whopping sixty-two paintings on show. Was it preposterous even to think that the accused rapist could have devised such a scheme? Not so much, really, since Cosby was an artist himself—though of a different kind.

Cosby's art involved raping his victims with their consent. Andrea Constand testified[49] that, Cosby "passed her three blue pills," saying they were "friends to help you relax"—pills she freely took, which made her so weak and limp "that she could not push him away." Such was Cosby's persuasive skill level and refined artistic technique.

According to the same *Hollywood Reporter* article, Dr. Richard Kurin, who had worked at the Smithsonian "for decades," continued to rush to the defense of the museum and its justification for holding the exhibit. "'We certainly don't condone his behavior,' Kurin said. 'We're just as deeply disturbed and disappointed as I think everybody else. But it's not about Mr. Cosby. This is an art exhibit.'"[50]

Well, of course, Dr. Kurin, anything you say, Sir!

It is easy to get bogged down in the salacious details of the Smithsonian scandals, and we are by no means done with those. But feeling somewhat defiled after Cosby's and Kurin's scheme, a cleansing is in order. And what better way to sanitize the mind and spirit than with a true story of dedication, integrity, and virtue?

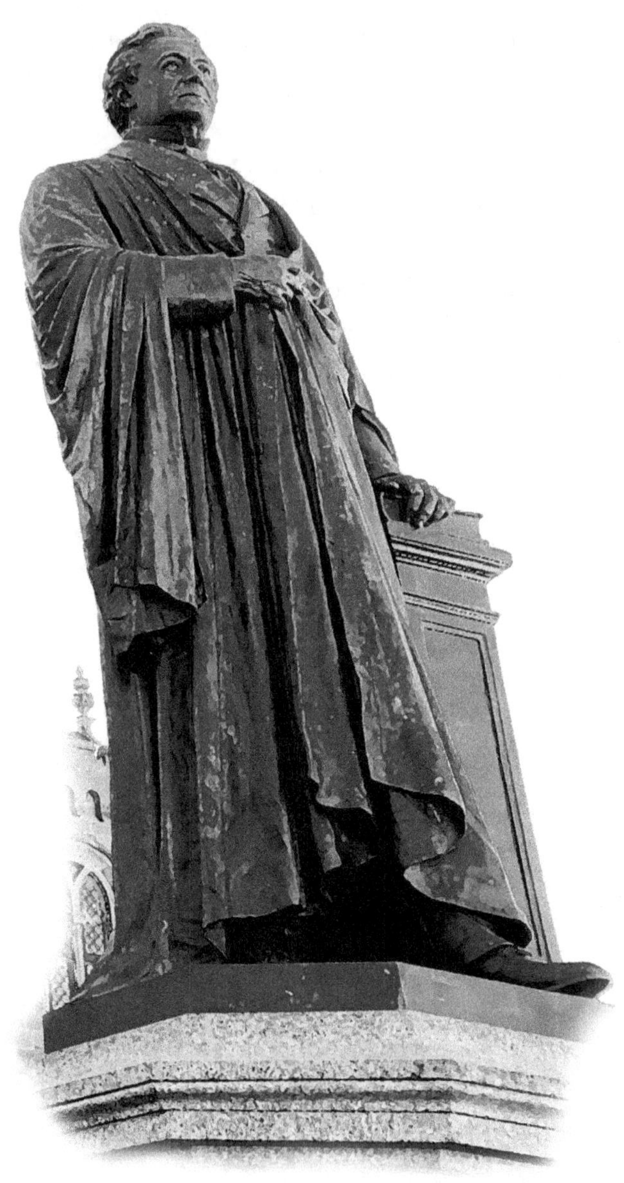

The Father of American Science, Joseph Henry

Chapter Thirty-Five

THE FATHER OF AMERICAN SCIENCE

AT DEATH, A PERSON'S LIFE IS LEFT TO THE LIVING TO DEFINE. Some lives require careful summations to find and highlight the aspects of that life that are worth remembering. Other lives leave legacies that speak for themselves. The living are left to catalog those exploits for the blessing and benefit of posterity. The eulogies for the Father of American Science, the first Smithsonian Secretary, Joseph Henry, are such a treasure. Professor Henry's life is a much-needed source of refreshment, strengthening the resolve to continue this rotten autopsy.

The Reverend Dod now helps us cross over into that place of the sublime and the ineffable:

> Into the kingdom of nature he entered as a little child, and she laid bare her secrets before him; she opened the leaves of her wonderful book, and he read therein, and told us some of her most marvelous secrets, which others had but dimly guessed.
>
> So also into the kingdom of heaven he entered as a little child, and in the same simplicity and sincerity of faith with which he had accepted the truths of nature, he received the word of God.[51]

Without a doubt, people deeply loved Smithsonian Secretary Joseph Henry. After reading the soul-stirring eulogies, which bring you to tears of longing for such character to be once again cherished and celebrated sea to sea in our illustrious institutions, one cannot but come away with a singular picture of the man Joseph Henry. Neither his scientific abilities nor his genius, his intellect nor his stewardship of the Smithsonian, nor any of the other positions that he once held, made him so beloved. And make no mistake, those elements were always undeniable in his life. However, front and center was his

> purity, simplicity, benevolence!… He was simple as a child, without folds, without dissimulation, without guile. He was not smart, as some men count smartness. Neither was his Savior…. His mind was the crystal depths of our Northern lakes, not the noisy course of the shallow and frothy river.[52]

Ahhh, how wonderfully invigorating and restorative, reestablishing faith in humanity! Joseph Henry's character illustrated something specific about American scientific identity, which is often mocked by academic elites. There is a great divide between the cold, immoral, arrogant haughtiness of godless academics and the gentle, humble, and guileless character of those brilliant minds who have bowed throughout history in reverence to and confession of nature's Great Designer and Creator.

This conflict and divide, especially in the scientific world in Henry's time, was the beginning of the war on the Christian faith and God. The war has brought us today's atheist apologists, in the likes of Richard Dawkins, Sam Harris, and the late Christopher Hitchens, as well as the staggering moral and spiritual decline of our sophisticated, scientific, and technological age. Darwin's *On the Origin of Species*, published in 1859, was about to flood the European scientific community during Joseph Henry's tenure at the Smithsonian, extinguishing many fires of faith and eventually washing up on American shores.

Reverend Samuel Dod spoke of this war on the Christian faith and God in his eulogy of Joseph Henry:

There are some who, in these days, tell us that if a man believes in God as his maker, in Christ as his redeemer, in the Holy Spirit as his sanctifier, and in the word of God as the guide for his life, he is no more to be ranked among scientific men, nor fit to be trusted as a student of nature. Where then shall we place this father of American Science? Who that vaunts his skeptical conjectures before the world today, as the badge of his scientific acumen and liberty of thought, can show so wide, and free, and fair a record of high scientific and beneficent work for his day and generation, as this avowed Christian philosopher?[53]

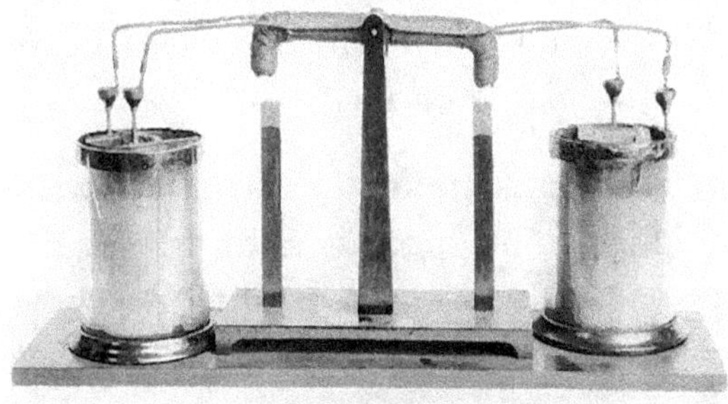

Oscillating Beam Motor, Joseph Henry

Joseph Henry and Michael Faraday are the founding fathers of the electrical industry and electrical technology. Electric motors, generators, transformers, radio and the telegraph all function on electromagnetic principles discovered by these men who worked on opposite sides of the Atlantic. Henry not only pioneered electrical technology almost 50 years before Thomas Edison, but led the Smithsonian, National Academy of Science and occupied important positions such as President Lincoln's science advisor.[54]

Fast-forward to an evolutionary and free-speech scandal at the Smithsonian Museum of Natural History involving Dr. Richard Sternberg in 2005 (that will come up later), and you will be left wondering what the modern Smithsonian would have done to the Honorable Joseph Henry. The Committee on Government Reform Staff Report from 2006 in the U.S. House of Representatives declared about the Smithsonian actions:

> Given the attitudes expressed in these emails, scientists who are known to be skeptical of Darwinian theory, whatever their qualifications or research record, cannot expect to receive equal treatment or consideration by [Smithsonian] NMNH officials. As a taxpayer-funded institution, such blatant discrimination against otherwise qualified individuals based on their outside views and activities raises serious free speech and civil rights concerns.... Some [Smithsonian] NMNH officials apparently believe that they have the right to use their official positions to punish scientists who in their outside activities express skepticism toward Darwinian theory.[55]

Raising one of the fundamental issues in my lawsuit, the Reform Staff Report weighed in on specifics about the Smithsonian Institution's actions that were directly related to the First Amendment's free-speech clause. Joseph Henry lived in a scientific era when faith in God and science were compatible, and yet the tide had begun to turn. But what Dr. Sternberg's case and my own reveal is that the Institution that existed for the increase and diffusion of knowledge has become hostile toward certain types of knowledge that are now forbidden.

And rightly did the Reform Staff Report investigate the free-speech scandal, because of the millions of taxpayer dollars that were being used to fund the Smithsonian. As I read the eulogies delivered at Joseph Henry's funeral, I thought to myself, "There is no way on earth that the atheistic, left-leaning Smithsonian has *not* in some way tried to tear down the stature and statue of Joseph Henry, 'the Christian'." Have they?

Chapter Thirty-Six

LEFT WITHOUT REDEMPTION

Sure enough, my research uncovered an article on the Smithsonian website, "Joseph Henry, Scientist and Christian," by Albert E. Moyer, in which we find the takedown:

> But as I dug still deeper into the historical record, I discovered that, of course, Henry was not too good to be true. As might be expected, the archives revealed a more fallible, if not flawed, Henry.[56]

Moyer's revelations are probably all accurate and true. His digging in the Smithsonian dirt uncovered that Joseph Henry was a man like all men, born in sin and prone to weakness and failure even against his best efforts to be otherwise. What a surprise! That is precisely why Joseph Henry needed a savior, to save himself from his fallibility and flaws. This is what was repeated in Henry's eulogies—that Joseph Henry was a humble man, in that he recognized his need for the Savior. And this is the glorious difference between people of faith and unbelievers—that is, the humility to admit one's flawed and fallible condition by confessing one's need for a savior.

Unbelief and a lack of redemptive themes prevail in leftist and elitist ideology, although not always married to hard-core atheism (but apparently so under today's Smithsonian banner). Redemption and God have no place in the leftist worldview. Today's self-righteous "wokeists" and cancel-culture proponents are similar to the new atheists in their dogmatic hostility and intolerance toward Biblical faith in God and morality. This intolerance has poisoned American institutions, creating a hostile environment toward people of faith and conservative Biblical values. The fields of science and the arts are examples in the Smithsonian of this hostility today, and Moyer's takedown is an example from the nineties of digging up a man's bones in search of his crimes of the past to delegitimize his influence in the present.

Leftists these days think that anyone who has not arrived suddenly, at birth, at their mandated standards on a potpourri of causes—especially sexuality, race relations, and socialistic policies—cannot be redeemed from their past sins and indiscretions. They ignore the fact that Jesus Christ dealt with these issues two millennia ago. Christ bludgeoned many societal sins, including racism, by teaching people to love their neighbor as themselves and to forgive as God forgives. But leftists, in their Bible-free system, cannot help but stray into the absurd with their ultrasensitivity consciousness, microaggression preventions, safe spaces, genderlessness, multi-pansexuality, and socialist wokeness campaigns, etc. Some of their social band-aids are external mechanisms aimed at curtailing humanity's same old inner sinful diseases, which they despise, while others are aimed at unshackling their preferred sinful cravings. No one in history is spared from today's wokeists, who scrutinize people's pasts for wokeness failures. No one's personal history can be tolerated by these ultra-"tolerant" wokeists if it is discovered that someone—me, you, or anybody, way back when or whenever—had some whiff of "failing." According to their arbitrary manual of wokery, if the slightest indiscretion is discovered, or even a hint of an accusation of one, you are eternally canceled. I wonder if Moyer would have argued for canceling Joseph Henry back in the day at the discovery of his fallibilities and flaws? Considering that Moyer wrote a book on the life of Joseph Henry the scientist, in which he documents Henry's scientific discoveries, that may be a stretch. Still, it is worth asking, since he obviously was eager to mar Henry's legacy of faith.

In American academic circles, those Euro-influenced elitist standards were well established long ago. They were first enshrined in the glorious, academic halls of anti-Christian, atheistic Europe, from which people of faith have fled over the centuries. Yet, some Americans today seem to crave the rarefied affirmation and perpetually yearn to return to taste the refined air of those prestigious European institutions. It reminds me of some great old story of deliverance from slavery and how freed slaves yearned to return to their land of slavery—strange! (Just read, for example, Numbers chapter 11 or Exodus 16 in the Bible.) Moyer ultimately scoffs at Henry's American successes because "he failed to attain even an honorary, foreign membership in either the Royal Society of London or the Paris Academy, the foremost scientific societies of the two countries with which he maintained strongest ties. Most British and French savants did not deem him another [Benjamin] Franklin."[57]

Moyer's unsurprising takedown, at its root, attacks the source of Henry's character—the source of his success—and that is Jesus Christ Himself:

> As his letters and other writings clearly show, Henry believed the rationale—believed that he was selflessly fulfilling a moral obligation. For decades, he had been placing duty and altruism at the core of his personal value system. This stance was an expression of, however, not merely his innate temperament or American culture's prevailing republican and Protestant values. The stance also had psychological shadings traceable to childhood traumas.
>
> The traumas, which Henry kept hushed most of his adult life, arose from a tragedy in his working-class family: his father's alcoholism and death due to delirium tremens. Henry emerged

from a troubled youth with a deep need for approval and affir-mation. But he masked public expressions of this egocentric side of his personality. Instead, he imposed on himself a regimen of service to others. Cloaking his personal desires, he consistently invoked what he perceived to be his moral duty as his motive for following a particular course of action—whether in professional or personal endeavors.

And lest any hint of self-fulfillment or self-gratification should surface publicly, he routinely offered self-abnegating reconstructions of the circumstances behind his actions. Thus, he repeatedly justified his acceptance of the Smithsonian sec-retaryship in terms of self-sacrificing duty to the nation and science rather than, as he unguardedly intimated to friends and relatives, increased salary and deserved recognition.

Moyer concludes:

To replace idealized images of Henry with historically based portrayals is not to demean his life and career. Instead, we start to fathom how a boy from a family of modest means in a nation of scant scientific resources attained national and international distinction in the esoteric field of natural philosophy.[58]

This elitist professor was perturbed because he could not fathom "modest" Joseph Henry's successful life; it did not add up. I imagine Henry's elevated bronze statue (which Moyer mentions in detail), his scientific discoveries, and the remarkable accolades and eulo-gies (also mentioned as the reason for the takedown) spoken after his death were too much to bear—after all, he was a Christian. Somehow, for Moyer, the discovery of Henry's administrative sins, shortcomings, and failures undermine Henry's successes. No, Sir! Henry's failures and successes were all part of a redeemed and sur-rendered life that glorified God as he lived and, in the end, glorified God in his death. It is God who raises people from "families of modest means" to impact the world for Christ. St. Paul, in the first chapter of the first book of Corinthians, explained this mystery when he said, "God chose things the world considers foolish in order to shame those who think they are wise. And he chose things that are powerless to shame those who are powerful" (NLT). God exalts the humble, something that professor Moyer obviously could neither fathom nor personally know. He would rather tear down Henry than celebrate him together with his faith, the source of his redemption and success. He had to do this because if he didn't, in the end, Moyer too would have to glorify God, becoming like Joseph Henry.

Militant atheists and leftist activists continually resist morality and ideas that they despise, tearing down faith and leaving a barren wasteland of immoral and valueless chaos in their wake. They have to rewrite everything or tear down even statues of Abraham Lincoln because they do not have any other options in their set of ideas, as the concept of redemption is foreign to them. History can serve as a tool from which we can learn, redeeming the past, changing the present, and charting a course for a better future through the lens of redemption. Not for the Left, though.

As for some of those statues in public places of honor that glorified Confederate generals, which represented slavery, racist hatred, and oppression, there is no doubt they had to go. Their stories should be accurately told in museums, where people can learn from the past and judge. But it is how we carry out those historic corrections in a civilized, democratic manner that expresses how people and society today have grown beyond that individual's sins of the past. Taking the uncivilized, undemocratic route, blinded by self-righteous rage, the lawless protesters have just morphed into another form of hatred. Was that what I too experienced at the hands of Smithsonian Director Kim Sajet?

We can choose to either learn from history through a redemptive worldview, in which the awareness of our sins, fallibilities, and flaws plays a part in interpreting the sins and failures of our history and its characters, or we can resist, erase, and tear down the history and the ideas that we despise. Being left without redemption, the Left's only option is to edit and revise history at their own peril, ensuring they themselves are then extremely likely to become the objects of the same searing scrutiny, and worse, to repeat the same old history.

The National Portrait Gallery of the Smithsonian Institution is a museum of history whose purpose is to increase and diffuse knowledge of the stories of historically significant Americans, through portraits. It might have functioned as one of the antidotes for our present maladies. Unfortunately, rather than being the antidote, the Smithsonian continues to purge forbidden ideas, silencing free speech. So much so, in fact, that its scandals, when layered on top of each other, resemble a very well-known story of revolutionary freedom that ended up in oppression.

ALL ARTISTS ARE EQUAL
BUT SOME ARTISTS ARE
MORE EQUAL THAN OTHERS

Chapter Thirty-Seven

SMITHSONIAN FARM

Senator Grassley's "Bend the Rules; Break the Rules; Change the Rules" experience with Chancellor Roberts and the Smithsonian Board of Regents identified a prevailing culture of corruption operating deep within the Smithsonian Institution. As my research increased, I scoured the Internet for related legal cases. I discovered stories that unsettled me by their eerie similarity to the old allegorical tale of farm animals that rebelled against their human masters.

One case in particular, involving the California Science Center, caused me to think of some of the animal characters in the revolution on the farm. Strangely, they were the same individuals that were involved in my case—from 2010, nearly seven years before my case. This was evidence that there was a hierarchy of individuals in the Smithsonian who had been in "the family" for a long time. They were calling the shots. They were neither the Smithsonian secretary nor Regent trustees, who came to resemble figureheads disconnected from the real power and operations of the machine.

Enter Linda St. Thomas, Smithsonian Institution Spokesperson. In the *Daily Caller* article relating my story, "Smithsonian Says 'No' To New York Artist's Trump Portrait,"[59] St. Thomas added Shakespeare's black snake's forked tongue, bat's fur, and a lizard's leg to the steaming brew hypnotically spinning in Sajet's cauldron of lies. "You don't apply to have portraits or artifacts taken into the Smithsonian," St. Thomas said, completely contradicting the written policy regarding the "rigorous selection process" and "careful consideration" given to artifacts submitted by the public to the museum. After that interview was published and I filed my lawsuit, the wording on the FAQ page of the Smithsonian website mysteriously changed. The key words that contradicted word for word what St. Thomas had said in the interview regarding the submission of art were redacted, removing Sajet and St. Thomas from legal jeopardy. This discovery was also documented in the *Washingtonian* article from August 2019.[60]

St. Thomas continued, "We had the original art work for that [Obama] poster. We had no paintings of him or other works. So we used that for the inaugural space…. In this case, in our collection, we had a photograph [i.e., apple-tossing Trump] of President-elect Trump and that's the one we're using."[61] (Notice the curious use of the plural pronoun *we*, indicating a role seemingly more significant than that of just a spokesperson for an organization.)

My stomach tightened as I reread those falsehoods that seemed to flow so easily off the tongue of St. Thomas. The Obama poster was donated to the Smithsonian in January 2009, just days before the inauguration, for the Obama inauguration, by D.C. superlobbyists Tony and Heather Podesta. Tony was the brother of John Podesta, Hillary Clinton's former campaign manager and then the transition-team co-chair at Obama's inauguration. Podesta even said on January 7 in a 2009 interview with the *Washington Post* that "it seemed like a historic moment for the country, and a chance to do something for art and Democrats."[62] Ok, there it is.

St. Thomas's claim that they had no "other works" depicting Obama at the time was another hissing lie. On December 16,

2008, in the *Smithsonian Magazine* online, this article was posted: "Barack Obama is the Man of the Moment at the Portrait Gallery,"[63] displaying a large photographic portrait of Barack Obama. Yes, the Obama photo was already on show a month before the inauguration, and it remained on show through 2009. In either case, It did not matter whether they had works prior to the inaugurations of Obama or Trump; what mattered was that the will of Smithson had to be fulfilled by an increase and diffusion of knowledge, not a regurgitation of the past. St. Thomas's rationale that the old Trump photo was used instead of my painting because it was in stock was absurd and a breach of trust.

Now, back to the California Science Center story, and who pops up? Linda St. Thomas, back in action as the mouthpiece now opposing the intelligent-design community. An anti-Darwin group, the American Freedom Alliance, rented the IMAX theatre to show a documentary called *Darwin's Dilemma*. As I read the story[64] of how St. Thomas zealously drove to shut down the showing of *Darwin's Dilemma* at the Smithsonian affiliate institution with a cease-and-desist order—forbidding any notion of the Smithsonian having any association with intelligent design—a vision of Orwell's squealing propagandist pig rushed through my mind. St. Thomas the Squealer could not fit the part more perfectly; it was as uncanny as it was haunting.

Smithsonian Museum Affiliate Director Harold Closter, the same Harold Closter with whom I'd filed a complaint against the Rockwell Museum in Corning, New York, also was part of the Science Center story. He fit Boxer's role on the farm—the cart horse, dedicated and loyal to the cause. Interestingly, once again it is none other than Dr. Richard Kurin who enters the scene. Kurin was always the go-to guy who called the shots, who had been in the Smithsonian for "decades." The ever-changing Smithsonian secretary was obviously busy raising money somewhere.

According to the report, when the Smithsonian Institution pressured the California Science Center to cancel the American Freedom Alliance's contract to use their IMAX theater to show the documentary *Darwin's Dilemma*, it was Dr. Richard Kurin whom Harold Closter tried to reassure that the California Science Center was still anti-intelligent design.[65] That demonstrated that Kurin, too, had a perfect role on Smithsonian Farm—that of Napoleon, the tyrannical bully. Let's see who else was on Smithsonian Farm? You can't have a real *Animal Farm* without tyranny, intrigue, false accusations, paranoia, and ultimately assassinations—let's see some of that too!

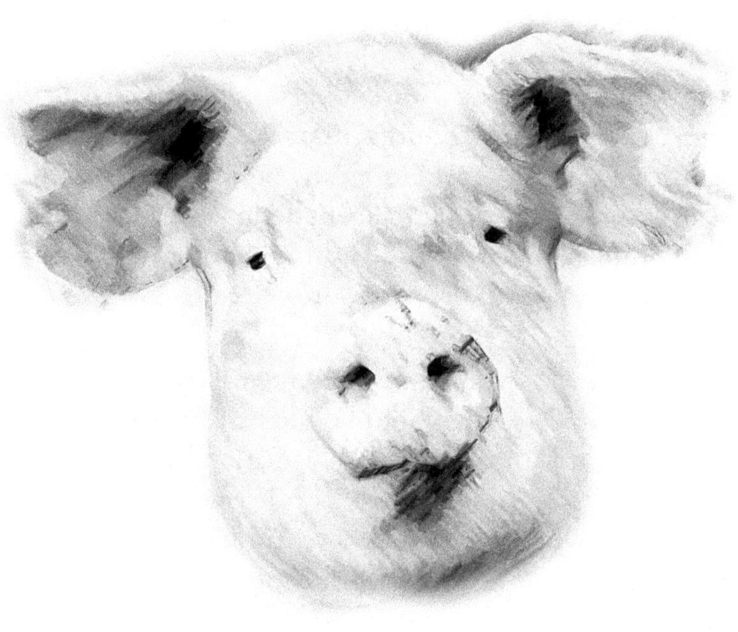

Chapter Thirty-Eight

MICRO MURDER

THE INSPIRATION BEHIND THE 2008 DOCUMENTARY, *EXPELLED, No Intelligence Allowed*, by actor and economist Ben Stein, was the vindictive, anti-intelligent-design, anti-Christian, and anti-conservative politics of personal destruction within the Smithsonian Institution. In his own words from his website, Dr. Richard Sternberg, who holds a Ph.D. in microbiology, said:

In 2004, in my capacity as editor of The Proceedings of the Biological Society of Washington, I authorized "The Origin of Biological Information and the Higher Taxonomic Categories" by Dr. Stephen Meyer to be published in the journal after passing peer-review. Because Dr. Meyer's article presented scientific evidence for intelligent design in biology, I faced retaliation, defamation, harassment, and a hostile work environment at the Smithsonian's National Museum of Natural History that was designed to force me out as a Research Associate there. These actions were taken by federal government employees acting in concert with an outside advocacy group, the National Center for Science Education. Efforts were also made to get me fired from my job as a staff scientist at the National Center for Bio-technology Information. Subsequently, there were two federal investigations of my mistreatment, one by the U.S. Office of Special Counsel in 2005, and the other by subcommittee staff of the U.S. House Committee on Government Reform in 2006. Both investigations unearthed clear evidence that my rights had been repeatedly violated. Because there has been so much misinformation spread about what actually happened to me, I have decided to make available the relevant documents here for those who would like to know the truth.[66]

I encourage you to go and read all of the documents on his website to get a fuller picture of the institutional corruption responsible for the destruction of Dr. Sternberg's career. The Smithsonian Institution eventually investigated, once the smoke had cleared, and discovered that Dr. Sternberg had done nothing wrong. Yet simultaneously, they ignored all of the wrongdoings that had been done to him. They never apologized, never compensated him, or any such thing. And once again, the same anti-God, viscious intolerance was unleashed upon this faithful steward who was just doing his job, fulfilling the will of Smithson by increasing and diffusing knowledge, and who in fact had followed all of the protocols and procedures for publishing peer-reviewed articles.

In the U.S. House Committee on Government Reform, from December 2006, in a staff report[67] prepared for Congressman Mark Souder, the conclusive evidence was laid bare, pointing the finger of justice once again in the face of the Smithsonian Institution. Citing the U.S. Office of Special Counsel's investigation into Sternberg's claims by Attorney James McVay, the report highlighted the laundry list of Smithsonian crimes. Not only are the crimes spelled out in black and white, but the same old systemic putrefaction that persists till this day was revealed:

The staff investigation has uncovered compelling evidence that Dr. Sternberg's civil and constitutional rights were violated by Smithsonian officials. Moreover, the agency's top officials—Secretary Lawrence Small and Deputy Secretary Sheila Burke—have shown themselves completely unwilling to rectify the wrongs that were done or even to genuinely investigate the wrongdoing.... The failure of Small and Burke to take any action against such discrimination raises serious questions about the Smithsonian's willingness to protect the free speech and civil rights of scientists who may hold dissenting views on topics such as biological evolution.[68]

In a letter from Senator Rick Santorum and Congressman Mark Souder addressed to Secretary Small and his assistant, Secretary Sheila Burke, on April 7, 2006, they waste no time in getting to the crux of the matter:

> We have read a copy of the letter, however, and are extremely disappointed with the Smithsonian Institution's bureaucratic stonewalling and lack of responsiveness in correcting what were clear actions of hostility and discrimination against Dr. Sternberg for his scientific viewpoints. It is apparent to us that the Smithsonian is guided by an authoritarian ideology that suppresses free scientific inquiry and intellectual curiosity that are so essential....
>
> The failure of the Smithsonian to take this matter seriously— as demonstrated by your letter to Dr. Sternberg—heightens our concern about the pattern of bias and discrimination we have observed at the Smithsonian....
>
> Finally, we find it unbelievable that you continue to ignore the findings of the Office of Special Counsel in its "pre-closure" letter to Dr. Sternberg.[69]

Attorney for the U.S. Office of Special Counsel, James McVay, who initially investigated Sternberg's claims, also ran into the Smithsonian's mysterious legal structure that blocked the OSC from obtaining documents from the Smithsonian via the Freedom of Information Act and even blocked them from cooperating:

During our initial investigations, OSC has been able to find support for many of your allegations. However, the SI is now refusing to cooperate with our investigation. OSC is not able to take statements and receive further paper discovery that would allow for final conclusions. The SI may in fact maintain documents that place our current information in a different context.[70]

Notice that the United States Office of Special Counsel in Washington, D.C., was unable to "take statements and receive further paper discovery." They could not even file for the documents under the Freedom of Information Act. What evil churns behind the impenetrable walls of the Smithsonian Institution? Dr. Sternberg's reputation was destroyed, as he was professionally assassinated for following the established procedures and for doing his job, as was concluded by the investigation. What insanity—being coddled and protected, those perpetrators in both Sternberg's case and mine still have their jobs today after butchering the First Amendment, violating the will of James Smithson, breaching the trust placed upon them, trashing the people they swore an oath to serve, and utterly failing to fulfill their responsibilities.

The link between the Smithsonian Farm and *Animal Farm* is nearly complete. Chapter 5 in *Animal Farm* is where Snowball is banished, as was Dr. Sternberg, chased off by vicious dogs (atheistic scientists) with no justification. The authoritarian Napoleon (in this scene, Smithsonian's Dr. Rafael Lemaitre, who is still the Smithsonian's Research Zoologist and Curator of Crustacea) shuts down the debating. No more "new" ideas, as Napoleon urinates on Snowball's plans. This is similar to Lemaitre's outrage at Sternberg's publication. Lemaitre took it upon himself to start the inquisition against Darwin-dissenting Dr. Sternberg for daring to publish dangerous new ideas contained in the intelligent-design paper by Dr. Stephen Meyer:

NMNH [Smithsonian's National Museum of Natural History] officials conspired with a special interest group on government time and using government emails to publicly smear Dr. Sternberg; the group was also enlisted to monitor Sternberg's outside activities in order to find a way to dismiss him.[71]

In *Animal Farm*, Snowball is further maligned as a traitor and a criminal by Squealer, ensuring institutional compliance, strikingly similar to St. Thomas's role in the California Science Center controversy, pressuring the California Science Center into lockstep with the Smithsonian's atheistic agenda. In Sternberg's case, Smithsonian officials took it upon themselves to destroy Sternberg's reputation. St. Thomas, true to form, held the ideological line, speaking in the third person once again to make it easy to imagine a barn full of animals all speaking at once in echoing unison, saying, "We do stand by evolution—we are a scientific organization."[72] St. Thomas was seemingly oblivious and indifferent to the will of Smithson that defines the Institution as one that exists for the increase and diffusion of knowledge and prohibits no fields of learning within the scientific field, including intelligent design. It was even broad enough to include religion.

In the emails documented in Appendix 96 to the Congressional Report, found on Dr. Sternberg's site, one can read firsthand how scientists who were still working at the Smithsonian in 2017 conspired against, mocked, slandered, and ridiculed the doctor for his presumed faith in the Bible and conservative politics. Their disdain and contempt for any hint of faith, belief in God, creationism, or consideration of intelligent design provoked an unrestrained spew, as if from the Smithsonian castle's deep, dark dungeons. Their contempt was revealed in their frenzied back-and-forth email chains.[73]

The rise of revolutionary authoritarian power illustrated in *Animal Farm*, based upon the atheistic Russian Revolution, ended in totalitarian Leninist communism. The similarity with the spirit driving the godless leftists of today is dangerously real. When making a comparative study, the critical, essential difference between the Russian, French, and Cuban Revolutions on the one hand and the principled American Revolution on the other is telling. The former revolutions devolved into abject tyranny at the hands of the revolutionaries. They destroyed the Christian faith, its symbols, and its representatives, as well as incarcerating, killing, and murdering their own people. The American Revolution, on the other hand, granted religious freedom, inalienable rights, and freedom of speech to the People. The nexus of American revolutionary liberty was the result of one simple ingredient—faith in God, the transcendent accountability partner necessary to restrain evil in the hearts of even well-intentioned revolutionaries.

Mollie, Orwell's vain, irresponsible, and lazy mare, finds her modern-day parallel on the Smithsonian Farm in Kim Sajet. Sajet refused to do her job when my application arrived in her inbox. Mollie could care less about her fellow animals, just as we see in Sajet's treatment of me. Instead, Sajet preferred to fill the Internet with photos of herself fawning and gushing over leftist celebrities, who were both participating and being subjects of display in her museum. Sajet also tweeted and posted to the official Smithsonian website a picture of herself proudly wearing a "p**sy" hat at the anti-Trump protest, only to remind me of the red ribbons Mollie in *Animal Farm* put on view for everyone to see as she sat at the front of the meetings. In the 2019 *Washingtonian* article by Ben Wofford regarding my lawsuit against the Smithsonian, Kim Sajet was interviewed:

> Wearing broad cat-eye glasses in electric turquoise and matching statement jewelry, she told me about her vision for the museum—a six-year effort, she said, to "go big or go home."… "There was this persistent, and completely wrong, perception that the Gallery was about stuffy old history and dead white men."
>
> The week she arrived in DC, Sajet distributed an internal list of values. One edict commanded never to tell a lie.… Her artistic notions, too, pushed the boundaries: The museum installed a massive American flag imbued with portraits meant to be seen with Google glasses.… "Portraiture is now hip," she says, "but it wasn't in 2013."

Sajet had managed to advance her own kind of populism, one that did more to situate multicultural and underprivileged views in the museum…. The partisan blood feud gradually spilling into Sajet's world was entirely unnatural to her. Sajet said she couldn't comment on anything involving Julian Raven. But she seemed to treat the incident like the natural culmination of these events. Looking back on accepting the job, she playfully scoffed at her own ingenuousness.

"Never once, for a second, did I ever think about what it would be like to be part of the Smithsonian," she says. "It didn't even occur to me—so stupid."[74]

Mollie is eventually lured off the farm by the opportunities of material prosperity. Could this perhaps allude to that special day when Sajet leaves America to return to her native Australia? How ironic that Sajet's lawless resistance against me and my patriotic painting, in true leftist fashion, devolved into *Animal Farm*–like authoritarianism all its own.

What is the answer to the Smithsonian disease? One of the characters from *Animal Farm* comes to the rescue.

Chapter Thirty-Nine

MOSES THE RAVEN

MOSES THE RAVEN, THE FINAL CHARACTER OF IMPORT FROM *Animal Farm*, fills the role of those at the Smithsonian who represent the Christian-faith worldview today. The raven believed in Sugarcandy Mountain, where all animals went when they died. This aspect of the raven character alone serves the analogy well.

John Quincy Adams was Moses the Raven. He believed in Sugarcandy Mountain, as shown in his eloquent defense of man's attainment of knowledge in his speech in favor of accepting James Smithson's bequest:

> On him [man] alone is bestowed, by the bounty of the Creator…, the power and the capacity of acquiring knowledge. Knowledge is the attribute of his nature, which at once enables him to improve his condition upon earth and to prepare him for the enjoyment of a happier existence hereafter. It is by this attribute that man discovers his own nature as the link between earth and heaven; as the partaker of an immortal spirit.[75]

John Quincy Adams's argument to persuade the congressional committee to accept the funds rested on acknowledging that God alone is the source of all knowledge, the increase of which was the purpose of the Smithson bequest. How staggeringly vile it is to see the culture of today's godless Smithsonian.

Eminent scientist and Smithsonian founding Secretary Joseph Henry was also Moses the Raven, stating in a letter that

> after all our speculations, and an attempt to grapple with the problem of the universe, the simplest conception which explains and connects the phenomena is that of the existence of one Spiritual Being—infinite in wisdom, in power, and all divine perfections.[76]

Reverend Mitchell, who eulogized Professor Henry, described the last conversation he had with him and the final words Henry spoke before he died, as the professor's breath rapidly shortened:

> As to the Christian scheme in its main outlines—that there is one God, an infinite Spirit; that man is made up of body and soul; that there is an immortal life for man reaching out beyond the present world; that the power and love of God are brought into relation with the weakness and sinfulness of man in the Lord Jesus Christ—of these great truths, I have no doubt. I regard the system which teaches them as rational beyond any of the opposing theories which have come under my view. Upon Jesus Christ—[and here his eyes filled with tears and his voice broke as he repeated the words]—upon Jesus Christ, as the One who, for God, affiliates himself with man, upon Him I rest my faith and my hope.[77]

Joseph Henry did not shy away from the truth; he was not ashamed of Jesus Christ. He, too, believed in Sugarcandy Mountain, to the outrage and torment of the atheist pigs. In his final words, Professor Henry, the Father of American Science and the Smithsonian, condemned all of the "opposing theories" that had come before him as irrational. Henry purposefully took a tacit shot aimed at Darwin's theory of evolution, which had stunk up the scientific world during his time. In that golden age of enlightenment, which rested faith upon man's reason as the final arbiter of truth, Henry stood his ground on the Rock of Christ.

Was this the reason Henry's funeral was so unusual, attended by so many dignitaries, politicians, academics, writers, and professionals, etc., who were drawn to Henry's light while he was alive? Could it be they all showed up when his light went out as if to get one last glimpse of a man they knew and admired because he was unashamed of his faith and lived his faith, unlike so many?

O God, have mercy upon us—please raise up such men and women again in America!

There have been others in our modern era who have also been like Moses the Raven. In his role, Dr. Richard Sternberg was Moses the Raven, banished from the farm at the hands of the pigs, maybe even to return one day, as was the case with the banished raven of *Animal Farm*.

The American Freedom Alliance was also raven-like in its "poking-Darwinian-evolution-right-in-the-eye" plan to show the documentary *Darwin's Dilemma* at the Smithsonian Affiliate, the California Science Center, enraging the pigs at the farm. The AFA won a $110,000 settlement from the California Science Center, one of the few victories in the war with the pigs.

How ironic that years after Secretary Henry's death, the Smithsonian Institution would be hijacked by the atheistic evolutionary pigs. They would appropriate large amounts of dollars from the federal government, who got their cash from the taxpayer, to fund their "monkey-man" science exhibit. In time, that exhibition would travel the country, infecting American minds both young and old in schools and libraries from sea to sea with their monkey-man delusion. This new, irrational enterprise would ride on the back of the institutional machinery that Joseph Henry built. He believed and professed what years later would have gotten him too banished (or in today's vernacular, "canceled").

In 1978, ravenish former missionary Dale Crowley Jr. sued the Smithsonian in one of the very few constitutional lawsuits against the Smithsonian on record. Crowley's suit was based on the argument that the federal government violated the establishment clause in the First Amendment, which prohibits Congress from establishing a religion. By Congress funding the teaching of evolution at the Smithsonian, he claimed a religion was being established. Crowley's contention was that Darwinian evolution is a religion. The courts disagreed, and the lawsuit was thrown out.

Smithson's will did not prohibit any particular types of knowledge (see point 6 of the Smithsonian "Programme of Organization"[78]), but he did specify the increase had to be made of "new truths." How could one's knowledge increase without new truths? I suppose one could increase knowledge with lies, but are lies knowledge? Smithson was a scientist, specifically a geologist, who discovered the mineral Smithsonite, which was named after him. If the Institution were to have been strictly scientific, the will of Smithson would have said so, but it did not. Thus, the will was open for interpretation by the trustees. If the government-appointed trustees banned certain types of knowledge, it would have been in violation of the trust and the First Amendment since it was a publicly funded trust. (Now, that could have been a better argument for Dale Crowley to have levied against them in court.) Since the Smithsonian was a trust but treated as a federal agency, there was no basis to sue because of the continued entity confusion, since no laws could correctly be applied to it.

Demanding equal opportunity and funding for a different, alternative, and contradicting scientific theory could have been a more successful route for Crowley's case. That alternative analysis, conclusion, and presentation of the fossil record would have allowed for debate, furthering the increase and diffusion of knowledge. Since the Smithsonian uses taxpayer dollars, why not fund an alternative scientific theory and let the People decide?

The presentation of a one-sided argument and its belabored conclusion is dogmatic and contradictory to science in the first place.

It takes little effort to demonstrate how the theory of Darwinian evolution has become absolute, rigid, and dogmatic. Just look at Dr. Sternberg's experience.

By default, this confirms Crowley's earlier contention that Darwinian evolution has a religious nature, embodying its own orthodoxy and orthopraxy. Its central deity is "Time," without a will or a mind, which can make anything evolve. If Time chooses, even nothing can be made into anything. And Time's son, the demigod "Chance," performs spectacular miracles. For example, small, land-based, dog-like mammals become giant blue water whales; scaly, crawling reptilians become delicately feathered, flying birds. The religion has famous prophets (Darwin, Dawkins, Dennett, Hitchins, Hawking, Harris, and Dillahunty, et al.), written doctrines and creeds (*On the Origin of Species*, *The God Delusion*, etc.), seminaries and indoctrination camps (universities), temples of worship (the Smithsonian), even a priestly class of ordained inquisition-thirsty men and women in white robes (Smithsonian scientists).

People have "faith" in the theory of evolution; they "believe in" something they cannot see or observe, such as evolution in progress. They just accept on faith what their priests tell them about how nothing became something because of nothing and for no reason at all. And all this violates the scientific method, since it is impossible to prove the theory and observe the unseen mechanics of the proposition in action, making it a believed creed rather than an established fact. The courts, unsurprisingly, were not willing to allow Crowley's case to proceed, on the basis that evolution could not be officially defined as a religion. Semantics saved the Smithsonian since the religious elements of evolution are deliberately and deceptively disguised in scientific terms.

Maybe the courts and Congress will eventually catch up one day, vindicating Dale Crowley and Dr. Richard Sternberg. Prominent British science writer and critic, 5th Viscount Matthew White Ridley, was quoted recently, skewering the scientific community in a *Wall Street Journal* article by Tunku Varadarajan:

"Conformity," Mr. Ridley says, "is the enemy of scientific progress, which depends on disagreement and challenge. Science is the belief in the ignorance of experts, as [the physicist Richard] Feynman put it." Mr. Ridley reserves his bluntest criticism for "science as a profession," which he says has become "rather off-puttingly arrogant and political, permeated by motivated reasoning and confirmation bias." Increasing numbers of scientists "seem to fall prey to groupthink, and the process of peer-reviewing and publishing allows dogmatic gate-keeping to get in the way of new ideas and open-minded challenge.... In Mr. Ridley's view, the scientific establishment has always had a tendency "to turn into a church, enforcing obedience to the latest dogma and expelling heretics and blasphemers.... The space for heterodoxy is evaporating.[79]

Crowley serves as a reminder of how few legal successes are on record against the legally impenetrable Smithsonian Institution. Crowley was right to try to puncture the veil of the Smithsonian because his intent was righteous, especially since the Smithsonian is funded by the taxpayers. The People's money continues to be used to propagate a one-sided increase in knowledge. Darwinism on our dime is an eloquently and convincingly presented *theory*, a mere interpretation of the fossil record, and yet is proclaimed as conclusive. Could the promotion of Darwinian evolution really be federally funded propaganda? Could the official Smithsonian orthodoxy actually be federal orthodoxy, or in legal speak, "government speech"? Or, is it as Smithsonian Assistant Secretary William Warner wrote in a speech for then Chancellor Chief Justice Warren Burger:

The Smithsonian has made and will continue to make its most significant research and educational contributions to the needs of the public precisely because it is not an organizational part of the federal government.[80]

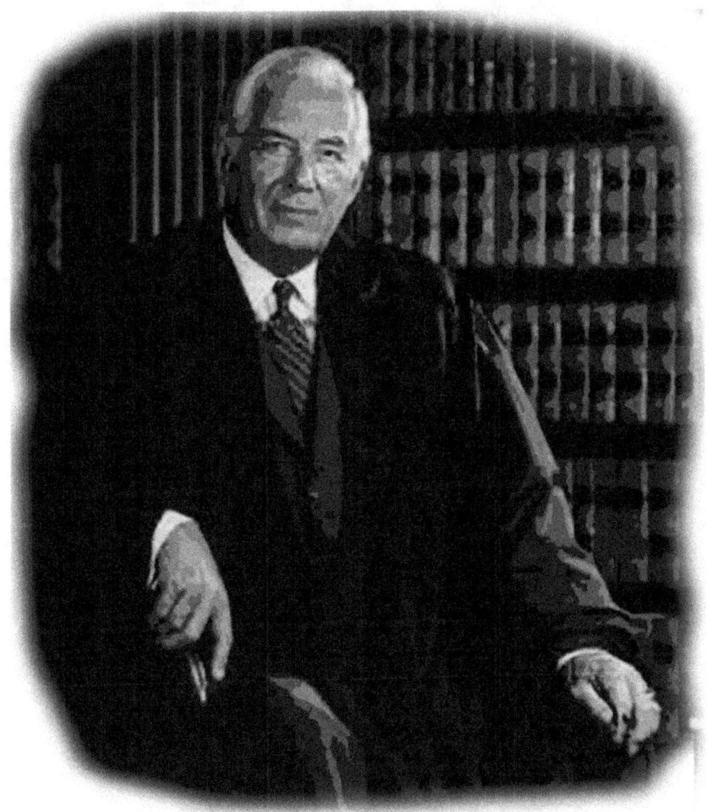

Chief Justice Warren Burger (1907–1995)

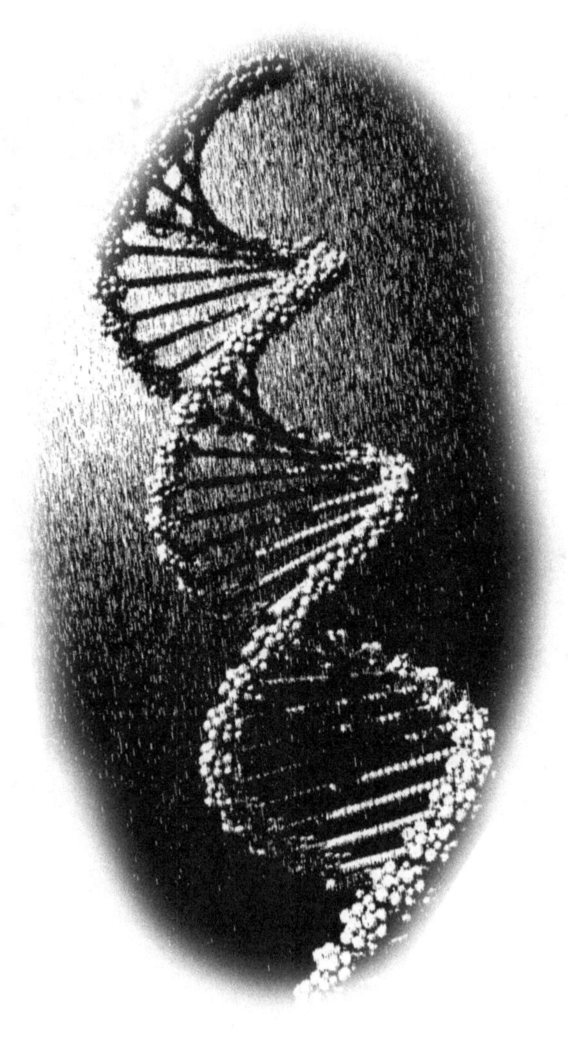

SMITHSONIAN DNA

OVER A CENTURY AND A HALF HAVE DEEPENED THE SMITHSONIAN mystery. The persisting legal conundrums' consequences continue to increase the invulnerability of the Institution. Following on from Crowley and Sternberg, these questions must be answered: What laws govern the Smithsonian Institution? What laws affect the conduct and discretion of the Board of Regents and Congress itself, since Congress is the principal fiduciary trustee of the will of Smithson? Can they be held accountable? Who can hold the Smithsonian to account? Accountable to what?

The lack of a clear legal definition of precisely what the Smithsonian Institution is—the entity status, in legal jargon—is the root problem. Just what animal is it? Unless defined, you cannot find a body of laws under which to sue the Smithsonian and its trustees, bringing them to account. This legal no-man's-land is precisely the problem with the Smithsonian Institution. For now, this ongoing and confusing ambiguity has served as the license for seemingly endless parades of corruption, scandals, and lawless conduct by officials, without any accountability.

It is nothing new that people with access to so much money, prestigious titles, and power will not voluntarily give them up if asked politely. Neither would they willingly invite review, correction, or reform by external legal probes that might end in constraints. Why would they wish to shut down their own party? We can learn why the Institution remains an enigma, protected in a no-mans'-land, by looking at who exactly is dancing at the party.

The Smithsonian Institution, over time, has evolved into a social, academic, and cultural paradise for the D.C. elite and beyond. The Smithsonian is a playground, the after-party for the wealthy and celebrity social crowd, including Hollywood actors, academics, celebrity scientists, politicians, judges, and the like. In the Smithsonian, power and influence are funneled through donations, on top of the seven hundred million dollars in yearly appropriations. Roughly three hundred million dollars a year are raised through private parties, creating a massive "charity" enterprise. The millions of dollars in donations do not flow in without rewards. (Just ask Amazon billionaire Jeff Bezos about his two-hundred-million-dollar donation.[81]) The perks are part of the game because everyone who is anyone or wants to become someone wants everyone to know that they gave and how much they gave. The gifts purchase position, titles, access, plaques on walls, paintings in galleries, names in records, and statues in yards, and they ultimately immortalize the donors—humanly speaking, that is.

The rich love to give publicly because donating makes them look good while they are still alive and immortalizes them once they die. Some institutions love to receive the money so much they are willing to turn a blind eye to the donor's character. Stretching this unfortunate effect that wealth can have into a view of eternity, this system of conveying power, position, and supposed immortality is necessary for them because many (especially, it seems, at the Smithsonian Institution) reject the Source of genuine immortality. The great immortality paradox for the rich is that eternal life is free for all people—rich and poor alike—if only they will humble themselves, believe it, and receive it.

Yes, sadly, this scenario is reminiscent of early warnings when the Smithsonian Institution came to be. Remember Senator William C. Preston in 1836? One of his chief objections to receiving Smithson's gold was that it would serve to immortalize some foreign, illegitimate vagabond—someone who happened to be rich, a descendant of so-called royalty, who had never even been to America. His objection was outvoted, and James Smithson was immortalized because he donated his massive treasure of gold, of unknown origin.

Can you imagine this happening today? Just imagine for a moment Congress debating the establishment of the "Pablo Escobar Institution" in Washington, D.C., dedicated to the study of Columbia's national coca plant. (Escobar was the wealthiest drug lord in history.) What a bottomless font of dollar bills that would be, inspiring a torrent of gravity-defying and back-bending justifications, leaving the hallowed chamber full of contorted bodies strewn all over the dais. It would be a circus.

You get the point. We're still left with the unanswered question: who should legally define the Smithsonian, finally ending this ambiguity and bringing legal clarity to this lingering problem?

Chapter Forty-One

CERBERUS RISING

The answer to the Smithsonian entity question (What type of animal is it?) can be found at the establishment of the Smithsonian Institution back in 1846. In its composition of heads of all three branches of the government and the public, the Smithsonian Institution's Board of Regents resembles no other institution except maybe the local pub in Washington, D.C., on a Friday night. It is plausible that the chief justice, the vice president, members of Congress, and the public could all be found at the bar of the same local pub on a Friday night after a tough week. Seriously though, that scenario—the assembly of members of the three branches of the federal government and the public—only happens during the State of the Union Address.

The representatives of the three branches of the federal government do not sit together in conference as the Smithsonian Board of Regents does. Far from it. In fact, the State of the Union is an adversarial gathering where policy decisions are not made. Instead, the separateness and interdependence of the three branches are often aggressively flaunted and displayed in loud vocal disagreement, in silence, or sometimes even by the indifference of nodding off.

If the leadership composition of the Smithsonian Board of Regents, including members of the executive, legislative, and judicial branches as well as unelected members of the public, were an expression or agency of a merged federal government, it would be a whole new and different form of government, or "animal" in need of a name.

Scientist Joseph Henry was tapped to take on the role of building the vision of the Institution. On December 8, 1847, Secretary Henry presented the Board of Regents with the blueprint of the Smithsonian vision. The Board of Regents ratified the "Programme of Organization" on December the 13, 1847. That founding day is still celebrated every year as Smithsonian Day. Clearly stated within that foundational document was the identity of the Smithsonian Institution. All of the members of the Board of Regents agreed with it; there was no opposition. In articles 2 and 3, Secretary Henry defined the DNA of the Institution:

> 2. The bequest is for the benefit of mankind. The Government of the United States is merely a trustee to carry out the design of the testator.
> 3. The Institution is not a national establishment, as is frequently supposed, but the establishment of an individual, and is to bear and perpetuate his name.[82]

Nothing ambiguous here. The government is "merely a trustee"—nothing more, nothing less. Nothing else to say. Here is the most critical part: "The Institution is *not* a national establishment." Notice that Henry had to include the warning against the problem of government overreach, already existing even back then in 1846. It was a privately funded public institution for the benefit of mankind, not a government institution for government objectives and purposes. It was from a private individual and was to bear and perpetuate the individual's name—hence the name Smithson-ian Institution, after James Smithson.

The entity status or legal organizational structure has never changed. Henry's warning regarding government overreach continues to apply to the present day, since it has been a constant problem. So much so, in fact, that today the institutional drift has caused most people to be uninformed as to what the Smithsonian is or to whom it belongs. Most people assume it is a national museum, an agency, or an arm of the federal government.

As the entity enigma has grown because of a lack of the diffusion of knowledge regarding the Smithsonian status, different authorities have spoken up, attempting to clarify the sticky matter. The mysterious anomaly of the Board of Regents' unique composition, if left legally unexplained, appears like the mythical three-headed beast, Cerberus. The following explanations regarding the Smithsonian status by the highest authority on the subject should once and for all dispel the myth.

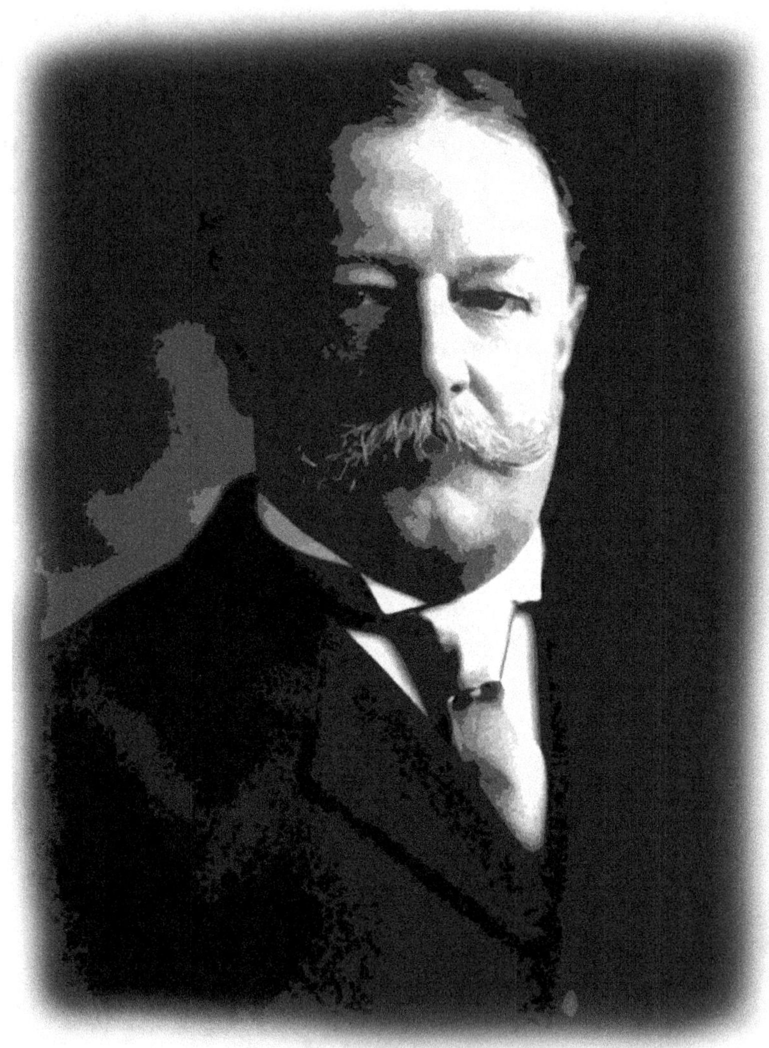

William Howard Taft (1857–1930)

Chapter Forty-Two

AMERICAN TAFFY, AMERICAN TAFT

AMERICA IS A NATION OF REMARKABLE INVENTIONS AND STORIES of remarkable people from humble beginnings. From the 1800s came the enduring yellow or pink stretchy, chewy candy called taffy. Unrelated but also from the 1800s came an enduring man named Taft (September 15, 1857–March 8, 1930). He was another man like Joseph Henry, born into a family of modest means. Yet Taft's destiny would take him down a political path that would make him a political behemoth. William Taft's parents were driven, pushing him and his brothers to become the best that they could be. His story paints a portrait of Taft as a hard worker—maybe not the brightest, but obviously also driven, landing him second place in his class of 121 students at Yale. He was a jolly and popular character in both school and sports. Also, he was a member of the Skull and Bones secret society, which his father actually co-founded at Yale. Taft was known as a man of integrity, and he was devoted to his wife Nellie for forty-four years. They had three children.[83]

Taft became president of the United States and the most often-cited authority on the Smithsonian-status matter, and you are about to see why. Taft also was: chief justice of the United States Supreme Court, the 42nd U.S. Secretary of War, the First Provisional Governor of Cuba, Governor-General of the Philippines, Judge of the U.S. Court of Appeals for the Sixth Circuit, the 6th Solicitor General of the United States, and also, by default at the time of his being chief justice of the U.S. Supreme Court (after he was president), he was the chancellor of (Yes! You guessed it! Come on down, William Howard Taft!) our very own Smithsonian Institution's Board of Regents. What an eye-popping, distinguished, historic, and enduring political career for a man from a family of modest means.

It is understandable that when inquiries along the Smithsonian road arose, requiring clarification as to what in the world the Smithsonian Institution was, people turned to the man named Taft. Because if Taft did not know the answer, nobody knew!

Acting as the Smithsonian Institution's Board of Regents chancellor, Howard Taft declared in multiple documents at the Department of Justice that the Smithsonian was "a historical and legal anomaly."[84] After acknowledging the confusing nature of the Institution, Chancellor Howard Taft dispelled the myth with an unambiguous statement: "The Smithsonian Institution is not, and never has been considered a government bureau. It is a private institution under the guardianship of the Government."[85]

The Department of Justice was defending the Smithsonian Institution against me by arguing that the Smithsonian is not a private institution but the federal government in action and speech.

Howard Taft's declaration was not a Supreme Court ruling, but pretty close, since he was also the chief justice. *Not* and *never* are pretty final and absolute words, especially the word *never*. It seems that words have lost their power since President William Jefferson Clinton called into question the meaning of the word *is*.

Chapter Forty-Three

IDEAL AMBIGUITY

You WOULD THINK THAT WITH CHANCELLOR TAFT'S UNAMBIGuous declaration from 1927 as to the Smithsonian identity, the issue would have been cleared up. Nope! With each successive generation, the problem persisted, and Howard Taft's words ended up buried somewhere, leaving the Smithsonian open for interpretation until someone took the time to dig them up. Some fifty years later, in the era of Chief Justice Warren Burger, the issue resurfaced, needing to be addressed again. The chief justice, in his capacity as chancellor of the Smithsonian Institution, had the task of setting the record straight again.

A speech was to be given on September 6, 1971, for the 125th Anniversary of the Smithsonian Institution. The chief justice never presented the address, and it somehow ended up archived at the prestigious Cosmo Club in Washington, D.C. It was written by Pulitzer Prize–winner William W. Warner,[86] assistant to the Smithsonian secretary at that time. In the speech, Warner asks the age-old and never legally resolved question. He then begins to answer the question thoroughly before driving home his rebuttal to the issue of the day. The reason why we have these declarations and the nagging issues persist is that the issues require a ruling from the U.S. Supreme Court itself to create a law that then will govern policy:

The Question and the Answer

But just what is the Smithsonian Institution? Why does it look and operate the way it does? It most certainly *is not* a government agency, *nor* a component of the executive branch of the federal government. It *is not* a part of the Congress or the Judiciary.

The speech was refreshing and crystal clear from the start, immediately addressing the pressing issue. "It most certainly is not" most certainly is not ambiguous. Critical to the question is the immediate nullification of the idea that the Smithsonian is a government agency, shutting down the possibility that the Smithsonian acts or speaks for the federal government:

The Trust

The Smithsonian Institution *is* a unique trust instrumentality for the benefit of the public…. Trust instrumentalities are fictions created in English common law and find their roots primarily in the preparations by nobles and other landowners for the Crusades. It was a means of providing for continuity of legal ownership and care of their lands while they were absent for long periods, and might well not return. Trust law is extremely complicated and difficult to understand and apply, even to this day.

The Mystery

Moreover, the Smithsonian Institution, *as a trust* instrumentality, *continues to confuse* members of Congress, the courts, and the executive branch. Nevertheless, the founding fathers knew exactly what they were doing….

With surprising regularity, elements of the executive or legislative branches discover the fact that the Smithsonian is a non-governmental institution operating with a mix of private and public funds to pursue its purposes. Nevertheless, the Institution receives a preponderance of its support from federal appropriations and this discovery, realized by members of Congress on occasion, has led to the conclusion from time to time that there may be something wrong with this arrangement, and they have decided that steps must be taken to correct it.

"On occasion," when Congress took the time to look closely at the Institution and its unusual arrangement, efforts were made to correct the problems. But as can be seen by the fact that this speech had to be written, those steps failed to clarify the confusion. The fact that this speech was never given may also explain the continual confusion today. Because if this speech was designed to confront congressional overreach in the 1970s and yet was tabled, that only contributed to the persistent problem:

The Example of Confusion

One of the most important of such misunderstandings occurred in 1927, when it was proposed that the funds employed for research coming from the Smithsonian's private endowment should be federalized, or possibly even turned over to the various states in what today we might call a matching or grant-in-aid program....

Justice Taft then explained that it was probably because the Institution administered for the federal government several of the public bureaus it created, by which he meant the Smithsonian's major museums, that many people supposed the private research activities of the Smithsonian also to be part of the government.

If this all seems ambiguous, then I must say it is an ideal ambiguity. Why? In answering this question, it's useful to make a comparison with the establishment of the Peace Corps. The story is told that early in his tenure as secretary of state, Dean Rusk was asked by a somewhat skeptical reporter how the Peace Corps would relate to the Department of State, and what it might contribute to American foreign policy. Secretary Rusk thought a moment and replied; "The Peace Corps will best contribute to the foreign policy of the United States *by not* becoming part of it."

The Conclusion

In similar fashion, the Smithsonian has made and will continue to make its most significant research and educational contributions to the needs of the public precisely because *it is not* an organizational part of the federal government. The Smithsonian *is and ever should remain*, in my opinion, a center for the independent pursuit of knowledge for its own sake, i.e., basic research under a form of limited federal guardianship.[87]

"Precisely because it is not an organizational part of the federal government" is cited as evidence of the independence of the Institution, giving way to private inquiry based upon a private vision and purpose. The absolute, unambiguous language used in the description of the institutional entity status looks like a clear attempt to chop off any tentacles that had latched onto the Institution in an attempt to subvert its private purpose.

"Ideal ambiguity" is an apt description of the Smithsonian mystery. Coming from the assistant Smithsonian secretary at the time and written for the acting chancellor and chief justice of the United States Supreme Court, one could confidently conclude this to be an authoritative definition of the entity status of the Smithsonian Institution that would undergird any legal action against the Smithsonian today. Ideally, Chief Justice John Roberts is on the hook for a twenty-first-century restating of the definition of the Smithsonian, coming from the bench of the U.S. Supreme Court. That decision then must become the basis for a Congressional amendment to the Smithsonian Act of Congress that would clear up the ambiguity once and for all.

My federal lawsuit against the Smithsonian Institution was just about to test whether the institutional dilemma had been resolved. Judge Trevor N. McFadden had my case. What would be his ruling?

Chapter Forty-Four

COURTS CONTINUALLY CONFUSED

IMAGINE THE TYPE OF WILD PAJAMA PARTY YOU MIGHT FIND GOING on in the federal court system were they to discover that what William Warner just described was in fact the truth. The Smithsonian's glaring problem is clear. Confusion regarding the status of the Smithsonian was and is widespread, affecting all branches of government. Surely not the courts, though, right?

Without an official Supreme Court ruling clearly establishing the Smithsonian status and the laws that apply to the Institution, its status is anyone's guess. Would I encounter status-quo clutching, out-of-thin-air guessing, and finger-in-the-wind divining as the primary defense of the Smithsonian presented by the Department of Justice? What else would they have to offer, especially if they ignored the answers within their own documents, ignored the history, and disregarded the Smithsonian founding documents? Who would know the difference?

Certainly not the unknown, unqualified, uneducated pauper and pro-Trump artist. What a fool—representing himself pro se against the full legal might of the United States Department of Justice, the same Department of Justice that happened to be defending the Smithsonian as if it were the very United States of America. The pro se artist just had to be wrong—he must be wrong before he could even set foot in the courtroom, and they, of course, had to be right, "just because they said so."

According to William Warner, the federal courts have been continually confused regarding the nature of the Smithsonian. That is an indictment against the courts at the highest level. He did not say "often," or "sometimes." He said the Institution "*continues* to confuse." That statement is crying out for an intervention and explanation. Former Department of Justice prosecutor and then thirty-eight-year-old Federal Judge Trevor McFadden, with no experience in adjudicating cases involving trust law or the mysterious Smithsonian, was obviously wading into uncharted and confusing legal territory.

Would a rookie judge presume some special knowledge of these matters beyond what Taft and Burger asserted in their lesser capacities as chancellors of the Smithsonian Board of Regents (rather than as Supreme Court justices)? Or would he arrive at the same conclusion as the pro se artist, in harmony with those sage justices, finding himself in a monumental legal pickle at odds with the status quo and DOJ representing the Smithsonian? The safest route would be to run hard into the arms of the status quo, knocking the ball into someone else's court. But in toeing the status-quo line, McFadden would have to deny to one of America's citizens certain inalienable rights and blessings of liberty guaranteed under the First and Fifth Amendments to the U.S. Constitution.

What would Judge McFadden do? What would you have done?

Chapter Forty-Five

VERY GAY PORTRAITS?

Can you see where this Smithsonian mystery, this "entity confusion," is leading me up Mount Justlaw? In other words, can you see the constitutional problems that arise because of the legal confusion? You have no rights if there is no law granting you such rights. We have certain inalienable, God-given rights that tyrants have trampled since the beginning of time. But in America, many of those rights—especially the quintessential right to free speech—are enshrined in the First Amendment to the U.S. Constitution. The amendments guarantee and protect those rights against a tyrannical government and its officials. And it is the job of the courts to enforce the Constitution and defend the People, administering justice. If the courts are confused, then what?

The freedom-of-speech clause was written to protect the People from the government when the government abridges, restricts, or prohibits free speech in places where the People are free to speak— i.e., parks, sidewalks, etc. Any place the government is in charge, by the will of and consent of the governed, the Constitution is in force restraining the government. The type of public forum dictates the type of activities and freedoms the People enjoy therein. Therefore, in those forums, the People are able and should always be able to express themselves freely, according to the type of forum.

Thus, there are limits to free speech in certain places where the government is in control and can by law restrict or limit free speech—for example, in public schools. In those forums, the government can determine the time, place, and manner of the People's speech. Likewise, there are places where only government speech occurs. For example, you cannot run into Congress when it is in session and start speaking about or shouting out whatever you want. The government can stop you, silence you, and arrest you since you have no free-speech rights in Congress. In that forum, we have elected representatives that speak for us.

So, the question now arises: Do We the People have any free-speech rights in, for example, the Smithsonian National Portrait Gallery? What is the role of the government in the Smithsonian Institution? Is it a free-speech forum? Is it like Congress, where only government officials can speak?

Right before Christmas, in December of 2010, a new controversy erupted at the Smithsonian National Portrait Gallery. This time, the liberal art world was outraged, with protests erupting as far as California, because the Smithsonian National Portrait Gallery removed a video that was part of the exhibit, "Hide/Seek: Difference and Desire in American Portraiture." A particular work in the show enraged Catholics and especially the Catholic League's Bill Donohue.

The exhibit positively promoted homosexuality and fluidity of gender identity and featured same-sex-attracted artists like Andy Warhol, Georgia O'Keefe, Jasper Johns, and Annie Liebowitz. An ABC News article quoted a CNS (Catholic News Service) News article headline that read, "Smithsonian Christmas-Season Exhibit Features Ant-Covered Jesus, Naked Brothers Kissing, Genitalia, and Ellen DeGeneres Grabbing Her Breasts."[88] The political outrage that followed at the time forced Speaker John Boehner and

Majority Leader Eric Cantor to threaten an investigation into Smithsonian funding. This looming financial threat yanked then Smithsonian Secretary Wayne Clough's chain hard enough that he yanked the "offensive" video.

You can see a video that I made of the Smithsonian Institution's video that was made of the exhibit, comparing the exhibit's content with the written standards for portraiture acceptance.[89] Looking closely at the video, you will see images of sexually aroused men holding towels in a bathhouse, a painting of naked young boys swimming in a river, paintings depicting same-sex attraction, and other strange "portraits." They are strange not because of the questionable morality of the images but because since when did a painting of sexually aroused, towel-covered naked men in a bathhouse constitute portraiture? They even displayed a pile of sweets, although it was impossible to determine whom it represented—yes, a literal pile of candy (please watch the video linked above[90])—and this was a portrait? The written standards say that a portrait is to be the best likeness of the historically significant subjects—not candy, not their genitals, but their faces—likenesses of their faces!

Catholics were outraged by a video on a small TV screen depicting Jesus Christ on a crucifix, lying in the dirt with blood and ants crawling all over Him. Now again, did this exhibit abide by the written standards? This exhibit should have been canceled before it started because it did not meet the portrait gallery's written criteria, regardless of its salacious content.

If the exhibit had consisted of portraits—you know, images of the face, head, and shoulders, maybe from the waist up, maybe full length, of people who had privately struggled with or even embraced being attracted to others of the same sex and yet who had done great things for America, then so be it. Their sexual issues, if not made "full-frontal" and center, would not have been the issue; what the individuals had accomplished would have been. And if what they had accomplished was viewed by some as advancing the rights and political and social agenda of people with same-sex attractions, then that subject matter could have opened the conversation, creating debate—as long as in that setting, the paintings were portraits. The museum could have shown both sides of the argument, giving people for and against the controversial issue a chance to express themselves and further increase knowledge and its diffusion. That would educate and inform, allowing the People to make up their minds about the individuals, their sexual preference, the art, the artists, and the artists' content.

The fact that the exhibit just bulldozed through the written standards and "no one said a dicky-bird" is revelatory. The exhibit was presented solely as a collection of all manner of sexually themed imagery from a same-sex perspective. One can only conclude that the Smithsonian, and the exhibit organizers who sought out a venue, only had one thing on their minds—use the legitimizing power of the Smithsonian Institution's rubber stamp of authentication to normalize homosexual imagery and themes without any question. That was social reengineering and the manipulation of the public at the taxpayer's expense. It used both the fame of the artists and the fame, prestige, and authoritative voice of the Smithsonian Institution to attempt to sanctify homosexuality. Talk about propaganda! And as for perspective, try to find an exhibit of portraits of—say, heterosexual couples celebrating five thousand years of monogamy and their platinum wedding anniversaries. Good luck!

While we are on the propaganda subject, here again in the ABC story by Devin Dwyer is our old friend Linda St. Thomas, better known as Squealer, popping up to masterfully rush to the defense of the display of the blood and ant-covered crucifix, while at the same time minimizing the art's perceived offensive nature. She simultaneously did not directly condemn Secretary Clough and subtly called into question the decision to remove the art (notice the lack of the third person pronoun *we*):

Smithsonian Institution spokeswoman Linda St. Thomas said the removal of Wojnarowicz's work was unprecedented.

The gallery has never before pulled a piece out of an exhibition because of public outcry.

She said that prior to publication of the CNS article the museum had received no complaints about the video, which she described as a small part of the show.

"It was a small screen in an alcove of the exhibit, and you had to push a button on the screen to activate it," said St. Thomas.[91]

The most revealing and pertinent information to come out of this controversy for my case was what Smithsonian Secretary Wayne Clough had to say on his cross-country, post-art-yanking apology tour. He had a tough job for sure appeasing both sides, lest government funds dry up on one side and liberal donations on the other. Yes, he had to go out and calm the enraged left, lest the Smithsonian become known as anything but the on-demand rubber-stamp institute for all liberal agendas and causes.

Referring to the Smithsonian National Portrait Gallery, Clough said, "We're not out to censor anything; we are dealing with this issue of free speech, rights of free speech, and protection. Protection of certain individuals and allowing for free speech."[92]

Well into my climb up Mount Justlaw, in 2017—when Attorney General Jeff Sessions injected the Department of Justice into the ongoing free-speech university scandals[93] happening across the country simultaneously with my lawsuit—I appealed to the Attorney General. I was curious if his concern for free speech extended to the local federal government in D.C. I was appealing for his involvement in my free-speech case to confront the abuse of the First Amendment at the Smithsonian Institution, which was similar to what was occurring at the universities, where they were making it impossible for conservatives to speak freely.[94]

Well, as you might imagine, if the DOJ was defending the accused (the Smithsonian), it was going to be hard for them to charge the Smithsonian with violating my First Amendment rights of free speech. Letters of appeal went out, accompanied by copies of the portrait, to all manner of officials at the Department of Justice at that time. I suppose I was naive to think that the free-speech clause of the First Amendment applied to everyone, especially people like me, in Washington, D.C. I never received a reply.

While on the subject of responses to petitions, look at this next impressive example of how the Smithsonian National Portrait Gallery director *should* respond.

Chapter Forty-Six

BLOODY SANGER RACIST

SOMETIMES GIVING CREDIT WHERE CREDIT IS DUE, *IS DUE*, EVEN if that means acknowledging Director Kim Sajet's job done right. This next Smithsonian controversy is an example of Director Kim Sajet setting the right example of how to respectfully treat people with whom she disagrees, while denying their petition to the Smithsonian National Portrait Gallery. Here is how this exemplary behavior unfolded:

> "We do not want word to go out that we want to exterminate the Negro population, and the minister is the man who can straighten out that idea if it ever occurs to any of their more rebellious members." (Margaret Sanger commenting on the "Negro Project" in a letter to Gamble, Dec. 10, 1939).[95]

> "By all means, there should be no children when either mother or father suffers from such diseases as tuberculosis, gonorrhea, syphilis, cancer, epilepsy, insanity, drunkenness and mental disorders. In the case of the mother, heart disease, kidney trouble and pelvic deformities are also a serious bar to childbearing. No

more children should be born when the parents, though healthy themselves, find that their children are physically or mentally defective." ("Woman and the New Race," 1920, chapter 7)[96]

Margaret Sanger endeared herself thus to Black America, to you, me, and the "feeble-minded," whom she wanted to see sterilized. Sanger advocated for "the gradual suppression, elimination, and eventual extinction of defective stocks—those human weeds which threaten the blooming of the finest flowers of American civilization."[97] Is it any wonder, then, that permanently exhibiting a beautifully cast, classic bronze bust glorifying Margaret Sanger produced outrage? Especially after billing the "feeble-minded" taxpayer for the exhibition—especially at the Smithsonian National Portrait Gallery, the People's Gallery.

Don't be silly! Absolutely not! You must be a narrow-minded imbecile not to see past Sanger's slightly embarrassing indiscretions and KKK associations and being a downright evil witch. For goodness' sake, look at all the good she did! (I was trying to employ Squealer's propagandist skills of minimizing offenses—did it work?)

But Smithsonian National Portrait Gallery Director Kim Sajet, on the other hand, managed to parse Sanger's "foibles" and unfortunate flaws without any trouble. Bishop E. W. Jackson, a highly respected and well-known Black American minister, was naturally horrified that such a woman would be granted a place of honor in the People's Gallery. Raising his voice in protest, he rallied Black ministers far and wide, including politicians Senator Cruz, Senator Louie Gohmert, and others.

They raised 14,000-plus signatures of members of We the People (American citizens and beneficiaries of Smithson's will), demanding the removal of the bust. But to no avail. Foreign national Kim Sajet denied the American citizens' petition, though to her credit, she responded professionally and courteously (in writing) on official Smithsonian-letterheaded paper to Bishop Jackson's petition requesting the removal of Sanger's bust.

Sajet's treatment of my letter and application in denying my Trump-portrait participation in the People's Gallery was slightly different, as you know. Would not plain decency, civilized discourse, and written procedural policy require that in all cases a polite and respectful denial in writing, with an official explanation, be given? (Remember, my application was publicly supported by elected officials representing two hundred thousand citizens of New York.)

On the other hand, when dealing with the Bishop, Sajet was extremely helpful in explaining that the museum is for people (sometimes depicted as candy) who have made a "significant impact on this nation's history and culture—both positive and negative."[98] Let's take a look at what the codified law concerning the purpose of the Portrait Gallery says:

> The Gallery shall function as a free public museum for the exhibition and study of portraiture and statuary depicting men and women who have made significant contributions to the history, development, and culture of the people of the United States and of the artists who created such portraiture and statuary. 20 U.S. Code §75(b).[99]

Does "significant contributions" imply good, or evil, or both? Truth be told, the statute does not require or specify a "positive" or "good" significant contribution, but we know already how Sajet likes to bend the rules for her own purposes.

Does Sajet's interpretation open up a can of worms where someone as controversial as Margaret Sanger is honored because she fits Sajet's personal feminist ideology and political agenda? And why was that same standard not applied to my painting, considering that some people saw controversial Trump as a man who could have saved America, while others saw him as a pig and worse?

Sajet goes on to say:

> There is no "moral test" for people to be accepted into the National Portrait Gallery. Instead, we try to draw attention to

those who have made a significant impact on American history and culture, and that includes both the accomplished and reprehensible. We recognize Sanger's advocacy…whilst acknowledging her sometimes deplorable beliefs.[100]

How about this deplorable artist and his painting of the deplorable president-to-be? Shouldn't that deplorable quality perfectly square with Sajet's interpretation, guaranteeing my portrait's acceptance?

Sadly, here we go again with the "do-as-I-say-not-as-I-do" leftist complex, as Sajet equivocates, saying, "We attempt to acknowledge past mistakes, engage in open and civilized discourse, and set a path towards a better future."[101] (This was August of 2015.) Acknowledge past mistakes? Open and civilized dialogue? Did I read that correctly?

As of April 17, 2021, Planned Parenthood has finally owned up to its vile defense of Margaret Sanger in the past. In an Op-Ed written in the *New York Times*, Alexis McGill Johnson, president and chief executive of the Planned Parenthood Federation of America, said:

> We must reckon with Margaret Sanger's association with white supremacist groups and eugenics.… Up until now, Planned Parenthood has failed to own the impact of our founder's actions. We have defended Sanger as a protector of bodily autonomy and self-determination, while excusing her association with white supremacist groups and eugenics as an unfortunate "product of her time."… We don't know what was in Sanger's heart, and we don't need to in order to condemn her harmful choices.… We will no longer make excuses or apologize for Margaret Sanger's actions.[102]

Kudos to Alexis!

It was my hope that Kim Sajet and her Smithsonian were in line for a reckoning all of their own at the hands of Judge Trevor McFadden up on perilous Mount Justlaw.

Chapter Forty-Seven

GREASY GOLDEN PIG CATCHING

WAKING UP ON THE MOUNTAIN AND STARING BACK OUT ACROSS the vast landscape was a reminder of just how far I had come. My nose hairs bristled as my lungs gulped down the fresh morning air. I winced as my steaming black tea bit my tongue. I glanced up at the intimidating wall of rock awaiting me. It jolted my senses far beyond what my sweet and fragrant tea attempted to do. Ascending perilous Mount Justlaw was already a monumental challenge for someone without any mountain-climbing experience. But then, that challenge seemed to be morphing into a full-on modern-day medieval quest. Like in the olden days, you know, crossing seven oceans, slaying ten beasts, and climbing numerous mountains to rescue the princess—except in my case, I was trying to rescue myself! And as always, along the journey in those mysterious ancient odysseys, the heroes would encounter new and unexpected challenges and tests around every corner. For example, today you must climb across a worn-out, rickety rope bridge, swaying in the wind over violently rushing rivers deep in the gorges below. Or another day you might have to carry the rare tiny flower between your teeth up the icy mountain to some mysterious monk in the monastery. (Undamaged, of course!) Some challenges were just absurd, like having to cut down a mighty tree with a fish or having to answer seven strange questions posed by a cranky, bearded old man lest ye be tossed into yonder gorge. Yes, my journey had ballooned into one of those full-blown holy grails, à la Monty Python.

Well, no sooner had I forged ahead on my climb that morning on Mount Justlaw, far enough to where I could no longer see the woods and the world behind me because of the dark clouds that had swept in, that a new task was added to my climb. Yes, an impossible new task on top of the already narrow, slippery, and steep paths up the first stages of Mount Justlaw. And it was as if I heard it spoken in a strange archaic John Cleese English voice: "You must cut down the mightiest tree in the forest…with…a…herring!" No, sorry, wrong quest! Try again. And it was as if I heard it spoken in a deep booming voice, like that of James Earl Jones:

"Julian Raven, you must catch the golden grease-covered pig that dwells somewhere on Mount Justlaw and bring it to the summit…. Alive! Ha Ha Ha Haaaaaa!" Dun dun dun duuun!

"You have got to be kidding me!" I replied.

"No, I'm not!" the deep voice replied.

I sort of laughed and grimaced at the same time, since from day one of my lawsuit, I'd had to rapidly and repeatedly change course, as every legal assumption of mine came crashing down. It was like trying to catch a golden, greased pig—or worse, trying to pin the tail on a moving donkey, blindfolded. I reached a place on the mountain where the wall of rock flattened out, opening up a steep, long winding path ahead of me. The golden pig was before me, and I gave chase. Every time I caught and gripped the squealing pig in my arms, I could feel its wriggling, greasy body just slip out of my grasp. Because my case was unprecedented, no guideposts were directing me on how to accurately base my claims against established laws that applied to the Smithsonian.

The first challenge was defining what types of crimes had been committed and what types of laws had been broken. I scoured the Internet and discovered what I thought to be the perfect federal law (assuming that federal laws applied to the Smithsonian) that would help me define Sajet's actions. Bingo! This law, called the Administrative Procedure Act (APA, 1946), was perfect. It addressed the many administrative and procedural failures of the Smithsonian Institution's Board of Regents, Dr. Richard Kurin, and of course, Ms. Kim Sajet. The law came into existence to hold federal agencies to account in abiding by the federally defined procedures and processes which govern the functioning of their particular government agency. The law was expansive, covering all sorts of details of procedural lawlessness and their appropriate legal remedies. Joyfully, I would say to myself, "That is exactly what Sajet did and what happened to me," as the law defined the specific actions taken against me.

Soon enough, though, to my utter surprise and disappointment, I discovered that the Smithsonian Institution did not qualify as a federal agency in that way and thus did not fall under the jurisdiction of that law. Even Judge Victor J. Wolski, from the U.S. Court of Federal Claims, transferred my case to the District of Columbia's District Court on the basis of my claims made against the APA. He did not even know himself that the law did not apply, further proving the courts are continually confused about the status of the Smithsonian Institution. But that misunderstanding served my case, so I was glad.

My discovery meant that there were no federal process laws that applied, but did the Fifth Amendment not apply? Even the very founding Smithsonian Act of Congress, which contained plenty of process law to be followed, could not be enforced if the Smithsonian was not classified as a federal agency under the APA, which it was not. That meant there was no way to hold them accountable for violating the clearly written federal procedures and processes within the Smithsonian Institution.

Lying there in the dust, I could see the golden pig's squiggly tail and galloping black trotters as it took off at full speed, squealing further up the mountain, out of my grasp, out of sight, and covered in grease.

In 2008, Senator Chuck Grassley introduced legislation,[103] in the form of the "Open and Transparent Smithsonian Act," that would compel Smithsonian board meetings to be open to the public and make records available to the public upon request. He did this because, along with the APA, not even the Freedom of Information Act (FOIA) applied to the Smithsonian Institution. Well, as of today, Grassley's Transparency Bill has still not been passed.

Surprise, surprise, our old friend Squealer is back, speaking in the third person again, in the *Washington Post* story by James V. Grimaldi on July 19, 2008, covering Grassley's FOIA Bill:

> The Smithsonian's attorneys have opposed applying FOIA to the institution. Spokeswoman Linda St. Thomas said, "The Smithsonian's governance reforms have resulted in greater transparency and accountability, and our FOIA policy is consistent with the approach taken by organizations that report to Congress such as the Library of Congress."…
>
> Patrice McDermott, a public-records advocate who is the director of OpentheGovernment.org, has participated in those talks. She said Leahy has worked hard to make the Smithsonian more transparent but called the Smithsonian's FOIA policy "a mess" that contains many more exemptions than the federal law. "They want the public to think they are acting in accord with FOIA, but they are not," McDermott said.
>
> St. Thomas countered by saying that a recent Government Accountability Office report on Smithsonian governance found that the institution's policy is consistent with FOIA.
>
> But Melanie Sloan, director of Citizens for Responsibility and Ethics in Washington, said there is no appeal if the Smithsonian refuses a FOIA request; if the FOIA exemption were removed, disputes could be resolved in court. "The reason they want to keep the exemption is they want to hide problems from

the public," Sloan said. "The Smithsonian isn't really interested in transparency."[104]

"No appeal!" Does that sound familiar? Talk about trying to catch a greasy pig!

Chapter Forty-Eight

PIN THE TAIL ON THAT DONKEY

THERE I STOOD ON MOUNT JUSTLAW, STARING AT THE WINDING path in front of me, and suddenly, I heard that deep booming voice again. "Now, Julian Raven, you must pin the tail on that donkey—actually, it is a Spanish ibex mountain goat, the most agile, sure-footed, and swift mountain-climbing creature on earth, way over there, up that very steep, sheer, unclimbable jaggedy mountain crag."

"That's impossible!" I said.

"You are right, just kidding—stick with the greasy pig; it's more fun watching you and the pig!" the voice replied. "Ha Ha Ha Haaaaaaaa!" The deep booming voice now faded behind a small curtain hanging on the mountainside, painted to look just like the mountain. 'Twas a strange place indeed upon which I had ventured.

Since the process claims slipped through my arms, I now tried to pin a civil-rights violation on the Smithsonian for Sajet's actions and upon Sajet herself. Ah yes, the historic Civil Rights Act of 1964, 42 U.S. Code § 1983, seemed to fit the civil constitutional violations committed. The act was created to allow citizens to sue the accused officers individually. Since they acted in the name of the government entity, they could be sued for violations of the U.S. Constitution and of laws. My hopes spiked as I lunged once again at the pig, firmly grabbing the squirming creature with my arms and legs. I got you now, O greasy one!

The Civil Rights Act was the perfect law to pursue my First Amendment free-speech claims and Fifth Amendment due-process claims. It certainly was a perfect law, especially if the offending officer worked for any of the fifty states or the District of Columbia. In other words, the law did not work against officers who worked directly for the federal government. Nooooo! I was in disbelief as the greasy pig popped once again. How could this law not be applied to the federal government as well? Simple. Congress created it only for the states, not for itself.

So naturally, when I found that out, I reasoned that Congress must have created a similar, codified civil law that served the identical purpose and yet applied to federal-government employees and officers—a law facilitating American citizens to recover monetary damages against federal officers who violated their constitutional rights. Right? Obviously, I had just made a mistake and cited the wrong law and code. So, off I went searching for the right law code with which to correct my filing. Well, I searched and searched and searched some more. Talk about discovering an absurd challenge on my quest.

I tried every type of Google query, based on the wording of the state law code, and all I found was the same §42:1983 Civil Rights code. There had to be a civil law for collecting monetary damages, not a criminal law. No, and yes! It's called the U.S. Constitution. But that does not allow you to sue individuals like Kim Sajet; you can only sue the United States, for whom she works, without recovery of damages. You need a separate law designed for the recovery of damages. But then Congress must have passed such a law explicitly applying the U.S. Constitution to individual actions taken by federal officials, right?

Wrong! No such law existed. I was stumped. No way! But there must be a way! The golden, greasy pig just popped right out of my hands again, squealing as it ran off into the distance. The truth is, it is rare that We the People (in general) come in contact with federal officers, other than maybe federal law-enforcement agencies like the FBI or the ATF. But we sometimes do, and we sometimes get violated.

That being the case, I learned that the Supreme Court had created a law (legislating from the bench) because Congress had not done so. This was accomplished by a ruling in favor of a claim that clearly violated the U.S. Constitution, which was compelling enough to cause them to hear the case. Webster Bivens had his home illegally searched by FBN (Federal Bureau of Narcotics) agents, was arrested, and had his stomach pumped, etc. He claimed in court that the agents' actions violated the Fourth Amendment's "unreasonable-searches-and-seizures" clause. The federal government, in defense of the officers, said there was no law to make a claim for monetary damages effective against the individual federal agents, since only a state law existed. Bivens had his case dismissed at the district-court level, and again on appeal, his case was dismissed again. Finally, the Supreme Court decided to hear his case.

In the U.S. Supreme Court, on June 21, 1971, Justice Brennan, writing the opinion for the six-to-three majority, said that the Supreme Court would "rule to infer a right of action for monetary damages where no other federal remedy existed for the vindication of a constitutional right based on the principle that for every wrong there is a remedy."[105]

Sweet music to my ears, "For every wrong, there is a remedy." Even if all else failed, at the tippy tippy top of Mount Justlaw I would find a remedy. I just had to make it to the top. The *Bivens* remedy for the First Amendment free-speech violations and Fifth Amendment due process and equal rights under the law would have to work for me. One would think that the preeminent free-speech clause in the First Amendment would work by default, causing the judges and justices to sit up in their seats, even jump up and eagerly wave their proverbial staffs of approval in the air. The justices would be eager to hear dismissed claims of free-speech violations—because there was no federal law or cause of action that citizens could use against federal officials for monetary damages. Right?

My study of the *Bivens* law led me to another hurdle to overcome. The law would block me from trying to sue federal officers for the same violation using a different set of laws to try to recover monetary claims twice—which makes sense, to prevent suing twice for double the payout for the same offense.

The law barring double recovery was quite bizarre in its application, as I was to discover. The shocking story I found illustrates a choice I would have to face further up the mountain. Steven Manning sued two FBI agents. Manning was an FBI informant. Things went sour, the FBI agents set him up for murder, and Manning was convicted and sentenced to jail for murder. Can you imagine what a nightmare? Manning managed to sue the FBI agents under the *Bivens* remedy and won six and a half million dollars and his freedom from a jury verdict. For some unknown reason—maybe greed, anger, vengeance, or stupidity—he decided to sue them some more. He used another recovery law, the FTCA (Federal Tort Claims Act), which allowed him to sue the government for torts caused by the individual officers, which law came with an explicit warning label. No matter what the FTCA lawsuit's outcome would be, whether he would win big or lose big, it would cancel out any other monetary awards he may have won prior to the FTCA lawsuit. It was a six-and-a-half-million-dollar gamble. Manning knew that going into his lawsuit. One can only imagine that he was blinded by greed, thinking that because he had just won a verdict with a jury, he would win a better verdict with a judge. Well, he lost the FTCA lawsuit. As a result, the judge vacated (deleted) his six-and-a-half-million-dollar judgment. Can you believe it? Manning went from six and a half million dollars to zero with the bang of a gavel.

Was I glad to learn that early on in the climb! If my case moved forward, at some point, I would have to drop one side of my monetary claims. If I didn't, I would blow myself off the side of Mount Justlaw. So what was the FTCA all about, and would it apply to my case?

The FTCA, or Federal Tort Claims Act, became my subsequent discovery. And that time, the Smithsonian did comply with the act, because Smithsonian employees, for the most part, are federal employees. But then, I discovered that the part of my filing that was based on the FTCA was deficient since it had not been properly filed at the Smithsonian. And once again, right before the DOJ could respond to my claims, attempting to get the judge to dismiss them, I learned that I could dismiss them myself before they had a shot. Meaning I could withdraw my FTCA claims before they were legally disqualified. So I did, obviously without any opposition from the Department of Justice. Then I returned my FTCA claims to the Smithsonian as the law required.

The Federal Tort Claims Act was created to allow the federal government to be sued in the event that any of its agents, officers, or employees cause the public injuries, called torts, not for violations of rights based in the Constitution. For example, if the postman, when delivering your mail, drives over your foot with his car, you can sue the government through the FTCA, claiming compensation for a broken foot. You cannot sue the individual postman through this law, but you can sue the government—the U.S.A.

The winding path ended. A tremendous gorge slashed into the mountain waited for me. The gaping crossing was dreadfully wide, carved by a rushing, violent river that thundered below. There were two tight ropes stretching across the chasm, one to walk on and one to hold above my head. With no other options and filled with trepidation, I began inching myself along the swaying cables with nothing but mist and roaring far below. More than at any time before, I wondered if I would survive.

The FTCA law required a special form to be filed with the offending institution for which the individual worked before you can go to federal court. After that, 180 days (six months) had to pass, exhausting all administrative remedies at the same institution (i.e., making use of all and any available solutions within the offending institution to right the wrong). Then I could file, or refile in my case, my claims and join them to my already-ongoing case. I just had to cling on in the district court with my other claims, which I did.

After six months, I returned to the court with my FTCA claims. Unsurprisingly, the Department of Justice now opposed my FTCA claims being rejoined (reattached) to my pending case at the district court. The judge now suspended his decision on whether or not to allow the FTCA claims back until other issues were resolved on the docket at that time and until his final decision was made regarding whether or not my case could move forward.[106]

To my delight, I succeeded in crossing the gorge of certain doom. Energized, having survived, I was greeted by the stern grimace of the sheer rock face of Mount Justlaw. Without hesitation, I attacked the rock face with my boots, spikes, and ropes, aggressively scrambling up the mountain.

Chapter Forty-Nine

CONSTITUTIONAL CONTORTIONS

A TERRIBLE, HOLLOW FLOATING SENSATION FILLS YOUR GUT when a piece of rock-climbing hardware, with all your weight on it, fails. Arms flailing, your hands wildly grab at anything, catching fists full of air. Tumbling helplessly downward, the next piece of hardware along the rope line snags your fall with a jolt of whiplash. If that too fails, and the next one, you have to rely on the main anchor point secured to the rock wall to break your fall. If that too fails, pray you get your wings.

All of the laws that I tried to pin to the Smithsonian donkey failed like defective rock-climbers' cams. But regardless, I knew I was anchored. My assurance was in the U.S. Constitution, and I was confident it would break my fall, securing me justice. My constitutional claims of First Amendment free-speech and Fifth Amendment due-process and equal-protection violations all hinged on one pivotal question, though. What did Judge Trevor McFadden of the District Court for the District of Columbia believe the Smithsonian Institution was? If the entity distortion came at the judicial level, then the court would be guilty of schmeering the already-greasy golden pig with even more grease in its ruling. All of my attempts to grab that greasy, golden pig would be futile.

I found further structural support for my constitutional arguments in another case involving four artists, their free-speech claims, the Constitution, and a government art entity. The four artists tried to bend and twist the law, refusing to accept the standards in a particular speech forum created by the government. They claimed the Constitution gave them broad free-speech rights that superseded the standards set by the government, in the landmark Supreme Court case *National Endowments for the Arts (NEA) v. Finley.*

The standards in the NEA were quite clear:

> No payment shall be made under this section except upon application therefor which is submitted to the National Endowment for the Arts in accordance with regulations issued and procedures established by the Chairperson. In establishing such regulations and procedures, the Chairperson shall ensure that—
>
> (1) artistic excellence and artistic merit are the criteria by which applications are judged, taking into consideration general standards of decency and respect for the diverse beliefs and values of the American public; and
>
> (2) applications are consistent with the purposes of this section. Such regulations and procedures shall clearly indicate that obscenity is without artistic merit, is not protected speech, and shall not be funded.[107]

The artists sued the NEA, claiming their First Amendment free-speech rights were violated because the obscenity standard that barred their participation was "vague." They claimed a vague standard could be arbitrarily applied, ending up discriminating against their viewpoint. That could be true in a world where obscenity had become ambiguous. The artworks in question unsurprisingly involved different degrees of nudity, homosexuality, and sexually themed subject matter.[108]

The founding of the National Endowment for the Arts was illuminating for my case because it shed light on the Smithsonian entity question when comparing the establishment of the two entities and the participatory rights and procedures for artists. I could not rely on the opinions of Chief Justices Taft and Burger alone, since theirs were not legal rulings. I needed to demonstrate by comparing institutions how drastically different they were, showing how the Constitution applied. The establishment of the NEA paints a clear picture of what a "through-and-through" government agency looks like. This is relevant because the entity's nature is essential to determining if free-speech rights existed in both the NEA and the Smithsonian. The National Endowment for the Arts, 20 U.S. Code § 954 was established by an Act of Congress in 1965:

> An Act To provide for the establishment of the National Foundation on the Arts and the Humanities to promote progress and scholarship in the humanities and the arts in the United States, and for other purposes....
>
> [Sec. 2] (2) The encouragement and support of national progress and scholarship in the humanities and the arts, while primarily a matter for private and local initiative, are also appropriate matters of concern to the Federal Government....
>
> (5).... Public funding of the arts and humanities is subject to the conditions that traditionally govern the use of public money. Such funding should contribute to public support and confidence in the use of taxpayer funds. Public funds provided by the Federal Government must ultimately serve public purposes the Congress defines.[109]

"National Foundation," "national progress," "matters of concern to the Federal Government," "use of taxpayer funds," "public funds...public purposes," "Congress defines"—these terms clearly define the object and purpose of the NEA and whose will it was to form it. It was the will of the federal government. The will of Congress, comprised of elected representatives of the people, pioneered that institution.

Regarding First Amendment free-speech rights, there was no argument made by the Department of Justice that the four artists did not have free-speech rights; the rights were limited by the established standards. Neither did the Department of Justice argue that the selection of art by the NEA was government speech.

In striking contrast, and as a reminder, read how differently the Smithsonian Act of Congress reads:

James Smithson, esquire, of London, in the Kingdom of Great Britain, having by his last will and testament given the whole of his property to the United States of America, to found at Washington, under the name of the "Smithsonian Institution," an establishment for the increase and diffusion of knowledge among men; and the United States having, by an act of Congress, received said property and accepted said trust; Therefore, For the faithful execution of said trust, according to the will of the liberal and enlightened donor…[110]

Notice the key differences: a private foreign citizen's will, private funding, Congress received the money, the institution was to bear the name of that private person not a national name, Congress accepted the duty as trustee to faithfully carry out the will of the private donor—i.e., it would be a government-run private trust for the benefit of the public.

Regarding First Amendment free-speech rights in the Smithsonian in my case, the Department of Justice argued against me, saying that I had none—that there is only government speech in the Smithsonian. That is right, in the private Smithsonian Institution, it is only the government speaking through the selection of art—and yet in the genuinely government-created NEA, it is the artists speaking. Really?

The NEA has written standards restricting obscene art, and those standards were followed faithfully by the officials when they considered the artwork and then reached their decision, putting it down in writing. Do you see the difference between that and what happened in my case? There were written standards. There were no standards restricting the size or the political speech. The written standards were ignored and twisted by the Smithsonian officials in order to block my participation. Also, there was no written opinion citing the standards or identifying the reasons my painting failed. And the Department of Justice argued I had no free-speech rights, basically justifying that they violated their own rules, standards, and procedures.

The Supreme Court in *NEA v. Finley* ruled that the government did not have to accept and display obscene material that was in violation of their written standards. There was no free "obscene" speech when there was a standard barring obscene speech. It was at the discretion of the chairperson/board to decide what was obscene according to general standards of decency.

Notice the elements and make a note of them, please: 1. There was a written application. 2. There was a written response and official denial citing written standards. 3. There was a lawsuit and judgment. 4. There was an appeal to the U.S. Supreme Court, who heard the case, answering an unanswered constitutional question dealing with federal law, and 5. The Supreme Court made a binding decision and interpretation regarding the congressionally created law.

Clear written standards and abiding by them through strict processes are necessary for the government to function. The government, after all, is serving us for our benefit. In another Supreme Court case, we see that the court at that time understood that clearly. In *Southeastern Promotions v. Conrad*, in a six-to-three ruling, the court declared:

> The Court has felt obliged to condemn systems in which the exercise of such authority was not bounded by precise and clear standards. The reasoning has been, simply, that the danger of censorship and of abridgment of our precious First Amendment freedoms is too great where officials have unbridled discretion over a forum's use.[III]

In my case, here are the questions that arose that needed to be answered:

- Was Kim Sajet, and by extension, the government (Congress), the one making the decision when acting as Smithsonian trustee?
- Why in my case did Kim Sajet/the government (Congress acting as trustee) not have to follow the Smithsonian written standards?
- Can they (i.e., the Smithsonian officials) arbitrarily pick and choose what standards to follow depending on how they feel on any particular day?
- If the government was just acting as trustee, did their failing to follow the terms of the trust constitute breaches in trust by the government?
- Did Sajet's conduct constitute breaches of the duty of care and the duty of loyalty?
- And if Sajet, a government employee, did breach fiduciary trust, did her actions forbidding my political free speech constitute violations of my First Amendment free-speech and Fifth Amendment due-process rights?

The agenda-driven artists with their obscene images tried to bend the Constitution to their salacious will, forcing, as we see more and more these days, the blurring of the lines of decency. A line that once is compromised will forever fail. No more will there be decency or indecency, since the underlying rock of moral values, held by the People, are rejected as archaic and irrelevant. If these activists had their way, our taxpayer dollars would be used to fund every impulse of their unrestrained sexual appetites and their immoral expressions, all under the banner of free speech.

Chapter Fifty

LET THERE BE LIGHT

DANGLING BY A FINGER OR TWO AT THE END OF A TUMBLE WAS not uncommon for me during the first half of my climb. I was constantly in way over my head, barely able to hang on. Sometimes, especially when the Department of Justice would reply to my court filings, I would tremble. It was hard enough dealing with the court system's complexities and my own efforts to formulate my arguments and stay within the law and rules of the courts. But when I received one of those large, thick, orange manila envelopes stamped from the Department of Justice's Assistant U.S. Attorney Marina Braswell, my heart sank. The envelope sat on my desk for days before I could open it. I dreaded reading what it would say, as initially I knew I would not even understand what it was saying. Once I mustered up the courage to open the envelope, then the stapled pile of papers sat on top of my desk, on top of that envelope, staring at me. I slowly took small bites out of the document, flipping through a few pages at a time, squinting to protect my eyes in my attempts to make heads or tails of what they were saying. Each time I read a section, I would be driven back to reread, trying to decipher what word after word meant.

Legal concepts that were extremely difficult to understand presented themselves, and I found I was coming up against an overhanging darkened slippery rock face on Mount Justlaw. I stretched wide, reaching with my arms, running my hands along the surface, feeling the cold, smooth rock face and trying to grab at something—anything—but there was nothing. There seemed to be nowhere for me to grab or to put my foot.

One such concept that was hurled at me from the DOJ bunker was that Kim Sajet was protected by "qualified immunity." What in the world was qualified immunity? How did the government shield its officers behind that? At first reading, it sounded like an impenetrable force field that—no matter what happened—protected Sajet. I learned that it is for government officials who make honest mistakes in the line of duty and then are protected against prosecution as individuals. How in the world did the DOJ think what Sajet did was an honest mistake? Naively I thought the Department of *Justice* would stand on the side of *justice* no matter where justice lay. Using qualified immunity was like a smokescreen that O. J. Simpson's lawyers would have used. Another similar concept was "absolute immunity." The president of the United States and even judges, when functioning in their official capacities, have absolute immunity, meaning there is no way to sue them for their failures on the job (either as individuals or as officials). Here was a totally smooth wall. I could understand the need for immunity because I could imagine the litigious nightmare that would be unleashed if you could sue judges or the president. But what good is the law if corrupt officials and their lawyers can use a legitimate protection to protect unlawful actions? I was foolish enough to believe that the DOJ would look at their egregious actions and compel Sajet to confess to her misdeeds and do the right thing.

Director Kim Sajet did not make a mistake in how she acted; neither did Richard Kurin or any others involved. We are dealing with something completely foreign to accidents and far more nefarious than negligence. We are dealing with animus, willful hostility, and the deliberate actions that followed as a result. Darkness had come in to obscure their guilty deeds behind just laws. It was immensely difficult for me to process how the DOJ defended their sins—which they never denied but rather justified.

No free-speech rights, no due-process rights, no equal protection under the law. I was owed no duty of any kind, since the DOJ ignored the Smithsonian was a trust. Kim Sajet was immune from prosecution. "Throw him off the mountain," the Department of Justice demanded of the judge.

Just then, bursting white light cut through the clouds. Pure ecstasy-producing illumination always came to my rescue like spotlights in the night. The sunlight created shadows from the hidden seams and cracks that would appear like a secret ladder climbing up the once-unclimbable rock wall. No longer hidden, a pathway up became visible under the light of the sun. The views I enjoyed when the thick cloud cleared were nothing but spectacular. These discoveries were marvelously amplified because of the constant pressure that I was under not to fall off the mountain. When light broke through, my hope was renewed, affirming my intuition and fueling my determination.

Stumbling upon the Supreme Court case called *Lebron v. National Railroad Passenger Corp. (Amtrak)* was resplendent indeed.[112] The case involved Amtrak, another federally created enigma at the time. An artist by the name of Michael Lebron (who was a Democrat) wanted to display a political advertisement on the 150-foot spectacular Amtrak screen in Pennsylvania Station in New York City. His display was refused, and Lebron subsequently sued the government for violating his free-speech rights. The similarities between Lebron's case and mine were uncanny. *Lebron* was all about artistic, political free speech by a Democrat; I was all about conservative artistic free speech as a Republican.

However, the specific difference between the two cases was that Amtrak (National Railroad Passenger Corporation) was a federally created "national" entity for a national purpose, similar to the National Endowment for the Arts. The Smithsonian was not. Oddly, Amtrak claimed that it was not a government entity, insisting the First Amendment could not apply. Thus, they claimed, Lebron could not have any protected free-speech rights, as Amtrak was completely private—divorced from government involvement. The unresolved legal question that developed as a result of those claims was, What exactly was the entity status of Amtrak? Was it a purely private entity or business (where the Constitution does not apply), or was it a federally run instrumentality, applying the Constitution—in Lebron's case, the First Amendment?

The case ended up in the U.S. Supreme Court when Justice Antonin Scalia was on the bench. The court took the case because it had to. It fulfilled one of the purposes of the Supreme Court, which is to settle unanswered questions of federal law and legal controversies in general. It was an "aha" moment that gave me the confidence that no matter what happened, the Supreme Court would and had to ultimately decide my case, because the cardinal issue with which I was dealing was identical, except it was regarding the entity status of the Smithsonian Institution.[113]

I argued in my briefs (Haha! Turns out the boy fighting in his underpants really happened! Actually, briefs here mean written filings at the court) that the Smithsonian Institution was a private institution for the benefit of the public, established with private funds (the Smithsonian owns its own property) but operated by the federal government. The Department of Justice argued that the Smithsonian was a completely federal agency exercising government speech, thus depriving me of my First Amendment free-speech rights. In *Lebron*, it was bizarre that the defense strategy to deprive the artist of speech rights was to deny that Amtrak had anything to do with the government. In my case, the DOJ argued that the Smithsonian was absolutely and ultimately a government agency through which the government alone speaks, like the Department of Motor Vehicles in Texas.

One of the prominent cases used to bolster the DOJ's arguments against me having speech rights was *Walker v. Texas Division, Sons of the Confederate Veterans.* In that case, the Supreme Court decided in a close five-to-four ruling that the State of Texas could discriminate against personal viewpoints. Any custom-license-plate content the state-run Department of Motor Vehicles found objectionable could be refused if the application violated the written rules. That seemed reasonable, except that custom plates were paid for by private individuals. It was not like the NEA doling out the cash; it was the other way around. But once again, there were written standards and a process of consideration and then an official ruling in writing. The head of the DMV in Texas did not call up the Confederate Veterans off the record in a hostile manner, twist the rules, ban their participation, and then hang up the phone.

The Smithsonian Institution, a private charity named after a Brit who had never even come to America, founded with his donated private fortune, was compared to the Department of Motor Vehicles agency of the State of Texas in governmental purpose, power, and authority. The DOJ argued that the Smithsonian could discriminate against political viewpoints it did not like, even though it had shown other contrary political viewpoints, because the private Smithsonian, in its selection of artwork, speaks as the federal government. The Supreme Court in the *Walker* case ruled the custom-license-plate program was not a limited free-speech forum but a government agency speaking through the license plates it selected.

One of the cardinal differences, other than the glaring entity-status difference between the DMV and the Smithsonian, was that in the *Walker* case, there were written standards that were followed and public considerations of the offending license-plate-design application. In other words, there was a rigorous and lawful selection process held up against written standards. The design failed to abide by the written standards and was rejected. In my case, there was no rigorous selection process as mandated by law, just egregious violations of the law, but nobody seemed to care.

The bizarre comparison the DOJ made with my case and the *Texas Confederate Veterans* was not just a stretch but akin to a legal Hail Mary. How in the world can the selection of political art, one of the highest forms of personal free expression and speech, be even close to paying to have a symbol printed by the government on a government-made tin license plate? Well, it happens when a desperate legal strategy is employed to deprive one of one's free-speech rights.

According to former Justice Souter, the government-speech doctrine is messy, "is relatively new, and correspondingly impre-cise."[114] Also, the cases cited by the DOJ did not involve political free speech. Imagine the government silencing political speech from the opposition—let's say it permitted a Democrat donkey license plate but forbade a Republican elephant one by appealing to its government speech superseding the First Amendment—what hogwash! No need to imagine the case; mine was precisely that scenario, but worse.

My case presented a perfect unprecedented and unanswered free-speech question that needed to be settled just like in the Amtrak case—there was no comparison with tin license plates. The outcome in *Lebron* was not surprising. In an eight-to-one-ma-jority slam-dunk decision in Lebron's favor, the court ruled Amtrak was responsible for protecting the People's First Amendment free-speech rights under the U.S. Constitution. Amtrak's selection and display of art in the form of advertisements did not speak for the federal government. So how in the world could the private Smith-sonian charity speak for the federal government? Lebron's case was sent back to the lower court, where the unexpected retrial further bolstered my case.

Lebron surprisingly then lost his case on remand (once sent back to the lower courts for retrial) because even though he had discovered he had certain speech rights in Amtrak, Amtrak had the discretion to decide what type of speech could happen in that limited free-speech forum. And since Amtrak had never sold space for a political advertisement before, it did not have the "practice" of displaying politically themed art in the form of advertisements. Thus, Lebron could not compel them to show his political art. Lebron lost.

That surprising ruling inadvertently supported my case. It demonstrated that if speech rights for political viewpoints were not permitted in a government-run limited-speech forum, yet that same entity did at some subsequent point display political speech, they had created a public forum for *all* political speech.

Also, further buttressing my case was another Michael Lebron free-speech case from 1984, in which he won against the Washington Metro Area Transit Authority. The appeals court ruled that since the Metro had accepted political art and displayed other political messages, they had created a free-speech forum. And thus, Lebron's political speech could not be restricted:

> There is no doubt that the poster at issue here conveys a political message; nor is there a question that WMATA has converted its subway stations into public fora by accepting other political advertising…. Political speech may not constitutionally be restricted in a public forum…. We reverse the district court and hold that WMATA violated the plaintiff's first amendment right of free speech.[115]

Another glorious moment of legal revelation happened when I discovered a Supreme Court case related to *Lebron*. The case supported my trust and constitutional claims against the Smithsonian trust. In that marvelous case, a trust was bequeathed by a private individual and entrusted to the government to be run by the government as trustee. The government, acting as trustee, not only owed the beneficiaries fiduciary duties, but since the trust had a government-appointed board, that involvement activated the protections of the U.S. Constitution.

In *Pennsylvania v. Board of Trustees*, Stephen Girard, illiterate yet the wealthiest man in America at the time of his death in 1831, left a six-million-dollar (nearly twelve times bigger than James Smithson's bequest) fortune in trust for the creation of an orphanage to the City of Philadelphia.[116] The state and the city carried out the provisions of the will. The will was for the care and education of White male orphans between the ages of six and ten years. Fast forward to the 1950s. Two boys, Foust and Felder, were denied participation in the trust because they were Black. The state's actions were deemed in violation of the "equal protection of laws" in the Fourteenth Amendment to the U.S. Constitution, which states that:

> No state shall make or enforce any law which shall abridge the privileges or immunities of citizens of the United States; nor shall any state deprive any person of life, liberty, or property, without due process of law; nor deny to any person within its jurisdiction the equal protection of the laws.

No matter what the will of Girard said, if the state was to continue to administer the trust, it could not discriminate against Black American boys. The Supreme Court concluded, to my sheer delight, that even though the government-appointed board was acting as trustee, its refusal to admit the boys because they were Black was discrimination by the state and in violation of the Fourteenth Amendment:

> Therefore, even though the Board was acting as a trustee, its refusal to admit Foust and Felder to the college because they were Negroes was discrimination by the State. Such discrimination is forbidden by the Fourteenth Amendment.[117]

That was crystal clear. There was no effort to deny the trust was a trust. It was a trust, in the same way that the Smithsonian Institution is a trust for the public's benefit. In the Girard case, the Supreme Court decision bound the trust to the Fourteenth Amendment's equal-protection-under-law clause in its selection of participatory beneficiaries of Girard's will. They could do this since the trust was being administered by the government through its appointees. The Supreme Court clarified that private entities could sometimes be regarded as government actors for constitutional purposes. The Girard trust had a board of trustees made up of government appointees, which made it constitutionally liable:

We have held once, *Burton v. Wilmington Parking Authority*, 365 U.S. 715 (1961), and said many times, that actions of private entities can sometimes be regarded as governmental action for constitutional purposes.[118]

Even though my case was unprecedented (in that the Smithsonian Institution had never before been raked over the coals, being exposed and ultimately defined by a U.S. Supreme Court ruling), virtually identical cases in principle did exist, validating and illuminating my arguments. These were glorious discoveries. I knew I was right no matter what anyone else said.

The time was getting close to when Judge McFadden himself would weigh in on the matter. It had been nearly two years from the time I began my climb up Mount Justlaw in search of justice. What would the District Court for the District of Columbia decide?

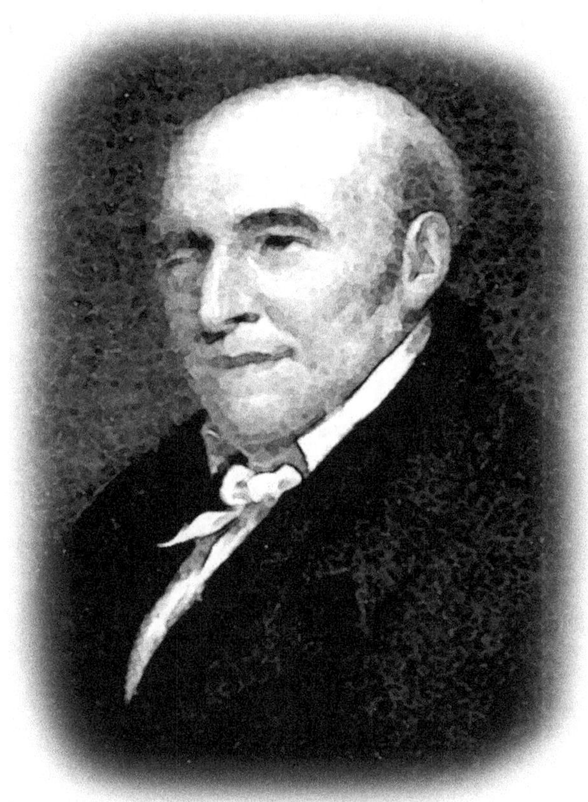

Steven Girard (1750–1831)

Chapter Fifty-One

THE BEAUTY OF MOUNT JUSTLAW

Steven Girard's life was another fantastic American story, but also a story overcast by the shadow of slavery and racial discrimination. Girard's indifference to young boys of dark skin color was a tragedy of the era. Still, the power of just law expressed in the U.S. Constitution would eventually beautify and straighten out his bent and twisted notion about race. The Girard Trust case ruling did precisely that. It also created other questions for me about how it could apply to my case. If the Smithsonian was simply a trust, then the trust should operate for the benefit of the public. The question then became who could participate in the Smithsonian public trust if it was not clearly defined in the will. Should anyone be allowed to walk into the public Portrait Gallery and hang their painting on the wall without a process? Was the trust an active or passive trust, meaning, would trust beneficiaries actively participate in fulfilling the testator's will or just passively enjoy the trust benefits? Who were the Smithsonian beneficiaries and how would they participate? Also, what laws would govern their participation? The answers to these questions are essential to the faithful administration of the trust.

A deeper understanding of trust law would help me, the layman, answer those questions. In the *Lebron* case, the justices often cited A. W. Scott's *The Law of Trusts*. Google no longer worked for me in my research, as I could not gain access to Scott's *Law of Trusts* online. Purchasing was not an option for this costly multi-volume set. The local library did not carry a copy. They directed me to the local law library, but they did not carry it either. To my great joy, the law library managed to locate a copy of the Scott series somewhere else in New York State and had it shipped.

Getting the call from the law librarian had me running to my truck and zipping over to the law library. Excitedly I bounded in, grinning ear to ear. She must have thought I was some sort of nut, watching me skipping (sort of) out of the library with my multi-volume set of *The Law of Trusts*. A. W. Scott was the authority to whom the Supreme Court looked; now I would do the same. Mr. Scott did not disappoint. Scott absolutely vindicated me. It was thrilling to read the pertinent portions of this expansive series on the law of trusts. Who would have known that I would find myself buried in this set of reference books dealing with trust law, only to be filled with joy? What an odd place to find joy!

What treasure had I uncovered that was the source of this joy? O sweet, beautiful, and just law! Moments like these are precious, framing our existence with truth and undergirding our lives as individuals and our society with righteousness. These moments reminded me of the psalms of King David, who proclaimed: "The law from Your mouth is more precious to me than thousands of pieces of silver and gold" (Holy Bible, Psalm 119:72 NIV). Even though I was dealing with man's law, it was just law and was better than gold.

Majestic "just law" is sublime. Law, as an architectural structure, undergirds and frames the physical world. Intellectually, spiritually, and practically, just law creates order, balance, and symmetry out of the havoc of lawlessness. Rightly applied, just law restrains evil madness and chaos, enthrones truth, and establishes justice, producing security. It releases peace and joy in an exquisite symphony, weaving and holding together the fabric of our fragile human experience.

This power of just law remained distant from my Smithsonian saga due to the constantly unattended legal confusion that had created the antithesis of just law—namely, darklaw.

These unanswered issues and questions of law clamored to be harmonized, equalized, categorized, and made beautiful in the United States federal court system.

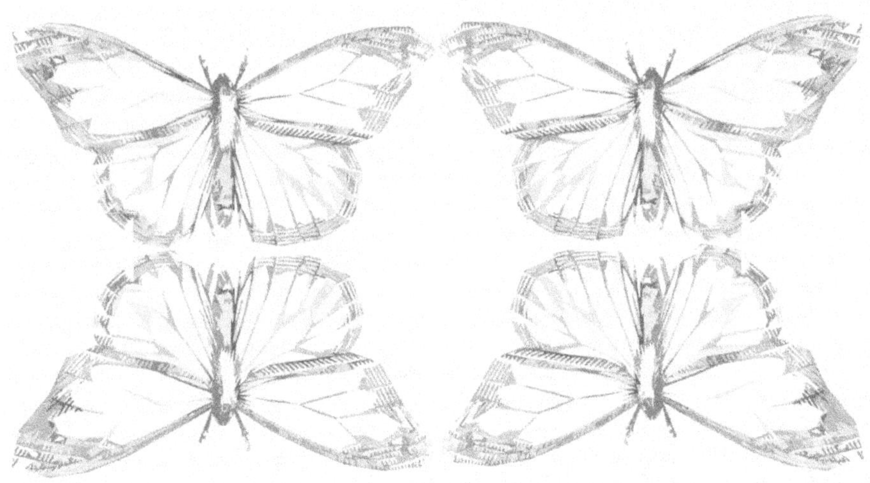

Chapter Fifty-Two

TRUST OR TRUST NOT?

As an American citizen and beneficiary of the Smithson will and as an artist, I believed I had a right to actively participate in the Smithsonian trust. But If I could not prove that I had a particular, participatory interest in the Smithsonian trust, expressed in the Smithsonian National Portrait Gallery, then my claim could fail. Without a legally valid interest, it would be like requesting to be seated and served at a fine restaurant without a reservation—or better still, trying to play golf at a private club without a membership or trying to enter the United States without a visa.

That was one of the principal arguments used by the government against me, as they distorted the Smithsonian's trust-entity status. This is why the entity-status definition was so fundamental and why they had to claim that it had changed. If the Institution's identity was deformed from a trust into a strictly government agency, then the DOJ could claim, as they did, that as a member of the public, I had no right to participate in the government agency.

To further understand how public trusts work, let us take a look at various court cases where these trust issues have been dealt with already. Trusts for the public's benefit do not usually name individual beneficiaries; they usually name groups of people. In Steven Girard's trust, he specifically named orphaned White boys between the ages of six and ten as beneficiaries. The Smithson will calls for an "increase and diffusion of knowledge among men." *Men* was a generic term for men and women and would be confined to Americans, as the bequest was given to "men" of the United States of America. That was a broad and vague mandate that the trustees could interpret and define as they saw fit, but their discretion had to remain within the guardrails of the law of trusts and the U.S. Constitution under which the trust was established. That was demonstrated in the initial vision statement written by the Smithsonian's first secretary, Joseph Henry, in his "Programme of Organization," in which he stated in sections 4–6:

> 4. The objects of the Institution are, 1st, to increase, and 2d, to diffuse knowledge among men.
>
> 5. These two objects should not be confounded with one another. The first is to enlarge the existing stock of knowledge by the addition of new truths; and the second, to disseminate knowledge, thus increased, among men.
>
> 6. The will makes no restriction in favor of any particular kind of knowledge; hence all branches are entitled to a share of attention.[119]

Before the Smithsonian opened its doors, its halls were empty. Where did the Smithsonian get all the artifacts, specimens, relics, sculptures, and paintings? The government did not create them or commission them using taxpayer funds. No, the Institution's content came from We the People through gifts, donations, bequests, and eventually acquisitions. So right away, the American people played an active part in fulfilling the will of Smithson by being actively involved in the creation of the collections in their public Institution.

What laws would then govern the process of accepting donations? People could give anything in the fields of knowledge the trustees decided to increase. Maybe it was rock samples and minerals, skeletons, or fossils—possibly artifacts like old tools, weapons, books, maps, toys, antiques, or memorabilia. Perhaps photos of people or paintings of landscapes, for all of which the government-appointed trustees would have to determine if the submission fit the gap in the record of knowledge they were creating and looking to increase.

But what if someone gave a photo of a political leader and it was accepted as part of the historic catalogue of American political figures? And for example, if someone else wanted to give another photo of another political leader whom the trustees disliked— would they have to accept it? What if that happened? If the museum was for the benefit of the People, and now some group was being denied participation because their political beliefs clashed with the government-appointed trustees, then what?

Now, if it were solely a private museum or gallery, created by a private bequest, run by private citizens with the discretion to fulfill the private will however they wished, they could do what they wanted within the law and there would be no argument. The Constitution would not be involved. But if the constitutionally constrained government acted as trustee of the private will—being the government hand in the Smithsonian glove, and the Smithsonian then barred different political views—operated by the government hand—could the public redress that, and how?

You see, James Smithson gave his gold to the United States for the benefit of the People (on the condition that he could get his name in lights). The representatives of the People received it in trust on the People's behalf. For the government to play a part other than that of a neutral manager would change the nature of their fiduciary duty into something contrary to the donor's will.

James Smithson never made a distinction in the type of knowledge to be increased in the will, so the government as trustee could decide what knowledge to increase. But since the government was constrained by the Constitution, the minute they displayed political speech from one person's viewpoint, they then had to display all political viewpoints; they could not discriminate. But Steven Girard did distinguish the kind or skin color of the boys he wanted to benefit from his trust. That racial distinction ended up causing the government to violate the U.S. Constitution under the Fourteenth Amendment, which regulated the government's actions regarding American citizens of different skin color. And this had to be remedied.

In another case in the Supreme Court of Hawaii, regular citizens legally challenged the administration of a public trust—in their case, a public park—and the court ruled in the citizens' favor. Beyond even a specific group's interest in the public trust, the last line of defense in the administration of a public trust is the general public. If the administration of the trust goes bad—and even the attorney general who should be representing the public joins the corrupt administration—then it's up to the members of the public, the beneficiaries, to right the wrongs:

> If Kapiolani Park is the subject of a charitable trust,…where a trustee of a public charitable trust is a governmental agency,… in such a case, the attorney general as parens patriae, has actively joined in supporting the alleged breach of trust, the citizens of this State would be left without protection, or a remedy, unless we hold, as we do, that members of the public, as beneficiaries of the trust, have standing to bring the matter to the attention of the court.[120]

On May 1, 1906, Congress established another private trust in the District of Columbia, Edes Home, providing perpetual succession for a home for aged and indigent widows. In the bylaws, the Board of Trustees established additional admission criteria beyond those set out in the will and charter.

Back in 1990, the District of Columbia Court of Appeals in Washington, D.C., understood trust law. Since Edes Home was a government-established trust, the court had to determine what laws governed the administration of the trust. The court declared that "although Edes Home is technically a charitable corporation chartered by an Act of Congress, the trial court concluded, and the parties agree, that rules applying to charitable trusts govern the standing issue."[121] This is identical to the Smithsonian Institution and binding as to the law the Smithsonian should follow and which should have been applied in my case as I claimed. The Uniform Trust Code governs charitable trusts in the District of Columbia for the District of Columbia.

The court also went on to describe how, in order to prevent litigious chaos against a public trust (since potentially, every Tom, Dick, and Harry could bring suits for any reason), the court, based upon the broad and expansive Restatement of Trust Law, narrowed the criteria for those who could bring suit against trustees of a public trust. The court determined that the classification may be of uncertain scope without a definition, but a clearly intended beneficiary would have a justiciable interest in the enforcement of the law. That is, if the trust specified the particular group of people it was to benefit, those people could bring suit against the trust. They further defined the "special interest" as a "particularized interest distinct from that of members of the general public." Also, the group would be sharply defined, and its members would be limited in numbers. They also indicated that bylaws created by the trustees would be critical in identifying the special-interest group.

Finally, the court declared that the representative of a class of special-interest beneficiaries must be aiming to vindicate the collective interests of the entire class, not just him or herself having a personal grievance. This would ensure that once settled, there would be no more vexatious litigation:

> Because the will, charter, and by-laws of the corporation establish a set of criteria identifying a limited class of potential beneficiaries of the charitable trust, we conclude that members of that class have a "special interest" in the trust distinct from that of members of the public at large, notwithstanding the Trustees' discretion to exclude them from the trust benefits.[122]

Now let's read the purpose of the Smithsonian National Portrait Gallery:

> (b) The Gallery shall function as a free public museum for the exhibition and study of portraiture and statuary depicting men and women who have made significant contributions to the history, development, and culture of the people of the United States *and of the artists* who created such portraiture and statuary.[123]

Did you see the special-interest group in the Smithsonian National Portrait Gallery? Would the judge see it? The back and forth between the DOJ and myself came to an end. The court had rebuffed my efforts for in-person hearings and oral arguments by denying my motions for the same. It was finally up to Judge Trevor McFadden to rule on my claims and arguments. He would have to pick a side. The DOJ had motioned the court to throw out my case and McFadden was about to render his opinion on the Department of Justice's counterarguments in defense of Kim Sajet and the Smithsonian Institution.

Back on Mount Justlaw, the weather had deteriorated to the point where I could only see ten feet of sheer rock above, while distant tiny trees and vastness fell away beneath. I was forced to end my climb for the day. The crag of the rock was secure and shielded from the driving rain, allowing me to set up camp on the side of the mountain. Anchored in, with just air supporting me, I hung my swallow sack, zipping in for the night.

Chapter Fifty-Three

CERBERUS ROARING

Daily, I would log on to the federal court's online docket, anxiously scrolling in search of the judge's order. I could see when a new document was added to the docket, but I could not open them as a pro se litigant. McFadden's order was going to take awhile, and my patience had improved greatly during my ascent up the mountain, having adapted to its rhythm. But I was eager to know my fate. Camped on the side of the mountain, I had no choice but to wait until the storm clouds cleared to find out in which direction my next steps would be.

On September 19, 2018, I noticed on the docket that Judge Trevor N. McFadden in the District Court for the District of Columbia had handed down the court's judgment. But I could not read the file, requiring me to hang on longer.

Yes, my political free speech had been silenced, but it was more than that, and the judge knew it. An entire group, that of citizen artists, was explicitly named in the Smithsonian law as a participatory special-interest class of beneficiaries in the Smithson trust. Since my artistic free speech had been silenced, it was my duty to fight not only for my rights but for the rights of the whole group of artists. If not, the trustees and their agents would continue to silence artists with whom they disagreed.

Anxiously, I waited for the court's opinion to arrive in the mail. Had McFadden agreed with me in his ruling and decided that the Smithsonian was merely a trust and subject to trust law and the U.S. Constitution, granting me beneficiary-participatory standing? How could he not? My case would move forward into the discovery phase. The court would subpoena all of the officials involved. Those would include Director Kim Sajet, Dr. Richard Kurin, and Chancellor John Roberts, as well as every other official and Board of Regents member to whom I had appealed.

The lawsuit's discovery phase would give me access through the court's subpoena power to request all electronic conversations, either by email, phone, or text. In the deposition phase, part of the discovery phase, I would be able to depose, in person, in Washington, D.C., and under oath, Director Kim Sajet, Dr. Richard Kurin, and Supreme Court Chief Justice John Roberts in his capacity as Smithsonian Board of Regents chancellor. Take a moment and imagine the legal circus that would be!

There I would be, a barely born U.S. citizen, a nobody-artist from Elmira, New York, deposing the Smithsonian royalty. I was not a lawyer, neither rich nor influential, but a self-representing pro se litigant with forma pauperis status, which granted me all of the financial assistance needed to carry out every facet of the discovery process. Was I about to get the green light or not? What a paparazzi party, as the sitting chief justice of the United States Supreme Court would be deposed under oath—by me. Chancellor Roberts would be questioned about Kim Sajet's multiple violations and his fiduciary duty to care for my appeal, since he apparently handed it off to Dr. Kurin. Also, he would be questioned about what happened to the appeal follow-through and what position he had taken regarding the silencing of my political free-speech rights.

Can you imagine hearing Director Kim Sajet trying to justify her conduct as a fiduciary agent whose conduct should have abided by the strictest moral duties of the trust on behalf of the beneficiaries? Can you imagine the look on Dr. Richard Kurin's face when asked in the light of Sajet's hostility why he ignored the appeal enumerating Sajet's egregious and injurious conduct that he was appointed to resolve? And also how he (Kurin) could have concurred with Kim Sajet's egregious behavior? At this point, the fabrications and lies would have bubbled up as the parties involved began to deflect and defend themselves, throwing each other under the bus.

The scales of blind justice and resulting legal jeopardy were precariously tilting to the right. On the right side of the scales, there was me, the nobody artist, with my silenced political speech, my abused due process and trust-beneficiary status, and my injured emotional condition. On the left side of the scales, there were Kim Sajet's breaches of trust, violations of law, and abuse of power, inseparably chained to the chief justice, Smithsonian Chancellor John Roberts, the Smithsonian Institution, and its national prestige.

Did something have to give? Would that something require a man to subtly put his finger on the left side of the scales, forcing an outcome out of view of the blindfolded Lady Justice? Was the legal peril just too great? Did another choice have to be made to shift the seemingly inevitable and shocking embarrassment away from the highly revered, mysterious Institution and away from the esteemed government officials involved?

If so, that something would have to be the law itself. Somewhere, a decision would have to be made either to toe the status-quo line, distorting the law, or to green-light the unsettling discovery phase of the case—a case that could set off a cascade of legal ramifications that would disturb the fragile equilibrium, causing far-reaching and historic consequences. Judicial decisions are sometimes amazing and courageous acts of justice. Other times, they are pernicious acts of the will of men who, because of other controlling forces (from the preservation of personal power and prestige to the preservation of the status quo of the times to deeply held prejudices), bend the law under the human will to their self-preserving ends.

To illustrate this, look at this case and see just how deeply and catastrophically the will of man can subvert written law. In the Supreme Court's majority eight-to-one ruling in *Plessy v. Ferguson* from 1896, one of the worst judicial decisions was made. The historic Supreme Court case established the constitutional doctrine for racial-segregation laws for the next half-century. That's right, and it was the legal gymnastics, status-quo bias, and deep-seated prejudice of overtly racist jurists that managed to legally split society in two, based on the color of one's skin, with a veneer and appearance of justice. Yes, so long as there was the equal quality of the facilities and services citizens could enjoy—whether they be buses, schools, or restaurants—segregation by skin color was lawful, and the Constitution could apply to their legal pretzel. This is a grave and sobering reminder that men and women in black robes can and often do fall short of truth and justice because of political peer pressure and personal prejudice.

But one courageous justice dissented against the other eight in *Plessy v. Ferguson*. Justice Harlan's dissent argued:

> In view of the constitution, in the eye of the law, there is in this country no superior, dominant, ruling class of citizens. There is no caste here. Our constitution is color-blind, and neither knows nor tolerates classes among citizens. In respect of civil rights, all citizens are equal before the law. The humblest is the peer of the most powerful. The law regards man as man, and takes no account of his surroundings or of his color when his civil rights as guaranteed by the supreme law of the land are involved....
>
> In my opinion, the judgment this day rendered will, in time, prove to be quite as pernicious as the decision made by this tribunal in the Dred Scott case.[124]

That travesty of justice took over fifty years to correct in the 1954 case of *Brown v. Board of Education of Topeka*, when *Plessy v. Ferguson* was overturned. Over fifty years! My case may seem insignificant in comparison, yet Justice Harlan's dissent applies just as aptly. Violating someone's constitutionally protected political free-speech rights is egregious, no matter when or to whom or by whom the violation is committed. All citizens are equal before the law. The U.S. Supreme Court ruled that there is "practically universal agreement that a major purpose of that [the First] Amendment [is] to protect the free discussion of governmental affairs."[125] Additionally, "expression on public issues has always rested on the highest rung of the hierarchy of First Amendment values."[126]

To my dismay, however, Judge Trevor McFadden threw out my case. In his memorandum opinion, he chose to agree with the Department of Justice and deny the Smithsonian Institution was a trust, deny my rights of participation in the Smithsonian trust as an artist, deny there were any breaches of trust, deny there were breaches of the duties of loyalty, care, and impartiality, deny the First Amendment applied, deny my political free-speech rights, deny my Fifth Amendment due-process rights, deny my Fifth Amendment equal-protection-under-law rights, deny that Kim Sajet violated any federal laws regarding lying, impartiality, or following procedure as a federal employee, deny my injured condition, and deny justice itself as he dismissed my case. The remarkable public-trust-extinguishing memorandum opinion all hinged on this one fundamental question, that of the Smithsonian Institution's entity status. Once the judge deformed the Smithsonian's entity status, he doomed my case, justifying his ruling as he did. Judge McFadden ruled as follows:

> The Smithsonian is a government institution through and through....
> ...(The Smithsonian was created "pursuant to a trust bequest," and "the United States, as trustee, holds legal title to the original Smithson trust property and later accretions"). But even if "the increase and diffusion of knowledge" was originally a private goal, Congress ratified it, and the United States now has complete discretion in how to fulfill it.[127]

Notice the subtle use of language used in the creation of McFadden's "ratification" theory: "But even if," and then "was originally a private goal." For a moment, he acknowledged everything I argued, but relegated it to the past. But the judge could not allow my arguments to stand, so he alone determined that it was no longer a trust; it had evolved. If the private trust had been lawfully extinguished (which can happen to trusts in certain circumstances), the status change would have been due to a federal-court ruling or a congressional act. Obviously, because no such thing ever happened to the Smithsonian, the judge cited nothing—no ruling, no law, and no act.

Now let's remember and compare those words to what then-Supreme Court Justice and Smithsonian Chancellor Taft said in 1927: "The Smithsonian Institution is not, and never has been considered a government bureau. It is a private institution under the guardianship of the Government." This statement by Chief Justice and Chancellor Taft was made to counteract any notion that maybe the Institution had changed into something belonging to the federal government or an arm of the federal government. Also, remember the speech made for Chief Justice Warren Burger, which affirmed: "…precisely because it [the Smithsonian Institution] is not an organizational part of the federal government." But Judge McFadden ruled the Smithsonian was the federal government "through and through." What we have here, ladies and gentlemen, is a case of acute judicial schizophrenia.

Like a proclamation by a king and not by the force of law, Judge McFadden decreed his ratification theory into law. He had to do this because he neither had a legal precedent nor an act of Congress that he could cite. The ruling reversed the terms upon which the trust was accepted. Originally, the government's role was merely to act as trustee. McFadden changed Congress's role into a federal mandate, without a congressional act. He chose to make that declaration because it was the only way to protect the Smithsonian and its eminent officials. In essence, the judge declared that when the United States received Smithson's private property in trust, the government was in effect being deceptive and had no intention of fulfilling the private will of Smithson.

By his ruling, McFadden was saying that the original transaction between the Smithson estate and the U.S. government did not really involve acceptance of the duty of a trustee but that the transaction was "ratified" such that the government would become the recipient and beneficiary of the gold. According to McFadden, Smithson's private property would become nationalized property, now belonging to the federal government for a strictly governmental purpose: government speech. (So why did Congress, upon receipt of the gold, borrow it from the trust and pay 6 percent interest, if the gold was the government's money?[128])

The truth is, the property was bequeathed to the United States, not to the federal government! Congress, the branch that could accept the trusteeship, simply agreed to accept the bequest on behalf of Smithson and the United States to carry out the will of the private citizen James Smithson. With the judge's ruling, the private will of James Smithson would now be absorbed into the federal government, who would assume the will and now make the will its own, extinguishing the will and free speech of the private person. Explaining why the Institution was still called the Smithsonian Institution, a precondition of the private will, would require another Jedi mind trick and sleight of hand, telling the people that what the will of Smithson actually said, and what the Act of Congress actually said, did not actually mean what they actually said.

By that declaration, the judge could then justify most of his other arguments that appeared to be sound—if in fact, the Smithsonian Institution was, as he said it was, a completely federal entity "through and through," on par with the National Endowment for the Arts. Except his Smithsonian government-speech assertion would run into a problem, as we shall soon see. Unless McFadden's ruling is overturned in the courts (or Congress is compelled to act), it will remain the law of the land.

McFadden's theory had significant constitutional consequences. If the private will of James Smithson, speaking in the voice of private free speech, no longer existed, then who was now speaking? Truth be told, when I read this bizarre opinion, I wondered whether McFadden's legal pretzel was his deliberate attempt to force my appeal up the legal ladder. My appeal would have to then compel a higher court to make a judgment that would have the force of precedent that the district-court decision did not have. Or, in contrast, was the judge just going along with the status quo to preserve his own skin?

Stretching out the consequences, McFadden's theory caused the creation of a Cerberus-like form of the federal government. In McFadden's memorandum opinion, he said, "It is true that the Smithsonian, Cerberus-like, sports heads from the Executive, Legislative, and Judicial Branches."[129] What in the world was the judge saying? He went on to say, "That conclusion brings us close to deciding Mr. Raven's speech claim, because when the government speaks, the First Amendment's Free Speech Clause does not limit what it says."[130] According to the government-speech theory, what McFadden says is true when it legitimately applies to the federal government. But that is not the case with the Smithsonian. How else could Smithsonian Secretary Clough proclaim the artist had "rights to free speech?"[131] There cannot be both. The whole point of representative government is that the people give their voice to the elected representatives to speak on their behalf. This government speaking must be according to and within their elected positions and spheres of authority. But the Smithsonian Institution is James Smithson speaking; that is why it was and continues to be named after him.

To make it worse for McFadden, even the U.S. Supreme Court in *National Endowment for the Arts v. Finley* stated in their decision that "the Government freely admits, however, that it neither speaks through the expression subsidized by the NEA."[132] This contradicts McFadden's government-speech theory that he applied in defense of the Smithsonian Institution. If the selection of art by the truly federally created government agency, the National Endowment for the Arts, does not constitute government speech, how on God's green earth does the selection of art by a private charitable trust, merely run by the government, constitute government speech?

Would the Court of Appeals for the District of Columbia and the U.S. Supreme Court allow the lower-court ruling at the hands of rookie Judge McFadden to stand when it contradicts the Supreme Court decision in *NEA v. Finley*?

Let us take a moment and examine how McFadden's three-headed Cerberus-like federal beast speaks. The federal government, made up of three separate but coequal branches, was established to restrain the abuse of power by creating checks and balances through the three separate branches. McFadden created out of the three a new singular form of the tri-part federal government that speaks as one, with one unified voice. How else could it speak? Would the different heads of the three branches take turns speaking while the others are playing golf, yielding to one another on different days of the week?

The Constitutional conundrum untangles itself if the law is simply applied; yes, of course, but at what cost to the beast? You see, in order for the Smithsonian to function under the Constitution and under trust law, the individuals—when acting in the capacity of trustees who also happen to be elected or appointed members of the three different branches of the federal government—had to remove their robes (their authority, so to speak, whilst remaining government appointees) before entering the Smithsonian board room as Regent trustees of Smithson's will. The officials who established the Smithsonian understood this because, as Justice Jackson opined in 1952, "The Constitution...enjoins upon its branches separateness but interdependence, autonomy but reciprocity."[133] Thus, you cannot have "separateness but interdependence" and "autonomy but reciprocity" when the three branches of government sit at the same Board of Regents table, making decisions as one unified body. There would have to be three separate Boards of Regents, and they would have to sit at three separate tables, meeting in three separate rooms... Or else, as James Madison wrote in the *Federalist Papers*, "The fundamental principles of a free constitution are subverted" because "the whole power of one department is exercised by the same hands which possess the whole power of another department."[134]

Further adding fuel to the Smithsonian separation-of-powers dilemma, the daughter of Smithsonian Provost Dr. Richard Kurin, an attorney named Jaclyn Kurin, posted an essay online in 2017 (coincidently, around the same time as my lawsuit): "Unconstitutional Limbo: Why the Smithsonian Institution May Violate the Separation of Powers Doctrine." In the essay, Attorney Jaclyn lays out a comprehensive record that paints a very similar picture to what I argued in my briefs against the Smithsonian—just with sharper legal skills.

No one exercises their federal-governmental authority when acting in the capacity of a trustee executing another person's will. They are, in effect, by proxy, becoming that person, to do that person's will with his property. They act as neutral trustees like regular citizens, regardless of their status at their day jobs, just like church members acting as trustees of a church.

Imagine if these elected members of Congress, the Senate, the vice president, and the chief justice all happened to go to the same little old church. The church has about thirty old-timers as members, and these powerful officials happen to sit on the board of trustees of the tiny church.

Can you imagine John Roberts, acting as chief justice, arguing over the color of the choir robes for their five-member choir, saying, "Historically, our robes have been black, so precedent establishes the color of the choir robes. The robes will be black—I'm the chief justice of the Supreme Court after all!"

And then Vice President Harris chimes in with a head bob, hand on her hip, and a side-to-side wave of her finger, "Excuse me—I'm speaking, I'm speaking. Well, I was actually elected, not appointed, and I'm the vice president, so I'm making an executive decision: they're gonna be pink, Baby—that's right, pink!"

The three members of the Senate and the three members of the House huddle for a minute, and for once in their careers actually agree on something, replying in unison, "Oh no you don't, VP

Harris! You're not going to pretend you are President Biden. You have no executive authority here. We have a super, super-majority here!" With some hearty congratulatory backslapping, their nightcaps on, and sleeping bags under their arms, they continue, "We are just going to camp out here in the church where the Speaker cannot find us and filibuster for the next week. We cannot decide what color the robes should be, and this will serve as an excuse to not get anything done!"

This was now Judge McFadden's creature—his Cerberus-like leadership of the Smithsonian Institution. Oh, and let's not forget the now-eight regular citizen members of the Board of Regents. They must be like the snakes on Cerberus's back. The citizens are not elected officials—they are ordinary citizens appointed from the public to be on the Board. And now, when the Board of Regents acts in a quorum, in the capacity to make decisions requiring eight board members to be present, do these unelected members speak as the federal government too? This would be like Nancy Pelosi appointing her gardener to be Speaker of the House for a week while she is on vacation. Any combination of the mixture of elected, appointed, and regular citizens now would constitute a new multi-headed federal agency that would be speaking as the federal government. Now that is no longer a conundrum; that is a beast—a three-headed beast with snakes on its back, by the name of *Cerberus*!

Stretching his ratification theory into the absurd in order to justify his fabrication, Judge McFadden claimed that political accountability existed and thus validated his Smithsonian government-speech theory. He ruled that some of the members of the Board of Regents could be defenestrated, or removed, from the Board by public elections. That is, if the public actually knew who they were and what they were supposed to be doing. My experience has shown me that most people do not know anyone who sits on the Board of Regents. Government accountability, compelled by free elections, is the critical component of any elected democratic governmental institution. If the public does not like the performance or direction an elected official has taken, they can remove and replace them. Please note that nine of the sixteen members of the Smithsonian Board of Regents are *not* removable via elections, including the chief justice, who is appointed to office. Only seven officials could actually be changed. These include the vice president, three "appointed" members of the House, and three "appointed" members of the Senate. So, even if the People miraculously managed to vote all seven simultaneously out of office, thus removing them from the Board of Regents, out of the seven electable officials, the only official who is guaranteed to sit back down on the board is the vice president. The other members of Congress are randomly appointed to serve on the board, thus giving no guarantee who you vote in would sit on the Board of Regents. Can you remember the last time you heard any candidate running for office claiming they were also going to sit on the Smithsonian Board of Regents if elected?

The Board of Regents requires eight members to be present to make binding decisions. So just how does McFadden's so-called political accountability work if the voting super-majority of nine members cannot be removed via the election process?

This is the extreme to which Judge McFadden distorted reality in order to buttress his government-speech theory, erected to protect the Smithsonian and deny me my First Amendment guaranteed rights of political free speech. Unwittingly, did McFadden just include himself in the judiciary part of his Cerberus analogy as the defender of the Smithsonian?

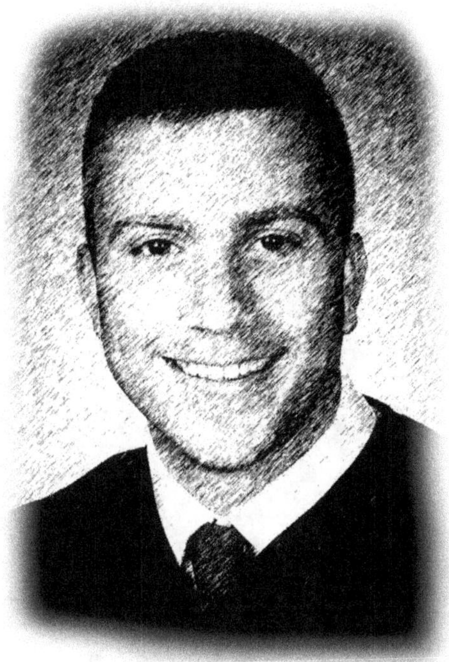

Judge Trevor McFadden (1978–present), (photoshopped)

Chapter Fifty-Four

CERBERUS UNCHAINED

CERBERUS STOOD UNCHAINED ON THE STEPS OF THE Smithsonian Institution. That image was the source of inspiration for the illustration on the front cover of this book. Judge McFadden once again contradicted his ratification theory. He revealed his ignorance of the matter and confused the issue some more when he declared, "It is true that the Smithsonian acts as a 'trustee,' in that it administers 'the original Smithson trust property and later accretions.' Dong, 125 F.3d at 883."[135] The Smithsonian is the trust, not the trustee. That is why the Smithsonian is not the federal government. Congress is the trustee of the Smithsonian trust. Congress would not need to be trustee if the Smithsonian were, as McFadden said, "the government through and through."

McFadden went on, "But as explained above, the Smithsonian's management has complete, unfettered discretion to determine how best to pursue 'the increase and diffusion of knowledge among men'."[136] This statement seemed designed to excuse the Smithsonian and its officials from any accountability. Yes, the trustees had complete discretion regarding how to fulfill the will, but it was not unfettered. McFadden did not follow up with the laws the Smithsonian had to follow. Thus, in effect, he unchained the beast to do whatever it wanted. You see, he could not say that they had unfettered discretion to fulfill the "will of Smithson" because he would have acknowledged the Smithsonian Institution was a trust which he had just hollowed out (although he still paid the trust lip service as if it still existed—like a shell, just without any applicable laws). For the judge, the increase and diffusion of knowledge had become a government mandate.

That proclamation violated the very Smithsonian Act of Congress that declared in its first section the establishment's purpose was

> for the increase and diffusion of knowledge among men; and by that name shall be known and have perpetual succession, with the powers, limitations, and restrictions, hereinafter contained, and no other.[137]

Congress established the legal boundaries contained in the Act declaring that Congress would faithfully execute the trust "according to the will of the liberal and enlightened donor."[138]

The will of James Smithson fetters the Smithsonian trust. The law of trusts fetters trusts; that is what defines them as trusts and keeps them as trusts. The written standards for portraiture acceptance fetters the Smithsonian directors. The judge blew through those standards as well by refusing to find Smithsonian Director Kim Sajet in violation of the written standards. The U.S. Constitution fetters the Smithsonian management as a government-run facility. If Congress wishes to change the law, it may, as stated in Section 11, and it would have to be done by a legal amendment. But at all times, individual rights are not to be extinguished:

> SEC. 11. And be it further enacted, That there is reserved to Congress the right of altering, amending, adding to, or repealing, any of the provisions of this act. Provided, That no contract,

or individual right, made or acquired under such provisions, shall be thereby divested or impaired.[139]

Contrary to everything I argued, nowhere did the judge indicate any set of rules by which the Smithsonian management was to abide—no trust laws, no federal laws, no standards, no fiduciary duty, no constitutional accountability, no administrative procedure law, no Freedom of Information Act—nothing. The beast was loose and remains on the loose.

In using the "Cerberus-like" analogy, the judge unwittingly gave me the title to this book. He alluded to the story of Hercules, who, in his final and most difficult labor, had to subdue and chain up Cerberus, the three-headed hound-like beast that guarded the gates of hell. I was encouraged by the story, since the beast does eventually get defeated and chained. Like Hercules, though, I first had to get my hands on Cerberus.

Chapter Fifty-Five

HERR ODIOUS DIREKTOR

JUDGE MCFADDEN HAD TO DO TWO THINGS TO SHELTER THE Smithsonian and its officials: 1. Distort the entity status and thus remove any legal grounds for my constitutional claims to stick against the Smithsonian Institution, and 2. Minimize the conduct of the Smithsonian trustees and their agents so as to place them beyond the risk of conviction. By paying lip service to the trust as something that once existed, the judge extinguished the Smithsonian trust's legal obligations. By extension, he also extinguished the trustee duties of care and loyalty. It is so hard to fathom his ruling, when right in the Smithsonian Statement of Values and Code of Ethics the Institution says this about itself and its standards of conduct:

> The Smithsonian Institution is a public trust whose mission is the increase and diffusion of knowledge. The Smithsonian was established by the United States Congress to carry out the fiduciary responsibility assumed by the United States in accepting the bequest of James Smithson to create the Smithsonian Institution. We are accountable to the general public as well as to the Smithsonian's multiple stakeholders in carrying

out this responsibility. We recognize that the public interest is paramount.

Serving the Smithsonian is a privilege and those who work on its behalf have a responsibility to maintain the highest standards of honesty, integrity, professionalism, and loyalty to the Institution....

This Statement of Values and Code of Ethics establishes the standards and principles for ethical conduct that apply to the Institution collectively and to all members of the Smithsonian community, which includes Regents, staff, volunteers, advisory board members, fellows, interns, research associates, affiliated individuals, and others who have been entrusted to act on behalf of or in the name of the Smithsonian....

Given this unique and special status, the Smithsonian must be mindful that it is a public trust operating on behalf of the American public.... As such, the Smithsonian will be guided by the principles of the federal sector in the conduct of its activities whenever appropriate and consistent with its mission and trust responsibilities. In all other cases, the Institution will follow the principles and best practices for fiduciary stewardship in the nonprofit sector.[140]

In all honesty, as I reread this now, I am still struggling to reconcile the judicial schizophrenia that is shorting out my mind, and my heart is infuriated. Are we even talking about the same institution? The Smithsonian admits it is "accountable to the general public" but refuses accountability—and the courts even agree. It is genuinely dreadful that this confusion exists when the district court had the chance to clear it up. Because of this ongoing confusion, those officials keep on living off the back of the taxpayer, and they all still have their jobs. But the little guy, the simple citizen, is shut out and deprived of his constitutional free-speech rights, equal-protection rights, and beneficiary rights and benefits of participation in the People's Institution.

The actions of federal employee, covered executive, and Smithsonian National Portrait Gallery Director Kim Sajet were denounced as "partisan"[141] by Judge McFadden, yet somehow perfectly legal. Except, does not Federal Regulation 5 CFR § 2635.502 apply? It states:

> You must take appropriate steps to avoid any appearance of loss of impartiality in the performance of your official duties. Beyond the conflict of interest law discussed at 18 U.S.C. § 208, ethics regulations require all employees to recuse themselves from participating in an official matter if their impartiality would be questioned.

I imagined myself arguing with the judge in court:

"Your Honor, surely a federal employee impartiality law like 5 CFR 2635.502 or 19-1308 of the trust law must apply to this?"

"No!" the judge snapped back.

"But you just ruled her actions were partisan," I countered.

Digging in, he replied, "Yes, they were, but no laws apply!"

"So Smithsonian government officials can be partisan in their official decisions when the law says they cannot?" I jabbed back.

"Yes, that is what I just said yesterday! The Smithsonian Institution is a private charity today and federal law does not apply," the judge firmly replied.

"Your Honor, that is ridiculous!" I snapped. "Since you found Sajet's conduct to be partisan, at a minimum, order the Smithsonian to reprocess my application and reconsider my painting according to written Smithsonian standards."

"Absolutely not!" the judge replied, "Director Kim Sajet and the Smithsonian Board of Regents did nothing wrong!"

"I'm going to appeal your decision. Somewhere a judge will agree with me that the law is the law," I sternly responded.

Raising his voice, McFadden doubled down, "I am the judge of the District Court for the District of Columbia. Your arguments will go no further; you can appeal it all you want!" as he pounded his gavel.

Not even the Smithsonian's standards of conduct applied, because Smithsonian bylaws are not federal laws, as it is a private institution when necessary, and as we learned, it is not a federal agency under the Administrative Procedure Act (APA). But McFadden said the Smithsonian was the government "through and through," so the bylaws were then federal laws that could be violated.

Smithsonian law states:

All members of the Smithsonian community have a duty to act in the best interest of the Smithsonian rather than in furtherance of their personal interest or for private gain. We must avoid apparent or actual conflicts of interest and ensure that potential conflicts of interest are disclosed and managed in accordance with applicable guidelines, directives, and standards of conduct.[142]

How about the breach of the duty of impartiality spelled out in Section 19-1308 of the Uniform Trust Code for the District of Columbia? *"The Duty of Impartiality; the trustee shall act impartially."* Sorry, I forgot, the Smithsonian is apparently not a trust anymore; right now, at the moment, it has been ratified.

Chief Justice John Roberts, acting as chancellor, and Dr. Richard Kurin, his agent, who concurred with Director Sajet's partisan actions, must be liable, right?

How about applying the First Amendment free-speech clause or the Fifth Amendment's due-process and equal-protection-under-law clause of the Constitution to this partisan conduct? This too fails because trust beneficiaries supposedly have no rights of participation in their own Institution.

This was just another layer of grease applied to that golden pig, making it impossible to catch. Judge McFadden went on to further contradict himself and then deny me my opportunity to let the jury decide whether or not I had been injured by Sajet's "partisan" actions, as required by law according to the decision in *Harris v. Jones*:

It is for the jury to determine whether, in the particular case, the conduct has been sufficiently extreme and outrageous to result in liability.[143]

How else could the injuries be determined—by the judge alone? By the judge reading my claims on paper, without anyone hearing a single word of testimony under oath? What? Would writing my claims in my own blood have been more persuasive? The whole purpose of a jury is to determine liability based upon the established facts, upon hearing evidence. What would be the point of a case going to trial before a jury if the judge had already determined the facts and decided for the jury? It made no sense. But it did in my case, when every claim of mine was denied and dismissed before it ever could get to trial because of who and what was involved.

The judge further dug his absurd ruling into the ridiculous when he spoke for the jury by saying:

> No impartial jury could conclude that the Defendant's politically-biased rejection was "so outrageous in character, and so extreme in degree, as to go beyond all possible bounds of decency, and to be regarded as atrocious, and utterly intolerable in a civilized community."[144]

How could Judge McFadden speak for the jury as if to know their minds? Had he never read the First Amendment regarding the freedom of speech? According to the judge, "politically biased" silencing of free speech by the government is not "outrageous"— sorry I forgot, I had no free-speech rights. That, ladies and gentlemen, is outrageous! In my claims, I clearly described the crushing depression, personal frustration, and embarrassment I had experienced after being silenced by Kim Sajet. I did not make up the stunning paralysis in my soul that gripped me, lingering for days after the tongue-lashing I received on the phone that fateful day when Sajet came for me. Those claims regarding the injuries I suffered were for a jury to hear and make a factual determination. Confusing the matter further, McFadden did get it right by ruling Sajet's actions to be partisan, but not just partisan—the federal judge ruled the director of the Smithsonian Institution's actions were also "*odious.*" Odious actions cause severe injuries to people; that is why they are called odious. A jury made up of regular citizens was deprived of their opportunity to determine the liability of the injuries based upon hearing the odious evidence. To top it off, Kim Sajet, represented by the Department of Justice, never denied a *single word* in my claims.

It is personally and emotionally tough for me to relive these facts of my case since the unresolved issues at law remain. Rereading my legal briefs makes me angry, as I can see how justice was miscarried. It is extremely disappointing. But there is hope. Yes, while we still live and breathe, there is always hope to pursue a righteous outcome.

After McFadden said that what I had endured did not rise to the level of being "extreme" or "outrageous," he contradicted himself and ruled Sajet's actions were "odious." In order to avoid invoking the trust and giving life to my breach-of-trust claims, the judge had to avoid defining Sajet's actions as breaches of the fiduciary duty of care or the duty of loyalty. In effect, McFadden said Sajet's conduct as a trustee could be odious and yet simultaneously not be a breach of trust, or not extreme or outrageous. *Odious*, by Webster's definition, means "hateful." *Odious* is as strong an adjective as one can find; it is synonymous with the word *evil*, for goodness' sake. Some other synonyms for *odious* as defined by *Webster's Dictionary* are: *abhorrent, abominable, repugnant, scandalous, shocking.* Sir Winston Churchill further filled in the meaning of *odious* for us in one of his most famous speeches, when he said Adolf Hitler's advances towards Great Britain were accomplished by "the odious apparatus of Nazi rule."[145]

So, according to Federal Judge Trevor McFadden, odious, shocking, scandalous, repugnant, abominable, abhorrent actions by a government official do not "go beyond all possible bounds of decency,…to be regarded as atrocious, and utterly intolerable in a civilized community." So let me ask you, Judge McFadden, what would you call, or how would you describe, conduct that does? Try to find those adjectives and not use the word *odious*!

For Judge McFadden to excuse Sajet from any legal consequences, he had to minimize and recategorize what Sajet had done. He had to squeeze her actions under the legal bar, justifying the legal pretzel he had twisted in his ruling. He had to reduce Sajet's actions to simply a "professional insult."[146] Yes that is right, silencing someone's free speech and breaching fiduciary trust is simply insulting.

The question then arises: Can a government-paid official, a director of a federally run institution, entrusted as an agent of a public trust with trustee fiduciary duty, simply insult you or me professionally? Sajet could insult another director or colleague. A work colleague can insult you, a man on the bus can insult you, your spouse can insult you, I can insult you. But when dealing with a government representative, can that official insult you or me when acting in their official capacity? Or is it called something else? Since there is a position, authority, and power discrepancy involved, and since they are not your colleague standing on a level playing field, can their words simply be a professional insult? In a lawsuit from 1977 in Maryland, we find our answer.

> In cases where the defendant is in a peculiar position to harass the plaintiff, and cause emotional distress, his conduct will be carefully scrutinized by the courts.... The extreme and outrageous character of the defendant's conduct may arise from his abuse of a position, or relation with another person, which gives him actual or apparent authority over him, or power to affect his interests.[147]

Do you think that in my case, Judge McFadden "carefully scrutinized" Sajet's odious actions in relation to the abuse of the power of her position? Imagine trying to justify and excuse King George's tyranny by saying he had a bad day on the job. The twenty-page court decision dismissing my case from the U.S. District Court for the District of Columbia came with a wallop.

As I looked up at the path I was about to climb on Mount Justlaw, a sudden gust of wind slammed me into its angry face. Losing my footing and grip simultaneously sent me into an uncontrollable dangling spin. The rope twisted itself into a knotted lump that popped the cam out of the rock, and straight down I plummeted, landing hard with a whump on a rock ledge. Lying there gasping and barely able to breathe, my right hand slid over the cold, damp stone until I felt the jagged edge of the ledge. Peering down over my shoulder at the hungry chasm spinning below, I saw just how close to disaster I was. Rolling my head back and staring up, the mountain spun into a white blur, and then—black.

I could not help but question myself, demanding answers and understanding, as my situation severely tested my will to continue. Was it worth it? All that effort to be knocked out with a stroke of the pen? Could I continue? Did I even want to continue? Was there a way back up? I was stunned.

People around me who did not know or understand what I knew extended commiserations, as if to say, "We knew you were wrong, but nice try—that was a noble effort." Even going back on Frank Acomb's radio show, I had to get ahold of my situation, bandage my wounds, and chart my way back into the federal court system.

Yes, I was going to appeal. I would not stop until I received justice. After all, the ruling only enforced the root issue. Even the courts continually got the Smithsonian's entity status confused. That issue, once and for all, needed to be determined at the appeal-court level, since those decisions would become binding precedent and would finally unravel the mystery of the Smithsonian.

Chapter Fifty-Six

CONSERVATIVE POLITICAL ART CONFERENCE

Aafter getting spurned by the Smithsonian National Portrait Gallery, I tried to figure out another way of displaying my Trump portrait in Washington, D.C. A venue at that time never materialized. That remained the case until a couple of years later, after a major left-leaning online news outlet covered the lawsuit story in 2019. That story was picked up by every reputable art-news site across the country and Europe: *Artnet News, Hyperallergic, Art Critique, Design-Taxi, Art@Law,* and many other art-related blogs. Their stories ranged from a couple of serious articles asking the right questions to the downright evil and slanderous, engendering vicious mockery and hatred.

The art magazines' Facebook and Twitter posts lit up with a mix of outrage and ridicule, thousands of comments, and thousands of shares. It got so bad that Internet trolls started to pop up on my Facebook page, spewing hatred on everything I posted. There were so many at one point that it felt like I was playing whack-a-mole, as I deleted their vile posts continuously as they popped up. Personal threats began to increase, and I even had my children remove their surname from their pages, lest they too become victims of those vicious Internet trolls. What had I done? Where was the support in the art community for artistic free speech?

The hatred for Trump was visceral; people could not control themselves in the way they reacted. There was little if any serious dialogue coming from the Left. The concepts of being curious, objective, constructively critical, and respectfully opposed, and maybe even reserving final aesthetic judgments until one saw the original painting, were figments of my imagination. How could anyone judge the giant original painting based upon a tiny photo on a small screen or maybe a laptop? They just saw Trump, the eagle, and the flag, and they hated it. Rather than honestly debating the implications of perhaps the painting's prescient nature or its symbolic accuracy that put it in a class of paintings all of its own, the preferred response was to frenzy.

2019 was to be an epic year, starting off with a blast. I was accepted to participate as a vendor at CPAC (Conservative Political Action Conference) 2019. This conference was the very apex of national conservative political activism, and this was where I would next display my Trump painting. This was huge for me. Not only was it an exciting opportunity, but it was a desperately needed pick-me-up after the many months of agonizing and discouraging litigation. Getting accepted to CPAC was huge. Getting the giant painting to the conference would become another unexpected and extreme challenge.

The road to CPAC had begun a few years earlier. Back in December 2015, Congressman Tom Reed wrote an official letter of support for my application to the Smithsonian at the recommendation of Joe Sempolinski. (Joe was Reed's assistant at the time and was very supportive of my work.) Since 2016, I had been inviting Tom Reed, who was my congressional representative, to view the Trump painting in person at my studio in Elmira. His endorsement could finally compel him to act on my behalf in the House of Representatives. He could have invoked my case and used it to echo support for the other House bills pressing hard for Smithsonian reform. He never did. Reed was very cautious and unwilling to engage me or my legal cause against the Smithsonian. I petitioned him multiple times to fight for my constitutional rights in Washington, even as we had discussed the case once over the phone. Publicly, he would discuss federal issues affecting his constituents (me)—for example, veterans' benefits and their poor treatment by the Veterans Administration. But for some reason, an artist's shocking treatment by Smithsonian officials was not a significant enough struggle for him to take up in the House, and he said that he could not get involved with my lawsuit.

Smithsonian prestige is a persuasive power exerting tremendous peer pressure for anyone considering upending the status quo by poking the beast. I neither wanted nor asked for his involvement with my lawsuit. Instead, I was looking for him to pressure the Smithsonian through his seat in Congress, especially after I informed Reed that he was also a trustee of the Smithson will as a Congressman. This was news to his ears. Reed even personally knew the Smithsonian secretary at the time, David Skorton. Skorton was formerly the principal of Cornell University in Ithaca, New York, about forty minutes away from Elmira, where I lived. I had previously unsuccessfully appealed to David Skorton. Reed told me that he had spoken with Skorton about my situation. Still, nothing had ever happened. Reed did nothing; David Skorton did nothing, just talk—probably about that pesky and persistent Raven. What Skorton did do several months later, surprising even officials at the Smithsonian, was abruptly resign. Out of the blue, he broke his nine-year commitment after only three and a half years. That was an extremely unusual departure at that level of leadership. The veil of prestige was apparently fragile, as Skorton's inaction in my case created a risk of embarrassing exposure. Was his resignation a case of legacy preservation breaching contract and fiduciary duty?[148]

After many months of my persistence, including the possibility of me publicly rescinding my vote for him, Congressman Reed finally did accept my invitation and saw my painting in person.

Then he took the initiative and wrote an official letter supporting my artistic efforts. I was very grateful. The letter, dated September 14, 2018 (my birthday), arrived, greatly encouraging me since I was to receive Judge McFadden's ruling by mail not many days later. He also informed me that President Trump was aware of my fight. This letter of recommendation helped pave the way for my painting to be shown at CPAC 2019. Securing a spot at CPAC took over three years to achieve. All of my previous efforts since January of 2016 had never received a response, as I came up against the ongoing artistic confusion in the conservative movement. CPAC would be historic, as it would catalyze an astonishing chain of events that were to take place in 2019.

CPAC is the Conservative Political Action Conference held annually, usually around the Washington, D.C., area. There are a limited number of spots in the giant vendor's hall. Most of the vendors were nationally known, bona fide, conservative organizations. The National Rifle Association, the *Washington Times*, Regnery Publishing, Judicial Watch, and Turning Point USA were represented. There were also microorganizations—and one solo artist, me, displaying my brobdingnagian portrait of President Donald Trump. (I just had to use that word!)

You just can't buy your way into CPAC—it's an exclusive political club of sorts. CPAC vets your conservative credentials, and if you pass, then you get to play. It is also very costly, well beyond my means at the time. No surprise, same old artist's story of woe, but everything I needed fell into place once I was approved. My dear mother was able to forward me the four thousand dollars on loan. (Later on, the loan was to become a gracious gift!)

This experience again demonstrated the conservative struggle with the arts; Conservative Political Art Conference—dreaming! I offered to show my work if CPAC had walls to spare and at no cost to them. They did have plenty of bare wall space, but they could not get it together to grant me permission to hang my painting for free. The vendor option was offered—you had to pay to show. I agreed and was honored to participate in such an auspicious and historic event.

That year, CPAC was held in the splendid Gaylord National Resort and Conference Center at the National Harbor in Maryland, drawing none other than the president himself, the vice president, and every other politically relevant politician, pundit, or celebrity in the conservative movement. My lawsuit was in full bloom, having been dismissed in the district court, then bumped up via my appeal to the three-judge United States Court of Appeals for the District of Columbia Circuit, one step beneath the U.S. Supreme Court. The year 2020 was fast approaching, and that 2019 CPAC conference was the big one, really launching the 2020 campaign efforts for the conservative movement, then entirely in President Trump's camp. It had not been so Trump-friendly previously, as could be understood. Trump was never a conservative. That probably explained CPAC's ghosting in my previous efforts to display my painting. But in 2019, after two years of President Trump in office, conservatism, in the form of the Republican Party, had morphed into the Trumplican Party. They were fired up. The economy was catching fire, and things in the country were probably at their best at that time under President Trump.

CPAC was a two-class system. The vendor hall downstairs was composed of political novelty freak-show types like me, which conservative celebrities avoided, lest they get mobbed by the masses of commoners and bottom-feeding riffraff. The speaking arena for the stars was upstairs, where the glitz twinkled and the paparazzi circus unfolded. Access, of course, was granted only to those who had the proper credentials. There were booths representing major TV networks, as well as radio. Radio Row, as it was called, was jammed with people trying to get on a show. Trump cabinet members Kellyanne Conway and Sebastian Gorka basked in their glory, as they were orbited by a flock of journos, camera-wielding fans, and well-known TV presenters. There were also wannabe YouTube celebrities and lesser-known politicians walking around with entourages varying in size. The bigger the star, the bigger the entourage, the bigger the circling flock of vulture-like journalists. Since I had the credentials, I wandered around freely, drinking in the political theatre, enjoying the buzz. There was a palpable atmosphere of excitement and expectation of better days, as things at that time were going well for President Trump.

Back downstairs, a commotion erupted, and people in the vendor's hall all started running in one direction. I could see the throng of people causing a ruckus. Cameras flashed, and people screamed, yelled, and jumped up to see who it was they mobbed. There had to be a celebrity somewhere in that scrum, yet nobody seemed to know who it was. This organic parade was heading my way, snaking its way down through the exhibition's displays toward where my painting hung. Behind the towering wall of Shrek-sized ogres, strategically positioned like centurions on all sides, I could just make out through the wall of flesh that it was Don Jr., the president's son. Whether he could not see over the wall of security, was too busy, uninterested, or deliberately ignored the painting to snub me (remember, I rescinded my offer of the Trump painting as a gift to President Trump way back in 2016), I don't know. Junior walked right past my towering Trump painting without stopping. The top of the painting was ten feet off the floor and sixteen feet wide, with its massive, ornate eight-by-eight-inch glistening gilded frame. I had paid particular attention to the lighting, and the display incorporated carefully selected light-temperature-calibrated spotlights to accentuate the painting's different warm and cool areas. It was a mega-watt attention-arresting display.

Those moments at CPAC were alive and entertaining, as people would just lose their minds. The exceptionally well-lit vendor's hall with scarlet-carpeted floors was an excellent stage for political theatre. Showtime's *The Circus* host, Mark McKinnon, turned up in the vendor's hall in search of footage for the show. He triggered substantial attention, being famous for his political TV show, campaign savvy, and distinguished hat, which he wore all the time. Filming for an upcoming episode (by the way, I had no idea who he was at the time), he made a beeline right to my painting, since it was the star of the show in the vendor's hall. Video-camera operators jostled for the best angle, while soundmen with giant afro-shaped microphone covers on the ends of their boom poles dangled and waved them in the air like kids fighting for the best spot at a fishing derby. Journalist cameras flashed, bouncing light off every glistening edge of the ornate acanthus leaves and egg-and-dart-decorated picture frame. The gold-leaf-covered opulent frame surrounding the Trump portrait, set against the scarlet red carpet, was a visual feast, not to mention the content of the painting. The commotion was great, as Mark's circus caused a large crowd to gather around my painting. Mark McKinnon interviewed me in front of the painting, concluding that the painting was "Trumpian"—especially the gold. That interview was cut from his show—he was not a Trump fan—but the image was incorporated into an episode of *The Circus*. *Time* photographer Mark Peterson took a stunning black-and-white photo of a blurred Mark McKinnon standing in front of the painting. It featured on *Time* magazine online. What a *Time* moment that was. Later, Mark Peterson threatened to sue me for breach of copyright because I used his photograph of my painting in a press release. I laughed—a photo of my copyrighted image was now his copyright? I welcomed the lawsuit, but of course, it never happened. I was eager to hear how he could defend his "fair use" of my image and at the same time deny my fair use of his![149]

CPAC 2019 was one of those events on my odyssey that had an incredible impact on the painting's cachet. Thousands of people and scores of media saw the painting, told the story, interacted with it, took photos, and generally enjoyed the painting. The most enjoyable part for me was sitting off to the side and quietly watching people engage with each other while considering the painting. People would stand, waving their arms, pointing and gesturing as they navigated the imagery in the painting, explaining to their friends what they thought it meant. Others would pace back and forth, traversing the space as they tried to absorb the image. That was the power of art at work, as it drove conversations and furthered discussion that could be educational, challenging, and redemptive. That is also why what the Smithsonian's Kim Sajet did was so odious. She shut down speech, debate, and meaningful conversation from all political perspectives—especially from opposing viewpoints—whereas, there was no controversy at CPAC. It was primarily attended by conservatives who supported the content of the painting. In the end, the conference was one of those events that I will never forget.

Getting to CPAC was an ordeal all its own. There would be no scale issues, as the conference center was massive. What I had to do was reconfigure my painting display to comply with the union rules and regulations that controlled the vendor area. If my display required power tools to install, I was obligated to hire the union workers at $150 an hour per laborer. Self-setup was prohibited; if there was any contractor-type work involved, they had to do it. What a racket, I thought! But then again, that was their gig, so they could do as they pleased. Money was tight, as usual. The display was tweaked, requiring only hand tools to assemble. I attached all the sections with snapping clamps and added two manual winches to hoist the massive painting up and onto the ten-foot wall. My sixteen-year-old daughter Victoria and I did the installation all by ourselves. The wall consisted of four four-foot by ten-foot panels on their stands that bolted together to create a ten-foot-tall by sixteen-foot-wide wall upon which the painting would be bolted and hung.

We arrived at the Gaylord Conference Center without incident. The vendor floor director, a pleasant, plump fellow, leaned back comfortably in an open-topped golf cart. He steered with one arm, the other hanging relaxed over the back of the seat, while he whizzed around and directed the furious setup activity going on all over the vendor hall. Forklift trucks, alarms beeping and yellow lights flashing, zipped up and down the aisles from the loading docks, schlepping crates loaded with booth components, fake plants, lighting, and merchandise for the massive displays. All of the work was union controlled and executed. I thought they would compel me to hire their guys, a few of whom were hanging around, idly staring at me and waiting. The director waved Victoria and me through as we wheeled our many display components to our set-up area, carefully avoiding getting run over by the speeding forklift trucks driving in reverse. He allowed us to set up without union assistance once he saw the subject of the painting. He was the only union Trump guy there, "the only one," he said, as everyone else in the union there was a Democrat. I also told him that the painting was worth a fortune, and it was best to let me handle it myself to prevent any costly mishaps. I could imagine the indifference and carelessness, had a bunch of unsupervised D.C. Democrat union workers been assigned the task of handling the massive portrait of President Trump. That would have made a great photo op, though. The director was ecstatic to get a signed print as a gift once the show was over, zipping away on his golf buggy.

Victoria was an invaluable help over the four-day event. It was her turn for a trip with her dad. Daily, she got to dress up, making herself look beautiful. She interacted with the throngs of people, holding conversations, taking photos, selling prints, explaining the painting, and helping with the setup and takedown.[150] The takedown was easier once Gloria and my son Jeremiah arrived. They were on hand to help load the truck for the long drive home. On the last day, waiting to go home, Victoria could barely stand up, resting her head on a nearby table most of the afternoon. She was featured in many of the photographs that would appear in the media, making it a memorable experience.

We stayed at a nearby Airbnb. It was a regular-sized house with a large converted basement, where our whole family would meet up. My wife and son from upstate New York, our other daughter, Johanna, and her friends from Liberty University in Lynchburg, Virginia, and even my mother flew in from Spain and stayed in a room upstairs in the same house. That was fun. Parking in their small driveway in the oversized twenty-six-foot yellow Penske box truck was comical, as there was no street parking. After a couple of conversations, the Russian homeowners turned out to be pro-Trumpers and only too glad to get a framed Trump print in exchange for the cost of my mother's room.

Media exposure was excellent, with the image of the Trump painting being the main image used to represent CPAC 2019 in most prominent papers, from the *New York Times* to the *Washington Post* and beyond—even appearing in Finland. The majority of the coverage was either neutral or positive from within CPAC. National Public Radio (NPR) did an exclusive on the painting, and it appeared on the front page on their website across the country. After an interview with radio host Tony Katz, the painting and I were also featured on Fox News, on Dana Perino's *The Briefing*, to my delight. My phone rang, with my friend Jerry Drake on the line, bouncing on his sofa with excitement, as he watched my painting live on Fox News as it happened. Twitter also went berserk with the painting, as different journalists posted photos, and the image took off. An animated gif was even created of the face of President Obama hijacking the painting, and it was widely circulated on Twitter. A couple of photographic journalists would hang around the painting all day, waiting for the perfect moments when crowds would gather, creating spontaneous happenings to catch in their lenses. Those photos would end up on stock-photo sites like Alamy, where they sold for top dollar, over five hundred dollars a pop, making them more money than I made. Many of those photos ended up in periodicals for weeks, months, and even years—even as recently as March of 2021.

CPAC was an action-packed event. The exposure and attention to the painting made the investment worth every penny—although, strangely, I could not get any attention to my Smithsonian case. It was another encounter with the power of the Smithsonian myth that made the subject of the lawsuit taboo—as if the words *lawsuit* and *Smithsonian* were not permitted in the same sentence.

But one particular story about my Smithsonian lawsuit came out as a result of CPAC that would ignite the liberal art world in a frenzy of slander, mockery, and protest and open the door to the next legendary stages in my odyssey. The seemingly impossible set of unforeseen events that were about to unfold throughout 2019 made the year historic. Before CPAC started, I had received interest in my Trump-painting story from a journalist named William Sommer from the *Daily Beast*. I knew the *Daily Beast* to be a well-read, left-leaning, tabloid-ish online political-news outlet, but he sounded like he was genuinely interested. He called me right after CPAC ended. He wanted a follow-up story, but once he learned about the Smithsonian lawsuit, that was all that he was interested in.

Chapter Fifty-Seven

SERVANTS
OF
SLANDER

THE *DAILY BEAST* WAS HOT ON THE TRAIL OF MY SMITHSONIAN lawsuit story. Journalist Will Sommer tracked me down and scribbled away on the other end of the call. The interview lasted about an hour and went very well, I thought. It was thorough, and Sommer did a good job asking the questions. It seemed like he sincerely cared about the legal issues with which I was grappling. Well, Sommer's article set the liberal art world on fire. The story was woven in a typical tongue-in-cheek liberal style. It was written more to provoke ridicule and incredulity than create a constructive conversation surrounding the issues about the Smithsonian, the subject in the story.

Hypocrisy was one of the most surprising responses to come out of the *Beast*'s story. Radical leftists and liberals, in general, are always gung ho about speaking truth to power, especially in the arts. If you stand up to power as an artist on the left, you become an instant folk hero, with the liberal art world rolling out the red carpet for you. To the Left, powerful institutions and officials are always beasts, the authoritarian enemy that needs toppling, the oppressive overlords needing a takedown. But, when it came to a conservative like me speaking truth to power, that was a whole different story. My free-speech lawsuit against the left-leaning Smithsonian, with Trump as the theme of my painting, galvanized the Left against *me*, not against the beast. Like lemmings, they all sided with the government-run Institution because of their hatred for Trump. Suddenly, no one on the Left cared about artistic free-speech rights, justice, or how I had been treated; they just hated Trump. That meant that if you supported Trump, you had no free-speech rights anyway. The story in the *Daily Beast* article was twisted into this subtitle: "Trump superfan Julian Raven has been locked in a years-long battle to force the gallery to put up his work. He thinks he might even get a hearing before the Supreme Court."[151]

The critical issues from the interview were ignored. The story was spun to create ridicule rather than stick to probing the constitutional questions and issues, especially the silencing of speech. Subtly, Sommer transformed the victim into the villain, as mean old Raven tried to force his way into the poor little Smithsonian. The sweet, lawful, and innocent government-run gallery had to endure this nonsense—how could you not have sympathy for the government-run Smithsonian!

All I was fighting for were my rights and for my application to be lawfully processed and given full consideration according to Smithsonian standards for portraiture consideration. The result, in my opinion, would have been the display of my painting, as I knew it qualified. But following the law was what was most important to me—just doing the right thing. And if Sajet responded according to the procedure, rigorously considering the painting according to written standards, and denied the application in writing by demonstrating where the painting failed to meet the bar, then so be it, case closed.

This type of slanderous mockery was, unfortunately, what I experienced throughout the liberal press. It was so prevalent that I got used to it after a while, resolving that this was the fire walk I had to pass through to get my story told. If I didn't, no one would know.

The coverage in the conservative press was generally thin, as art lacks its conservative commentators. But when stories were written from the right, they were usually very straightforward and an honest reflection of the facts. One such article early on was written by Matthew Walther, writing for the *Washington Free Beacon*. His story, "Immigrant Christian Abstract Expressionists for Trump,"[152] from way back in January of 2016, made an effort to stay true to the interview and was always the consolation in the midst of all the twisted stories.

The significant part of all this was that God was to use the good, the bad, and the ugly to open the doors to the subsequent events on my Trump-painting journey. Early in April of 2019, I received a call from a journalist called Ben Wofford. He was the staff writer at the *Washingtonian* magazine. I learned the *Washingtonian* was a prestigious, glossy-print magazine in Washington, D.C., that was the city's monthly gossipy, political, and cultural magazine. It was the go-to magazine to find out what to do, where to go, and where to be seen at cocktail parties and gallery openings, featuring the likes of presidents, their wives, politicians, top lawyers, doctors, restaurants, and cultural institutions. It was also the magazine that Washingtonians in D.C. read and left sitting around for months on coffee tables and in doctors' offices. Just go into local D.C. businesses and you will see framed copies of the *Washingtonian*'s front covers on the walls—featuring, for example, the Obamas or other famous personalities. This magazine covered the D.C. socialite pulse. The *Washingtonian* is all about power, prestige, wealth, food, and art.

The article that Wofford wanted to write was at first a small follow-up to the *Daily Beast* article, as it involved the Smithsonian Institution. The Smithsonian is consistently featured in their magazine on the never-ending "to-do" and "places-to-go" lists. The left-leaning magazine was no friend of President Trump or conservatives, nor was Wofford. They must have thought this would be an excellent opportunity to score some political points with my story, using me as a pincushion. That was the risk, and I knew it.

Well, once the interview began, it was as if it never ended. Wofford's journalistic skills started to mine the depths of my story, and the more of the story he heard, the more he called me. Before long, he had his editor on the line with him, listening in, as something big was developing. I told my story in detail, and Wofford just kept on scribbling. Eventually, he informed me that the editors had heard enough. Since Wofford was a staff writer, he was also in charge of writing the long-form feature stories, which were featured monthly in the magazine. It was not long before I was informed that my story would be the feature story in an upcoming print edition. I was floored. Wofford had previously interviewed D.C. Attorney General Karl Racine for one of their long-form feature stories. He had also interviewed Jeff Bezos,[153] Washington's newest resident—the new owner of the *Washington Post* newspaper and the world's richest man. He had also interviewed Sy Hersch, a famed investigative journalist. Then, for some strange or fortuitous reason, he interviewed me, Julian Raven.

It was somewhat disconcerting and exciting all at the same time. I told Wofford that he could call me whenever clarification was needed as he was writing his ten-thousand-word story, and that I would spend as much time as necessary with him so that he could write the story exactly as I told it. Ben called me often.

The more I researched Wofford and his stories, the more curious I became, wondering if I would get a fair shake. An artist painting a portrait of someone can distort the face to resemble a completely different expression or another person with the slightest changes in critical details. I knew that was true in journalism as well. I found articles that indicated that Wofford was a D.C. swamp creature and that it would be a long shot to hope for a long-form fair shake. Online, doing my research, I discovered that Wofford was the grandson of well-known politician Senator Harris Wofford, originally from Pennsylvania. According to the *Washington Post*, Senator Wofford was peers with President John F. Kennedy. He also was a presidential assistant on civil rights and was close to Martin Luther King Jr. In later life, after his wife of fifty years died, Senator Wofford fell in love again—this time with a man fifty years younger—eventually marrying his newfound love at the age of ninety.[154]

Would Wofford the journalist tell my story straight? We got on well, I thought, and I liked him. But maybe gaining my confidence was Wofford's tradecraft. I had nothing to hide, so I told him the story similarly to how I'm telling you. Would his liberal family context and the left-leaning *Washingtonian* be able to stomach the conservative Christian's Trump story? I may be naive, but I believe in giving people the benefit of the doubt. The truth of the story, I believed, would prevail and eclipse any prejudices Wofford might have. After all, he was spending many hours every week calling me on the phone and interviewing me.

Chapter Fifty-Eight

WASHINGTONIAN'S OTHER DARLING

The interviews continued for three months and over thirty hours of phone calls, plus multiple in-person interviews. There would be two photoshoots and breakfast at a fine French patisserie, then lunch on the terrace of the upscale The Smith restaurant while I was in D.C. preparing for the upcoming highly controversial art show.

Yes, my painting was to be part of another art show, the preparations for which were in full swing at the time. (And I bet you could never guess where that art show was to be held?) Ben told me his editors had told him to do whatever was necessary to get the story, giving him the green light to invite me for meals, over which he could interview me. When I was in D.C., Wofford followed me around like a puppy. He would go on to question the guests at the show once it opened and the other artists. Wofford even interviewed my daughter Johanna. He called upstate New York and interviewed Frank Acomb, the talk-show host. I think the only person he missed was my mother. But Wofford expressed interest in interviewing Mom too.

The Smithsonian Institution was venerated in Washington, D.C., holding sacred stature akin to a Greek temple to the deity of knowledge. What I was doing in suing the Smithsonian was offensive and sacrilegious to many, especially as a Trump supporter. "How dare you!" I would hear as if I were desecrating a beloved idol. But I trusted that people would see past their prejudices and that justice in our nation's capital would prevail, no matter who was involved. I thought people would empathize with me and express solidarity and outrage. But boy, was I wrong! As one person in D.C. put it, what I was doing was like another assault on the status quo and the Washington swamp "à la Trump." Rather than create a point of unity, a rallying cry for institutional reform, and a cause that people could get behind and support, the opposite happened, and I became the *Washingtonian*'s other darling of infamy, I think by design.

At times, I thought Wofford could have won the Pulitzer Prize if the magazine had printed the story the way I told it, since the facts draw hideous conclusions that demand official institutional investigation and reform. I wondered if Wofford would or even could buck the left-wing institution to tell the whole truth and nothing but the truth. I even discussed eventually writing *Odious and Cerberus* and invited Wofford to assist me once his story was printed, since he was a skillful writer.

Wofford was also skilled in playing his guileless subject. He used the powerful lure the prestigious magazine's media coverage could offer me, setting up a potential juicy showdown with Kim Sajet at the Smithsonian. He suggested I create a scene in the Portrait Gallery with his photographer there. He set the stage, openly suggesting a group of journalists, flashes going off, follow me into the museum, inflaming the controversy. It was ego tempting for sure, because controversy can drive the message, and it would have been a lot of fun to be followed around by camera-wielding journos capturing my every move. But it was just an ego trap. I felt like a fish staring at a juicy worm wriggling on a shiny, barbed hook buried deep within its flesh. Taking the bait would have been used to demonize me. Wofford, by his questioning, tried to depict me as an alt-right-wing nut job but failed when I condemned the far-right and individuals like conspiracy monger Alex Jones. If I had taken the bait, it also would have thrown shade over my pending lawsuit, painting me as the villain. But his trap didn't work.

Instead, he then suggested we walk the National Portrait Gallery together and consider the artworks in the light of Sajet's objections. We spent the good part of an afternoon in the Portrait Gallery, and, one by one, we found all manner of paintings there that trumped the director's arbitrary objections to my painting. The stroll was delightful and educational. I enjoyed the political art, the bad art, and the likes, as well as giant paintings that dwarfed my own. But there was nothing of President Trump on display. In addition, most of the contemporary, non-presidential portraits were of liberal icons. The presidential gallery was also a mixed bag of scale, quality, and content, completely discrediting Sajet's objections.

At one point, Wofford found an art installation that was an old fax machine actively printing out a news feed in a massive pile of paper all over the floor. He stood there thumbing through the hundreds of feet of unrolled printed paper on the dark-green carpeted floor until he found the name Trump. "Yes," Wofford proclaimed out loud, finding a tiny mention of Trump in the museum after all. I kept my distance at that point, as it was only a matter of time before he might have created the commotion he wanted all by himself by messing with and vandalizing someone's art on display in the gallery.

It was hard for me to believe that the *Washingtonian* would print the story the way I told it, as it could have far-reaching ramifications for the Smithsonian Institution if they did. However, what gave me a boost of confidence was that, as Wofford told me, the *Washingtonian* used an independent fact-checking service to verify the story after it had been written and was out of Wofford's hands. Wow, I thought, maybe my account would be told accurately. But often, Wofford would also allude to the "editorial overlords" who would have absolute control over the story, as if to tell me that they could do to it whatever they wanted once the story was out of his hands.

Chapter Fifty-Nine

KIM SAJET'S BACKYARD

DESPITE THE NEGATIVE SPIN, THE *DAILY BEAST* ARTICLE HAD SURprising reach and results. So much so, in fact, that I received another email in early April of 2019 that caused me to walk away from my desk in disbelief, again. This time it was hard to believe because of what was transpiring regarding my lawsuit. Since December of 2016, I had sought a venue to show my painting in D.C. to counteract the lies the Smithsonian director had said. I wanted to give the public a chance to see the painting and decide for themselves what they thought rather than have some bureaucrat decide for them, but to no avail.

The email was from Charles Krause, the owner and director of the Center for Contemporary Political Art in Washington, D.C. He was in the throes of setting up an anti-Trump art show and—mischievously, as he admitted later—wanted my painting in the show. Two other artists were involved; one was an academic, the other a seasoned political cartoonist. They all despised Trump.

Artist Jim Boden is Professor Emeritus of the Art Department in Coker College, Hartsville, South Carolina. He was going to exhibit a whole series of small Trump-skewering, multi-techniqued collages. Tim Atseff is a political cartoonist from Syracuse, New York. His career spans many decades. He was to show seven large paintings that depicted Trump's "Seven Deadly Sins."

Coincidently, I received an invitation to show my painting at a pro-Trump donors dinner at a yacht club in Erie, Pennsylvania, around the same time. The organizer and her husband were very active and successful in selling Trump merchandise and were then raising money. The husband told me that his wife wanted to make me famous in the MAGA world by flying me to Florida to meet with big-money Trump donors and be the star with my painting on show at their big-money donor dinner. It was very tempting to go the route of potential money, ego stroking, and celebrity (they wanted to purchase a pile of prints to give away to the donors). Or instead, I could choose the D.C. anti-Trump art show, where conflict was guaranteed, flattery would be exchanged for mockery, and maybe even right-wing scorn to boot for daring to participate in the blasphemous event. Although my painting would be locked up for months in Washington, D.C., it would be in D.C.—and right next to the Smithsonian Institution. The art-gallery-show cachet prevailed over the Erie Yacht Club. For me, a contrarian by nature, the allure of the challenge of overcoming hostility and adversity prevailed over the gushing celebration.

Krause was surprised that I was so willing to join the prickly party. He assumed that I would be offended and not dare set foot into his Trump-bludgeoning and Trump-butchering art show at his gallery. Far from it! For me, it was just another opportunity to tell my story and let the truth speak for itself. I am not easily offended, after all, and intense political artistic tension is the name of that game, for art's sake. I am drawn to where ideas clash, always curious to hear the most challenging arguments against what I believe. Welcoming the challenge, I am hungry to learn from those with whom I disagree, cultivating understanding and fine-tuning my own ideological positions.

Charles Krause had a fascinating story that made me stand back in awe at the uncanny confluence of events that were rapidly materializing in front of me. Krause had a very long history in the media. He was a *Washington Post* staff writer back in the '70s. As a journalist, Krause covered one of the most sadly memorable tragedies in contemporary American history—the Jonestown massacre. Not only did he cover the story, but he survived the story. Krause was one of the journalists who flew out to Guyana with Californian Congressman Leo Joseph Ryan Jr., investigating rumors of human-rights abuses at Jim Jones's People's Temple Agricultural Project, better known as Jonestown. A delegation of family members, other journalists, and staffers accompanied Ryan.

Congressman Ryan and others were gunned down, murdered in cold blood on the tarmac of the airstrip by Jones's Red Brigade. Krause described the events over dinner one night in D.C. After being shot, he pretended to be dead, fearing that what had happened to Congressman Ryan might happen to him. Ryan was shot dead from close range over twenty times. Krause, a Jew, survived and struggled since that time with the questions of existence and why he was spared, answers to which I told him he would find in the Jewish Messiah, Jesus.

That was fascinating for me personally because I had done extensive studies involving cults during my apologetics season in preparation for ministry years before. As a result, I had studied the Jonestown massacre. Speaking to a survivor made this seemingly distant and hard-to-fathom tragedy now all the more real and alarming. Krause's obsession with Trump and his palpable hatred of the man might have been in some way connected with the still-raw trauma he experienced at the hands of Jim Jones. Krause seemed obsessed with skewering Trump with all and any accusations that would brand him as a cult leader. My painting definitely played into his fears about Trump, as it could easily be misinterpreted as filling the "must-be-propaganda" rationale, if that was what he was looking for. The art show was ultimately called "The Good, the Bad and the Ugly: Portraits of our (*Unindicted*) Leader."

If that was not already an interesting-enough backstory flowing into the current political debate at the time, what Krause went on to tell me next left me flabbergasted. On my Smithsonian journey, most people I spoke with were utterly ignorant of what the Smithsonian Institution was, legally speaking. Which was understandable considering the enigma I had discovered and that it continued to be. Most people just thought it was a government museum. Krause coincidently knew differently, and I was dumbfounded. As the *Washington Post*'s staff writer, Charles Krause, back in 1977, when I was just a seven-year-old boy living and playing on the beach in the Mediterranean in Southern Spain, had been involved in investigating another Smithsonian scandal, this time involving another Smithsonian secretary. To my delight, Krause wrote not just one article but a series of twelve investigative articles, of which I would find copies on Lexis Nexis. His investigation got so deep into the corruption and unaccountable slush funds laundering taxpayer money, which ran amok within the impenetrable Smithsonian walls, that the *Washington Post* editorial powers eventually shut down his investigations at the *Washington Post*. He told me that story with a look in his eye as if to warn me about just how much power and influence the Smithsonian wielded.

One of Krause's investigations from 1977 surrounded then-Smithsonian Secretary S. Dillon Ripley. The controversy began with large amounts of cash (about $280,000 in today's money) being paid to Ripley's son-in-law Robert S. Ridgely, married to Ripley's oldest daughter, Julie. The son-in-law also received a camper, purchased by the Smithsonian. Once Krause began to press for answers about how this all happened, he experienced the same old Smithsonian stonewalling. The Smithsonian could not explain how the son-in-law had managed to become the recipient of the funds, and they denied it had anything to do with his father-in-law being secretary. Other Smithsonian employees who were interviewed at the time

> cited the Ridgely case as an extreme example of a general condition.... "We are an elitist, WASP-type organization."...

"For a long time, you had to have gone to Yale and breathe rarefied air to get a job here. Now, you just need to know someone who went to Yale."

This employee said she was once told that, "we need someone with class" when she asked what qualifications were necessary to fill a particular job.

Other employees say the Smithsonian is run through an "old boy" network.[155]

In the uncovered slush-fund scandal reported in the *Washington Post* on April 1, 1977, the U.S. General Accounting Office (GAO) auditors concluded that

> the controversy about the Smithsonian's use of its public and private money stems from its unusual constitution. It is neither a U.S. agency nor a fully private museum and research complex....
>
> The Smithsonian is separate from, but under the care of the U.S. government.[156]

Krause's slush-fund-controversy reporting in the *Washington Post* continued to expose the Smithsonian rot as the GAO dug deeper. We read from April 19, 1977, that

> the GAO audit found that the Smithsonian has created two private corporations to convert millions of dollars of federal money into "private money" each year, which the Smithsonian then spends without regard to federal restrictions....
>
> Yet, Peter G. Powers, the Smithsonian's general counsel, said yesterday that virtually all Smithsonian properties, including the museums on the Mall in Washington, legally belong to the Institution and not to the federal government—despite the fact that hundreds of millions of dollars in federal money has been spent over the years to build, improve and maintain them.
>
> Asked by Stevens whether it is the Smithsonian's position that it could sell off these properties without Congressional approval, Powers responded unequivocally: "Yes . . . although I can't believe we'd do it" without informing Congress first.[157]

Notice how convoluted the district-court ruling by Judge McFadden in *Raven v. The Smithsonian* was in denying me my First Amendment free-speech rights by ruling entirely in opposition to this statement by the Smithsonian Attorney Powers in 1977 to Congressman Stevens. You see, if the Smithsonian property is private and is merely run by the federal government, then full speech rights for citizens exist, and McFadden's ruling falls apart. McFadden ruled that

> the National Portrait Gallery has historically communicated messages from the government, in the sense that it compiles the artwork of third parties for display on government property.[158]

On May 4, 1977, Congress began to react to the controversy:

> More in sorrow than in anger, Sen. Ted Stevens (R-Alaska) said yesterday he still believes Congress should conduct legislative hearings to clarify the Smithsonian Institution's relationship to the federal government.[159]

On May 14, 1977, in another article, as a result of the growing scandals, Krause reported:

> The Regents of the Smithsonian Institution are in negotiation with Phillip Samuel Hughes, a retired assistant comptroller general of the United States, to conduct "a scholarly, constitutional study" of the Smithsonian's relationship to the federal government.[160]

This was the same response that occurred thirty years later to the Secretary Small champagne-bubbly scandal in 2007. Reports are good if they produce reform. The 1977 report did confirm the same old Smithsonian issues that had provoked the investigation. Primarily, institutional-identity confusion—"the confusion as to the nature of the Smithsonian (whether it is 'private' or Federal for example) seems to have come about because the Regents and the Secretary have several kinds of funds at their disposal"[161]—provoked the investigation, especially since taxpayer money was just vanishing without congressional oversight. Adding further weight to the need for legal clarification from Congress or the Supreme Court is that taxpayer money—now in the amount of seven hundred million dollars—is appropriated each year.

The problem with these private-sector reports is that in the end, they have no legal teeth. They lack the power to force change, as they can only make recommendations to the Board of Regents but not mandate change. They are also unable to accurately interpret and legally define the Institution as it is. Instead, in the end, they defer to the status quo. A good example is how Hughes interpreted Smithson's will regarding who the United States of America is. He interpreted the United States of America to mean the government, which would seem to be a conveniently biased interpretation, since the federal government is the government of the United States of America. Smithson would have said that he gave his bequest to "the United States of America" government, which he did not. I would contend that the bequest was given to the United States, which is a federal republic of fifty states made up of American citizens. I am not a lawyer either, further highlighting the need for an accurate interpretation.

Hughes concluded that Congress was in the dark as to how the federal appropriations were being spent, emphasizing the GAO's recommendation "that there should be firm, specific policies for the uses of Federal and trust funds." One obvious problem Hughes highlighted was that "there has been no really generic legislation with respect to the Smithsonian since the 1846 act,"[162] amplifying the need for the legal status to be defined so as to determine the laws by which the Smithsonian must abide. Those laws, when applied, compel transparency, which until today the Smithsonian has evaded.

After reading these articles Charles Krause wrote, I was stunned. How amazing was that—out of all the people I had met along my journey, here was a man who knew what type of enigma and beast I was facing. Krause had read my story in the *Daily Beast*, and when he read that my painting was barred for being "too political," he wanted to show it in his gallery. And guess where his gallery was located in Washington, D.C.? Yep, you guessed it. After three years of seeking a venue, Krause's gallery was less than a couple hundred feet down the street from Kim Sajet's Smithsonian National Portrait Gallery. This was more than fantastic. Standing in front of his gallery, you could throw a stone and hit the western wall of the National Portrait Gallery. (What is also of note is that Krause's Center for Contemporary Political Art was a new gallery in 2019 and closed some months after "The Good, the Bad and the Ugly" art show.)

Would this art show, of all political art shows—in the shadow of my ongoing federal lawsuit in Washington, D.C., on the heels of CPAC 2019 with its extensive media coverage involving the uber-prestigious national art gallery—become a major controversy of the day? The show's "star" was the sitting president of the United States, Donald J. Trump, the most controversial and well-known political figure in the world at the time, and a major figure in all of history. Trump lived only seven blocks down the street in the other direction from the gallery. The show held no punches; it was raw and uncensored and was sure to be the source of all controversial news stories of the day. Or was it?

Only a couple of months before the opening, Nancy Pelosi, the Speaker of the House, was in Krause's gallery at an art show about gun control. "Walls of Demand" featured art from Manny Oliver, the father of Parkland shooting victim Juaquin Oliver. The media was there in droves, especially the mainstream media. Also in attendance were Rep. Joe Kennedy, Rep. Jamie Raskin, Rep. Ted Deutch, and even Rep. Debbie Wasserman Schultz. Krause was putting his gallery on the map, and this next show at the CCPA could be a political-art coup.

Fighting for justice for the innocent victims of gun violence is a noble cause, no matter where you stand on the issue of guns. Would justice for the innocent victim of political tyranny pull on the heartstrings of those social-justice warriors yearning to speak truth to power? Would Nancy Pelosi, the Speaker of the House of

Representatives, return to condemn the abuse of power in my case, regardless if Trump was the subject or not, simply because it was the right thing to do? Would even the president himself come down to the gallery and champion his efforts to drain the swamp right there in Washington, D.C., as my Smithsonian cause was further proof of the swamp that was resisting Trump behind the scenes?

As I hope you can imagine, I was bursting with excitement, despite the fact that President Trump had declined my offer to display his portrait in the People's House.[163] My painting on show in Washington, D.C., at the Center for Contemporary Political Art! WOW! But, for all or any of that to happen, I first had to get the painting to D.C. for me to be included in the show. And as you know by now, the size of my painting always made any effort to show it extra challenging. As soon as I found out where the gallery was, I anxiously googled it to scope out the access. From the address Krause gave me, Google maps showed me the front of the building, and it looked fine, with street access to large double entry doors. Phew! But as Krause followed up his emails with more detailed photos, things changed dramatically. My heart sank as his photos revealed his gallery was located next door to the main double-doored entrance I'd seen on Google maps, through a small single-entrance door. The gallery was on the second floor, up a flight of stairs that doubled back on itself as soon as you entered the foyer. It was impossible to get my eight-by-sixteen-foot painting in, make the turn, and go up those stairs and then over the railing at the top of the stairs. My painting weighed over one hundred pounds when in its frame; there was no way on earth it was going to make it in one piece.

For a moment, I teetered and my stomach tightened as I contemplated the possibility that I would not be able to show my painting after all. O, that hollow, sickly feeling—how awful! Once again, what seemed like a huge opportunity began to slip away in my mind as I considered declining the invitation to show because of the hurdle. There was a solution; I had to completely reconfigure my display. "Unafraid and Unashamed" was no ordinary painting. It required careful planning to get it in place wherever I took it.

This new challenge, however, was one for the ages. If I was to get my painting to D.C., I would have to take the whole painting apart, and the two layers of framing, unstretch the canvas, and roll it up—something that I dreaded doing. I then would have to build an identical new seven-by-fifteen-foot stretcher frame that would have to remain unassembled until I assembled it on site, without glue. Then it would need to be disassembled all over again when the show was over. I then had to build a whole new decorative frame in four pieces that would seamlessly lock together in the gallery once the painting was unrolled and stretched on the new stretcher frame. The painting needed to be rolled on a large cardboard tube and transported in a heavy-duty, 24 x 24 x 85-inch custom padded plywood carrying case that I would build in order for it to get up the stairs safely. (You can see a time-lapse video of me setting up.[164])

Showtime! Fortuitously, I had sold a painting that summer, so I had the money for the trip. I rented a sixteen-foot Penske truck, this time in white, loaded my tools and my painting, and took off to Washington, D.C., by myself, into hostile territory, politically speaking. Gloria was working, and the kids were in school. For an excellent weekly rate, I stayed with a Hispanic family in a tiny room in an affordable Airbnb outside Washington. After the long drive from New York, I arrived at the Center for Contemporary Political Art in D.C. Ben Wofford from the *Washingtonian* magazine was waiting for me when I arrived at the gallery. He wanted to cover the whole story of me arriving with the painting, getting set up, the show itself, and every juicy drop of the story he could extract. Krause had a couple of helpers at the gallery who assisted me with carrying up the components to the painting, the large crate, my tools, and its new frame, now in two eight-foot and two sixteen-foot pieces.

Once the components were unloaded, immediately the hostilities started. I was expecting plenty of flack, but I had only been there for twenty minutes. One of Krause's helpers was a Cuban

American chap who was no fan of Trump. He was miffed that he had to help me, and no sooner had he put down the last item than he began to get in my face. He was thrown off guard after he griped about being part of the persecuted Hispanic minority, insinuating that I was a racist, White imperialist and the cause of his suffering. He went quiet when he heard that I too had tasted some of that poison as a minority, White, English Jewish kid growing up in Spain. To him, the American flag was a symbol of oppression. I could and could not understand that, because to me, the good that America has done far outweighs the evil. Old Glory is the symbol of freedom and opportunity. Perspective is everything, I told him, as we shook hands.

It took a day to build the new stretcher frame and get set up. Not only was I hanging the painting but also installing the spotlights necessary for the painting to be thoroughly enjoyed. By the time I was done, artists Tim Atseff and Jim Boden had arrived, and we got to meet each other. We were all very excited. The tension was palpable and increased as the other powerful images were hung next to mine. Also, the political divide was evident, and interpersonal tensions awkwardly manifested. We were, after all, unapologetic political adversaries. Here you had this enormous and unashamedly pro-Trump portrait, and one by one, Tim Atseff began to hang his large "Seven Deadly Sins of Trump" pieces on the bare wall next to it. This was followed by Jim Boden's horde of smaller yet equally deadly Trump collages. It was tense! Artistically, they were very well-made works of art. Jim and Tim had been at this for decades. They had thoughtfully developed their styles and techniques, elevating the show's quality. Many of the anti-Trump works that I had previously seen were generally rubbish in quality. This art was serious art by serious artists and genuinely worthy political opponents.

The art show would also have individual artist presentations, explanations, and even a three-man debate. I had resolved not to fall into any snares that were designed to feed their prejudices, as provocations loomed. Dealing with hostility was not foreign to me, having been an evangelist for many years, also supporting Trump for the previous four years. Diffusing people's anger, showing them respect regardless of our disagreements, and making peace was my challenge. It was my strategy to deflate their prejudices. After a few days, the initial tensions began to subside somewhat, and we all started to get on with one another. Their left-leaning mindsets were expecting a red-MAGA-hat-wearing, racist, homophobic bigot, spewing hatred and vile poison. That person would have given them plenty of reason to hate the Trumping artist.

My biggest concern with the show was the safety of the painting, causing me to plan and design a glass/acrylic enclosure that I would have had to erect. However, that was way out of my budget. My other backup plan was to insure the painting. I began to look around for fine-art insurance. No one would insure the painting without a certificate from an art-insurance valuation expert.

Victor Wiener Associates LLC popped up on Google as the fine-art appraiser and highly reputable art consultant that I needed in order to get my painting appraised for insurance purposes. They had been involved in many fine-art-related lawsuits as expert witnesses and were reputed to be at the industry's top. I called them up and spoke to appraisal expert David Shapiro. I explained my situation and concerns about the upcoming show in D.C. and my painting. To my surprise, he knew all about my painting and the Smithsonian lawsuit. That is how far-reaching my story had traveled into the art world. It made me glad, since that alone gave me the credibility to get my work appraised.

Their cost to appraise and certify my painting came back at $7,500. Well, that was well out of my budget. Nevertheless, I continued with the inquiry as I learned of their litigation participation. I asked Shapiro if, since his firm was prepared to appraise the painting, they would also make a historical appraisal based upon the backstory and join that with the insurance appraisal so that I could use it in my lawsuit. No, they responded. Although that is precisely the type of service they offered, they would not do it in my case. I was astonished. What could be the reason? Would it damage their prestige and cause them to be blacklisted for making a historical appraisal of the Trump painting "Unafraid and Unashamed," just in case they helped me win? Now, they were a private company that could do what they wanted, but it just revealed the prevailing current against which I was swimming. But then again, if Jack Phillips, the Christian baker, could be sued for discrimination for declining to bake a wedding cake for a couple of homosexual men because he personally opposed same-sex marriage, maybe there were grounds for a discrimination case? The problem with that was that I agreed with their right to turn me away, since they were a private company run by private citizens.

Their no was a no for history, but they were still willing to make the insurance certificate and charge me $7,500. The certificate would state that its valuation had no bearing on the painting's historical importance or value, barring me from using the certificate as expert testimony in my lawsuit. How could a painting's historicity be divorced from its value? I wondered. Once again encountering bias, I shook my head. Merely stating the painting's historical value was a bridge too far for these folks, as it could have positively influenced my lawsuit. As it turned out, the federal government, particularly the Department of Justice, was one of their biggest clients.

This historicity issue would arise later when Wofford conducted follow-up interviews for his story. Because of the nature of the article, Wofford was given all of the resources and authority to dig and interview whomever he could relating to art, law, and the Smithsonian, etc. One day, Wofford called me up from Krause's gallery to tell me that he was standing there in front of my painting with an art historian. He never told me her name, but she had joined him at the gallery to opine on the historicity question. He told me she wholeheartedly agreed the painting should have been accepted into the Smithsonian for its historical significance. Would that positive and vindicating academic opinion make it into the *Washingtonian* article in support of my case and expose the revisionism of history at the hands of Kim Sajet? I wondered, excitedly hoping it would.

There was a no-go on the insurance end, obviously, for two reasons: bucks and bias. Now I had to decide to trust Krause and his gallery security guard, a no-fan-of-Trump man named Troy. Krause thought if the painting did get vandalized, it would increase its art value anyway and interest in the art show. He probably cared little because of his animosity toward Trump. If I had not gone, there would have been no show for me. It was undoubtedly high risk due to the potential hostility, especially in Washington, D.C., but the show had to go on. Deciding to go was most certainly a high-bar mental challenge for me to overcome, adding to the dynamics at play.

The show was to take place from May 8 to June 28, 2019.[165] The printed catalog made by Tim Atseff was an excellently produced document, even though biased in the anti-Trump artists' direction. I was the "good"-Trump representing artist, so I might have been placed as the first painting in the catalogue, but my painting was last. Both Tim and Jim's work took up the whole catalog after Krause's introduction. Their coverage was about forty pages. My painting, the most recognized and well-known painting of the show, received just two pages at the back of the book. The show ended up staying open for four months. The good news was that after all that time, my painting remained undamaged, and it continued to command respect—even from the haters.

When the show was about to open, I was nervous, excited, and dreading the social occasion all at once. Introverts naturally want to run the other way when there are crowds of people among whom they have to socialize. But duty called, and I had to go even if I had to drag myself there. (Life has taught me how to be a situational extrovert.) My eldest daughter, Johanna, came to help me this time; she was a first-year student at Liberty University's pre-law program. We stayed together in a different Airbnb and got all dolled up for the opening. Because I was representing the "good" Trump, it made sense to dress up, so a white tux became the order of the day—rented, of course. For me, it was the most important art show I was to attend. The nation's capital, Washington, D.C., called for the best I could give. Who knew who might turn up?

We arrived a few minutes late, just in time to coincide with Krause's arrival and help him carry up the broccoli tray and dip. I expected a full house, causing a spring in my step as I climbed the stairs. The turnout was decent but by no means packed. Holding a tray of broccoli and dip, dressed in trepidation and my white tux, I made my entrance into the art gallery. I would have been very comfortable being anonymous, pretending to be "le garçon," politely serving the guests their crunchy vegetables rather than chit-chatting. But that was not to be—I was the culprit of the political monstrosity hanging on the wall. One Hispanic academic loudly denounced it in his Spanish accent as "propaganda!" as he walked out, making sure I saw him. It was hostile territory. I had to try to mingle. The only political friendlies to attend who dared to reveal their identities and introduce themselves were Sam Patten and his wife, Laura. I had heard of his story, which he was proud to share with me; he wore it like a badge of honor. He was the first person Special Counsel Robert Mueller charged in the Russia probe, and he pleaded guilty and received a three-year suspended sentence. Was I next on Mueller's list, I wondered? Anyone could have been disguised in that crowd, even Mueller himself, sniffing out Russian propaganda, since I was definitely guilty of the charge of painting the Trump portrait. This was Washington, D.C., after all, not Elmira, New York.

The media was a no-show, which was disappointing, except for photographer Jeff Elkins from the *Washingtonian* magazine and the journalist of the hour, Ben Wofford. Without letting the disappointment crumple my face too much, I smiled and greeted, doing my best to socialize and attempting to win over my political adversaries. Wofford declared that he was glad no other media was there, as he said this was his story. I was not glad at all! I wanted the whole world to know about the show. Wofford's long-form story would not be out for a couple of months. I wanted the show to be front-page news so that it would shine a light on my war with the Smithsonian. At least people would know and could come and see the painting for themselves, making up their minds. After all, this was a portrait, the only positive portrait to my knowledge of the sitting president of the United States of America on display at that time in all of Washington, in an art gallery that was open to the public. The mainstream media, even the conservative media, ghosted the show.

The dynamic of having these powerful paintings from strikingly opposite points of view was obviously too much for the poor media's sensibilities. It appeared that the Smithsonian, a left-leaning ideological acropolis dedicated to the arts, needed protecting by not shining a light on the conservative artist's free-speech cause. Not even covering the juicy and merciless anti-Trump bludgeoning paintings by themselves could lure the media into the gallery. I suppose ignoring my painting would have exposed their bias.

If the right-leaning media covered the show, would it offend Trump because of Tim Atseff's "Seven Trump Sin" pigs? What was fascinating about the show was that it was a well-rounded portrait of Trump; he was depicted as a sinner and as a type of savior of America. He was desperately human and desperately in need of God. The anti-Trump art was energized by fierce political judgment, personal convictions, and condemnation because they did not have the slightest redemptive theme in their work. To Tim and Jim, there was nothing good about the man. My painting, on the other hand, was patriotic, celebrating America and steeped in salvation, redemption, and hope themes. Trump's strengths and accomplishments were evident and needed to be championed, but at the same time, I neither excused nor defended Trump's sins. I proclaimed Trump's need for a transcendent Savior. The same Savior America needed, the same Savior I needed.

During the debate, it was clear my painting had struck a nerve. Charles Krause objected to my invocation of God in politics and my art. "That was like Hitler, putting 'Gott mit Uns' (God with us) on the buckles of German stormtroopers," Jim Boden retorted with genuine concern. Krause protested even further with the "separation-of-church-and-state" objection. I agreed with him, asking who would want the church meddling with the state? The separation of church and state was what it said it was, but Jefferson did not mean the separation of God and state. Silence prevailed after my rebuttal. And what was curious was that it was okay for the Left to indirectly invoke God by pointing out Trump's seven deadly "sins," thus using a purely theological concept to condemn Trump. Still, any mention of God with Trump in the positive, hopeful sense was verboten and propaganda of the worst kind. But of course, championing the idols of the Left in Che Guevara–esque portraits and injecting existential messianic concepts like "Hope" in the Obama poster is, of course, totally fine—just ask Kim Sajet.

The notion of mixing God in with the dialogue about Trump made people very uncomfortable, primarily because of Trump's moral failings. I can also see why there was concern, since there was no doubt that the God-with-Trump factor could be used illegitimately to manipulate opinions and votes, invoking ye olde "divine right of kings." But it does not have to mean that, if people would take time to listen, because "to the pure, all things are pure; but to those who are defiled and unbelieving, nothing is pure, but both their mind and their conscience are defiled," according to Paul's letter to Titus (1:15). People assumed that if God was with Trump, it meant Trump was like Christ, the sinless Savior. No doubt, some people could not see the line and crossed over into the cult of Trump worship, which was and continues to be an abomination in God's eyes. But that was not where I stood. And that concept is admittedly complex for people from all sides to grasp, as we wrestle with how God uses people, both good and evil, in positions of power. That is why the art show was so powerful—because it allowed for that dialogue. I think those in the secular media who could not find the balance chose to ignore the story so as to compensate for their own inability to comprehend the divine dynamic at play, leaving it behind the walls of the church. The risk was too high of inspiring the possibility of the same idea in other people's minds. Rather than create dialogue and raise challenging questions about God's dealing with man, the general media chose to edit out that conversation entirely, protecting people from such a dangerous idea. A nation whose people carry legal tender in all their pockets with the words "In God We Trust" on it surely should be able to handle the question, Was God with Trump?

The art show played out perfectly, exposing the media's status-quo bias and prejudices. Covering it from the left, no matter how hard they spun the story, would give credence to Trump because the giant portrait was a persuasive and influential image all by itself. That could never be allowed to happen. O, the danger that something positive and pro-Trump might slip through the filter and get on and defile their screens! Tim Atseff, who had been involved with New York media for forty years, shared how not one of his contacts or friends in the media responded to his invitations to cover the show. Tim later admitted to me privately that my blackout and ghosting claims were true; he could not fathom the complete blackout.

"The Good, the Bad and the Ugly" was a balanced show, powerfully exhibiting both sides of the fierce political debate. We were serious artists who remained civil and engaged in open dialogue about our differences, sharing our ideas and increasing understanding and modeling constructive discourse around the controversial subject of President Donald Trump. Freedom of political speech does not get much better than that, held in Washington, D.C., the capital of American freedom. The dialogue was desperately needed, especially in the dangerously divided climate we were in back then (and continue to be in), when pro-Trump politicians in D.C. were being harassed while simply eating out. Some were even chased out of restaurants. Troy, the gallery security guard, admitted that some woman genuinely offered him a thousand dollars to turn a blind eye so she could take a sharpie and deface the painting with a Hitler mustache on Trump's face. Troy pressed me for a backhander to compensate him for doing his job. He assumed I was rich. I gave him what I had, twenty bucks! I think that in general, because there was so much anti-Trump art in the show, the intense feelings that might lead one to deface my painting were mitigated, as the other artists had done a pretty thorough job of defacing Trump by themselves. The paintings appeared to neutralize each other—a fascinating effect.

Why not tell that story—that these fiercely opposing political views were practicing civil and respectful political discourse in the age of Trump? It was powerfully countercultural. But O no, just too positive, too good, no blood, no screaming, no hateful insults. We all actually got on well and liked and learned from each other. I suppose it was too boring in the end. No ratings there, as today's salaciously media-conditioned mob needs the blood of the Colosseum to be continually entertained.

The most significant show shock happened once the event opened. There was a time when the artists would make their presentations and debate each other. Krause invited a journalist named Hunter Schwartz to use the show to help launch his new political art blog called *Yellozine*. Schwartz had worked for CNN and other outlets and was trying to get going with his new digital publication. He had already written some political-art articles, one on Democrat candidate Kamala Harris, including a flattering portrait of her. He spent the whole day in the gallery listening to the presentations and to the debate, which was moderated by Ashok Panikkar, a local mediation expert and democracy advocate with whom Gloria and I built an ongoing friendship.

We imagined Schwartz's coverage could shed some light on the show, highlighting the issues and being, as he explained to me, "purple"—that is, fair to both sides, neither blue nor red. We all waited and waited and waited some more for his article. Because other than the *Washingtonian* magazine, he was the only other journalist to write a story. Weeks passed and nothing. Maybe he was just busy?

When he finally posted an article regarding something completely different, dated after his attendance at the show, the other artists' and my fears were confirmed. Schwartz decided to completely ghost the show—not even a single word or mention. The other two artists were shocked, even in disbelief, as all my blackout claims were proving true.

The ghosting would be complete as Krause extended the show into August to coincide with and capitalize on exposure from the *Washingtonian* piece, which was to come out at the end of July. Wofford finally handed his article over to a fact-checking charade that turned out to be conducted by one of their own journalists (who no longer works for the magazine) and not an independent fact-checker, as I had originally been given the impression it would be. The very things I had contested as factually inaccurate remained in the article after it was printed, with only a couple of corrections. At first, I had believed the *Washingtonian* magazine would print the truth and tell my whole story, giving me a fair shake. But as time went on I began to have severe doubts as to whether they would even print the article at all. Then, right before it went to press, my gut instinct was that it was impossible for the story to be published in such a left-leaning magazine as I had told it. Even as excited and nervous as I was, nightmare scenarios still played out over and over in my head. I was naive to think that the magazine would side with the conclusion where the facts led; Wofford would tell the story as he wanted.

August 2019's *Washingtonian* magazine was first published online during the final week of July. Then the over one hundred thousand subscriptions went out as the magazines flooded the stores. Their monthly readership was over 430,000 people. My story was the feature article, although they kept me off the front page. The story sprawled across a total of thirteen pages in the magazine, including many photos, and it did mention the show. The article opened on the inside front page with a photo of the three artists laughing together in front of my painting. For me, that was a triumph, although the editors might have meant it to be something else—it depends on the degree of cynicism through which one sees the world. The sense I got was that my story was a direct threat to certain ideals that people had regarding the Smithsonian, as what I was doing was an affront to the sacred cow. The risk was too high to go and see for themselves, just in case I was right and they would have to side with me—what an awful prospect. Rather, it was easier to ignore the controversy that risked nakedly exposing further institutional anti-Trump bias. And as was revealed in the thousands of comments online in the art forums, people were glad my painting was banned in the gallery because of Trump, regardless of whether I was wronged or artistic speech was silenced. The gallery-attendance needle barely moved as a result of the article, so I was told, as people here and there only trickled into the gallery.

I concluded the magazine was unable to stomach the repercussions of an honest, positive, passionate pro-Trump story that might have sunk their magazine in a world where printed glossy color magazines are fast becoming relics. The risk of offending their majority-liberal D.C. readers was just too significant. They twisted the story just enough to please themselves and their readers, giving them enough of my blood to placate their wrath and, at the same time, daring to expose and embarrass the Smithsonian, which they did do, to their credit. They even nailed Kim Sajet's actions as "odious," citing Judge McFadden. But they had to make me look bad in order to do that. Wofford told me directly that he had to "knock me down to size; your story was just too good," he said. In other words, they could not justify exposing the sacred Smithsonian National Portrait Gallery and its socialite leftist director without smearing me as well. By doing this, they were forced into creating an anticlimax by ensuring there were no heroes at the end of the story, just villains. This is the dilemma that blinds agenda-driven ideologues as they always struggle with plainly telling the truth. And so it was. Even though it was very well written and it did make me laugh at times, it was also cynical, condescending, and deliberately mischaracterizing of me in a way that could only be described as diabolical. After the magazine came out and I expressed disappointment with the manner in which I was represented, Wofford retorted, "I told you I was a Democrat!" as his justification. Fancy that—I thought he was a journalist! I told him it felt like I was being used as a sacrificial lamb for their own hatred of the president. He was silent. Wofford no longer works for the *Washingtonian*.

The CCPA art-show opening evening ended with the curator and the artists breaking bread at a new classy joint called Dacha at the Navy Yard, at Krause's expense. The meal was delicious. My daughter Johanna looked beautiful and was very impressed to be eating out in such a well-to-do place. I was still dressed in my white tux, provoking the maître d' to come over and thank me for dressing up as a dandy in order to patronize their fine establishment. Little did they know that our dueling-Trump-portrait war was the real reason for the tux. I am sure if they had known which side of the duel I was on, not even my pearly white tux would have been able to draw out such flattery. The restaurant's goal, she told me, was to attract my type of style in their trendy new establishment— if only she knew!

Gloria, too, would get to see the painting in D.C. with some of her friends, along with my daughter Victoria. Victoria was on a class trip from Breesport, New York, and visited the gallery with her whole class, making that D.C. trip the trip of a lifetime for her. And, as always, my good son, Jeremiah, helped me dismantle the painting and schlep it downstairs out of the Center for Contemporary Political Art and back into my truck. And another Raven-family adventure came to a close.

There existed a general institutional reluctance to challenge the Smithsonian Institution, to protect it rather than exposing its problems. But the *Washingtonian* story did mention the Hatch Act investigation by the U.S. Office of Special Counsel into Kim Sajet's political activity protesting the inauguration of President Trump. Sajet posted tweets to the official Smithsonian Twitter page about her participation. Surely that was a violation of the Hatch Act? Would the U.S. Office of Special Counsel find the Smithsonian's Kim Sajet guilty?

Chapter Sixty

SPECIAL-COUNSEL HATCHET JOB

NOT EVEN THE THREE-MONTH JOURNALISTIC INVESTIGATION that unearthed anti-Trump bias and putrid corruption at the Smithsonian Institution, some of which was included in the *Washingtonian* magazine's story, could get Washingtonians to throw up their arms in outrage. It appeared that corruption was permissible if swatting off the conservative Trumpist was necessary.

In my research, I had discovered the Hatch Act,

a federal law passed in 1939, limits certain political activities of federal employees, as well as some state, D.C., and local government employees who work in connection with federally funded programs. The law's purposes are to ensure that federal programs are administered in a nonpartisan fashion.[166]

The Hatch Act facilitated another way for me to expose Sajet's partisan actions in my attempt to force Smithsonian accountability. The law demonstrated how Sajet's actions were illegal and how she abused her office by using it to promote the partisan protest against President Trump, who had just been sworn in.

Concerning President Trump, Kim Sajet's actions, caught in tweets and then under investigation, perfectly revealed her political bias and the cause of her animus and state of mind in my case. That evidence vindicated all of my claims. Sajet herself handed me all the evidence I needed to prove she was an anti-Trump activist, enforcing her partisan political agenda, arbitrary rules, and biased views in the People's Smithsonian.

I had appealed to the U.S. Office of Special Counsel for their intervention in Sajet's blatant partisan political activity using her taxpayer-created power and position of authority for her personal political activity:

> The U.S. Office of Special Counsel (OSC) is an independent federal investigative and prosecutorial agency. Our basic authorities come from…[inter alia,] the Hatch Act.[167]

The day after President Trump's inauguration, January 21, 2017, the Women's March, a social-welfare organization with IRS 501(c)(4) status, put on an anti-Trump protest in Washington, D.C., right behind the White House. At the rabid protest, pop star and singer Madonna, in between her use of four-letter expletives, proclaimed that she was thinking a lot about "blowing up the White House," obviously with the newly elected president in it.

Leftist activist Michael Moore laid out a game plan of political resistance, sealing his strategy by tearing up the newspaper with President Trump's inauguration story on its front page. Hollywood actress Ashley Judd said that a yellow toupee had replaced Hitler's mustache. Meanwhile, discredited anti-Semite activist Linda Sarsour screamed how she would never respect President Trump. All the while, Smithsonian National Portrait Gallery Director Kim Sajet made her presence known at the anti-Trump protest. She gleefully tweeted from the anti-Trump rally, proudly wearing her purple "p*ssy" hat, directly to the official Smithsonian National Portrait Gallery director's Twitter page.

Absolutely nothing wrong with that, OSC's Hatch Act Chief, Ana Galindo-Marrone,[168] said, after citing only half of the Hatch

Act regarding social-welfare organizations' participation in partisan politics, because "a 501(c)(4) organization may participate in some political activity," and she closed the investigation. Fine, a 501(c)(4) could participate in politics, but according to the Hatch Act, not federal employees. I researched further and discovered the second part of the act Galindo-Marrone had conveniently ignored. I protested in a letter addressing the missing section of the law, and Galindo-Marrone never replied. Case closed! That law warned federal employees, saying:

> Employees should be cautious about engaging in any 501(c)(4)-related activity while at work…. For example, the Hatch Act would prohibit an employee from forwarding an email from a 501(c)(4) organization if that email advocates for or against a political party, candidate for partisan political office, or partisan political group.[169]

According to U.S. Special Counsel Chief Galindo-Marrone, Kim Sajet could lawfully tweet to the official Smithsonian @NPGDirector's page about how much she loved being at and participating in the vicious, angry, vulgar, and partisan anti-Trump political protest. Sajet tweeted the protest was really what "democracy looks like," echoing the founder Linda Sarsour. She also tweeted images of other partisan political portraits on display. She concurred with Michael Moore's instructions on leftist political anti-Trump activism—totally fine! All this somehow was not advocating for a "partisan political group"? O of course, I'm sorry—it was just a social-welfare organization.

Chief Galindo-Marrone also confirmed my accusation regarding the once-official Smithsonian/U.S.-government-claimed and copyright-protected Twitter account, "@NPGDirector," when it mysteriously changed to "@KimSajet." But not a problem there either. The Smithsonian covered their tracks by changing present legal reality to cover for Sajet's illicit use of the Twitter feed that had been brought to light. All the Smithsonian National Portrait Gallery director's tweets, photos of art, portraits, paintings, and what was once declared to be the property of the United States was now, at the click of a mouse, Kim Sajet's personal property, that of the Australian foreign national. Perfectly fine, moving on.

Senator Chuck Grassley's words, "Bend the Rules, Change the Rules," no longer only applied to the corruption scandal he was investigating back in 2007. Those words now applied directly to my case as well—just astonishing. Was I just imagining things or was there a concerted effort from within and without to protect the Smithsonian and its employees from prosecution? I had appealed to the U.S. Office of Special Counsel and that ended up being like pulling on the tail of a declawed and toothless tiger. Looking around, I wondered if there were any other tails I could pull.

Icy water began to sting my face, startling me. I lunged, I grabbed, and I pulled on something. The sound of the pitter-patter became louder and louder as I came to. My clothing was soaked. Opening my eyes, freezing rain like needles poured out of the grey skies above, racing toward me. Lying stiff on my back, that stone-cold slab had chilled me to the bone. Wrapped around my left hand, I could feel the braided climbing rope, as the dull throb of my freezing, numb fingertips registered in my mind. I was tugging on that rope in my dream, thinking it was the tail of the toothless tiger. Spinning, falling images flashed through my mind as I tried to recall how I had ended up where I was on that rock ledge.

My body began to shiver uncontrollably, warning me that if I did not react soon and get under the dry overhang a few hundred feet along that ledge, it was all over. Retrieving my pack hanging on the other line, I pulled myself up and staggered to the shelter. The silvery reflective thermal rescue blanket worked quickly, allowing my inner core to start to glow and warm up. I could see my new path up Mount Justlaw opening up at the end of the ledge. There was no time to lose; the mountain waited for no man.

Chapter Sixty-One

I APPEAL TO CAESAR

MY JOURNEY UP MOUNT JUSTLAW WAS FAR FROM OVER. AFTER an hour, the freezing rains stopped. I recovered sufficiently to resume my climb, since it was still early morning, with a whole day's climb ahead of me up the new mountain section I had discovered at the end of the ledge. It looked like another formidable stretch of mountain facade, but my optimism was up, and there was no time to lose. I latched myself onto the now-familiar rock wall without hesitation, clawing my way upward toward the summit.

The District Court for the District of Columbia and Federal Judge McFadden had tossed my case out. The time to appeal was a small window, driving me to find my way up to the appeals court.

The apostle Paul has always been an excellent example for me of using the privileges and rights of his Roman citizenship in the cause of justice—in his case, to further the Christian Gospel. In the book of Acts 25:11, Paul argues his case and concludes his only path forward is upward via appeal: "If, however, I am guilty of anything worthy of death, I do not refuse to die. But if there is no truth to their accusations against me, no one has the right to hand me over to them. I appeal to Caesar!" (BSB). If there was no truth to the actions of his adversaries, Paul knew that the issue had to be settled by the final, higher authority, and that was Caesar himself. Governor Festus replied, "You have appealed to Caesar; to Caesar you shall go," further encouraging me to keep on going upward on my quest for justice.

My studies focused initially on how in the world I would appeal my case to a Washington, D.C., appeals court. Again, there were many appeals courts in Washington, D.C. In which one would I have to file? Was it the U.S. Court of Appeals for Veteran Claims, the U.S. Court of Appeals for the Federal Circuit, the U.S. Court of Appeals for the Armed Services, the U.S. Court for the District of Columbia, or the U.S. Court of Appeals for the District of Columbia Circuit? And these are just some of the courts. What would appealing entail? After diligently researching, I found that my case had to ascend to the U.S. Court of Appeals for the District of Columbia Circuit. That was the court where Judge Merrick Garland presided at the time.

The U.S. Court of Appeals for the District of Columbia Circuit was the second most important court in the United States federal court system. It was just one step below the Supreme Court—now, that was a fantastic realization. The appeals court was made up of a three-judge panel. Those judges would hear appeals involving the actions of the federal government and other federal cases that arose from the district courts. It had its own court rules, plus there were new federal-appeal rules to follow, even down to the type of paper, font, margins, and line spacing that had to be used. It was different from the district court, where I was the plaintiff and the Smithsonian (U.S.A.) was the defendant. Now, I was the appellant and they were the appellees.

I had to take the first steps to alert both courts that I would appeal the district court's decision via a Civil Notice of Appeal. That had to happen within a specific time limit. It had to be followed by a Statement of Issues to Be Raised, a Certificate as to Parties, and a Statement of Intent to Use a Joint Appendix with

DOJ Attorney Braswell. Also, a new Certificate of Service had to be included.

After filing all of the correct documents and my appeal, the DOJ filed a motion for Summary Affirmance, basically asking the court to ignore my appeal and just affirm the lower-court ruling. It was signed and sealed by Julie K. Liu, a United States Attorney, R. Craig Lawrence, Assistant U.S. Attorney, and Marina Utgoff Braswell, Assistant U.S. Attorney.

Before my appeal was even heard, the DOJ fought to block my case by quashing my appeal and removing any chance of oral arguments. That was the legal maneuvering, seeking my early termination by requesting the judges to agree with Judge McFadden, and the status quo would remain unharmed. Representing yourself in court puts you into a particular category of people who are often considered some form of legal leper. You are either a prisoner with too much time on your hands, looking to overturn your conviction, or, as the old saying goes, you are someone representing himself, "who has a fool for a client." Add to that a Trump supporter and a nincompoop who dared to sue the Smithsonian Institution, including the chief justice. Ask yourself honestly, if you were one of the judges and the Department of Justice were to say to you something like, "Look, that guy is one of those 'pro se' pests. He's just antagonizing the system to get publicity. He has no case, and besides, Chief Justice John Roberts would be on the hook if this goes forward." Whom would you be inclined to believe? And also remember Cerberus, the three-headed beast running the Smithsonian—one of those heads was the judiciary, represented by Chief Justice John Roberts.

You see, the status-quo pressure is enormous. The Smithsonian has not changed in over 150 years, and its physical presence in Washington, D.C., is enormous. Thus, behind-the-scenes interests are involved that remain undisclosed because the Smithsonian is exempt from the penetrating gaze of the Freedom of Information Act. Many of the buildings on the National Mall between the U.S. Capitol and the Lincoln Memorial belong to the sprawling

Smithsonian Institution. The Court of Appeals for the District of Columbia Circuit, the court where my appeal would first arrive, sits only a few blocks from the Smithsonian. Interestingly, Chief Justice Roberts used to preside over that court too. Hmmm—such a tight-knit family.

The legal sparring began. It went back and forth as I exchanged blows with my sparring partner, Attorney Braswell. My opposition to the DOJ's motion for Summary Affirmance, once I understood what that meant, was carefully drafted, highlighting all of the legal anomalies and including Judge McFadden's abuse of discretion. As always, I was confident in my appeal and my arguments, even though I knew they were drafted by an amateur. I knew the judges had to look past my legal shortcomings to the heart of the issues, especially the free-speech issue, giving me greater confidence they would see things my way. Three judges would be able to see through the noise and make the right call finally. The nearly eight weeks it took to get a decision were filled with anxiety and uncertainty.

My efforts failed once again. The DOJ's motion for Summary Affirmance was granted, and I was stumped. Did they even look at my case, more than just a cursory glance, I wondered, or just side with the DOJ and the district court by default? This was very hard to bear. "God, please, give me justice!" I prayed. I was encouraged by Jesus's words in Luke 18:1–8, about the old woman who kept bothering the unjust judge for justice. In the end, she received justice, because she was a persistent pain:

> For some time he [the judge] refused. But finally he said to him-self, "Even though I don't fear God or care what people think, yet because this widow keeps bothering me, I will see that she gets justice." (Luke 18:4–5, Holy Bible NIV)

Well, I had to hang on and keep climbing because I had not yet received justice as I had hoped. What do I do? I wondered again to myself. Just give up and climb back down? Staring upward was ever darker and increasingly intimidating as the institutional powers increased in number. No longer just the U.S. Office of Special

Counsel, the Smithsonian Institution, and the U.S. Department of Justice but then not one but two federal courts and *four* federal judges in their black robes, arms folded, peered over the bench glaring down at me. My climb had become more challenging, but the truth was, I was becoming a better climber. And I was not about to start climbing down that mountain, no matter how hard it appeared.

Before I could change courts again and appeal to the nine Supreme Court justices, I had to appeal to the same appeals court again for rehearing, which was denied. Then I had to appeal to the entire appellate court. That appeal was called an "en banc" appeal—in other words, an appeal to the entire session when all the judges sat down at once, all *sixteen* judges together in the grand court hall of appeals. Remember, this is the same grueling process that all unresolved issues of law must pass through. Eventually they would reach the U.S. Supreme Court, having had their claims repeatedly denied in all of the courts below that court. It is incredible to think how all those judges could get it so wrong, requiring the Supreme Court to overrule them all. It makes you wonder how many times the lower courts get it wrong, how many times when appeals are denied justice is not served, and how many times an appeal is never even filed.

If appeals were never made, if people gave up on the strength of their convictions that they were right and that the law or the lower courts were wrong (even in the face of multiple courts and judges telling them otherwise), we would be living in a very different country. The mere fact that an appeals process exists in our judicial system is evidence that laws can be bad, and judges can get it wrong, do get it wrong, and get it wrong for various reasons. Under their black robes, judges are just broken, fallible people like everyone else. In their fragile, sinful humanity, although veiled by their robes, they deal with a multitude of often very complex issues that cannot always be resolved as quickly or rightly as one would like.

But this is America, not Somalia. Here, I believed truth and justice and the American way would prevail. Even as voices of doubt continued to echo around me each time I suffered a setback, I paid them no mind. Other than my dear wife and children and a handful of friends, most people just instinctively concluded I had to be nuts to try to climb Mount Justlaw, as I was sure to fall off.

The denial to hear my appeal by the U.S. Court of Appeals for the District of Columbia Circuit was another blow. Surprisingly, it did not have the devastating effect that I thought it would have. I was still on the mountain and still in the fight. There were a few more options, and I was going to exercise every single one of them.

The climb got steeper by the hour, as the precariousness and risk also increased. The rock structure changed. The climbing surface was extremely narrow, and there were fewer places to grab, fewer places to secure myself. I pressed on all the more, and I pressed on all the same. Looking over my shoulder, the view was spectacular from that elevated vantage point I had reached up Mount Justlaw; I could never have imagined being that far up the mountain. I was closer to the summit then than I was to the base of the mountain, and that alone encouraged and energized me, even though it felt like at any moment I would be swept off Mount Justlaw's precipitous face to my destruction.

Chapter Sixty-Two

EQUAL JUSTICE UNDER LAW

REGARDLESS OF MY ONGOING LEGAL SETBACKS AT THAT TIME, FOR a change, my hopes were higher after the initial denial of my appeal than they were before the appeal. As I aggressively pushed up Mount Justlaw, I believed that the section of ascent I was on would finally be *it*. There was now a football team of sixteen appellate judges who, I believed, had to step in and say it was time to deal with the Smithsonian enigma. My case was an unanswered question of federal law, sufficient to compel a judicial ruling that would begin to right the ship. All those eminently qualified appellate judges in the Circuit Court of Appeals were independent, righteously inclined individuals who loved truth and justice—they would see the glaring problems.

The pressing issues were no longer just the claims in my case; they also included abuses of judicial discretion at the district level and the circuit level. The three circuit judges, Tatel, Millett, and Rao, had not followed the law in their review of my case. They even went on to ignore whole portions of my arguments and deny my right to amend my briefs, excusing the Smithsonian from answering the trust-law questions, and they ignored a specific Supreme Court–mandated First Amendment review of my case.

Assuming the judges just followed the law and the rules because they were judges was probably naive on my part. I discovered that was not always the case. Judges are fallible people, susceptible to temptations of corruption, compromise, and capitulation. The question of how judges deal with issues that are not clear even for them, especially if they have legal consequences that will upset the status quo, remained unknown to me. Maybe I was naive to think that a ruling had to be made to clarify the law if there was evident confusion. And since there were already two Supreme Court rulings supporting my case, I expected the judges to make their ruling accordingly. But I had no idea how the thinking went behind those black robes. I had no idea about the behind-the-scenes culture and unwritten rules within the court system. A judge can pick and choose, deflect, and avoid specific issues the same way the DOJ attorneys could do in their arguments—judges are all lawyers, after all. And as we saw in *Plessy v. Ferguson*, the highest court in the land could be a cesspool of iniquity. A judge's decision bears their name indefinitely, which I imagine can be a badge of honor or a curse. Maybe ruling could boomerang back to bite them, causing careful calculation on their part. And remember, the Smithsonian Institution was a beloved playground, virtually their next-door neighbor, where I can imagine people would often go for lunch or a stroll on their lunch breaks. In the end, who knew what went on, but I learned enough to know that something did. No matter how good the system was or how good the judges may have been, they were simply people at the end of the day.

The history of the Smithsonian's entity confusion was presented in my case right in front of them in black and white. The three-judge appellate panel chose to leave it alone, further muddying the waters surrounding the untouchable issues. This pushed the issues further out of reach, even from the long arm of the law.

It reminded me of when my wife worked as a dialysis technician in a state prison in New York State. She interacted with medical staff, criminal felons, and state correctional officers. She soon learned that the culture within the prison was very different from what the law required. The officers would even admit it when she observed conduct that was just out of order. It was as if they were saying, "Yeah, we know that's what it says on paper, but this is what we have to do to survive in here."

Also, I kept considering that these judges could have been passing the buck to Chief Justice John Roberts to sort out. Did judges see issues and then deliberately deny them, forcing them up the ladder, knowing there had to be a Supreme Court decision to sort out the problems? The ramifications of my case were far reaching. Giving me an inch would have meant giving me what I needed to prevail. Those federal judges did not have to be concerned about their jobs if they blew it—they were on the bench for life. So really, they could do what they wanted without fear of losing their retirement benefits, except in extreme cases. Only fifteen judges have been impeached in just over two hundred years of the federal judiciary, and only eight judges have been actually convicted.[170] I also learned, to my surprise, that judges could focus on rulings that buttressed their position and ignore other authoritative Supreme Court rulings I had cited that contradicted them. The contradiction they created was either intentional, requiring a Supreme Court untangling, or it was the controlling status-quo bias, prohibiting them from even considering anything else. Perhaps they just wanted to shoo me away. Please note below, in the three-judge-panel opinion I was appealing, how they say "he" and "his" and not "Mr. Raven" or "appellant." At that level, you should not address anyone in that manner—it is disrespectful, as though you are deliberately pointing out that there is a dog in the court. Imagine calling an appellate federal judge "Buddy" in an official setting. Whatever it was, it was flat-out wrong. Take a look. The three-judge appellate panel said in their written ruling regarding the critical entity-status question that to the extent he contends the Smithsonian Institution is a purely private foundation, that is inconsistent with his contention that it is subject to the First Amendment.[171]

Yet I had argued and quoted the Supreme Court opinion in *Lebron v. Amtrak* that had already clearly ruled:

> We held that Girard College, which had been built and maintained pursuant to a privately erected trust, was nevertheless a governmental actor for constitutional purposes because it was operated and controlled by a board of state appointees....
>
> We have held once, Burton v. Wilmington Parking Authority, 365 U.S. 715 (1961), and said many times, that actions of private entities can sometimes be regarded as governmental action for constitutional purposes.[172]

How the judges could flat out ignore the Supreme Court's opinion on private entities being liable for constitutional constraints still confounds me. They were toeing the line already created in the district court below. The whole point of the Supreme Court–cited case in *Lebron v. Amtrak* was to show beyond a shadow of a doubt that specific private organizations run by the government, whether state or federal, were found to be constitutionally liable precisely because they were run by the government. The Smithsonian Institution was no different—it was a private trust, operated and controlled by a board of Congressionally appointed Regents, some of whom were federal officials and representatives. Therefore, the First Amendment to the U.S. Constitution had to apply. (Bear with me, please, while I have a short-circuit moment, as the wires short out in my brain! Aaaaarrrrrrrgggh!!!)

Also, what was clearly lacking in their ruling was their own Circuit Court–mandated First Amendment review of First Amendment free-speech claims mandated by the U.S. Supreme Court in *Bose Corp. v. Consumers Union*:

> In Bose, the Court set out the responsibility of an appellate court in cases raising first amendment issues: "an appellate court

has an obligation to make an independent examination of the whole record in order to make sure that the judgment does not constitute a forbidden intrusion on the field of free expression.[173]

In other words, any case that came before the Court of Appeals regarding any issues related to the First Amendment was to receive a special review. The three-judge panel was to review "the whole record"—i.e., the entire docket in my case. Not just my appeal document alone and the motion for Summary Affirmance from the DOJ. There was no mention of this "independent examination" of the whole record in their decision to deny my appeal. That was also judicial abuse of discretion. Those issues were now before the sixteen appellate judges en banc, boosting my confidence that the hammer would fall on my adversary at law and not on me.

My energized ascent caused me to think that I was close to the summit. I could see the approaching ridgeline above me with nothing else above it, just sky. Excitedly, I gained on Mount Justlaw's peak. But, being both inexperienced and overconfident caused me to find myself rushing over the edge, stumbling and tumbling down the backside of the mountainous ridge once again.

The en banc petition for rehearing was denied.[174] That was it—denied, no explanation. "O come on, give me a break!" I yelled up the gorge between the two mountain peaks in which I found myself after my tumble. "O, come on—O, come on—O, come on—," the mountain echoed back, mocking me.

Most cases that go the distance up Mount Justlaw are fueled by large coffers and have expert climbers, Sherpas, equipment, and endless supplies, ensuring that even if they get tossed off the mountain, the attorneys who have done the lion's share of the work walk away, pockets flush with cash. I, on the other hand, was on the other end of the spectrum, struggling to survive on fumes, with my wife working full time. I took contracting jobs here and there to stay afloat, while spending hundreds of hours studying. If I was eventually to be booted off the mountain, all I would have left would be my story. Now truth be told, I went to self-taught law school for those three years, which has greatly benefited my understanding of this world, our laws, and America. It has deepened my love for my country and American history. I gained a deeper understanding of the history of law and how it charts the ups and downs of our progress and decay in the cause of justice. Even my understanding of the sacred Scriptures dramatically increased because rigors of study and research reformed my thinking. But were my relentless studies helping my legal battle as I climbed Mount Justlaw? Did it even matter, since the more proficient I became and the more convinced I was of the truth, the more the institutional wall of opposition enlarged in front of me? I kept reminding myself that the Supreme Court cases that were critical to my case had all gone through the same arduous process. In my condition, that was both encouraging and exhausting to consider.

Finally, the clouds lifted just enough for me to unmistakably see the last stage of the climb up Mount Justlaw. It rose far above me up the sheer rock face on the other side of the gorge, its peak disappearing into the clouds. I knew without a doubt that it was Mount Justlaw's peak because I could see through the clearing in the clouds toward the east for the first time. The mountainous view was spectacular around the south side of the mountain, stretching out for hundreds of miles into the distance. Weather permitting, I would get to see the sunrise for the first time in the morning. Pitching my tiny tent, it was the perfect spot between the peaks to camp for the night before the grueling ascent in the morning. To the west, my view of the setting sun was blocked by the backside of the mountain ridge I had tumbled down earlier on. The weather cleared up as the day fled away, taking with it all of the clouds. I could see my breath as the deep velvet night fell. There was not a cloud in the sky—just crisp, crystal-clear air, with billions of sparkling stars framing the ominous jagged silhouette of Mount Justlaw's peak looming over me.

My wife and I decided around that time that we should move closer to the action. The hill country in Elmira was just a little bit too off the beaten path. The city of Alexandria, Virginia, located just outside of Washington, D.C., was beautiful. In the summer of 2019, when I was in D.C. for "The Good, the Bad and the Ugly" art show, I told myself that I would move to Alexandria if the opportunity arose. Alexandria looked very promising for my art. Alexandria was small enough that it was not D.C. and at the same time was very close to D.C. It reminded me of Nyack, New York.

Alexandria is a delightful river town on the shores of the Potomac. It is artsy and quaint, with plenty of interesting shops and coffee houses, as well as a yearly cherry-blossom festival that looked like the perfect setting for my new series of D.C. monument paintings, saturated with cherry blossoms. I reasoned that we could move to the area and capitalize on my story's exposure and the thriving economy, if it was God's will. That could become a welcomed and successful season of Washington-themed art sales.

Gloria had reached the end of a four-month-long substitute-teaching job in Elmira and had outperformed the principal's expectations. He was unable to secure Gloria a full-time position but wrote her a golden referral letter. Yet she sat on a bench outside the school looking very forlorn, with the golden letter hanging down in her hand like an ice cream melting in the sun when I picked her up that summer day. She was super bummed out that she had to leave a school where she had taught roughly seven hundred children a week in the art room, impacting their lives. Since we were in limbo as to where we needed to be workwise, I said, "Let's look for work in Alexandria, Virginia!" I sat down and googled "kindergarten teacher in Alexandria," and immediately, one position popped up on the job site called Indeed.com. Shiver me timbers! It was a kindergarten position at not just any school but a Christian school in Alexandria.

"Put the golden referral letter on the front page of your resume, and send it in like that," was my advice to my wife. Within the day, Gloria had a response. Within the week, a job interview. During that job interview with the principal and assistant principal, Gloria recommended they speak to the principal of the local Baptist school where our kids had gone to school for the last several years. Our children were highly respected there and had graduated with honors. They were reflections of Gloria as an educator and homeschool teacher when they were younger. Also, Gloria had substituted at their school a couple of times over the years. The principal interviewing Gloria asked her to repeat the name of the Baptist-school principal. She said slowly and deliberately, "Doctor. Michael. Drury," to which the principal responded by asking if Drury had a daughter named Kiley. Gloria replied in the affirmative, and he then asked if Kiley had a sister named Mary-Anne. "Yes, yes!" Gloria replied. The principal, now sounding wonderfully amazed, told Gloria that Mary-Anne Drury worked in their school (not their real names). That was most definitely the hand of Providence at work. That was all we needed, as the events in our life lined up as to the direction we sensed we should go. Gloria landed the job within the week, packed up, and took off to Alexandria with the kids, as the new school year was just around the corner. Our children got into excellent local schools, and our eldest was already in Virginia at Liberty University.

With our home now empty, I was able to remodel the property in preparation for renting it. Twenty acres of hard and softwood trees were ripe for the harvest after owning the property for thirteen years, and I discovered money did grow on trees for once in my life. The trees were harvested while I renovated the house for two months, and we successfully renting it out when complete. Now it was my turn to move to West Springfield, Virginia, where Gloria had secured a small apartment within the Fairfax County district, securing a seat in an excellent school for our son. It was costly for a small two-bedroom apartment, but it was worth it. Gloria could self-sustain while I finished up in New York and then made the transfer. I also secured a new art studio, a well-sized, semisubterranean garage space in Alexandria, hoping for a successful art season.

We then lived on the outskirts of Washington, D.C., about thirty minutes away—without traffic—from all the action. We were also neighbors of sorts with the Smithsonian Institution and the U.S. Supreme Court. It was inspiring to live in Washington, D.C., to be able to pass the time in our nation's capital, with so much to do, see, and learn. Also, as an artist, there was plenty of subject matter to use in my paintings from the drama of the seasons—white snow in the winter and pink cherry blossoms in spring, to spectacular scenes of the summer's setting sun unfolding behind the clouds and historic Washington monuments.

Bright orange light lit up the walls of my tent, causing my eyes to peek through the zipper of my sleeping bag to behold the glory of the orange fireball that blazed over the distant horizon to the east. The weather had held out, as piercing splintered sunlight cut through the morning fog and my steamy breath. My heart began to pound in my chest as the thoughts of the final climb filled my sleepy mind. There was no time to waste; the weather was perfect for once—cold but clear and dry.

The United States Supreme Court, then only miles away from my home, awaited my petition. As soon as I finished my Supreme Court research (which included all the new rules and filing formats that I had to follow) and, of course, wrote the petition itself, it was time to file. Since I lived so close, I filed everything in person at the Supreme Court, making copies for each of the justices—Roberts, Gorsuch, Kavanaugh, Kagan, Ginsberg, Breyer, Thomas, Alito, and Sotomayor.

That was to be my second direct appeal to John Roberts in his capacity now as chief justice. Beside the nine copies for the nine justices, there was one copy for the clerk and one for the U.S. solicitor general, often regarded as the mysterious tenth justice—he was the chief attorney that argued in defense of the United States at the Supreme Court. At the time, the solicitor general, Noel Francisco, was the fourth-highest attorney at the Department of Justice, with offices in the Supreme Court and the Department of Justice. I appealed directly to Solicitor General Francisco in a letter, asking him to recommend my case to the Supreme Court because of the unanswered question of federal law regarding the Smithsonian Institution. Out of approximately eight thousand yearly petitions for certiorari at the Supreme Court, mine could have been one of the seventy-five to 125 cases the court could have taken, since it was such a straightforward, unanswered question of federal law.

Other necessarily error-free application details comprised petitioning for a writ of certiorari (cert) to the U.S. Supreme Court. Otherwise, forget it—you would not even get your papers through the door. I had long thought about the potential of ending up at the Supreme Court. Yes, I would eventually walk up those iconic marble steps after all.

As it turned out, I first had to notify Attorney Marina Braswell at the Department of Justice. Together with my daughter Victoria, I set out early in the morning on November 7, 2019, for important business in our nation's capital and some extraordinary father-daughter time. This would be as exciting as it would be educational for both of us. After finding the right DOJ location, as there were many of them around D.C., we arrived and passed through the layers of security on our way up to Braswell's office. I wanted to meet her in person, as I had argued my case against her in writing and communicated via email and phone for over a year.

Braswell was not in that day, so we dropped off the filing with the attendant so that I could certify the Smithsonian and the United States had been served. Then it was time to skip across town and pop in to see U.S. Solicitor General Noel Francisco. Although I was dressed in a suit and tie and my daughter looked beautiful, I was carrying around a heavy red-and-white Staples bulk-paper-carrier box with all of the copies of my petition for cert to the Supreme Court. You can imagine all of the security around the Department of Justice's main headquarters. Well, I was carefully surveilled with my package that looked like it could contain something threatening, which it did. I probably raised suspicion by carrying the box very gingerly, as this was now my most significant legal work to date. All of my three years of study had been poured into this Supreme Court brief; it was a work of art.

Arriving at the Department of Justice's main entrance, from behind the snaking concrete barricades, a uniformed officer in a flak jacket squared up to me, sternly asking my business. I informed the officer that I was there to see General Noel. He asked if I had an appointment, to which I replied in the negative. It turns out that I could not even drop off my copy of the brief for the general, as it had to be mailed in to pass through security. Off we skipped to the post office, where we could mail the copy and certify my other filings were appropriately served with a notary public as required. We found the post office but had to wait for over an hour. We had lunch and waited some more, sitting outside the post office. For Washington, D.C., the pace of the post office worker strolling back to work after an hour's lunch was surprising and aggravating. His attention to my need was equally sluggish—there was no skip in his step, causing me to get just a little bit edgy. But that was my special day that I would not allow to be marred by sloth-like Mr. Postie. He finally notarized my document, and we swiftly took off, straight to the Supreme Court.

Now my heart started to pound, as the prospect of walking up those iconic marble steps approached. I had seen those steps in movies, the news, documentaries, and photos. I was about to climb them myself with my sweet daughter in tow. We parked near the Supreme Court after at least forty minutes of driving in circles looking for a spot. That area in D.C. is bustling and very tight, with barricades, security, and cars parked in every spot imaginable. Time was flying, and the court would close within the hour. We walked swiftly about four blocks, through the bustling congressional office buildings flanking the street, and at last, up the steps of the U.S. Supreme Court.[175]

As if commanded by the presence of the massive ornamental structure, I could not help but gaze up the steps ahead of me. My eyes floated up the sixteen massive fluted marble columns that created the portico underneath the pediment. I stood there in awe, my eyes dancing and twirling over the exquisite marble details. Having built and designed period-inspired fine furniture and custom cabinetry for many years, I was all too familiar with those Greco-Roman details, which many fine pieces of furniture embody. Standing still, staring at those few but beautiful and simple words, "EQUAL

JUSTICE UNDER LAW," was genuinely moving. Those four words were deeply chiseled and elegantly carved into the marble architrave, part of the relatively soft, off-white marble entablature.

The words filled my heart and mind with hope. I made it. The summit of Mount Justlaw was now within reach. After all, even the Supreme Court said this about itself:

> The Court is the highest tribunal in the Nation for all cases and controversies arising under the Constitution or the laws of the United States. As the final arbiter of the law, the Court is charged with ensuring the American people the promise of equal justice under law.[176]

We were directed around the side of the building exterior, since one cannot enter through the main doors—they are used as the exit after one passes through security around the back of the court. We were directed to a small metallic security-guard hut, where we were met by a very stern police officer wearing protruding, angular body armor under his white shirt, on which was displayed a bright brass chest-pocket badge. Wearing glasses, black pants, and a black peaked D.C. policeman's hat emblazoned with another brass badge, he glared at Victoria for daring to take photos. That was definitely not a tourist spot. He said very little and was determined to get me to dump out the contents of my box into a large clear plastic bag in the middle of the street. My finest work, dumped into a clear garbage liner—no way! O yes, or it was not going anywhere that day. Obviously, it had to clear security before getting into the court. (These days, it is rare that anyone files in person.) Unsurprisingly, I was the only one that day. The officer gave me a small ticket as a receipt and said now I could go inside to the clerk and complete the submission.

After passing through security, Victoria and I were impacted by the majestic and beautiful interior of the Supreme Court building. The dignified portraits of deceased justices were absolutely fabulous, a striking contrast with the presidential portraits in the

Smithsonian. Some of those Smithsonian presidential portraits just undermine the dignity, honor, and power of the office of the president. President Barack Obama sitting in a bush is a good example. Every hallway there, by contrast, was dripping with venerable history, which was highly relevant to me at the time. Victoria was impressed, as she realized that we were not tourists like so many others there that day; we had official business in the U.S. Supreme Court.

Yes, we did, and we carried it out, filing my petition for certiorari to the U.S. Supreme Court on November 7, 2019, and it went without a hiccup. Every "t" was crossed and every "i" dotted. The slightest administrative mistake at that level could get the petition rejected. I passed that bar on my first try, to my delight.

We took our time leaving, as we enjoyed the art and the individuals we recognized in the portraits, Justice Scalia and Chief Justice Howard Taft being among those most pertinent to my case. What a truly wonderful experience. And what an exquisite and dignified structure dedicated to such a noble and exalted cause—the cause of justice.

Yes, through opened double-access doors, we could look into the Supreme Court chamber, which at the time was not in session, where maybe I would end up arguing my case. A rope barrier barred our access to the inner sanctum of American justice. We could see the bench made of ornate and dark paneled wood. The tall crimson curtains reached the very high ceilings, over forty feet in some places. They hung between the four giant marble ionic columns, symbolic pillars of justice, behind the nine substantial leather chairs belonging to the Supreme Court justices. It was verging on the surreal, as my journey had brought me to such an auspicious and mysterious place.

Filing my petition for cert was a milestone for me, leading to a whirlwind of publicity that would document that accomplishment. Since 2016, I had been in contact with Kevin McVicker, vice president of a very well-connected public-affairs agency in Alexandria,

Virginia, by the name of Shirley & Banister. Craig Shirley was a well-known author of seven political books focusing on the life and presidency of Ronald Reagan, among others.

McVicker was not interested in my story in 2016, but by the time CPAC 2019 came around, the agency's interest was piqued, as McVicker was there at CPAC and saw my painting in person. After getting in contact with them after CPAC, I wanted to know if they could assist me in driving my story into the current D.C. political dialogue. I now had his attention.

The only hurdle was the funds, as their proposal was thousands of dollars out of budget. Reputable publicists are not cheap. I was stumped. Now I had a premier PR engine who could drive attention to my story but no way to harness their powerful machinery. I managed to get the word out on Frank Acomb's radio show, inviting people to assist me by purchasing my art locally, but nothing came of it. I refused to beg or ask anybody for anything. However, if they believed in what I was doing, they could support me by buying my art.

By the time I filed my petition for cert at the Supreme Court months later, Kevin McVicker was a partner at the agency, and he kindly made it possible for me to afford his services by giving me a price break and payment terms. He knew that if the Supreme Court took my case, it would be a publicity bonanza for both of us.

Now I had to generate the funds to pay McVicker. I had no choice but to return to New York in search of a contracting job that would help me cover my expenses in D.C., which now included the new studio space and my publicity agent. I planned to make it through the winter and get going with my new Alexandria-based art enterprise in the spring season of 2020. Things were very tight heading into the winter, and it could have been very bleak that year.

In Elmira, my friend and neighbor Jim was also in a bind at that time, trying to get his house renovated with funds from a trust his recently deceased parents had left to him. Although he was a contractor, the trust required him to hire a reputable contractor to do the work. I had the skills and insurance requirements he needed, and so I landed the contract.

The time together with Jim proved to be a huge blessing for both of us. We often prayed together, seeking God to help us order our lives and get through the winter. That season of prayer proved to be invaluable, as God would be preparing me for the momentous events that were just around the corner.

Funds began to flow again, and the bills were paid down in Virginia, including Kevin McVicker, who now put his Rolodex to work for me. The building contract with Jim lasted the winter, requiring me to stay most of the time in Elmira and visit my family on the weekends. Before long, Kevin landed a big interview. He connected with Alexandra Swoyer, a journalist who covers the Supreme Court for the very well-known and respected *Washington Times* newspaper in D.C. He pitched her the story, and her curiosity was piqued. After reading the briefs, she wanted to interview me.

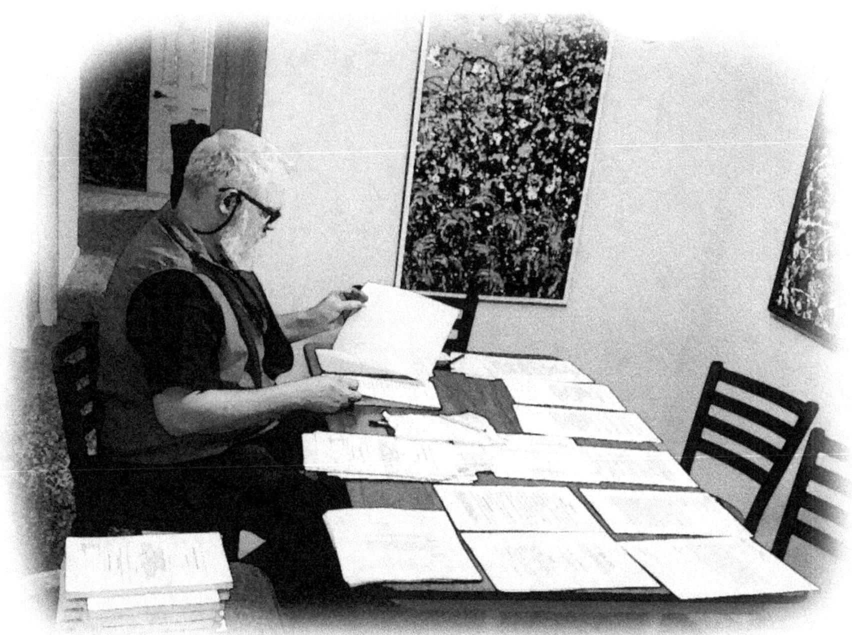

Preparing my petition for certiorari at the U.S. Supreme Court,
Fall of 2019, Virginia

Chapter Sixty-Three

PRESS'S POLITICAL PRESSURE

I T WAS SAID THAT PRESIDENT RONALD REAGAN READ THE *Washington Times* every day while president, saying, "The American people know the truth. You, my friends at the *Washington Times*, have told it to them. It wasn't always the popular thing to do. But you were a loud and powerful voice."[177] Alex Swoyer, from the *Washington Times*, called me at my studio in Alexandria to interview me. It was a great interview at a monumental time in my climb up Mount Justlaw. Having just filed my petition for cert at the Supreme Court, I needed all the media attention I could get focused on my case. Bringing awareness to my case in the public eye would drag the long-hidden mystery into the light. Climbing up Mount Justlaw was often a surprising source of light and joy, as I would stumble across sparkling, precious stones here and there. Holding them up to the light, I would admire their colorful and glistening illumination before pocketing them safely away.

The great Supreme Court Justice Louis Brandeis once famously wrote, "Publicity is justly commended as a remedy for social and industrial diseases. Sunlight is said to be the best of disinfectants; electric light the most efficient policeman."[178] I knew this to be the truth and knew that I needed a megadose of this "sunlight" to assist me in disinfecting the industrial disease I had been exposed to in the Smithsonian Institution.

On November 28, 2019, Swoyer's article appeared in the *Washington Times*[179] online. On Friday, November 29, it was in the print edition. That Friday coincided with my being in West Springfield. Early that morning, wanting to be the first one at the store, I went to the local Giant Supermarket, since they had a newsstand there. As I approached the newspapers, I could see the *Washington Times*. My heart started pounding as I stared intently at the paper. I could see my painting on the front page of the *Washington Times*! My story was on the front page![180] I was in awe, ecstatic, with my eyes heavenward, supremely grateful to God and Kevin McVicker. That special moment, all by itself, felt like vindication and victory. All of the twisted media stories I had endured just melted away like wax in the presence of the light of Swoyer's factual and spin-free account of my story. It made all of the struggles worth it and brought a surge of joy and courage to dig in further and prepare myself for the fight of my life that I believed was sure to come up the mountain. I stood there beside the newsstand, like the proud father of a newborn child. As people passed by, not paying me any mind, all I wanted to do was stop them, hand out cigars, and say, "Look at my baby! That is my painting; this is my story!" I had taken the fight all the way to the U.S. Supreme Court, and by the grace of God, I was going to win.

The story surprisingly generated just one email in support. I found that odd, but it was a good email nonetheless. Laurence Jarvik, the author of *PBS Behind the Screen*, an exhaustive exposé of the corruption at another taxpayer-funded institution, congratulated me. Jarvik was not surprised at reading the story. He had personally heard Kim Sajet speak and found her presentation at a Washington, D.C., club where he was a member disturbingly leftist.

Jarvik was aware of what I was up against and used his connections, contacting a well-known author and conservative activist, David Horowitz, in search of an attorney who could assist me. He did this of his own accord. I told him I was not opposed to help if they wanted to come along, but I had come this far by myself and planned to go all the way up Mount Justlaw.

Jarvik managed to get the attention of Cleta Mitchell, a very well-known conservative attorney, former Congresswoman, and political activist. Cleta put out the word to other attorneys who may have been interested in filing amicus briefs in support of my case. Those amicus ("friends of the court") briefs are written independently of the case but in favor of the case being granted certiorari at the Supreme Court. Time was short, since I had already filed my case, and Supreme Court consideration was fast approaching. That type of participation required intense preparation and prompt attention to the issue, as the amicus briefs were usually filed at the same time as the petition for certiorari, and those attorneys were busy people.

Jumping on board in support of a pro se litigant could come with all sorts of reputational complications. I imagined I was just too unconventional to partner with, especially as I made it clear that this was my fight and that I would take it all the way, not being prepared to hand it over to anybody. Well, the amicus briefs never came. Nonetheless, it was encouraging that someone, in this case, Larry Jarvik, took the time to try to generate assistance. He told me D.C. was an impenetrable fortress. No one could deny what he was saying.

Nevertheless, I had great faith that if my day in court came, I would ultimately triumph, because my trust was not in myself but in Him in whom our Founding Fathers trusted, "the Supreme Judge of the world."[181] Likewise, as a tiny stone flew from the shepherd boy David's sling right into the tiny space below Goliath's helmet, my case too could make it through the tiny odds and be heard. I, too, could be victorious, if only I could get my day on the field—if only I could get my chance to fight.

The only difference was that David could run right up to Goliath on an open field. There were no hindrances other than men's fears. Having rejected Saul's cumbersome and weighty bronze body armor, David charged into battle. In my case, I had to get through two massive seventeen-foot bronze doors that weighed thirteen tons. There would be no battle to win if I could not get through the doors and into the courtroom to fight. Would the doors open, and would my Goliath come out to fight?

The *Washington Times* story was no ordinary story. Every prominent political figure, especially on the conservative side of the aisle, including President Trump, would have known what was on the front page of the *Washington Times* that day. That would have been an excellent time for the president to tweet his support, but he never did. Also, the Supreme Court justices and their squadron of law clerks would probably have been made aware of what was soon going to appear on their desks.

The biggest takeaway from the story ended up being that the most reputable conservative-leaning political newspaper in Washington, D.C., and the country would put my story on their front page. They had their lawyers—including Alexandra Swoyer, who was an attorney herself—vet the story. They would not risk their reputation by embarrassing themselves with frivolous legal theatrics on their front page. (Also, remember the left-leaning *Washingtonian*'s feature article, which would never have been published earlier that year had the powers that be not recognized the truth behind my claims.) The game was now on. The pressure in the press had increased.

An energized Kevin McVicker went out to bat for me and began landing interviews on News Max, OANN, One News Now, PJ Media, and *The Schilling Show* with Rob Schilling, and even an Op-Ed on Townhall.com. Following a flurry of interest, a big interview materialized.

Kevin called late one evening. He said he had booked me on the Fox News morning show, *Fox and Friends*. They were sending a car to pick me up in the wee hours of the morning the next day. This was a heart-pounding moment. My story would get the national television coverage it needed, and the issues regarding the People's museum would now be front and center. That level of exposure would drive the conversation and the questions that my pending petition for cert had raised, especially the unanswered question of federal law. That national spotlight could put pressure on the justices to take the case as an unresolved federal legal dispute, a case which was in desperate need of a hefty dose of Supreme Court jurisprudence.

Everything was set, and my family was abuzz. My wife and kids called their friends to let them know and keep their eyes on Fox News. We were all waiting to pile into the limo Fox News was sending to pick us up and take us to the Fox News studios in D.C. We would make this another Raven-family adventure. It was electrifying, in all honesty. I was so excited to finally get the opportunity to appear on such a far-reaching show—to tell my story and inform millions of Americans of what was going on in their museum.

As we waited nervously, another hour passed. My phone rang. I tried to be calm and collected when I answered it. Kevin was on the other end. He called to say that he had not received a call confirming the pickup time. Something had happened; the call never came. We waited some more and then nothing. Something or someone had derailed the interview. That all-too-familiar gloomy disappointment filled our family, as we all felt dejected at being dropped without explanation. They never called Kevin back.

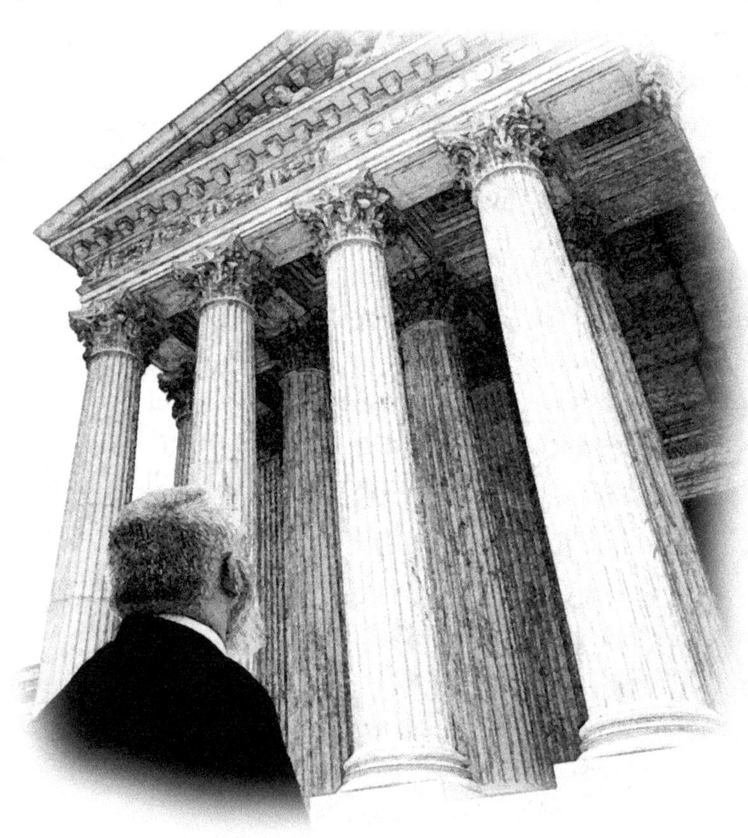

Filing my petition for certiorari at the U.S. Supreme Court, Fall 2019

Chapter Sixty-Four

SUPREME MOUNT JUSTLAW

Mount Justlaw's rocky summit was in focus. Its triangular jagged peak, made up of light grey boulders with patches of sap-green moss between them, momentarily peeked through the fast-moving storm clouds that rolled in from the west. Mountain winds whipped and whistled through the stacked craggy rocks jutting straight up on the way to the peak. The setting sun's fractured golden rays pierced through the clouds as the sun sank behind the jagged rock pillars. The rays painted menacing shadows on every surface. They were like wild and terrible silhouetted animals, like animated cave paintings stampeding across the rock face of Mount Justlaw. Camouflaged by the moving shadows, a barely trodden, narrow footpath meandered up ahead of me, snaking its way to the very top, several hundred feet away.

Suddenly, with a loud crack, like a spooked grouse on a hunting trip, the greasy golden pig appeared, crashing out of the thicket of dried thornbushes lining the winding path. The pig squealed hysterically. It bolted up the path ahead of me, causing my heart to skip a beat. Immediately, I gave chase, rushing with all my might.

My weary body, now flooded with adrenaline, had a mind of its own. My feet thumped the dirt as I gained on the fleeing pig. It would be within my grasp as I sprinted that winding path around a looming tower of black rock out in front of me.

All of a sudden, the golden pig vanished into a wisp of fast-moving cloud, upon which there suddenly appeared the terrifying silhouette of the beast, Cerberus. The clouds sped away as the growling, snarling three-headed hellhound now straddled the path in front of me. Grinding to a sudden halt, I rapidly composed myself, yanking from out of my backpack the three-chained spiked dog collars I had cold-forged in preparation for this moment. Cerberus rose up on its hind legs, as all three grotesque heads roared. I shook the chains violently in reply. The clashing sound of clanking, cold-forged steel alarmed the beast. "Roar all you want, but you're mine!" I yelled as the winds whipped and howled around me.

One of the three heads now raised itself above the other two as I rushed toward it. That head had nine eyes and one large horn. It opened its mouth and howled in terror as I lunged for its neck, stomping on the other two necks. Wrestling and struggling, I tried to secure the collar around its thrashing neck, only to have it slip through my grip. The winds immediately picked up and wrapped the beast in thick clouds, as it swiftly retreated into the falling darkness. Out of the darkness, a sinister laugh faded into the howling wind. Violent winds drove the racing clouds, completely enveloping the summit. Everything suddenly went black. I could not see the path right in front of my feet. Quickly, I threw myself down in the dust as the biting winds now screamed around me. Frozen in the piercing black darkness, I squeezed my eyes closed, covering my head with my hands. The winds crescendoed to a soul-shuddering screech—and then nothing. A lonely silence descended around my weary body as I drifted off into dreams.

Startled, the sounds of singing, cheery birds woke me. Opening my eyes slowly, the bright, golden light of the rising sun lit up the gently swaying wild grasses in the field around me. I lay motionless for a moment. To my surprise, I found myself once again way back down the mountain, at the foot of Mount Justlaw. Its peak I could see poking up through the clouds, miles away in the distance. Standing up, I brushed myself off, glancing one last time at the mountain. Shaking my head in silence, I walked away, back into the all-too-familiar woods behind my house.

On January 10, 2020, my petition for certiorari at the U.S. Supreme Court was denied. Sure, it could have been potentially embarrassing, uncomfortable, and destabilizing for the status quo and the justices to validate my arguments. There would have been far-reaching ramifications in granting my petition for certiorari, but it would have been equal justice under law. Granting certiorari would have focused the attention not only on my case but on the court itself as it deliberated, because of the chief justice's dual roles.

My case was unprecedented and historic because no other federal lawsuit against the Smithsonian had ever reached the legal altitude of the U.S. Supreme Court, but that no longer mattered. It felt like I was watching my sodden appeal float down a rain-filled gutter, pages flapping in the wind, never to be seen again. My precious Supreme Court brief, into which I had poured my heart, mind, and soul and which had consumed three years of my life, had been washed away. I had tried to prepare myself for the denial of certiorari, as I knew it was possible, but I had not wanted to believe it could happen.

Before 1925, the court had to hear all petitions for justice. Since 1925, under the Certiorari Act, the Supreme Court has been given the discretion to refuse most cases at will. After all I had read, studied, and discovered to be the truth, I reasoned that the truth, combined with the force of law, would have carried enough weight in themselves to guarantee the hearing of my case in the Supreme Court. But as it turned out, my legal naivete would have to grapple with the complexities of unseen and unspoken forces that influenced judicial decisions even at the Supreme Court level. Wasn't this the U.S. Supreme Court, where anyone—even me—could find equal justice under the law? Why was my case not heard?

This was the same court, after all, where even a drifter, petty thief, and prisoner by the name of Clarence Earl Gideon could study the legal system from his prison cell, represent himself, and scribble his petition to the U.S. Supreme Court. Gideon discovered by himself that his constitutional rights to legal representation under the Sixth Amendment had been violated. On March 18, 1963, the U.S. Supreme Court heard Gideon's case and ruled in his favor, guaranteeing his case would be retried. With a lawyer representing him, he won his freedom. Amazing! This, I sincerely believed, was the American justice system that glimmered on a distant hilltop for the whole world to admire, and this was the same court my case had reached. I knew Gideon's remarkable story. It had always intrigued me, leaving me in awe since the first day I heard it many years ago. It filled me with hope. There was even a movie made about him from the book by Anthony Lewis, called *Gideon's Trumpet: How One Man, a Poor Prisoner, Took His Case to the Supreme Court—and Changed the Law of the United States.*

But no, in my case, it was one more disappointment in over three years of repeated petitions, appeals, and denials of justice. People and the media had mocked me, and others had ignored me, sheepishly and safely siding with the government and concluding the government must be correct. By default, the Smithsonian-guarding status quo dictated that I had to be wrong, even though there was still no answer to the lingering entity-status question.

Four out of nine votes were necessary to grant my petition for certiorari. They would have laid the groundwork for the old unanswered question to be answered finally. Granting me certiorari guaranteed deep and penetrating scrutiny. Accountability would have come to the Smithsonian Institution. Director Sajet, Dr. Richard Kurin, and the chancellor/chief justice may eventually have been on the hook for violations of the First and Fifth Amendments to the U.S. Constitution and for breaches of fiduciary trust. Try to imagine what could have happened in the Supreme Court chamber while in session if the chief justice had to recuse himself publicly.

This "nobody" artist, a self-represented litigant, had charged him in his capacity as Smithsonian chancellor with breaching his fiduciary duties. (As a side note, pro se litigants can no longer represent themselves in oral arguments in the Supreme Court. They are assigned an attorney by the court.)

Even if my petition had been granted, the Supreme Court could not have determined if my rights were violated—that was for the lower courts to decide. All they could have done was define the laws, stating my rights, by which the Smithsonian Institution and its officers would have had to abide. And as I have already quoted several times, the court had already determined that the Constitution did apply to Amtrak and other government-run private trusts. They also would have had to rule that since the federal government did not and could not speak through its art selections at the National Endowment for the Arts, neither did it nor could it speak through the Smithsonian's selections of art. This would have granted We the People our speech rights.

At that time, I wrote an Op-Ed called "O, To Be a Fly on the Wall,"[182] which dramatically described the imagined dynamics at play during the nine justices' January 10, 2020, meeting. According to law, the justices would have executed the responsibilities that our elected representatives had appointed them to do by granting my petition and defining the Smithsonian Institution. Justice should be blind and impartial, especially in the hall where "equal justice" exists for all. If that was the case and the chief justice was found wanting in his performance as Smithsonian trustee, then so be it—nobody is above the law. Truth is truth, the law is law, and justice is justice. Sadly, I found out that "Equal Justice Under Law" is not absolute. Instead, it is a goal, and the inscription should read, "Equal Justice Under Law For Some."

In a different time, in one of the Supreme Court's most lasting and historic landmark rulings, in the case of *Marbury v. Madison,*[183] the Supreme Court had to inject itself into another pressing issue of defining federal law. In that case, Chief Justice Marshall established the principle of judicial review. This principle would give the federal courts the power to determine if any legislative or executive acts were unconstitutional.

Chief Justice Marshall wrote, "It is emphatically the duty of the Judicial Department to say what the law is." And this most certainly was the controlling principle overshadowing my case. *Marbury* defined the specific duty of the Supreme Court, which was, in my case, to review the congressionally created Smithsonian law and say what the law was. The fact that the Supreme Court has gotten away with ignoring this duty to this day still profoundly troubles me. Who then must hold the Supreme Court to account if We the People, through our elected representatives, stay silent? If we cannot compel judicial accountability, we are powerless in the face of supremely powerful, unelected judges whose rulings are redefining the very DNA of the United States. Judges should be executing their jobs by faithfully interpreting the Constitution and saying what the law is, not protecting the status quo.

The justices refused to do their duty for unknown reasons. Chief Justice Roberts, at the January 10 denial to hear my petition, recused himself.[184] That alone was an indicator of the conflict of interest and internal disturbance my case was causing. Simultaneously, Justice Roberts was about to preside in the Senate over the first impeachment trial of President Trump on January 16, 2020. Imagine if questions were allowed in the Supreme Court that called into question Chief Justice Roberts's conduct, especially if they related to a biased, anti-Trump sentiment that he had supported, either knowingly or unknowingly, at the Smithsonian Institution. How then would he be able to sit and preside over the impeachment of President Trump?

Rather than open my pro se can of worms, as the justices could see the far-reaching legal ramifications directly affecting the Supreme Court and the Smithsonian Institution (and the firestorm in the press that would ensue), the justices kicked the can down the road. They chose to decline my petition and leave a question of unanswered federal law unanswered to preserve the status quo, ignoring *Marbury v. Madison*!

Silencing one man's free speech and denying him his constitutional rights as guaranteed in the First and Fifth Amendments to the U.S. Constitution was the preferred sacrificial option and was the price they were willing to pay. Those nine justices swore an oath to God to defend the U.S. Constitution in all cases impartially, but somehow they managed to shirk and suspend their oaths and duty on that day, specifically in my case.

What they had not taken into account was that I, too, had sworn a similar oath of allegiance unto the U.S. Constitution and unto God upon becoming a U.S. citizen. I may not have been a famous lawyer, influential celebrity, wealthy Washington socialite, popular politician, or even a judge. Still, I was indeed a citizen of the United States of America. My oath read as follows:

> I hereby declare, on oath…that I will support and defend the Constitution and laws of the United States of America against all enemies, foreign and domestic; that I will bear true faith and allegiance to the same…and that I take this obligation freely, without any mental reservation or purpose of evasion; so help me God.[185]

Their decision did not extinguish my oath, my conscience, or my God-given duty to be faithful to my oaths. That oath now constrains my conscience to defend the Constitution until the present day. If not, what is the point of anything in America, if the integrity of our word just dissolves in the face of disappointment, seemingly insurmountable adversity, or even judicial abuse of discretion at the highest level of our judicial system? Does one just relinquish the duty to defend the Constitution simply because a bunch of unelected lawyers refused to hear one's case and do their jobs?

What is the point of America? What does it mean to be an American? In my case, by defending my rights and fighting for my First Amendment free-speech, Fifth Amendment due-process, and equal-protection-under-law rights, I was trying to win and thus prevent the rights of all future participants in the arts and any other fields of learning at the People's Smithsonian Institution from being odiously abused by partisan activists on the People's payroll. This is how We the People participate in the American experiment, each one of us adding our signature symbolically to the Declaration of Independence in defiance of tyranny, whatever form it may take.

Truth be told, that is not how I felt the day I received the call from my publicist Kevin McVicker with the terrible news that my petition for certiorari had been denied. That decision sent me into a tailspin of despondency that lasted for months. I was sickened, numb, and deeply disappointed. There were days when I was so discouraged that I did not want to be an American anymore. I felt betrayed. I wanted a constitutional divorce! At times, it was so bad that I was tempted to exercise the new concept that I had learned of in the first part of my oath of allegiance, which was to "abjure." Yes, to abjure an oath was to unswear and break the oath. When I became a U.S. citizen, I abjured my allegiance "to any foreign prince, potentate, state, or sovereignty," as I was formerly a British citizen, subject of the Queen of England and resident of Spain. In this case, I would be abjuring my oath to the U.S. Constitution. What a nightmare to be a man without a country!

At their refusal to hear my petition, I felt like my legs got kicked out from underneath me. It reminded me of a structure I saw when on a pilgrimage to Israel. On that trip, I visited the Yad Vashem Holocaust Memorial. Part of its odd, triangular, cone-shaped architecture jutted out from the rest of the building, cantilevered over nothing but a road that passed underneath it. The tour guide explained that this architectural feature expressed the feelings the Jews in Nazi Germany experienced. It was as if the ground under their feet had disappeared when their once-democratic government extinguished their rights as citizens. To be clear, in no way am I saying that what I experienced was anything like the horror that my Abrahamic brethren experienced as a result of losing their rights. Neither am I comparing the court's actions to those of the Nazis.

Instead, my analogy refers to the strange feeling of the ground, in my case the constitutional legal foundation upon which I thought I was standing, suddenly disappearing beneath me.

Life back in Spain would have been excellent, relatively simple, with great food, culture, and endless beaches bathed in the Mediterranean sun. Corruption was expected, so involvement in politics for a foreigner was pointless. Most people just enjoyed the uncomplicated life under the sun. I was very tempted to go back to my life in Spain. My family still lived there, so it would have been therapeutic.

Even in the dizzied condition in which I found myself, I knew I had to say something. They may have silenced me in the Smithsonian, but I knew I was free to speak elsewhere. I had to respond. Kevin McVicker called me up asking if I wanted to write an Op-Ed in response, but at the time, I could not bring myself even to do that. What could I have said that would have had any positive effect? I did not know what my next step would be. Once the Supreme Court brushed me aside, would anyone still care? Would the controversy end?

People naturally look to the court to determine justice. Their rulings usually seal one's fate, since they have the last word. Well, that was not justice in my case since I didn't get my day in court. Was there another court in which I could appeal? Would there be a way to try my case in the court of public opinion with an actual remedy at the end?

At the time, all I was able to do was repeatedly say how disappointed I was, with nothing else to offer. However, as time passed, in response to the emotional effect the ruling had upon me, I created a digital poster, "The Swampire Strikes Back."[186] It depicted and expressed how silenced and powerless I felt. Printed on the back was an outline of the Smithsonian legal story. The graphic was a spoof on the Star Wars episode, *The Empire Strikes Back*, when Han Solo was frozen in Carbonite. He would have to wait until he was free to fight again.

Chapter Sixty-Five

BOOK, FLIGHT, OR FIGHT?

Bᴀᴄᴋ ɪɴ Aᴜɢᴜsᴛ ᴏғ 2019, ᴡʜᴇɴ ᴛʜᴇ sᴘʀᴀᴡʟɪɴɢ *Wᴀsʜɪɴɢᴛᴏɴɪᴀɴ* article came out highlighting my Smithsonian saga, I tried in vain to secure a book deal. I needed an advance sufficient to buy me time to sit for three months and write *Odious and Cerberus*. My story had been distorted in the *Washingtonian*. My case had been denied, compelling me to seek ways to set the record straight. Despite how they spun the story, I reasoned that if the *Washingtonian* magazine took so much time to write and print my story in full color (which became one of their best reads of 2019[187]), my true story was worth turning into a book. But the financial pressure to make ends meet kept me from the creative zone where inspiration—in this case, in the form of book writing—happens. The waters of my mind and spirit were not at ease.

Somehow, the book had to be written. After three years of study, my accumulated knowledge had piled up. It could benefit, educate, and infuriate American citizens and hopefully inspire them to action. As challenging and discouraging as it often was, my experience on Mount Justlaw had benefited and equipped me enormously. Yet, I had no idea how to look for a book deal effectively. After soliciting various publishers and getting no response, that effort ended.

In February 2020, I began to seriously think about how I could reach the American people to share my story. A road trip made the most sense, I thought, even back then in my still-raw and wounded condition. If I did not inform and share with my fellow Americans everything I had learned, who would? A cross-country trip, from state to state and town to town, was calling to me. On the other hand, getting on the road might also help me run away from it all.

In February, I purchased an older-model 1997 motorhome,[188] intending to renovate and letter it up in vinyl. Citizens all across the country would be curious, I imagined, about a story informing on and exposing the Smithsonian Institution. People would be eager to listen and learn the facts of an American immigrant's true story, and ultimately, they would be as outraged about the whole fiasco as I was. There was one big problem—I did not have the book written, edited, published, or in hand. I needed to write my book.

The COVID-19 pandemic hit in March of 2020, throwing the whole world into a tizzy. As a result, my family and I left Virginia, as Gloria learned her yearly teaching contract would not be renewed. My new art-studio plans in the Washington, D.C., area fell apart, as everything was headed toward lockdown and shutdown, destroying the tourism industry. Since it would have been impossible to start up my art business during the pandemic, especially with the exorbitant D.C. overheads, we packed up and moved back to Elmira to live full time in our warehouse and motorhome. My wife and children and I worked together to renovate the RV, courtesy of the pandemic.

The plan was to get the RV roadworthy and just get out on the road, as the road was one of the best and safest places to be during the pandemic. If a book and tour of some sort were going to happen, it would have to materialize once we were on the road traveling the country. But until then, like everything else, it was on hold.

I had a deep longing just to go and enjoy the open road, as traveling can be a great panacea. The potential to live on the road, travel, and see the beauty, grandeur, and majesty of the national parks dotted across America was all that appealed to me. At times, I felt like a dying man in a desert, thirsting for that oasis of rejuvenating nature and spectacular scenery waiting for me out on the road.

After eight months of renovating the RV and my art studio in Elmira, New York, we were ready for the open road. The pandemic turned out to be a blessing for us, as we could renovate even our warehouse because I had no work and plenty of time on my hands. Gloria was hired to teach virtually. We sold our car and bought an enclosed trailer that we could haul behind the RV. I converted the trailer into an Internet-broadcasting studio from which Gloria could teach while we were on the road. In this way, we would have an income and could survive on the road as we traveled. If I could paint and sell paintings, then all the better. If that went well, we could take my brush all across the country, painting the scenery. It was December 17, 2020, with two feet of snow on the ground in New York, that we finally headed out on the road.

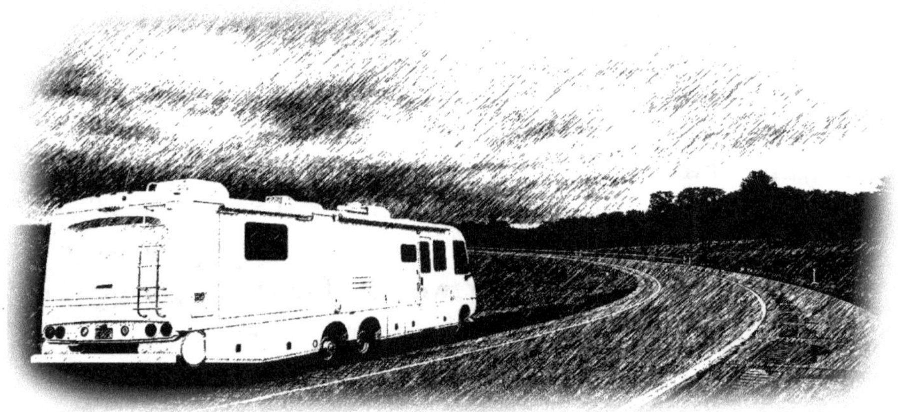

The open road, December 17, 2020

Chapter Sixty-Six

BEAUTIFUL AMERICA

WORDS FALL SHORT OF THE FULL POWER NECESSARY TO EXPRESS exactly how I felt seeing the scenery and learning some of the great histories of the American Southeast. Upstate New York, where I live, is truly beautiful and rich in rivers, wildflowers, tall trees, and waterfalls. These vistas culminate at the thundering and mind-blowing Niagara Falls in Buffalo, New York. But the South had an unexpected beauty all of its own. Part of the treasure we were to discover was the people. Although COVID limited our interactions, we still encountered the warmth and charm of the people in the South.

Since we did not plan our trip, we serendipitously followed the flow of available campsites and ended up in some truly magnificent places. Virginia's Outer Banks were absolutely wild and terrifying. We arrived there at night amid a storm. Our motorhome shook as we were lashed by the driving rain. The next day, the sun burst through the dramatic sky, illuminating frothy white waves as they pounded the golden beach set against the colorfully churned Atlantic Ocean. The Carolinian coastline was equally splendid, from

Holden Beach to the Crystal Coast, all the way down to Beaufort. The white, sandy beaches and tropical flora, bursting with palm trees all the way down to Florida, were astonishing to me. American history on the coast was riveting, as we learned of American heroes and Biblical-esque struggles and successes the likes of which I had never heard—in particular, the remarkable life and story of Robert Smalls. From slave to a member of the U.S. House of Representatives. Unbelievable![189]

The trees—O those magnificent trees covered in Spanish moss—took my breath away on multiple occasions. Some of the sprawling oak trees were gargantuan, filled with singing songbirds that left me speechless and totally in awe. I found many of the swamps to be exquisite—another completely unexpected discovery. The still waters within them created perfect, even kaleidoscopic images, as the mirror-like reflections crafted the illusion of mysterious netherworlds beneath the mercurial surface.

Our three-month adventure of over four thousand miles culminated in the Great Smoky Mountains. We camped by the Oconaluftee River in Bradley's Campground on Native American lands in the town of Cherokee. The Great Smoky Mountains, the national park, the magnificent views, and the giant yet graceful elk completely arrested my attention. I learned the gut-wrenching story of the Trail of Tears and the trauma the Cherokee Indians suffered. The Cherokees' admiration and reverence for creation were inspiring. Especially significant to me was their respect for the powerful, iridescent black bird, the raven, a symbol of a messenger from the spirit world.

Over massive moss-covered boulders, the rushing and crashing bubbly white, ice-cold rivers ran. Yet their waters were crystal clear. It was as if my wounded condition were being cleansed and washed away, far downstream, by the sublime and majestic wonders of God's artistry. I could not have predicted that the road trip where I feasted my mind on the glory of nature would have such a healing and restorative effect on me. And not only restoring my mind and spirit but also restoring my love for America, warming my heart and defrosting me out of my encrusted, carbonite-like paralysis (poignantly illustrated in my "Swampire Strikes Back" poster). I was genuinely reinspired and eternally grateful to be a citizen of such a beautiful America. I was ready for the fight. The "animating contest of freedom"[190] called to me once again!

Upon our return to New York, I discovered I indeed had been reset. After a few days of being back, the winds of inspiration fell

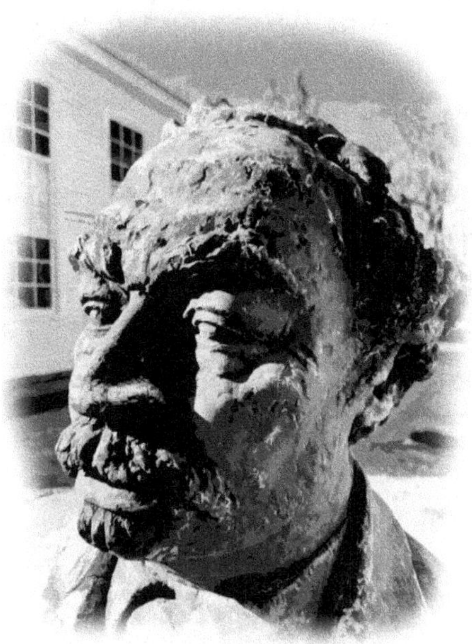

Robert Smalls (1839–1915)

upon me to write *Odious and Cerberus*. Financially, we continued to live on my wife's income alone. Peace came as a result. The book flowed from my fingertips like water gushing from a faucet morning, noon, and night until it was written. In two weeks, over one hundred thousand words poured forth as I told my story in the rough. The story then needed months of critical editing with the help of my wife and chief editor, Gloria, who is highly skilled in the technicalities of the English language.

Giants like Mr. Smalls never gave up. He kept on pressing into the cause of justice. His suffering and heartbreaking story had given me perspective in my wounded condition. His triumphant deliverance and overcoming persistence in the face of seemingly impossible obstacles were powerfully transformative.

Mr. Smalls's story demonstrated that terrible evils happen under the star-spangled banner of freedom, but God is not hindered in His ability to redeem our suffering under the same flag. Remarkably, America—more often than not—facilitates redemptive destinies that can happen if we choose to humble ourselves and embrace our cross of disappointments and injustice. This is, after all, our path in the footsteps of our Savior. This is, after all, the path to our own healing through His stripes. And this is, after all, the path on which the glory of the resurrection awaits at its end.

Thus restored, I began to resharpen my sword, eager to get back into my battle for righteousness. *Odious and Cerberus* was soon to be finished. The American People had to join me in my battle if there was any chance of securing justice.

"Hineni!"

Here I am!

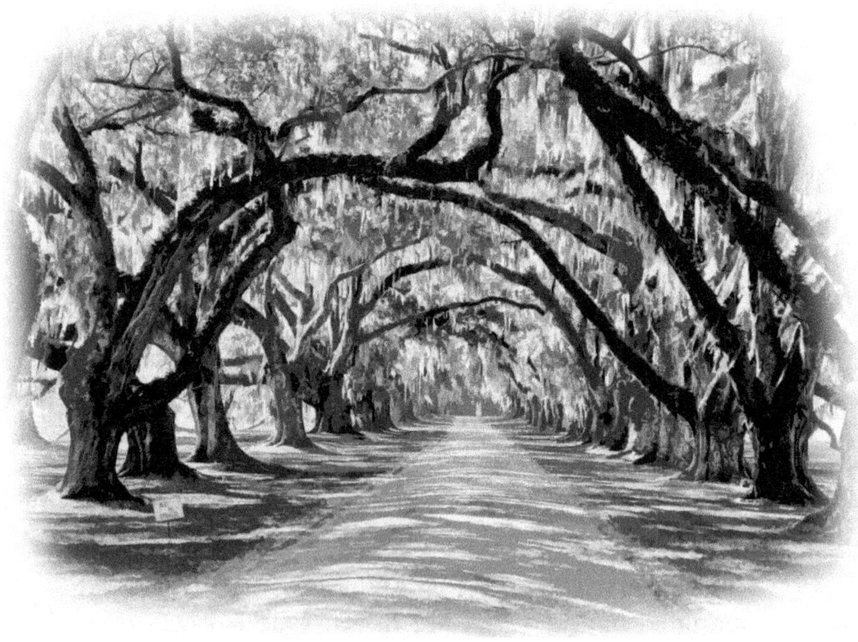

Giant oak trees covered with Spanish moss

Chapter Sixty-Seven

GRAVE VOICES

THE SUPREME COURT DENIAL WAS NOT THE END OF MY journey—it was just another challenge to overcome, another phase in my unfinished free-speech legal war. Some people conveniently forget that America was born not only out of agonizing resistance against oppression and tyranny but also out of resistance against corruption and injustice. Americans did not give up when King George thought that he was ending the dispute by denying the colonial appeals. Justice was still wanting, and the colonists knew they were in the right. The American spirit was forged in an unyielding and determined opposition to a tyrant king's refusal to humble himself and submit himself to his own laws. These continual injurious acts drove the suffering colonies to a place where they had no choice but to appeal and, in the end, no choice but to fight. Oddly enough, when one fights for one's rights today in federal court against a prestigious, untouchable, and ostensibly infallible institution, it is considered by some to be embarrassing and even offensive. People conveniently forget that power corrupts, even here in America—even in the most prestigious institutions.

Is it then beyond the ordinary citizen's reach today to do anything about homegrown corruption wherever it is discovered? To whom should we turn for guidance? I am reminded of that great scene in the movie *Amistad* when John Quincy Adams, played by Anthony Hopkins, echoes the captive Cinqué's sentiment to look to his ancestors in times of great trouble. Adams walks the marble busts lined up against a wall in the Supreme Court as a gesture to invoke the wisdom of Madison, Hamilton, Franklin, Jefferson, Washington, and John Adams. We must do likewise. According to Samuel Adams (whether one is a politician or not), is it not the American citizen's duty to be constantly involved in the "animating contest of freedom"? Or is that contest limited only to an elite few in specific fields of political activity? Does not the battle belong to freedom-loving people wherever freedom is denied?

Our government continually refused in my case—including the federal courts and the U.S. Supreme Court—to clarify the issues presented. Independently, and for other scandalous reasons, both houses of Congress (as we shall see in the next chapter) also refused to act in regards to the Smithsonian. The unresolved status-identity issues documented in this book have maintained the conditions for ongoing, unchallengeable corruption at the Smithsonian Institution. This corruption has expressed itself in the silencing of free speech and usurping the rule of law and thus has pushed the issues outside the reach of accountability. As a result, the unresolved issues naturally spill over into the national pool of ongoing institutional corruption, increasing its depth. That is, rather than serving as an example and restraining institutional aggression against free speech across the country, the inaction in this one sphere emboldens an ever-increasing and ever-broadening willingness to chill conservative and Christian speech. The liberal left-leaning press mocked my free-speech claims and ridiculed my lawsuit. What were people to conclude when the U.S. Supreme Court refused to hear my case?

By contrast, take, for example, the California Science Center case I wrote about earlier. We saw how the members of a scientific group in favor of intelligent design who wanted to show a film exposing evolution fought back in court and won in a settlement. However, they were still barred from showing the scientific film (speech). It serves as an example of pro-intelligent-design scientific speech being silenced under Smithsonian pressure.

Examining the bigger picture nationally may assist us in clarifying the duty placed upon us with the unresolved Smithsonian issues staring us in the face. The national trend away from free speech defines for us how we must respond when confronted by a free-speech-silencing story that continues to cry out for resolution. At some point, something has to change. And maybe the Smithsonian Institution can be the first domino to topple.

Looking deeper into our pressing national crisis, could it be that the unrestrained legal, moral, and spiritual disintegration we are witnessing from a front-row seat all across our country is precisely because of unchallenged institutional corruption? Thomas Jefferson, in the Declaration of Independence, correctly identified that the natural tendencies and weaknesses of good people, unfortunately, is to tolerate corruption. He said, "Experience hath shewn, that mankind are more disposed to suffer, while evils are sufferable, than to right themselves by abolishing the forms to which they are accustomed."[191] Imagine if our forefathers just sat back and licked the boots of the tyrant King George, capitulating in compromising submission? In the face of today's escalating corruption, what posture or course of action do the People owe to our Founding Fathers? What should be our attitude when we see this continual slide into corruption and American decay? Can we even restrain it?

The Declaration of Independence holds the answers. It is the ultimate "activist" guide for Americans to follow when dealing with corruption. It serves as the example of unrelenting legal and political action in pursuit of redressing governmental abuses:

> In every stage of these oppressions we have petitioned for redress in the most humble terms.

Not that we are at the stage where the use of force even needs to be considered, but rather, the Declaration of Independence serves as a reminder—a complete guide—indicating action must be taken "in every stage." Then, after every option has been exhausted, the Declaration clearly defines when and only when the use of justified insurrection should be exercised. Insurrection should never happen for "light and transient causes," like lies and conspiracies. Remember, the colonists were under the boot of tyrannical oppression. "Absolute despotism…absolute tyranny" is the bar to be reached before justified insurrection can even be considered. There is far too much talk today of skipping the long and drawn-out, often-tedious intermediary stages, as if the use of force were the only solution.

Today, we are not even close to being oppressed. In fact, our problem today may be the reverse—we are not oppressed at all but rather spoiled rotten with privilege, entitlement, comfort, and prosperity. And this condition has made us unfit for the battle of liberty, creating a climate where some constantly flirt with the obsession of a rush to arms as the quick fix to our problems rather than be engaged in the long, protracted, and drawn-out animated contest of freedom. Not until a patient and exhaustive lawful political, legal, and social full-court press has been made, playing out every single possible recourse while exercising the spirit of decorum, humility, and restraint, can force even be considered. One can see how the use of force is a juicy temptation for enraged people armed to the teeth with guns and bullets. But the American way, disposition, and character were marvelously modeled for us by our Founding Fathers as our example to follow. At the same time, they made it crystal clear:

> That whenever any form of Government becomes destructive of these ends, it is the right of The People to alter or to abolish it, and to institute new Government, laying its foundation on such principles and organizing its powers in such form, as to them shall seem most likely to effect their Safety and Happiness.[192]

The principle is clear: it is the duty and right of the People to correct governmental corruption.

At the time of this nation's founding, America had representatives who shared an underlying common set of values on both sides of the aisle and who would only bend so far in political compromise. They were people of a different character and creed from what we have today. Today, the divide between left and right has become virtually irreconcilable as a result of the breakdown both of absolute moral values and a core common faith on both sides.

Our Founders knew the level of commitment and determination required to accomplish freedom's victories. They also knew that if they had any chance of defeating the massing hordes of the British Empire, King George's red-coated army and the merciless Hessian mercenaries disembarking by the boatload on Staten Island's shores in New York, they needed help from above. Jefferson appealed to the "Supreme Judge of the world for the rectitude of our intentions…. And for the support of this Declaration,…a firm reliance on the protection of divine Providence." This has to be our first step; this has to be where our confidence resides as well. After they made the pledge of faith, the Founders signed the document and went to war. Thus, they put legs on their prayers and boots on their words.

Releasing and merging the power of the faith of a couple of million citizens in 1776, combined with courageous leadership expressing faith in God in concert, America was born. Today, we must make the same pledge of faith, harnessing the faith, power, and convictions of millions of free citizens in unwavering, tireless, and courageous actions on the front lines of these battles in the culture war. It is the only way we can hope to win and save America.

Without the pressure of a constant marshaled spirit upon the American People, we can only expect to lose America as easily "as a whale goes through a net." John Adams, on October 11, 1798, in a letter written to the Massachusetts militia, presciently warned us and speaks now from the grave, lighting another beacon to help illuminate our way in this present darkness:

While our country remains untainted with the principles and manners, which are now producing desolation in so many parts of the world: while she continues sincere and incapable of insidious and impious policy: We shall have the strongest reason to rejoice in the local destination assigned us by Providence. But should the People of America, once become capable of that deep…simulation towards one another and towards foreign nations, which assumes the language of justice and moderation while it is practicing iniquity and extravagance; and displays in the most captivating manner the charming pictures of candour frankness & sincerity while it is rioting in rapine and insolence: this country will be the most miserable habitation in the world. Because we have no government armed with power capable of contending with human passions unbridled by…morality and religion. Avarice, ambition [and] revenge or gallantry, would break the strongest cords of our Constitution as a whale goes through a net. Our Constitution was made only for a moral and religious people. It is wholly inadequate to the government of any other.[193]

Our system of government is simple. It was "made only for a moral and religious people." And what is the source of our common and historical religion and morality? What was that founding religion?

In his historic and often-read-in-Congress farewell address, President George Washington declared to the American people that: "With slight shades of difference, you have the same religion, manners, habits, and political principles." Unfortunately, we can no longer describe the fabric of the American socio-religious and political landscape in the same terms. Still, while there is breath in our lungs and hope in our hearts, we must light that beacon once again on our now-darkening path. And that light is the written source of the religion that once framed the worldview in which America was born and that once restrained the madness of sinful men and women.

On May 28, 1849, Former Speaker of the House Robert C. Winthrop, a contemporary of Smithsonian Secretary Joseph Henry, said:

> Men, in a word, must necessarily be controlled either by a power within them, or by a power without them; either by the word of God, or by the strong arm of man; either by the Bible or by the bayonet.[194]

President Lincoln is also an appropriate luminary to turn to at this time for guidance and inspiration. Although all men being created equal was the theme of his speech addressing the Civil War, the principles therein transcend that specific issue and press on toward the "great task remaining before us" as well. His Gettysburg Address defines our duty as "living" Americans today, which we must embrace:

> Fourscore and seven years ago our fathers brought forth, on this continent, a new nation, conceived in liberty, and dedicated to the proposition that all men are created equal.... It is for us the living, rather, to be dedicated here to the unfinished work which they who fought here have thus far so nobly advanced. It is rather for us to be here dedicated to the great task remaining before us—that from these honored dead we take increased devotion to that cause for which they here gave the last full measure of devotion.[195]

"The great task remaining before us" remains undone. We the living must "take increased devotion to that cause," as Lincoln said. He did not confine the task to political professionals or to an elite bourgeoisie, but to us, the American People. History tells us of Lincoln's reliance on the Sacred Scriptures during the dark days of the Civil War. Lincoln masterfully proclaimed this one nonexchangeable and fundamental truth: "That this nation, *under God*, shall have a new birth of freedom" (italics added). Submission to God alone brings freedom and facilitates the concept and the hope "that government of the people, by the people, for the people, shall not perish from the earth."

But government of the people can only happen if the underlying Source of self-government prevails. You see, you cannot have government of the people unless the people are firstly anchored morally to the same general transcendent objective standards and principles. Only then are they able to govern their own lives as individuals. And where do those standards and principles originate? The Bible is the critical ingredient for self-government undergirding our justice system. It is absolutely necessary as the source of absolute transcendent moral values required for the U.S. Constitution to function, as Adams instructed.

We will have no excuses left to tell our grandchildren if we openly and freely hand them an anti-Christian, leftist, socialist, atheistic, genderless, parentless, valueless, immoral America (with persecutions to boot). President Ronald Reagan understood the challenge and issued this admonition:

> Freedom is never more than one generation away from extinction. We didn't pass it to our children in the bloodstream. It must be fought for, protected, and handed on for them to do the same, or one day we will spend our sunset years telling our children and our children's children what it was once like in the United States where men were free.[196]

Is it too late? Has the persistent and tireless Left been so successful, under the liberties granted to them by the Constitution, that all is lost? No doubt, their aggressive, strategic, and well-funded efforts in media, the arts, academia, Hollywood, the music industry, and the Internet, etc., for the last fifty years have granted them significant gains (not all of which have been immoral). Even so, if the Left has accomplished what they have under our laws, then for goodness' sake, we must be able to undo the ills they have achieved using those same laws.

You see, we must look at ourselves and honestly ask, Have we made use of every available tool, spent every single available dollar, and employed every lawful means under the Constitution to promote, persuade, and resist at every turn the advances of the godless

Left? Has the massive body of conservatives (made up mainly of people of faith, especially Christians of different denominational stripes) been fully engaged at the forefront of the culture war in defense of traditional values? Have we been faithfully praying, voting, funding, participating, organizing, and protesting, creatively planning, and continually pushing back the indefatigable onslaught from the hordes of the godless, anti-Christ, anti-American hard Left, as well as the fascistic right-wing extremists? And not only pushing back, but pushing forward by promoting, propagating, and persuading hearts and minds to recognize and respect the Judeo-Christian and constitutional democratic-republican worldview we hold so dear?

I have closely observed how people I know who are professing Christians or politically conservative, holding to traditional American values, passively sit back and angrily yell at their TVs or radios. That sedentary and frustrated mindset creates a ticking time bomb that will one day explode. Principally, I believe this happens because many feel powerless or ill equipped, believing their efforts will be worthless. And this inability to act creatively is another cause of anger.

Another force that prevents people from trying is their fear of backlash, causing them to be petrified of the cost of getting involved, so they prefer to just hand it over to the professional religious and political class to do the job. Now, in an ideal, God-fearing, law-abiding America, that is how it should work. Unfortunately, not only is our America far from where we should be, but it has never been in such dire circumstances as it is today. Our Founding Fathers pledged their "…Lives,…Fortunes and… sacred Honor"[197] in freedom's struggle, setting the example of the high price of freedom. Today, just ask Jack "the Cake Baker" Phillips the far-reaching implications of prosecution by anti-Christian rogue state officials and judicial abuse of discretion in state courts and their impact upon cultural issues and his personal life. Are we prepared to pay that price?

John Adams even warned us in his letter to his wife, Abigail, on April 26, 1877:

> Posterity! You will never know, how much it cost the present generation, to preserve your freedom! I hope you will make a good use of it. If you do not, I shall repent in Heaven, that I ever took half the pains to preserve it.[198]

We cannot continue like this and hope things will get better by themselves. Just look at the rapid disintegration sweeping the nation: deceptive historical revisionism, arbitrary and punitive cancel culture, crippling political correctness, deceptive activist journalism, polluted primary- and general-school education, unrestrained political extremism, unaccountable judicial activism, unrestrained greed—even in the pulpit, medically certified gender dysphoria—now even in children, the elimination of God-created (science-defined) male and female genders, celebrated sexual perversion, hatred and unprecedented racial tension, rejection of God-created-and-ordained marital order, the distortion of the roles of husband and wife, mother, father, and children—and the list goes on. These are just some of our ever-increasing modern societal sins. They are continually undermining the Word of God, as well as our traditional, historical American values.

And just how does this erosion continue to happen? Every time laws, morals, standards, and values—i.e., the guardrails of a free society—are illegitimately breached and the people and the authorities refuse to mend the breach, disintegration and erosion happen. And the guarantee that this process will be complete is when the breached standards are converted into law by a Supreme Court ruling. For example, in the heyday of slavery, the 1857 *Dred Scott v. Sandford* decision was an example of despicable judicial activism. The perversion of human dignity and the preservation of the economic enterprise expressed through the institutionalization of slavery (the status quo at the time) had to be somehow justified under the U.S. Constitution. Chief Justice Taney, an unelected lawyer, slithered his way out of applying the Constitution to

African, or Black, Americans at the time. Whether slave or free, the court odiously ruled Black African Americans were not actually American citizens. In this way, the Constitution did not apply to them—genius! Thankfully, Congress was to have the last word. Three years after President Lincoln's Emancipation Proclamation in 1863, Congress enacted the Thirteenth Amendment, outlawing slavery. As a result of the congressionally created law, the Supreme Court decision in the *Dred Scott* case was overturned.

It is as if the current polite, Christian-conservative mindset refuses to get down-n-dirty, into the trenches of the culture war, where the Left seems to be at home. Don't get me wrong, there are many reputable individuals and organizations already in the fight, along with many noble activists, authors, politicians, and ministers who have been resisting and fighting. There are non-profits (e.g., the March for Life), legal and media platforms, religious organizations, and individuals engaged in different capacities in the fight for freedom. Some people pray, some organize, some give financially, some canvass during elections, and others volunteer. All of these are critical parts of the solution, which not only must continue but also must increase. But overall, we must resoundingly up our game. The time has come for conservatives to employ every legitimate means at our disposal to win back our country. We need to learn how to communicate persuasively, to make our message attractive to people who may be won over by an honest, reasonable, principled, compassionate, and creative conservatism.

To illustrate the acute irony of our times and simultaneously take a page out of the activist's playbook from "back in the day," take a look with me at the University of California at Berkeley anti-war and civil-rights protests in the sixties. Whether or not you agree with what they were protesting, they were successful in contending for justice because of their methods. In the free-speech movement on campus at that time, protests would take place with large numbers of students in "sit-ins," who demanded their rights under the Constitution to speak up on whatever topic they wished to speak. And they prevailed. In 1964, Mario Savio, a student leader, spoke passionately about the students' strategy to accomplish their free-speech goals. Pay attention to the words he used in reference to the "operation of the machine," so aptly applicable to the Smithsonian director and Board of Regents in silencing free speech:

> There's a time when the operation of the machine becomes so odious, makes you so sick at heart, that you can't take part! You can't even passively take part! And you've got to put your bodies upon the gears and upon the wheels, upon the levers, upon all the apparatus, and you've got to make it stop! And you've got to indicate to the people who run it, to the people who own it, that unless you're free, the machine will be prevented from working at all![199]

Liberals and leftists since those days have often cited this speech as inspiration for their protests. Occupy Wall Street is a somewhat recent example. Today, adherents to Biblical values and traditional, conservative family values must learn the lesson from these protests. It is not enough to rely on elected politicians who promise legislation that resists the Left. Every effort needs to be coupled with mass resistance through the mobilization of people putting our "bodies upon the gears."

Look at this other critical contemporary issue: the undermining and redefinition of society's once-fundamental, God-designed, and God-ordained institution of marriage. The upending of a cornerstone of civil society was accomplished in the U.S. Supreme Court decision in *Obergefell v. Hodges* on June 26, 2015. The radical ruling blew open the floodgates of America's recent and increasingly unrestrained sexual- and gender-identity insanity. With it, this Supreme Court ruling unleashed the systematic delegitimizing of the influence of the Bible, undermining its authority and its influence on American culture, and by extension, the Bible's influence on the world.

In *Obergefell v. Hodges*, the majority of liberal Supreme Court justices ignored the Tenth Amendment, which mandates the issue is reserved for the states. Then, like witches in black robes gathering around a steaming cauldron, they conjured up—out of a highly suspect, watery legal broth—a fundamental right for same sexes to marry. This they invented out of the due-process clause and equal-protection clause of the Fourteenth Amendment. Justice Kennedy, who cast the swing vote, tipped the scales into sin's bubbling broth of sexual anarchy, trampling five thousand years of human, marital, and religious history, along with all three of the world's great monotheistic religions' core ordinances. The sacred boundaries of the fundamental institution of marriage, the very cornerstone of civilized society, were ripped off by five unelected lawyers sitting in their marble temple in Washington, D.C.

This Supreme Court decision was a radical stroke of social reengineering, bowing to and in support of a group of people who have succeeded in promoting their ideology through years of militant activism. We would be remiss if we ignored the efforts and successes of their activism in the face of the constant defeats and setbacks on the Christian-conservative front. *Obergefell* was another stunning rout for our representative republic and historical Biblical, Judeo-Christian values in America. That law, now the law of the land, was created by judicial fiat. Somehow, Christian and constitutionally conservative Americans were incensed for only a couple of days. Then, it was as if they shrugged their shoulders in surrender and returned to their lives as usual, many even just accepting the ruling regardless that it was a divine provocation. The highest court on earth usurped divine authority, elevating itself above the Judge of the world, to whom Jefferson appealed for victory over tyranny. And we wonder why things are so bad in America! These aberrations of law may have already sealed our fate, since the Judge of the world may already have had enough of us, becoming deaf to our prayers.

What a mockery of the words of Jesus Christ, the final Judge, who will one day hold even the justices on the Supreme Court to account and who said in the book of Matthew:

"Haven't you read," He replied, "that at the beginning the Creator 'made them male and female,' and said, 'For this reason a man will leave his father and mother and be united to his wife, and the two will become one flesh'? So they are no longer two, but one flesh. Therefore what God has joined together, let no one separate." (Matthew 19:4–6, Holy Bible NIV)

Read Justice Antonin Scalia's dismay in his scathing dissent in *Obergefell*, in which he rebukes the overreaching Supreme Court, denouncing its majority decision and order as a

naked judicial claim to legislative—indeed, *super*-legislative—power; a claim fundamentally at odds with our system of government. Except as limited by a constitutional prohibition agreed to by the People, the States are free to adopt whatever laws they like, even those that offend the esteemed Justices' "reasoned judgment." A system of government that makes the People subordinate to a committee of nine unelected lawyers does not deserve to be called a democracy.[200]

Scalia continues, even making a tacit argument in favor of justified insurrection. He declares that a principle even more fundamental than "no taxation without representation" has been violated. By extension, if the colonies went to war over lack of representation in the British parliament as a taxpaying constituency, how much more justified the rush to war would have been for them over the violation of the more fundamental principle of "no social transformation without representation."

Scalia's dissent was not specifically even about the morality of same-sex marriage. It was about domestic relations and their definitions, which were outside the Constitutional purview of the Supreme Court, thus being subject only to the jurisdiction of the states. The issue should have been decided by the voting citizenry of each state, not mandated by the overreaching court. If this example of judicial tyranny has not further infuriated you, then what will? *Obergefell* became certified, documented judicial hubris—abuse of discretion in plain sight, at the highest level of our judicial system. But where were the protests over *Obergefell v. Hodges*? They should still be happening daily on the steps of Congress and the Supreme

Court. Conservatives give up too easily! Scalia's dissent redrew the line in the sand that was smudged by the nefarious ruling, yet his dissent had no legal power. However, what it did have was just enough raw indignation to blast every ounce of apathy out of the Judeo-Christian conservative mind for the next generation—yet where is our indignation?

One might have thought a nationally mandated societal transformation such as *Obergefell v. Hodges*, forced upon us without our consent, might have triggered a national outcry, but it did not. Can anything be done to right this ruling? Actually, yes! It would need a two-thirds-majority vote in the House and the Senate and a president who would sign into law the Twenty-Eighth Constitutional Amendment that would declare that marriage, by definition, is the union between one man and one woman. It might take fifty years to accomplish, but it is possible! That law would override *Obergefell v. Hodges*. Also, the Supreme Court could overturn the case itself.

This and so much more can happen when we Americans finally mourn and get on our knees and repent. Then, getting up revived, we turn the tide of our powerless state of being into courageous faith and the righteous activism necessary to reverse our sorry state of the union. We must heed the voice from the grave that said only "under God" shall this nation "have a new birth of freedom."

Could it be that the silencing of one artist's free speech will be the match in the powder barrel?

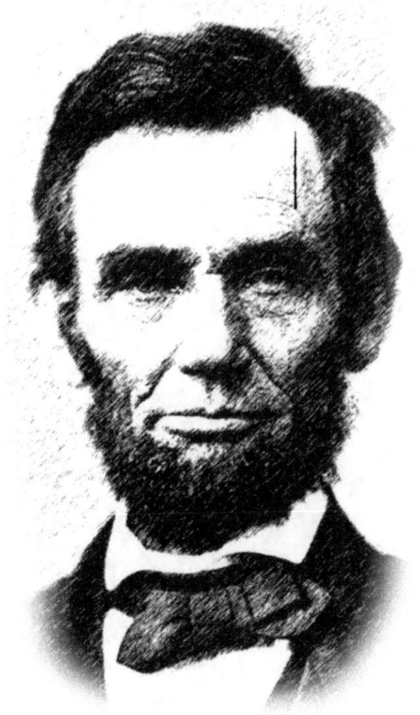

Chapter Sixty-Eight

MY FINAL APPEAL

LADIES AND GENTLEMEN OF THE JURY, HAVE YOU REACHED A verdict? My case was unjustly denied its day in court. That is why I have no more recourse but to appeal to you. My case can serve as an opportunity for you to act as a member of the jury of my peers, the American People. Your response can be a practical exercise in civic activism. A quintessential civil-rights violation, the silencing of our precious political free speech, has exposed ongoing corruption in our Institution that demands to be righted. It may just serve as the catalyst for Smithsonian reform. My case has created a moment of opportunity to enforce our rights by rebuilding a critical guardrail in an imploding America. The *Obergefell v. Hodges* case demonstrated the Supreme Court's reprehensible overreach in fabricating and changing law, reminding me of the book of Daniel chapter 7. The little horn in verse 8 arises and has human eyes and speaks boastfully. This is hard to understand for Daniel, so he gets angelic interpretation a few verses later in verse 25: "He will speak out against the Most High and wear down the saints of the Highest One, and he will intend to make alterations in times and in law." My case demonstrates the Supreme Court's refusal to say what the law is. Both are unacceptable when justice in America is in the balance.

If corruption and injustice do not inspire active resistance, then maybe it is already too late. Rather than trying to change things, perhaps the answer is for us to return to submission to the English Crown, as Samuel Adams suggested:

> If ye love wealth better than liberty, the tranquility of servitude than the animating contest of freedom,—go from us in peace. We ask not your counsels or arms. Crouch down and lick the hands which feed you. May your chains sit lightly upon you, and may posterity forget that ye were our countrymen![201]

In light of our current state of affairs, a measured dose of introspection may serve as part of the remedy necessary to shift the present frustration and Christian-conservative paralysis into action. Looking hard at ourselves and where our movement has failed and listening to our critics may provide us with some vital information necessary to develop a winning strategy.

For example, I can remember the uproar when Barack Obama observed and critiqued how people in small towns across the Midwest coped with job losses, saying it was not surprising that

> they get bitter; they cling to guns or religion or antipathy to people who aren't like them or anti-immigrant sentiment or anti-trade sentiment as a way to explain their frustrations.[202]

Conservatives were furious and felt insulted, but maybe he was somewhat right. Perhaps the default response of some conservatives when experiencing continual setbacks and losses is to get crippled by bitterness and rage. Some withdraw frustrated into the corner with guns loaded, far away from the battle of ideas, only waiting to blow up with bullets rather than with ballots. This is a crude defensive response to conflict and loss, like one would expect in—let's say—Afghanistan. But blind rage never truly resolves the pressing issues. It just destroys. That distorted last-resort response is certainly not winning the ongoing animated battle for freedom. We have to win on the battlefield of ideas.

Instead of bitterness and rage, even in the face of seemingly insurmountable opposition and setbacks, we should seize upon and celebrate our God-given liberties in this glorious land of freedom. Then, prayerfully and strategically work within our communities to facilitate and affirm American liberties and the rule of law, fueling brilliant policy, entrepreneurship, ingenuity, creativity, and faith, especially in tough times. We must not sit around getting depressed and frustrated, expecting the overpaid talking heads on television and the government to fix our problems. Getting right with God, then getting equipped and informed and having a practicable and realistic strategy to carry out a local actionable plan, are absolutely critical. Otherwise, it's all just angry talk that will bypass the creative-opportunity stage and rush headfirst into civil war.

Years ago, after I preached in a movie theater following the screening of Ben Stein's documentary, *Expelled: No Intelligence Allowed*[203] (a documentary about hostility against proponents of intelligent design in academia and in part addressing the Richard Sternberg debacle), Pastor John Cramer, from a local church in Corning, New York, came up to me and asked, "What should we do?" I said, "After you finish preaching on Sunday, lead the flock out of the church and into the community to speak up, protest, and campaign for our causes." I continued, "It's not enough just to hand out pizza. People need to respond, meet, organize, and strategize. Then they need to be led into the fray to drive righteous transformation and resist spiritual and moral corruption."

Every town hall and county public meeting—every public school-board meeting—should be swamped with participating citizens, parents, and people of faith and values—all lined up down the street and on street corners waiting for their turn to express their informed opinions and tempered outrage at the pressing issues of the day. This massive army of Christian citizens meets every week all over the country and then goes home and does the gardening. Their united voices must oppose the erosion of traditional Biblical values in the education, entertainment, economic, and political systems at every step. Start with just showing up, then read legally prepared statements that point out the issues, signed by hundreds of local residents. Then follow up with the repeated mailing of those petitions, phone calls, over and over and over again until compliance is achieved by the relentless pressure and persistence. Christian conservatives, for now, wield massive, influential voting power that if properly coordinated, withheld, or exercised can cause massive societal change.

Remember, it was dogged persistence that paid off when, in the Scriptures, the old woman sought justice from the unjust judge. But remember she had to be active in physically going to the judge and not giving up. This and many other full-court-press measures must be employed until we win. It might take many years, but we have no choice but to unwaveringly commit to the cause until we have the victory. It is the desperate hour. Individuals must rise up, speak up, get educated, get involved, get equipped, and get elected onto boards—leading them, influencing them, and resisting the continual slide into hell.

Today, finally, there are stories of parents who have had enough, stood up, and loudly spoken up at school-board meetings. Some have unfortunately gone from doing nothing to then exploding rather than the persistent and continuous full-court press. Some, though, have won seats on those boards and become actively involved in politics, embracing the battle for liberty. Look at the fantastic story of Mark Robinson, who made an eloquent and impassioned speech in favor of the Second Amendment on April 3, 2018, in front of the Greensborough City Council meeting. His speech went viral online, and before long, this average citizen became North Carolina's first Black Republican lieutenant governor. An amazing American story of rise from poverty to political power. What made the difference? He spoke up!

It is easy to excuse inaction and lay blame elsewhere before looking at ourselves to see how much of the blame we carry. If good people had been actively and constantly involved in animated prevention and resistance, could America have rotted to the core as it has? Like Trojan horses, tenured teachers and elected officials have abused our trust. Our children have been poisoned by activist educators who have executed their plan to reengineer America while decent and trusting people slept.

Desperately needed reform of institutions that belong to the American People presents a crisis of national import, survival, and identity. Look at the case of the Smithsonian Institution, which has become such a globally recognized and respected institution. The seal of the Smithsonian now serves as a seal of legitimacy upon any subject under its purview. With the Smithsonian seal, people automatically trust what they are being told and blindly believe it to be true. Do not think for a moment that those radical activists don't know this. They do. They know what they are doing. What type of chumps must *we* be to be financing their agenda to the tune of seven hundred million dollars a year?

When agenda-driven radicals who have become entrenched in the People's Smithsonian Institution use the power of the Smithsonian name and reputation to penalize and squash ideas and speech they despise—ideas related to Biblical values, political conservatism, and the scientific field of intelligent design—while acquiescing to, embracing, and promoting Darwinism, abortion, the radical sexual-anarchist agenda, and any other contemporary trends that threaten traditional values, our mission has been clearly defined.

What is exciting about this patriotic exercise before us is that it is totally within the power of the People, the average citizen like you and me, to accomplish. Who would *not* want to be part of righting the wrongs lurking in the Smithsonian as a great place to start participating in restoring America? Hopefully, you have been provoked and moved by my story to the point of action. You will be able to say to your grandchildren that you had an active part in an historic effort compelling the law to change for justice.

Join this just cause. Together, we can bring the beast into submission, chaining this Cerberus-like Smithsonian Institution to the U.S. Constitution and to law.

The court of public opinion is the last court to whom I can appeal.

This is my final appeal.

We the People

must win.

Chapter Sixty-Nine

THE SMITHSONIAN AMENDMENT AND REFORM BILL

REMEMBER WHEN SLAVERY FINALLY WAS ABOLISHED BY CONGRESS passing the Thirteenth Amendment to the U.S. Constitution in 1865? That amendment overturned the dreadful Supreme Court ruling in *Dred Scott v. Sandford*. Naturally then, our elected congressional representatives, whom we have sent to Washington to be our voices in our government, must do the same with the Smithsonian dilemma. That is, they must finally amend the 1846 Smithsonian Act, bringing the Institution into harmony with existing law. This is how We the People exercise our will. This is how We the People will reform and fix our Smithsonian Institution. This is how We the People overturn the ruling in *Raven v. Smithsonian*, and this is how the Smithsonian Amendment and Reform Bill came about.

Below is a draft of my bill that your congressional representative needs to read, refine, repurpose, and execute. Your congressional representative also needs a copy of *Odious and Cerberus* mailed to them. If new candidates are running for office, give them the same information, since they can make it part of their campaign.

The instructions, the introductory letter to be signed and mailed, and my version of the bill can all be found and printed out at: odiousandcerberus.com/the-peoples-reform-bill.

Tell your family, friends, neighbors, pastor/rabbi/minister, lawyer, colleagues, local business leaders, local politicians, and state politicians to do the same. Post the cause on Facebook, Twitter, Instagram, and other social-media platforms, using hashtags #odiousandcerberus, #Smithsonianreform, and #Smithsonianaccountability. Sharable links can be found at facebook.com/odiousandcerberus.

Follow-up suggestions and instructions on putting out one's own press releases are also available online. Contact local media and radio shows. If you or your lawyer can help in the final crafting of this bill, please email me: info@julianraven.com.

The People's Smithsonian Amendment and Reform Bill

A Petition to Amend the Smithsonian Act of Congress of 1846
- A Draft

We the People of the United States of America, beneficiaries of the will of James Smithson, petition the trustees of the Smithson trust, elected representatives and members of the United States Congress, according to the 1846 Smithsonian Act of Congress, to create a bill by the name of ***The People's Smithsonian Reform Bill.***

The Smithsonian Act of Congress of 1846 declares in SEC. 11.: "That there is reserved to Congress the right of altering, amending, adding to, or repealing, any of the provisions of this act," paving the way for this current amendment of said, in its fully realized and lawful version to be fully considered and passed into law.

The repeated scandals, corruption, and ongoing legal confusion about the Smithsonian Institution's entity status and the ongoing failed reform bills submitted by Congresswoman Eleanor Holmes Norton and Senator Chuck Grassley have failed to rectify these and other pressing issues. Congresswoman Holmes Norton stated that she

> introduced similar legislation in the three prior Congresses: H.R. 2622 (113th), H.R. 1786 (112th), and H.R. 4775 (111th). In the 110th Congress, Senator Chuck Grassley (R-IA) introduced a similar bill in the Senate, S. 3276, the Open and Transparent Smithsonian Act of 2008. No further action was taken on any of these bills.[204]

As a result of these and other failed reform efforts, ***We the People*** of the United States of America now intervene as citizens and trust beneficiaries.

In Section 1 of the Smithsonian Act of Congress, we read:

> James Smithson, esquire, of London, in the Kingdom of Great Britain, having by his last will and testament given the whole of his property to the United States of America, to found at Washington, under the name of the "Smithsonian Institution," an establishment for the increase and diffusion of knowledge among men; and the United States having, by an act of Congress, received said property and accepted said trust; Therefore, For the faithful execution of said trust, according to the will of the liberal and enlightened donor…[205]

For the United States of America to receive James Smithson's bequest, there was a need for a trust to be created and for trustees to be appointed to carry out Smithson's will. This role of fiduciary trustee the U.S. Congress accepted as the representatives of the People of the United States, the beneficiaries. Hence it is the duty of Congress as trustee to act in the best interests of both the testator, James Smithson, and of the beneficiaries of the Smithson trust, ***We the American People.***

For Congress to faithfully carry out this fiduciary obligation today, individual congressional representatives must take up their fiduciary duty and write a bill or cosponsor another bill calling for the amendment of the Smithsonian Act of Congress. This action is warranted for a multitude of reasons, including the multiple failed attempts to reform the Smithsonian Institution via failed bills. Serving as an example and bolstering this popular demand, in 2015, Congresswoman Eleanor Holmes Norton stated some of the systemic deficiencies crying out for a reform bill:

> "The Smithsonian Institution could not continue as the nation's foremost cultural institution without the 70 percent of its budget that comes from federal taxpayers," Norton said. "There is no reason why its operations and deliberations should be kept from the public. The Smithsonian is not a private club. Even publically-traded corporations must have public meetings, save specifically named exceptions. FOIA requirements are quite ordinary rules that all federal agencies in an open and democratic society must follow, such as making board meetings and administrative records, among others, publically available, except for traditionally confidential matters, such as internal personnel issues and trade secrets. The recent history of mismanagement at the Smithsonian took place out of sight in a tax-supported entity whose meetings and proceedings were closed to the public. The fiduciary responsibility of the Smithsonian Regents demands not only considerable attention to ensure appropriate oversight, but also ensuring the public the opportunity to assess both the tax-supported entity and its federal overseers."[206]

This statement should compel a special bipartisan committee to be formed to review the recommended amendments and then refine them according to appropriate laws. Once created, the bill must pass through the processes necessary to convert the amendments into law.

Not that American citizens need standing in Congress, but serving as legal support for this citizen intervention, the Supreme Court in Hawaii, in *Kapiolani Park v. City County*, ruled that "members of the public, as beneficiaries of the trust, have standing to bring the matter to the attention of the court."[207]

The U.S. Supreme Court in *Raven v. Smithsonian*[208] refused to hear Raven's case and answer the unanswered question of federal law, which was mandated by the Uniform Trust Code for the District of Columbia in § 19–1302.01, which reads: "(a) The court may intervene in the administration of a trust to the extent its jurisdiction is invoked by an interested person or as provided by law."[209]

It is clear that both as American citizens and beneficiaries of the Smithson trust, we have standing and the right to appeal to the United States Congress, as Smithson trustees, to act according to our wishes.

Also, according to the Uniform Trust Code for the District of Columbia, the trustee must administer the trust solely in the interest of the beneficiaries, the People of the United States of America. And when that duty has been violated, it is the right of the beneficiaries to call the trustee (in this case, the U.S. Congress) to account.

§ 19–1308.01. Duty to administer trust.

Upon acceptance of a trusteeship, the trustee shall administer the trust in good faith, in accordance with its terms and purposes and the interests of the beneficiaries, and in accordance with this chapter.

Amendment Goals and Considerations

Entity Status and Relationship between the Smithsonian and the Federal Government

Definition of the entity status of the Smithsonian Institution: This definition must include the Smithsonian Institution's legal composition, structure, and laws under which the Smithsonian Institution must function (i.e., Is the Institution a private institution to carry out the private will of its founder or a government institution to carry out the will of the federal government?). The definition must determine the role of Congress in relation to the Smithsonian Institution. The definition must specify the boundary of Smithsonian property ownership between the trust, the trustee, and the beneficiaries.

The independent and exhaustive 392-page investigation into Smithsonian Secretary Small's corrupt conduct in the 2007 IRC (Independent Review Committee) Report commissioned by the Smithsonian Board of Regents found (on page 29): "Unlike the vast majority of nonprofit organizations whose governance is informed by applicable state statutes and common law of fiduciary duties, there is no developed body of federal common law setting forth the duties and obligations of the Board."[210] These non-profit experts identified the glaring cause at the root of the then-current Smithsonian scandal and others, that no laws apply to the Smithsonian because the status of the Smithsonian Institution has not been defined by Congress, and the U.S. Supreme Court has refused to take up the matter.

The federal courts have continued to confuse the Smithsonian Institution's identity. In Federal Case number No. 1:17-cv-01240 (TNM), Judge McFadden ruled: "The Smithsonian is a government institution through and through," contradicting Supreme Court Justice William Taft, who declared in his capacity as Smithsonian chancellor that the "The Smithsonian Institution is not, and never has been considered a government bureau. It is a private institution under the guardianship of the Government."[211]

Board of Regents

Be it Enacted by the Senate and House of Representatives of the United States of America in Congress assembled: That the recommendations of the June 18, 2007, Independent Review Committee Report commissioned by the Smithsonian Board of Regents be adopted and implemented. Included in Congresswoman Holmes Norton's 2015 Smithsonian Modernization Bill is the dissolution of the Board of Trustees (the current members of the Board of Regents, being government officials, are far too busy to manage the Smithsonian properly) as it presently exists, to be replaced by twenty-one competent private-citizen trustees, who are professionals in all of the general fields of learning embraced by the Smithsonian Institution. Their composition, appointments, duration, and legal accountability to Congressional oversight require definition.

The objectives and other appropriate elements of the Holmes Norton and Grassley bills must be reconstituted in this new bill in light of the precise legal definition, including the submission of the Smithsonian Institution to the U.S. Constitution and all appropriate laws applying to public trusts that are administered by the federal government.

The Constitution and Free-Speech Rights in the Smithsonian Institution

The recommendation in support of the First Amendment's free-speech rights applying to the Smithsonian, written in the U.S. House of Representatives Committee on Government Reform staff report from December 2006, was titled "Intolerance and Politicization of Science at the Smithsonian" and said, "Because of the Smithsonian's continuous refusal to take action in the Sternberg case, Congress should consider statutory language that would protect the free-speech rights regarding evolution of scientists at all federally funded institutions."[212] The Congressional report's recommendation conflicts with the ruling in *Raven v. Sajet*, where Judge McFadden declared the First Amendment doesn't apply to the Smithsonian Institution, denying Mr. Raven his First Amendment free-speech rights.[213]

The question of who is speaking when the Smithsonian Institution's officers make executive decisions needs to be answered. Is it government speech or constitutionally protected private free speech? Does the Smithsonian violate the separation-of-powers doctrine when making decisions, since the Board of Regents is composed of members of all three branches of the federal government? In *Raven v. The Smithsonian*,[214] the court ruled Smithsonian decisions constitute federal-government speech.

Transparency

Be it further enacted: That all Smithsonian business meetings are to be open to the public, and that all records, minutes, resolutions, etc., be available upon request by beneficiaries and members of the public. That the Freedom of Information Act (FOIA) apply as well as the Uniform Trust Code for the District of Columbia §19-1308 regarding the Duty to Inform and Report (a).

Participation Rights

Be it further enacted: That the committee clearly defines the role of Smithson Trust beneficiaries as participants in the will of Smithson and their rights therein. The Smithson Trust beneficiaries have been actively participating in the trust since its inception and must continue to do so. That clearly written participatory criteria in every field of learning to be "increased" should be established for the Smithson beneficiaries.

Smithsonian Property Disclosure
and to Whom Does It Belong?

Be it further enacted: That the Smithsonian property in the amount of $541,379.63 loaned to the federal government at 6 percent interest per annum in 1836 (Smithsonian Act of Congress SEC. 2) be accounted for in the amount of approximately $28,000,000,000. The Smithson property or its interest should be returned to the trust fund to be used specifically for the operation of the Smithsonian Institution as initially directed. That amount may be sufficient for further institution operations, removing the necessity for yearly appropriations from the taxpayers. (See H.R.2979 - Public Broadcasting Self-Sufficiency Act of 1996.)

Clarification of the entity status will pave the way for appropriations accountability, ensuring that taxpayer money, if still needed after the return of the Smithson property, will be available for public scrutiny. As a result, the question of whether or not appropriations should even continue will then need to be answered. The American taxpayer should not be subsidizing a private, legally unaccountable organization wherein partisan agendas are pursued without any legal restraints.

In *Raven v. Smithsonian*, Judge Trevor McFadden erroneously claimed that the Smithsonian Institution and its buildings belong to the federal government:

First, the National Portrait Gallery has historically communicated messages from the government, in the sense that it compiles the artwork of third parties for display *on government property* [emphasis added].[215]

And yet, the Smithsonian Institution is known to be a private entity whose attorneys have claimed, for example, here in the *Washington Post*:

> Yet Peter G. Powers, the Smithsonian's general counsel, said yesterday that virtually all Smithsonian properties, including the museums on the Mall in Washington, *legally belong to the Institution and not the federal government* [emphasis added].[216]

Will of James Smithson

In the light of Secretary Joseph Henry's original "Programme of Organization" from 1847, we find a clear and concise interpretation and definition of the will, purpose, and goals of the Smithsonian Institution. Be it further enacted: That all relevant knowledge on controversial subjects deemed acceptable to be increased and diffused under the trust according to the original Smithsonian "Programme of Organization" be given equal funding and exhibition space. That specific trustees be appointed to manage a new (to be created) Smithsonian Department of Controversial Subject Matter.

The chief goal of the People's museum is to "increase and diffuse knowledge," thus ensuring the People have the choice of deciding what side of the issues of controversy they come down on based upon the best available information from differing points of view.

If the federal government wants to get its own National Portrait Gallery for its own agenda, speech, and governmental artistic objectives to be expressed, then let the government build its own gallery and call it, for example, the National Portrait Gallery, not to be confused with the Smithsonian National Portrait Gallery.

After reading this draft of the bill, follow the instructions online. The most effective strategy that will be refined over time will be to coordinate the mailings on the same date. That information you will find on the website too. This step is the beginning of the mission, which will take organization, determination, commitment, and patience to achieve.

Chapter Seventy

BIRD
OF
PRAY

MY DEAR READER, CONGRATULATIONS ON MAKING IT THIS FAR with me on this American odyssey. Thank you for taking the time to witness how the Father of our "inalienable rights" is not deaf to our prayers and has been at work in my life in this beloved country that we call home. The prequel to my story in *Odious and Cerberus* charts my conversion, among other relevant topics. From militant atheist to passionate Christian evangelist, it recounts how, on a mountain in Southern Spain, alone and having never heard the Gospel, I met God. The writing of that story is in the works. However, the sequel to *Odious and Cerberus* lies ahead of us. It is a story yet to be written—one in which you are invited to participate.

As people of faith, we know that the Bible alone is for the self-government of all peoples—in our case, the self-government of the American People, under the constitutional liberties entrusted to us. It is indisputable that the influence of the Word of God on the world, Western civilization, and especially America created the bedrock of faith, values, morals, and ideas that framed the modern Christian world. It may sound cliché, but the day has come and the time is now for people of faith, for the Church in America, to arise and act without wavering in the battle to restore the Bible to its rightful place of prominence and influence. Nothing else matters. The survival of Christianity in America, expressed in politics, education, the economy, the arts, and especially the family depends on it.

To accomplish that noble objective, we must prime the pump of righteous activism with this present objective, the reformation of the Smithsonian Institution. In support of our effort to seize this moment of telling the Smithsonian story coast to coast and coordinating the initiative to compel Congress to amend the Smithsonian Act, another level of organization is required for this task. For Americans like myself—and YOU reading this book—a deep, unsettling "knowing" is producing a burning inside. Not only from learning of my experience but from what is generally going on all over America. Our state of the union has produced an undiminished concern. The burden of getting involved and finally doing something to change the status quo will gnaw and nag the conscience until action is taken. It cannot just be another shoulder-shrugging moment.

But like most concerned citizens, you may have the desire but are unsure about the first steps. On our knees in prayer is where it all begins. In humble submission and repentance before the Most High God. We must cry out for mercy and forgiveness, then for wisdom, courage, commitment, and the resolve necessary to accomplish this critical objective.

Then, standing up, armor on, spear in hand, the tip being the Smithsonian Amendment and Reform Bill, we will need support, leadership, and organization. Without a command structure from which information, equipping, news, and strategic direction can issue forth, individuals alone will fail. We must be united. The establishment of the Raven Society, a 501(C)(4) non-profit social-welfare organization, is the next logical and practical step in the story. The

Raven Society will serve as the necessary organizational command structure for this objective and others to come. The Raven Society will function, with your prayers and help, as the backbone of all community-oriented, spiritual, educational, and political activities. Those will include lobbying the government locally, statewide, and nationally for our relevant and chosen causes. One of the Raven Society's chief missions will be to motivate and equip the American people with the tools necessary to be spiritually, socially, and politically aware, educated, active, and effective.

The principal objective of the Raven Society will be *to speak the truth in a time of national discord*. The Raven Society will be a refreshing and desperately needed operation, sparking action and dispelling today's inundating torrent of disinformation with the cutting edge of the truth. This purpose, posture, and function will, without a doubt, draw out all manner of misunderstanding, as is the case with the often-misunderstood bird, the raven. But tackling the confusion and the loss of trust head-on by reestablishing the plumbline of truth will serve our American society well.

The Raven Society derives its identity and purpose from the character in George Orwell's *Animal Farm*: Moses the Raven. He is the apropos symbol to represent the people of faith in God (especially the Christian faith). The raven, which Orwell initially used as a symbol of resistance against the communist, atheistic forces that spread from the Russian Revolution, is the perfect icon. (Orwell eventually went on to use the raven in the negative sense, depicting religion as a pacifying opiate of the masses used by the pigs, appropriately showing the dangers of powerless religious nationalism.) Christianity in the West today is again under assault from nefarious militant, Marxist/socialist, and atheistic forces that are undermining the fabric of traditional American Christian values.

The large, black, vocal raven is a highly intelligent bird adept at figuring out complex puzzles, symbolically fitting for our times. The raven in the Bible is used by God in First Kings 17:2–6 for feeding Elijah, the servant of God, with bread and meat in a time of divine judgment, national corruption, and division. This example serves symbolically for the educational mission of the Raven Society to "feed," or inform and educate, the Body of Christ and the public in matters relevant to the intersection of God and State in America, in order to accomplish the will of God expressed through American citizens. The Scriptures tell us that Elijah did what the Lord commanded, and that God "commanded" the majestic black birds and they also obeyed. It was a time of rebellion in Israel. Obedience to God created a strikingly clear contrast, demonstrating that without obedience, the perfect will of God is thwarted, but through obedience, great things happen.

In Native American spirituality, the raven totem is revered as a messenger from the spirit world. Likewise, the Raven Society will have a spiritual role. The organization can have no eternal value as a social-welfare organization unless its beliefs, values, and morals are firmly grounded in transcendent truths tethered to the Almighty. These truths we find in the Sacred Scriptures, the Holy Bible.

The terrifying raven is also a greatly feared and maligned creature. In Norse mythology, in Irish, Welsh, and Celtic lore, and in the traditions of many other ancient people groups, the raven is the prominent symbolic bird, appearing in ancient art and literature, remarkably, more than any other bird. It has represented death and the realm of the dead and was seen as the messenger between the worlds of the living and the dead.

On a lighter note, in American pop culture, Jimmy the Raven appeared in the beloved Christmas movie *It's a Wonderful Life*, playfully hopping around on the counter at the Bailey Bros. Building & Loan of Bedford Falls, New York. Jimmy the Raven appeared in one thousand feature films, even landing on the scarecrow in the American classic movie *The Wizard of Oz*. But the dark raven had already become part of American mythical lore through the 1845 poem by Edgar Allen Poe, "The Raven." That atmospheric poem still haunts, striking fear in its readers even today, appropriately depicting for us the ominous season into which America has entered.

There is no sugarcoating the times and seasons in which we find ourselves today. Like in the troubled days of a divided Israel and Judah, when God arranged for the ravens to feed the prophet Elijah (First Kings 14–22), we too in our time can take courage and expect the Lord's marvelous and faithful hand of providence to be extraordinarily manifested. The story of God's miraculous provision for the old woman and the raising of her son from the dead inspire increasing faith in God in desperate times. God's judgment on the false prophets of Baal, corrupt kings, and that evil witch, Jezebel, are all fitting ends awaiting the wicked—and even so during other, similar tumultuous seasons.

Today, America has navigated into ever-more-treacherous waters. Our future as a people has never been so uncertain, and as a result, our children's futures hang in the balance. Ultimately, what the future holds may be out of our hands, but that is never a reason to give up hope or to stop praying and doing.

My journey to America has taught me many things, but one of the most striking lessons has been about the faith and character of the American people in the face of adversity. That character created the environment in which some of our most outstanding leaders have flourished, especially in times of extraordinary turmoil. And as such, we can take courage that even in the midst of our present afflictions, we too, the American people, can rise up in faith and embrace our destiny and the challenges that have been placed upon us.

Our Founding Fathers experienced divine intervention because of their "firm reliance on the protection of divine providence," and America was born as a result. We too can do the same and trust that same God will not only protect us but also save our beloved America, "being confident of this, that He who began a good work in you will carry it on to completion until the day of Christ Jesus" (Philippians 1:6 NIV).

Maybe we will serendipitously meet one day, at the foot of some majestic mountain, camping at one of the many natural wonders that adorn America. Fluttering freely in the evening breeze, Old Glory's broad stripes and bright stars will be flying high above the park gate, anchored to its glistening steel flagpole. At sunset, we will sit around a crackling campfire enjoying a cup of tea. There, as they roast marshmallows, we will tell stories to our grandchildren about how we were part of a remarkable movement of free people who stood up and saved America.

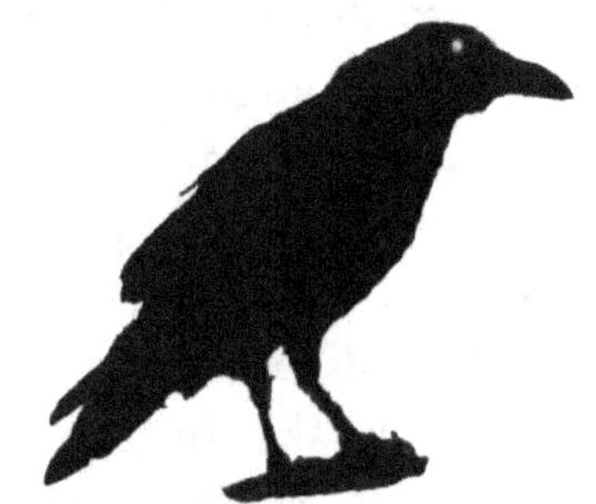

THE RAVEN SOCIETY

Speaking the Truth in a Time of National Discord

www.theravensociety.org

Endnotes

1. Eleanor Goldberg, "80% Of Central American Women, Girls Are Raped Crossing Into The U.S.," *HuffPost*, December 6, 2017, huffpost.com/entry/central-america-migrants-rape_n_5806972.
2. Eusebius, *The Conversion of Constantine*, Fordham University, sourcebooks.fordham.edu/source/conv-const.asp.
3. "Art at Donald Trump's campaign headquarters," CNN, November 12, 2015, cnn.com/2015/11/12/politics/gallery/donald-trump-headquarters-hq-art/index.html.
4. Lynne Patton, "The Trump Family That I Know," youtube.com/watch?v=lxaKUo5naoY.
5. Tanner Jubenville, "'Unafraid and Unashamed': Meet the Man Behind the Trump Painting," *My Twin Tiers*, March 13, 2016, mytwintiers.com/news-cat/unafraid-and-unashamed-meet-the-man-behind-the-trump-painting/.
6. Megan Zhang, "Local Artist Unveils Patriotic Painting Inspired by Donald Trump," Spectrum News 1, November 1, 2015, spectrumlocalnews.com/nys/binghamton/news/2015/11/1/local-artist-unveils-patriotic-painting-inspired-by-donald-trump.
7. Scroll down the listing of Politicon speakers and you will find me: *Politicon*, politicon.com/lineup/.
8. Jeff Horseman, "Politicon 2016: Brexit forces won't help Donald Trump in presidential race," *Los Angeles Daily News*, June 26, 2016, dailynews.com/2016/06/26/politicon-2016-brexit-forces-wont-help-donald-trump-in-presidential-race/.
9. Josh Brokaw, "Elmira Artist Prophesying Trump Win," *Ithaca Times*, July 20, 2016, ithaca.com/news/elmira-artist-prophesying-trump-win/article_1bbba378-4e9a-11e6-9f09-1327a0edc583.html.
10. Juliet Eilperin, Lisa Rein, and Marc Fisher, "Resistance from within: Federal workers push back against Trump," *Washington Post*, January 31, 2017, washingtonpost.com/politics/resistance-from-within-federal-workers-push-back-against-trump/2017/01/31/c65b110e-e7cb-11e6-b82f-687d6e-6a3e7c_story.html.
11. Smithsonian Institution Archives, National Portrait Gallery, siarchives.si.edu/history/national-portrait-gallery.
12. *Grayned v. City of Rockford* (1972).

13.　"Now on View: Portrait of Barack Obama by Shepard Fairey," Smithsonian National Portrait Gallery, npg.si.edu/blog/now-on-view-portrait-barack-obama-shepard-fairey.

14.　Visit "The Trump Portrait Unafraid and Unashamed," thetrumppaint-ing.com/smithsonian-lawsuit-docs for *Raven v. Smithsonian* documentation.

15.　Smithsonian Institution Archives, National Portrait Gallery, siarchives.si.edu/history/national-portrait-gallery.

16.　"Last Will and Testament, October 23, 1826," Smithsonian Institution Archives, siarchives.si.edu/history/featured-topics/stories/last-will-and-testament-october-23-1826.

17.　William Jones Rhees, *The Smithsonian Institution: Documents Relative to Its Origin and History: 1835–1899*, vol. 1, *1835–1887* (Washington, D.C.: Government Printing Office, 1901).

18.　Ibid., 130.

19.　Ibid., 131.

20.　Ibid., 132.

21.　Ibid., 134.

22.　Ibid., 137–38.

23.　Ibid., 139.

24.　"An Act to Establish the Smithsonian Institution, 1846," Smithsonian Institution Archives, siarchives.si.edu/history/featured-topics/stories/act-establish-smithsonian-institution-1846.

25.　Ibid.

26.　Ibid.

27.　The Judicial Oath, Supreme Court, supremecourt.gov/about/oath/oathsofoffice.aspx.

28.　*Meinhard v. Salmon*, Casemine, casemine.com/judgement/us/5914cd87add7b049348132d7.

29.　"English translation of Magna Carta," British Library, July 28, 2014, bl.uk/magna-carta/articles/magna-carta-english-translation.

30.　From "An Act in the Council of the District of Columbia To Amend Title 19 of the District of Columbia Official Code to Enact the Uniform Trust Code in the District of Columbia," code.dccouncil.us/us/dc/council/laws/docs/15-104.pdf.

31.　Dr. Richard Kurin Letter, *Odious and Cerberus*, odiousandcerberus.com/smithsonian-letters.

32.　"United States House of Representatives Committee on Governmet Reform, December 2006, Intolerance and the Politicization of Science at the Smithsonian," 26, 28, discovery.org/m/2008/02/IntoleranceandthePoliticizationofScienceattheSmithsonian.pdf.

33.　Smithsonian Institution, si.edu/FAQs, page currently unavailable.

34.　*Raven v. United States*, Court Listener, courtlistener.com/opinion/4397274/raven-v-united-states/.

35. "The Chief Justice of the United States: Responsibilities of the Office and Process for Appointment," *Every CRS Report*, September 23, 2005, everycrsreport.com/reports/RL32821.html#TOC2_1.

36. *A Memorial of Joseph Henry* (Washington, D.C.: Government Printing Office, 1880), 11–12.

37. Chuck Grassley, "Letter to Chief Justice Roberts," *Washington Post*, washingtonpost.com/wp-srv/nation/documents/smithsonian/Grassleyletter.pdf.

38. Ibid.

39. Charles A. Bowsher, Stephen D. Potts, A. W. Smith Jr., "A Report to the Board of Regents of the Smithsonian Institution," June 18, 2007, Smithsonian Institution, si.edu/content/governance/pdf/IRC_report.pdf.

40. Ibid.

41. Ibid.

42. Ibid.

43. "Summary of Report," Smithsonian Institution Archives, siarchives.si.edu/sites/default/files/pdfs/collections/000613/SIA_000613_B429_F06_D01_optimized.pdf.

44. "Smithsonian Institution Statement of Values and Code of Ethics," Smithsonian Institution, si.edu/content/governance/pdf/Statement_of_Values_and_Code_of_Ethics.pdf.

45. Kathryn Tully, "Smithsonian Funded Controversial Exhibition With $716,000 Gift From Bill And Camille Cosby," *Forbes*, July 13, 2015, forbes.com/sites/kathryntully/2015/07/13/smithsonian-funded-controversial-exhibition-with-716000-gift-from-bill-and-camille-cosby/?sh=7633748520c2.

46. Bradford Richardson, "Clarence Thomas Snubbed by Smithsonian's Museum of African American History," *The Washington Times*, December 7, 2016, washingtontimes.com/news/2016/dec/7/clarence-thomas-snubbed-by-smithsonians-museum-of-/.

47. Ibid.

48. The Associated Press, "Smithsonian Concealed $716,000 Gift from Bill Cosby Amid Rape Allegations," *The Hollywood Reporter*, July 13, 2015, hollywoodreporter.com/tv/tv-news/bill-cosby-smithsonian-concealed-716000-808311/.

49. Erin Brodwin, "Bill Cosby has been found guilty—here's what happens if you take the pills he described as 'friends to help you relax'," *Business Insider*, April 26, 2018, businessinsider.com/bill-cosby-andrea-constand-trial-verdict-pills-sex-quaaludes-benadryl-2017-6.

50. "Smithsonian Concealed $716,000 Gift from Bill Cosby," *The Hollywood Reporter*.

51. *A Memorial of Joseph Henry*, 146.

52. Ibid., 16–17.

53. Ibid., 147.

54.   M. Whelan, Edwin Reilly Jr., and Steve Rockwell, "Joseph Henry," Edison Tech Center, edisontechcenter.org/JosephHenry.html.

55.   "United States House of Representatives Committee on Government Reform: Intolerance and the Politicization of Science at the Smithsonian," December 11, 2006, discovery.org/m/2008/02/IntoleranceandthePoliticizationofScienceattheSmithsonian.pdf.

56.   Albert E. Moyer, "Joseph Henry: Scientist and Christian," The Joseph Henry Papers Project, Smithsonian Institution Archives, siarchives.si.edu/sites/default/files/pdfs/jhpp/JHP_Scientist_and_Christian.pdf, 2.

57.   Ibid.

58.   Ibid., 3.

59.   Kerry Picket, "Smithsonian Says 'No' To New York Artist's Trump Portrait," *Daily Caller*, December 13, 2016, dailycaller.com/2016/12/13/smithsonian-says-no-to-new-york-artists-trump-portrait/.

60.   Benjamin Wofford, "The Surreal Story of a Trump-Loving Artist's War With the Smithsonian," *Washingtonian*, August 4, 2019, washingtonian.com/2019/08/04/julian-raven-trump-artist-national-portrait-gallery-smithsonian/.

61.   Picket, "Smithsonian Says 'No'."

62.   Roxanne Roberts and Amy Argetsinger, "Fit for a T: Portrait Gallery Gets Obama 'Hope' Collage," The Reliable Source, *Washington Post*, January 7, 2009, voices.washingtonpost.com/reliable-source/2009/01/rs-portrait7.html.

63.   Anika Gupta, "Barack Obama is the Man of the Moment at the Portrait Gallery," *Smithsonian Magazine*, December 16, 2008, smithsonianmag.com/smithsonian-institution/barack-obama-is-the-man-of-the-moment-at-the-portrait-gallery-32753204/.

64.   Casey Luskin, "How Smithsonian Institution Pressured the California Science Center," *Evolution News*, October 12, 2010, evolutionnews.org/2010/10/how_smithsonian_institution_pr/.

65.   Ibid.

66.   Richard Sternberg, "Smithsonian Controversy," RichardSternberg.org, richardsternberg.com/smithsonian/.

67.   "Intolerance and the Politicization of Science at the Smithsonian."

68.   Ibid.

69.   Rick Santorum and Mark Souder, "Letter to Lawrence Small and Sheila Burke," April 7, 2006, discovery.org/m/2008/02/Smithsonian-Staff-Report-Appendix.pdf.

70.   James McVay, "U.S. Office of Special Counsel Letter," August 5, 2005, RichardSternberg.org, richardsternberg.com/smithsonian/letter/.

71.   "Intolerance and the Politicization of Science at the Smithsonian."

72.   Michael Powell, "Editor Explains Reasons for 'Intelligent Design' Article," *Washington Post*, August 19, 2005, washingtonpost.com/wp-dyn/content/article/2005/08/18/AR2005081801680.html.

73.   Santorum and Souder, "Letter to Lawrence Small and Sheila Burke."

74. Wofford, "The Surreal Story."

75. Rhees, *The Smithsonian Institution*, 132.

76. *A Memorial of Joseph Henry*, 24.

77. Ibid., 19.

78. "'Programme of Organization' of the Smithsonian Institution," December 13, 1847, Smithsonian Institution Archives, siarchives.si.edu/history/featured-topics/stories/programme-organization-smithsonian-institution.

79. Tunku Varadarajan, "How Science Lost the Public's Trust," *Wall Street Journal*, Opinion, July 23, 2021, wsj.com/articles/covid-china-media-lab-leak-climate-ridley-biden-censorship-coronavirus-11627049477.

80. William W. Warner, "The Smithsonian Institution and Science," September 6, 1971, cosmosclub.org/journals/2002/warner.html.

81. Leslie Albrecht, "Exclusive: Jeff Bezos's $200 million, 50-year naming-rights deal with the Smithsonian does not include a 'morals clause'," MSN *MarketWatch*, January 31, 2022, msn.com/en-us/money/companies/exclusive-jeff-bezos-s-200-million-naming-rights-deal-with-the-smithsonian-does-not-include-a-morals-clause/ar-AATeo1h.

82. "'Programme of Organization'."

83. Wikipedia; Wikipedia's entry on William Howard Taft, wikipedia.org/wiki/William_Howard_Taft.

84. Douglas W. Kmiec, "The Status of the Smithsonian Institution Under the Federal Property and Administrative Services Act," June 30, 1988, justice.gov/file/24096/download.

85. Ibid.

86. Warner, "The Smithsonian Institution and Science."

87. Ibid., emphases added.

88. Devin Dwyer, "Art or Hate Speech? Video of Ants Crawling on Crucifix Pulled from Smithsonian," ABC News, December 3, 2010, abcnews.go.com/US/smithsonian-removes-ants-crucifix-video-exhibit-sparking-debate/story?id=12305404.

89. Julian Raven, "Adult Content: Is There Free Speech in the Smithsonian? The Trump Painting Lawsuit," April 15, 2019, youtube.com/watch?v=EyBpIE9_-y4&t=7s.

90. Wikipedia; Wikipedia's entry on "Untitled (Portrait of Ross in L.A.)," wikipedia.org/wiki/Untitled_(Portrait_of_Ross_in_L.A.).

91. Dwyer, "Art or Hate Speech?"

92. Raven, "Adult Content: Is There Free Speech in the Smithsonian?"

93. Rebecca R. Ruiz, "Sessions Calls for 'Recommitment' to Free Speech on Campus, Diving Into Debate," *New York Times*, September 26, 2017, nytimes.com/2017/09/26/us/politics/jeff-sessions-campus-free-speech-georgetown.html.

94. Julian Raven, "An Amicus Curiae Invitation," November 26, 2019, *Odious and Cerberus*, odiousandcerberus.com/smithsonian-appeals.

95. Arina Grossu, "Margaret Sanger, Racist Eugenicist Extraordinaire," Family Research Council, May 5, 2014, frc.org/op-eds/margaret-sanger-racist-eugenicist-extraordinaire.

96. Ibid.

97. Brenna Lewis, "Senator Rand Paul Urges the Smithsonian to Remove Bust of Racist Planned Parenthood Founder Margaret Sanger," *Students for Life Action*, May 20, 2021, studentsforlifeaction.org/senator-rand-paul-urges-the-smithsonian-to-remove-bust-of-racist-planned-parenthood-founder-margaret-sanger/.

98. "Kim Sajet letter to Bishop E. W. Jackson," August 19, 2015, *Odious and Cerberus*, odiousandcerberus.com/smithsonian-letters.

99. "20 U.S. Code § 75b. Establishment of National Portrait Gallery; functions," Legal Information Institute, law.cornell.edu/uscode/text/20/75.

100. "Kim Sajet letter to Bishop E. W. Jackson."

101. Ibid.

102. Alexis McGill Johnson, "I'm the Head of Planned Parenthood. We're Done Making Excuses for Our Founder," *New York Times*, April 17, 2021, nytimes.com/2021/04/17/opinion/planned-parenthood-margaret-sanger.html.

103. James V. Grimaldi and Jacqueline Trescott, "Bill Would End FOIA Shield for Smithsonian," *Washington Post*, July 19, 2008, washingtonpost.com/wp-dyn/content/article/2008/07/18/AR2008071802938.html?nav=rss_print/style.

104. Ibid.

105. Wikipedia; Wikipedia's entry on *Bivens v. Six Unknown Named Agents*, en.wikipedia.org/wiki/Bivens_v._Six_Unknown_Named_Agents.

106. *Raven v. United States*, Court Listener, courtlistener.com/docket/6824689/raven-v-united-states/.

107. "20 U.S. Code § 954 - National Endowment for the Arts," *Legal Information Institute*, law.cornell.edu/uscode/text/20/954.

108. "Unessay," *Shameless*, March 26, 2016, hums334009.wordpress.com/.

109. "National Foundation on the Arts and the Humanities Act of 1965 (P.L. 89-209)," National Endowment for the Humanities, neh.gov/about/history/national-foundation-arts-and-humanities-act-1965-pl-89-209.

110. "An Act to Establish the Smithsonian Institution, 1846."

111. *Southeastern Promotions, Ltd. v. Conrad*, 420 U.S. 546 (1975), Justia, supreme.justia.com/cases/federal/us/420/546/.

112. *Lebron v. Amtrak*, C-Span, November 4, 1994, c-span.org/video/?61345-1/lebron-v-amtrak.

113. Julian Raven, "What Is the Status of the Smithsonian and How Can It Protect Free Speech Rights?" *Townhall*, January 6, 2020, townhall.com/columnists/julianraven/2020/01/06/what-is-the-status-of-the-smithsonian-and-how-can-it-protect-free-speech-rights-n2558956.

114. David L. Hudson Jr., "Government Speech Doctrine," *The First Amendment Encyclopedia*, mtsu.edu/first-amendment/article/962/government-speech-doctrine.

115. *Michael A. Lebron, Appellant, v. Washington Metropolitan Area Transit Authority, et al,* 749 F.2d 893 (D.C. Cir. 1984), Justia, law.justia.com/cases/federal/appellate-courts/F2/749/893/359468/.

116. Shannon Selin, "Stephen Girard, America's Napoleon of Commerce," *Imagining the Bounds of History,* shannonselin.com/2014/10/stephen-girard/.

117. *Pennsylvania v. Board of Trusts,* 353 U.S. 230 (1957), Justia, supreme.justia.com/cases/federal/us/353/230/.

118. *Lebron v. National Railroad Passenger Corporation,* Justia, supreme.justia.com/cases/federal/us/513/374/case.pdf.

119. "'Programme of Organization'."

120. *Kapiolani Park Preservation Society v. City County,* 69 Haw. 569, 751 P.2d 1022 (Haw. 1988), Casetext, casetext.com/case/kapiolani-park-preservation-society-v-city-county.

121. *Hooker v. Edes Home,* 579 A.2d 608 (D.C. 1990), Casetext, casetext.com/case/hooker-v-edes-home.

122. Ibid.

123. "20 U.S. Code § 75b.Establishment of National Portrait Gallery; functions," Legal Information Institute, law.cornell.edu/uscode/text/20/75b, emphasis added.

124. *Plessy v. Ferguson,* Legal Information Institute, law.cornell.edu/supremecourt/text/163/537.

125. *Burson v. Freeman,* 504 U.S. 191 (1992), Justia, supreme.justia.com/cases/federal/us/504/191/.

126. *FCC v. League of Women Voters,* 468 U.S. 364 (1984), Justia, supreme.justia.com/cases/federal/us/468/364/j.

127. *Raven v. Sajet,* 334 F. Supp. 3d 22 (D.D.C. 2018), Casetext, casetext.com/case/raven-v-sajet.

128. "An Act to Establish the Smithsonian Institution, 1846."

129. Ibid.

130. Ibid.

131. Raven, "Adult Content: Is There Free Speech in the Smithsonian?"

132. *National Endowment for Arts v. Finley,* 524 U.S. 569 (1998), Justia, supreme.justia.com/cases/federal/us/524/569/.

133. *Mistretta v. United States,* 488 U.S. 361 (1989), Justia, supreme.justia.com/cases/federal/us/488/361/.

134. James Madison, *The Federalist Papers* 47, The Avalon Project, avalon.law.yale.edu/18th_century/fed47.asp.

135. *Raven v. Sajet.*

136. Ibid.

137. "An Act to Establish the Smithsonian Institution, 1846."

138. Ibid.

139. Ibid.

140. "Smithsonian Institution Statement of Values and Code of Ethics."

141. *Raven v. United States of America,* No. 1:2017cv01240 - Document

54 (D.D.C. 2018), 20, Justia, law.justia.com/cases/federal/district-courts/district-of-columbia/dcdce/1:2017cv01240/187695/54/.

142. "Smithsonian Institution Statement of Values and Code of Ethics."

143. *Harris v. Jones*, 281 Md. 560, 380 A.2d 611 (Md. 1977), Casetext, casetext.com/case/harris-v-jones-16.

144. *Raven v. United States of America*, 20.

145. William Safire, ed., *Lend Me Your Ears: Great Speeches in History* (New York, London: W. W. Norton, 1992), 150.

146. *Raven v. Sajet*.

147. *Harris v. Jones*.

148. Tanner West, "Superstar Smithsonian Leader David Skorton Resigns after Less Than Four Years," *Artnet*, December 20, 2018, news.artnet.com/art-world/smithsonian-secretary-david-skorton-resigns-lead-medical-nonprofit-1426846/amp-page.

149. Ryan Teague Beckwith, "Inside the World of CPAC," *Time*, March 1, 2019, time.com/longform/cpac-2019-conservatives/.

150. Julian Raven, "The Trump Painting CPAC 2019 take-down time lapse," March 6, 2019, youtube.com/watch?v=T3JIvzqQKTo.

151. Will Sommer, "The Artist Behind the 16-Foot-Wide Trump Painting Wants It in the Smithsonian," *Daily Beast*, March 12, 2019, thedailybeast.com/the-artist-behind-the-16-foot-wide-trump-painting-wants-it-in-the-smithsonian.

152. Matthew Walther, "Immigrant Christian Abstract Expressionists for Trump," *Washington Free Beacon*, January 22, 2016, freebeacon.com/culture/immigrant-christian-abstract-expressionists-for-trump/.

153. Benjamin Wofford, "Inside Jeff Bezos's DC Life," *Washingtonian*, April 22, 2018, washingtonian.com/2018/04/22/inside-jeff-bezos-dc-life/.

154. Elaine Woo, "Harris Wofford, civil rights activist who helped Kennedy win the White House, dies at 92," *Washington Post*, January 22, 2019, washingtonpost.com/local/obituaries/harris-wofford-civil-rights-activist-who-helped-kennedy-win-the-white-house-dies-at-92/2019/01/22/026fe870-1e09-11e9-9145-3f74070bbdb9_story.html.

155. Charles A. Krause, "Ripley's Son-in-Law Given Smithsonian Aid for Work; Ripley's Son-in-Law Aided by Smithsonian," *Washington Post*, March 15, 1977, *Odious and Cerberus*, odiousandcerberus.com/smithsonian-investigation.

156. Charles A. Krause, "GAO Criticizes Smithsonian's Mixing of Funds; GAO Study Says Smithsonian Converts U.S. Cash to Own Use," *Washington Post*, April 1, 1977, *Odious and Cerberus*, odiousandcerberus.com/smithsonian-investigation.

157. Charles A. Krause, "New Probe Asked In Smithsonian, U.S. Relationship; Restudy of Museum Role Asked," *Washington Post*, April 19, 1977, *Odious and Cerberus*, odiousandcerberus.com/smithsonian-investigation.

158. *Raven v. United States of America*, 13.

159.   Charles A. Krause, "Smithsonian Congressional Hearing Backed," *Washington Post*, May 4, 1977, *Odious and Cerberus*, odiousandcerberus. com/smithsonian-investigation.

160.   Charles A. Krause, "Smithsonian to Study Its Federal Relationship," *Washington Post*, May 14, 1977, *Odious and Cerberus*, odiousandcerberus. com/smithsonian-investigation.

161.   Philip Samuel Hughes, "Study of the Relationship of the Smithsonian Institution to Congress," 1977, Smithsonian Institution Archives, siarchives. si.edu/sites/default/files/pdfs/collections/000613/SIA_000613_B429_F06_ D01_optimized.pdf.

162.   Ibid.

163.   Letter from Donald Trump to Julian Raven, July 19, 2019, *Odious and Cerberus*, odiousandcerberus.com/presidents-letter.

164.   Julian Raven, "The Trump Portrait Painting By Julian Raven Time lapse Set-Up Washington D. C. Art Show," youtube.com/ watch?v=3yhcQvf5joQ&t=66s.

165.   "The Good, the Bad and the Ugly," Exhibit catalog, yumpu.com/en/ document/view/62739265/the-good-the-bad-and-the-ugly.

166.   "Hatch Act Overview," U.S. Office of Special Counsel, osc.gov/Services/Pages/HatchAct.aspx.

167.   "About OSC," U.S. Office of Special Counsel, osc.gov/Pages/About.aspx.

168.   Julian Raven, "Investigation into Hatch Act Violations by Kim Sajet," March 7, 2018, *Odious and Cerberus*, odiousandcerberus.com/ smithsonian-investigation.

169.   "Hatch Act and 501(c)(4) Organizations," *IEC Journal*, Interagency Ethics Council: Standards of Conduct for Federal Employees, March 14, 2014, iec.typepad.com/iec/2014/03/hatch-act-and-501c4-organizations.html.

170.   Douglas Keith, "Impeachment and Removal of Judges: An Explainer," Brennan Center for Justice, March 23, 2018, brennancenter.org/our-work/ analysis-opinion/impeachment-and-removal-judges-explainer.

171.   "Court of Appeals District of Columbia Circuit: Denial," May 17, 2019, *Odious and Cerberus*, odiousandcerberus.com/smithsonian-appeals.

172.   *Lebron v. National Railroad Passenger Corporation.*

173.   *Michael A. Lebron, Appellant, v. Washington Metropolitan Area Transit Authority.*

174.   "Denial of En Banc Rehearing," August 12, 2019, *Odious and Cerberus*, odiousandcerberus.com/smithsonian-appeals, 3.

175.   Julian Raven, "Filing Petition for a Writ of Certiorari at the Supreme Court," *The Trump Painting*, thetrumppainting.com/the-petition-for-cert.

176.   "The Court and Constitutional Interpretation," SupremeCourt.gov, supremecourt.gov/about/constitutional.aspx.

177.   Wikipedia; Wikipedia's entry on the *Washington Times*, en.wikipedia. org/wiki/The_Washington_Times.

178. Louis D. Brandeis, *Other People's Money and How the Bankers Use It* (New York: Frederick A. Stokes, 1914), 92.

179. Alex Swoyer, "Julian Raven, Trump-inspired artist, fights national gallery to take portrait," *Washington Times*, November 28, 2019, washingtontimes. com/news/2019/nov/28/julian-raven-trump-inspired-artist-fights-national/.

180. Julian Raven, "Photo Gallery," *Odious and Cerberus*, odiousandcerberus.com/photos-%26-videos.

181. Declaration of Independence, National Archives, archives.gov/ founding-docs/declaration-transcript.

182. Julian Raven, "O To Be A Fly On The Wall At The January 10th 2020 SCOTUS Conference," January 9, 2020, julianraven.wordpress. com/2020/01/09/o-to-be-a-fly-on-the-wall-at-the-january-10th-2020-scotus-conference/.

183. *Marbury v. Madison*, 5 U.S. 137 (1803), Justia, supreme.justia.com/ cases/federal/us/5/137/.

184. "Letter from Supreme Court to Julian Marcus Raven," January 13, 2020, *Odious and Cerberus*, odiousandcerberus.com/smithsonian-appeals.

185. "Naturalization Oath of Allegiance to the United States of America," U.S. Citizenship and Immigration Services, uscis.gov/citizenship/learn-about-citizenship/the-naturalization-interview-and-test/ naturalization-oath-of-allegiance-to-the-united-states-of-america.

186. Julian Raven, "The Swampire Strikes Back!," *Odious and Cerberus*, odiousandcerberus.com/photos-%26-videos.

187. Kristen Hinman, "Washingtonian's Best Longreads of 2019," *Washingtonian*, December 23, 2019, washingtonian.com/2019/12/23/ washingtonian-best-longreads-of-2019/.

188. Julian Raven, "RV Motorhome 97 Fleetwood Pace Arrow Vision Exterior Restoration 3 Month 2020 Quarantine Project," February 12, 2021, youtube.com/watch?v=5UHinlw_EOw&t=196s.

189. Julian Raven, "Beautiful Beaufort South Carolina Fascinating History, Local Folk Interviews By Gloria Raven," March 14, 2021, youtube.com/ watch?v=Ry8Zf7bxHeY.

190. Samuel Adams, "On American Independence" (1776), bartleby. com/268/8/18.html.

191. Declaration of Independence.

192. Ibid.

193. John Adams, "From John Adams to Massachusetts Militia, 11 October 1798," National Archives, founders.archives.gov/documents/ Adams/99-02-02-3102.

194. Robert C. Wintrop, "Either by the Bible or the Bayonet" (May 28, 1849), in *3 Secular Reasons Why America Should Be Under God*, William J. Federer, ed. (St. Louis, MO: Amerisearch, Inc., 2004), 47.

195. Abraham Lincoln, "Gettysburg Address" (November 19, 1863), Cornell University, rmc.library.cornell.edu/gettysburg/good_cause/transcript.htm.

196.   Ronald Reagan, "Freedom Speech" (October 27, 1964), Reagan.com, reagan.com/ronald-reagan-freedom-speech.

197.   Declaration of Independence.

198.   John Adams, "John Adams to Abigail Adams, 26 April 1777," National Archives, Founders.archives.gov/documents/Adams/04-02-02-0169.

199.   Mario Savio, "Rage Against the Machine," Sproul Hall, University of California, Berkeley (December 2, 1964), youtube.com/watch?v=AgSr2iNXygo.

200.   *Obergefell v. Hodges*, Justice Scalia Dissenting, 5, supremecourt.gov/opinions/14pdf/14-556_3204.pdf.

201.   Samuel Adams, "Oration at Philadelphia," in *The Life and Public Services of Samuel Adams*, vol. 3, William Vincent Wells (Boston: Little, Brown & Company, 1865), 415.

202.   Ed Pilkington, "Obama angers midwest voters with guns and religion remark," *The Guardian*, April 14, 2008, theguardian.com/world/2008/apr/14/barackobama.uselections2008.

203.   Full movie, *Expelled: No Intelligence Allowed*, can be seen at youtube.com/watch?v=V5EPymcWp-g.

204.   "Open and Transparent Smithsonian Act of 2016," Congress.gov, congress.gov/congressional-report/114th-congress/house-report/864/1?s=1&r=47.

205.   "An Act to Establish the Smithsonian Institution, 1846."

206.   Press Release: "Norton Introduces Bill to Increase Transparency and Accountability at the Smithsonian Institution," July 29, 2015, norton.house.gov/media-center/press-releases/norton-introduces-bill-to-increase-transparency-and-accountability-at.

207.   *Kapiolani Park Preservation Society v. City County.*

208.   *Raven v. United States of America.*

209.   "§ 19–1302.01. Role of court in administration of trust," Council of the District of Columbia, code.dccouncil.us/us/dc/council/code/sections/19-1302.01.html.

210.   Bowsher, Potts, and Smith, "A Report to the Board of Regents of the Smithsonian Institution."

211.   "The Status of the Smithsonian Institution Under the Federal Property and Administrative Services Act," June 30, 1988, The United States Department of Justice, justice.gov/file/24096/download.

212.   "Intolerance and the Politicization of Science at the Smithsonian," December 11, 2006, discovery.org/m/2008/02/IntoleranceandthePoliticizationofScienceattheSmithsonian.pdf.

213.   *Raven v. United States of America*, 13.

214.   Ibid.

215.   Ibid.

216.   Krause, "New Probe Asked In Smithsonian, U.S. Relationship."

Index